Mujeres de Maiz en Movimiento

Felicia 'Fe' Montes, "Mujeres de Maiz 2020 Group Photo"

EDITED BY
Amber Rose González, Felicia 'Fe' Montes, and Nadia Zepeda

Mujeres de Maiz
en Movimiento

Spiritual Artivism, Healing Justice, and Feminist Praxis

THE UNIVERSITY OF
ARIZONA PRESS
TUCSON

The University of Arizona Press
www.uapress.arizona.edu

We respectfully acknowledge the University of Arizona is on the land and territories of Indigenous peoples. Today, Arizona is home to twenty-two federally recognized tribes, with Tucson being home to the O'odham and the Yaqui. Committed to diversity and inclusion, the University strives to build sustainable relationships with sovereign Native Nations and Indigenous communities through education offerings, partnerships, and community service.

© 2024 by The Arizona Board of Regents
All rights reserved. Published 2024

ISBN-13: 978-0-8165-5293-1 (paperback)
ISBN-13: 978-0-8165-5294-8 (ebook)

Cover design by Leigh McDonald
Cover art: *Hermana de Maiz: Portrait of Felicia Montes*, 1998, by Margaret 'Quica' Alarcón, oil and acrylic on asymmetrical handmade paper, approx. 28 x 20 in., p/c of Olivia Montes. Background texture of amate paper, Claudia Luna/Adobe Stock; Codex Azcatitlan (details), courtesy of Bibliotheque nationale de France
Typeset by Leigh McDonald in Warnock Pro 10.5/14 and BackOut by Frank Adebiaye and Ariel Martín Pérez / Velvetyne Type Foundry (display)

Library of Congress Cataloging-in-Publication Data
Names: González, Amber Rose, editor. | Montes, Felicia, 1975– editor. | Zepeda, Nadia, 1988– editor.
Title: Mujeres de Maiz en movimiento : spiritual ARTivism, healing justice, and feminist praxis / edited by Amber Rose González, Felicia 'Fe' Montes, and Nadia Zepeda.
Description: Tucson : University of Arizona Press, 2024. | Includes bibliographical references and index.
Identifiers: LCCN 2023027600 (print) | LCCN 2023027601 (ebook) | ISBN 9780816552931 (paperback) | ISBN 9780816552948 (ebook)
Subjects: LCSH: Mujeres de Maiz (Organization)—History. | Hispanic American women—Social networks—California—Los Angeles. | Hispanic American feminists—California—Los Angeles.
Classification: LCC HQ1161 .M854 2024 (print) | LCC HQ1161 (ebook) | DDC 305.48/68073079494—dc23/eng/20230815
LC record available at https://lccn.loc.gov/2023027600
LC ebook record available at https://lccn.loc.gov/2023027601

Printed in the United States of America
♾ This paper meets the requirements of ANSI/NISO Z39.48-1992 (Permanence of Paper).

To all our relations

We give thanks to our ancestors, our predecessors, our families, and those who have come before us, those in the present, and those yet to come. We call on their wisdom, strength, and love so that we may do this work in a good way and continue paving the road for future generations.

Mujeres de Maiz is immensely grateful to the generations of women who have paved the way in activist, artistic, cultural, community, and spiritual spaces. We give thanks to our guides, maestra/xs, femtors, and mentors who have guided our work throughout the years.

We have been blessed to have many amazing artists, performers, speakers, and healers grace our stages, pages, programs, circles, workshops, and events since 1997. As a volunteer-run organization, we offer thanks to the hundreds of volunteers, organizers, interns, community partners, supporters, and you. We are truly grassroots. There are too many individuals to name here, but many of them can be found throughout this book. We honor and thank you all from the bottom of our hearts.

We especially want to thank the Mujeres de Maiz throughout the years who have offered their energia and time to support the programming and Live Art Shows. We acknowledge the co-founders of the collective who had the vision and have carried this prayer for so long, including coordinating member and director Felicia 'Fe' Montes who has continued the vision and spread the initiative and invitation to so many. In addition, we want to thank Martha R. Gonzales, Michelle L. Lopez, and Norell Martínez for their work early on in this project and Megan Pennings for her support.

We wish to acknowledge that many may not be represented in this book, this Xicana codex, this prayer. There are so many more stories, experiences, art, ideas, and memories that are a part of our circle and they will be forever imprinted on our hearts, minds, and spirits.

This work, Mujeres de Maiz en Movimiento: Spiritual ARTivism, Healing Justice, and Feminist Praxis, *is our dedication, our prayer, our ofrenda, our living archive, our lineage, and our legacy.*

CONTENTS

Movimiento de Consciencia Xicana[x]   3
CELIA HERRERA RODRÍGUEZ

Todos Somos Mujeres de Maiz: An Introduction   5
AMBER ROSE GONZÁLEZ

Mujeres de Maiz: Seeds to Spiritual Artivism—An L.A. Herstory   28
FELICIA 'FE' MONTES

Mis Manos Solo Escriben   60
MARILYNN MONTAÑO

ROUND I. EMERGENT SPIRITUAL JOURNEYS AND HEALING SPACES

1. Danzando con el Fuego   65
   CLAUDIA MERCADO

2. Magandang Misteryo (Beautiful Mystery)   83
   LIZA COHEN HITA

3. Know Your Enemy: The Sham of Filipino Independence   90
   LIZA COHEN HITA

4. Reflections on Mujeres de Maiz   93
   LARA MEDINA

5. Coyolxauhqui Full Moon Circle: Self-Care as Community Care   97
   NADIA ZEPEDA

6. Mujeres de Maiz Arising: Shifts and Movement of Positioning Xicana-Driven Indigenous Spirituality   116
   ANGELA 'MICTLANXOCHITL' ANDERSON GUERRERO

7.	My Body Is My Sanctuary POVI-TAMU BRYANT	126
8.	For My Sister NATALINA ROSS	128
9.	Tamoanchan, Aztlan LUISA LEIJA	130

ROUND II. MOVIMIENTOS DE REBELDÍA

10.	I Am International Woman FELICIA 'FE' MONTES	135
11.	Re-Collecting D'LO	137
12.	Recollections: My Personal Journey with Mujeres de Maiz SKRYB ANU	151
13.	The Will of the Water MARISOL LYDIA TORRES	157
14.	Contusions FAITH SATILLA	167
15.	Cuscatlan LIZETTE HERNANDEZ	169
16.	farm for meme VIRGINIA GRISE	171
17.	Tortilla Warrior CLAUDIA SERRATO	173
18.	Revolutionary Rants MARIBEL MARTÍNEZ	175
19.	The Spiritual Activism of Mujeres de Maiz: Queering the Boundaries of Art and Action KAREN MARY DAVALOS	178

ROUND III. LA CULTURA CURA: ARTIVIST AESTHETICS

20.	Art Is Ceremony GINA APARICIO	205
21.	Queer Xicana Indígena Cultural Production: Remembering Through Oral and Visual Storytelling SUSY ZEPEDA	208

22. Bringing Art to the People: Decolonizing Art Spaces and Exhibitions　　234
    MICHELLE L. LOPEZ

23. Mythology of Flesh and Turquoise Serpents　　258
    DIANA PANDO

24. We Are　　260
    MARISOL CRISOSTOMO-ROMO

25. My Body: A Sight of Violence　　262
    MARIANA AQ'AB'AL MOSCOSO

26. Mi Querido 24th and Mission　　264
    MAYA CHINCHILLA

27. Femzines, Artivism, and Altar Aesthetics: Third Wave Feminism Chicana Style　　268
    NORELL MARTÍNEZ

28. Teatro Heals　　292
    JO ANNA MIXPE LEY

29. Poema Para Abuela: Escúchame　　296
    JO ANNA MIXPE LEY

30. Una Muñeca　　298
    XITLALIC GUIJOSA-OSUNA

ROUND IV. MDM EPISTEMOLOGIES AND PEDAGOGIES

31. In the Spirit of the Voluta　　301
    CRISTINA GOROCICA

32. *Conocimientos* from the Mujeres de Maiz Oral Herstory Project　　306
    GABRIELA MARTINEZ, PEDRO MARTINEZ, MEGAN PENNINGS, AND DIONNE ESPINOZA

33. Becoming an Activist-Scholar-Organizer with Mujeres de Maiz　　326
    AMBER ROSE GONZÁLEZ

34. Restoring the Mind, Body, and Spirit: Mujeres de Maiz and Social Media as a Tool of Spiritual Artivism and Education　　349
    MEGAN PENNINGS

35. The Bees. The Honey. The Humanity.　　371
    MARTHA GONZALEZ

36. Momma of the Soft Jersey T's　　375
    VICKIE VÉRTIZ

37. Revoloosonary Mama　　377
    PANQUETZANI

38.	I'm a Long Time Coming PATRICIA PAZ MOYA AND PATRICIA ZAMORANO	379
39.	dreamseeds of the women of the corn IRIS DE ANDA	381
40.	Makeover Manifesto IRIS DE ANDA	388

Contributors   *389*
Index   *407*
Color plates follow page   *166*

Mujeres de Maíz en Movimiento

Movimiento de Consciencia Xicana[x]

CELIA HERRERA RODRÍGUEZ

ABRIENDO ESTA puerta con vela y el humito. Calling Tunkashila/Tonantzin Abuelita/Abuelito. We call out to the Spirits of this land of this continent, those with form and those without. We acknowledge the strength, el poder de los Espiritos de cuatro puntos, cuatro caminos, y buscamos sus bendicíones en nuestro corazón. Llegamos aqui entre los vientos y aguas de la creacíon y reconocemos nuestra matrix, what surrounds us, source of life, animas. Lo de arriba y de abajo, luz y oscuridad, energia eterna. Damos gracias for those who came before us, those that follow, and those that walk beside us on this precious red road of life.

Segunda puerta is in gratitude for Mujeres de Maiz, for your thought, palabra, the corazón, determination, the huge amount of time and leadership that you have brought to this Amoxtli. Thank you for lighting this fire (and keeping it fed for decades) that has resulted in this collection of work created by and in community formed by this esfuerzo. This collection is the materia, the evidence of the values that are at the core of Movimiento: collective thought and work, the development of critical and social consciousness through art and cultural activism, and a commitment to making change with purpose and vision of a just world and future for us all.

Tercer puerta is asking la creadora for a return of energy freely given and time freely spent. Asking to make right what went wrong and the realization of wrong turns that brought life lessons and new possibilities to the manda of remembering. I ask for blessings for the families and loved ones and a lifting up of the prayers carried by the collective. I ask for healing, health, sustainability, new generations, and opportunities. I ask for letting go, a cleansing—a barrida de plumas y copal desde la cabeza, a corazón, a matriz, a pies, de enfrente y atraz. Un baño de agua bendita, un bocado de agua para limpiar la lengua, una sopladita a los oidos para abrirlos, a wiping of the eyes to clear the vision. A strengthening, a gentleness, a restoration of self as they/we go into a new day and cycle of life.

Cerrando la puerta: I see the staffs marking this beautiful road of life. The fierce Cihuateteo at the four corners, at the center, and at the crossroads. The brightest Tzitzimime, the sister-stars blazing bright light across the path. At this time when so many of our sisters have followed the sun's path to the west, I acknowledge their bravery, the love and sense of purpose that drove their work and their lives. I am reminded to be thankful for their flores y canciones that make walking this rocky path so precious. It is important to say that the influences are not only generational, who came before, or after, but who is walking alongside us.

We have agreed to carry these bundles of remembering, of daring to reembody, reanimate the spirit of life, by recalling our names, our gente, our pueblos, our humanity. It is our charge to challenge the conventions, to disarm the gatekeepers from within and without. This is my prayer for continuity of connection, embodiment, and consciousness of the spirit that remains alive as long as we remember in and through our practice. Y así cerramos esta puerta, and step into our prayer.

Todos Somos Mujeres de Maiz

An Introduction

AMBER ROSE GONZÁLEZ

On March 8, 2009, I hopped on the Pacific Surfliner from Santa Barbara to attend the twelfth annual Mujeres de Maiz Live Art Show, "La Sagrada" or "She, the Sacred," at the Metabolic Studio under the First Street Bridge in Yaanga.[1] Upon my arrival, I initially felt a sense of disappointment for having missed the opening sunset ceremony offered by all-women danzantes in the nearby community park known as "Not a Cornfield." However, as the evening unfolded, it became clear that the entire event was a ceremony.[2] After paying ten dollars at the door, I walked through the entrance that led to an enclosed art exhibit featuring beautifully adorned altars, vibrant paintings and photographs, and a multidimensional art installation of a life-sized "Mujer de Maiz" elegantly adorned in dried corn husks and live flowers (plate 9). Films were screening in an adjoining room, which I didn't get to see because I was beckoned by the allure of the excitement unfolding outside. Emerging from the art exhibit, I joined approximately eight hundred other audience members in the main outdoor area, and I was instantly enveloped by the energy buzzing all around me. The scene was alive as women of color artisans proudly showcased their creations, ranging from all-natural handmade beauty products to culturally inspired clothing, jewelry, and books. People were enjoying homemade Mexican food and telling jokes and stories while muralists and graffiti artists collaborated in creating a huge piece on a concrete wall in the background. I was captivated by an enormous blue and pink neon-light interactive installation that read: "Another city is Possible" (figure I.1). Parents watched their children as they laughed and climbed on four different ladders positioned directly beneath the sign. Others stopped to capture the moment by snapping pictures, and I thought that they must have been in as much awe as I was. The warmth of these interactions prompted me to think about the alterNative Los Angeles that I know and love—a city with a vibrant activist art and music scene, a strong sense of community, and people who care for one another.[3]

As I moved through the sprawling venue, I noticed people of all ages gathered around different stages; their anticipation was palpable as they eagerly awaited the electrifying performances by women musicians, poets, storytellers, singers, dancers, emcees, actors, and comedians who performed in rotation in three different areas. Diverse women of color were creating their art side by side, sharing in many languages, dissolving

FIGURE I.1 Lauren Bon and the Metabolic Studio. *Another city is Possible*, neon sign installation, n.d. Photograph by the author.

language barriers through stories that resonated across worlds. Many of them fearlessly transcended artistic boundaries, seamlessly intertwining various genres and styles like Skim, a queer Korean American hip hop artist, emcee, songwriter, and activist from Queens, New York, who incorporated traditional Korean drumming into her performance. I spent the next few hours trying to absorb all the sights, sounds, and emotions that I could. I shopped, I ate too much, I danced it off, I ran into old friends, I laughed, and my heart was full. By the end of the night, I was completely enamored with the Live Art Show space and the vibe MdM had created. They provided exactly what my spirit needed. Something special happened that night and I couldn't wait to return.

The next year, I recruited a few friends from my graduate program to take a road trip with me to attend the thirteenth annual MdM show, "13-Baktun Return of the Wisdom of Elders" at the Paramount Ballroom, formerly known as Casa Grande Salon, in Boyle Heights.[4] The day's events began with a free art walk along First Street with stops at local businesses including Eastside Luv and Primera Taza Coffee House and ended with live performances at Mariachi Plaza, named for the musicians who have gathered there since the 1930s in search of landing gigs at restaurants and private parties. We parked on Avenida César Chavez and walked to the nondescript building hoping that the clouds wouldn't bring rain, at least until we made it inside. We saw people we knew standing in line, waiting to get in, and so we chatted with them for a while. A few minutes later, a huge wooden door opened, and behind it were two women standing at a podium, collecting the twenty-dollar cover. After paying the entrance fee, my friends and I made our way inside to the first floor where women vendors were selling their merchandise at the Mujer Mercado. I spent most of my time talking with Dr. Elena Esparza, who had a booth with plants, herbs, essential oils, and pamphlets on acupuncture, flower essence healing, and holistic wellness.

Around 9:30 p.m. an interior door swung open, revealing the entrance to the main stage on the second floor. There were tons of people in a much smaller space than the previous year, leaving standing room only for an audience of approximately four hundred. People filled the aisles and the back of the room, eagerly awaiting the featured performance of award-winning Afro-Peruvian singer Susana Baca and her collaboration with Entre Mujeres, a transnational/translocal musical composition project between Chicanas/Latinas in East Los Angeles, California, and jarochas/ Mexicanas in Veracruz, Mexico (figure 1.8).[5] Women and children of all ages filled the stage, singing and dancing, and engaging the crowd in call and response. The pound of the drums and the harmonious blending of the women's voices reverberated in my body, opening my senses to take in the rest of the show. Another headlining act was Las Bomberas de la Bahia, an all-women Puerto Rican bomba troupe based in the Bay Area, California. The lineup also included Hermanas Canto Cura, consisting of Irma Cui Cui Rangel and Adriana Alvarez; D'Lo, queer/transgender Tamil Sri Lankan–American actor, writer, and comic from Queens, New York; Happy Frejo, Seminole Pawnee Xicana lyricist, dancer, filmmaker, and actress; the musical duo Indige Femme, comprising Tash Terry of the Navajo Nation and Elena Higgins of Māori and Samoan heritage; and Chicana playwright and poet Josefina Lopez.

The night felt magical. On the way home, my friends and I recounted our favorite performances, shared what we bought from the vendors, and laughed over the latest chismes. It was during that car ride home that I began to recognize the impact the Live Art Show had on me. MdM brought ancestral ceremonies and cultural expressions into the present, opened them up, and made them accessible to urban women of color and their allies—those interested in egalitarian, liberatory, and decolonial lifeways. I felt a sacred connection to the people in that space and understood the art beyond its aesthetic value. For me, it was also political and spiritual. The deep sense of belonging that I felt as a young woman of color from L.A. was new, and it was empowering. It was in that moment I decided that I too wanted to become a Mujer de Maiz.

I began organizing with MdM shortly after "13-Baktun," and in 2014 we began planning for the collective's twentieth anniversary. During our organizing meetings for the retrospective art exhibit and Live Art Show, the idea for an anthology emerged from a desire to document the work of the organization in a variety of ways. Since its inception, MdM has relied on a grassroots do-it-yourself model, self-publishing zines and producing multimedia art exhibitions and community events throughout the Greater Los Angeles area.[6] We continue this tradition through the creation of a retrospective anthology that foregrounds our voices and perspectives, weaving together diverse stories to collectively document MdM's herstory with attention to the larger sociopolitical context in which these stories take shape. The historical context for the emergence of Mujeres de Maiz is explored briefly in the following section.

FERTILE GROUND: THE EMERGENCE OF MUJERES DE MAIZ

> *Speaking and communicating lay the groundwork, but there is a point beyond too much talk that abstracts the experience. What is needed is a symbolic behavior performance made concrete by involving body and emotions with political theories and strategies, rituals that will connect the conscious with the unconscious. Through ritual we can make some deep-level changes. Ritual consecrates the alliance. Breaking bread together, and other group activities that physically and psychically represent the ideas, goals and attitudes promote a quickening, thickening between us.*
> —GLORIA ANZALDÚA, "BRIDGE, DRAWBRIDGE, SANDBAR OR ISLAND," P. 154

In the 1990s, Los Angeles had the highest concentrated populations of urban Indians and Latinxs in the United States—it was a city of civil unrest, a hotbed for political action, and a site of Raza and Indigenous cultural reawakening. A consequence of neoliberal capitalist economic restructuring and deindustrialization, L.A. was the most socioeconomically divided city in the nation and was facing major cuts to social programs and an unemployment rate near 50 percent. Gentrification was taking place throughout the city, especially in northeastern working-class neighborhoods. Uprisings erupted in South L.A. in 1992 following the acquittal of four police officers, three of them white, on charges of assault and excessive force against Rodney King and after decades of police violence and other social injustices in poor and working-class Black and Latinx communities. The LAPD's response was to unleash paramilitary policing tactics that were palpably aggressive toward poor communities of color. The decade also saw an upsurge in xenophobic white supremacist propositions in California, such as 187 and 209, used "to contain the power of the new nonwhite demographic majority [and] these propositions served as a model for the rest of the country."[7] Internationally, the decade marked the official conclusion of the Cold War, peace accords were signed to end the conflict in El Salvador, the prophecized Peace and Dignity Journeys connecting Northern and Southern Indigenous peoples were set in motion, and on the same day the North American Free Trade Agreement (NAFTA) was to go into effect, the Ejército Zapatista de Liberación Nacional (Zapatista Army of National Liberation, or EZLN), commonly known as the Zapatistas, rose up against the neoliberal Mexican State.

It was in this crucible that MdM emerged, alongside other Xican/x bands, visual artists, poets, and performers.[8] Los Angeles was fertile ground in the spring of 1997, and it was an auspicious time to plant the seeds that would become Mujeres de Maiz. Felicia 'Fe' Montes was enrolled in a Chicano art course at the University of California, Los Angeles, and she saw an opportunity to organize a women's collaborative art show as her final class project. She was joined by Lilia 'Liliflor' Ramirez, Lisa Rocha, Liza Cohen Hita, Skryb Anu, Sphear, Aida Salazar, and Victoria Delgadillo, diverse women of color from different L.A. neighborhoods, at the initial organizing meeting at the Aztlán Cultural Arts Foundation in Lincoln Heights. Felicia was also a founding member of the newly formed Indigenous Xicana performance poetry and song collective In Lak Ech, named in honor of the Maya worldview "You are my other me" or "Tu eres mi otro yo," along with Claudia Mercado, Liza Cohen Hita, Cristina Gorocica, Rachel Negrete Thorson, Marisol Lydia Torres, and joined by Marlene Beltran in 2004. In Lak Ech would go on to spearhead the efforts to establish Mujeres de Maiz and become a hallmark of the Live Art Shows.

The organizers decided to host an intercultural, intergenerational, multimedia event that would combine elements of an art exhibit, live performances, and ritual ceremony featuring women of color musicians, dancers, visual artists, artisans, poets, actors, filmmakers, and spiritual healers. They also decided to publish *Flor y Canto*, a literary and arts zine featuring the poetry and visual art of women of color from around the world to be released in conjunction with the Live Art Show.[9] The first zine, *The Birth of la Diosa de Maiz* (figure 1.2) was released at the inaugural show, which took place on June 29, 1997, at Centro Regeracíon, also known as the Popular Resource Center in Highland Park. Claudia,

MdM co-founder, recalls the PRC was "an energetic space" where local artists and activists held meetings, fundraisers, exhibits, and artistic events. Two noteworthy groups, Radio Clandestina and the National Committee for Democracy in Mexico, were permanent fixtures at the PRC. It was also a hub for Xicanx bands Aztlan Underground, Quetzal, Blues Experiment, In Lak Ech, Ollin, Quinto Sol, artists Nuke and Omar Ramírez, and later Mujeres de Maiz to gather and perform. The PRC was integral to the development of the East L.A. Xicanx artivist scene in the 1990s.[10]

The same summer as the first MdM Live Art Show, Xicanx artivists from L.A. participated in the Encuentro Cultural Intercontinental por la Humanidad y Contra el Neoliberalismo with the Indigenous Zapatista Mayan community of Oventic. Martha Gonzalez, cultural critic, MdM member, and lead singer, percussionist, and songwriter of the band Quetzal recalls the impact the encuentro had on her along with twenty artivists from East Los Angeles. Gonzalez remembers, "The Zapatista anti-imperialist message, as well as the use of a poetry-like approach to communicate their demands to the world invigorated the Xicana East LA artistic movement."[11] Gonzalez says the encuentro was significant because it demonstrated two things:

> One, how music and art could serve as dialectic tools between communities, and two, how the process of collective communal engagement drew out multiple subjectivities between Mayan and Xicano participants. Through communal artistic processes, our differences, although existing in multiple and intersectional ways in our daily life, were highlighted and deconstructed. Relationality and dialogue became the essential after-effect a creative convivial space engenders. As a result, artivista East Los methods and epistemologies reflect this emphasis on relationality and Indigenous pedagogies in the use of their art.

Gonzalez stresses that relationality, a core tenant of Zapatista philosophy, significantly influenced Xicanx artivist praxis, particularly the emphasis on building alliances with exploited and marginalized communities around the world. In the epigraph that opens this section, Anzaldúa calls for a similar collective process—embodied ritual practices that attend to the conscious and unconscious of our beings—to build bridges across differences and to thicken the bonds between us in order to "make deep level changes."

Felicia recalls learning the Zapatista mantras and poetic dichos "Everything for everyone" and "Todos somos Marcos/Ramona" (We are all Marcos/Ramona) while organizing at the Encuentro. MdM organizers refashioned the philosophy of relationality for their own context through the slogan "¡Todos somos Mujeres de Maiz!" (We are all Mujeres de Maiz). The phrase is often heard at events and organizing meetings, and is posted on the website, social media, and in the zine. Felicia explains, "After the 1994 uprising and especially after the [1997] gathering, Zapatista imagery, dichos, and philosophy" remain a prominent influence on Xicanx artivist's artistic, political, and spiritual practices.[12] In the chapter "Femzines, Artivism, and Altar Aesthetics," Norell Martínez points out how:

> Like the rebels in Chiapas, urban youth of color in L.A. also felt persecuted by the State and relegated to second-class citizenship. They too experienced low-intensity warfare and police violence and were living the effects of neoliberalism in their barrios. Chicana/o youth became inspired to organize political and artistic movements grounded in the Zapatista vision: "un mundo donde quepan muchos mundos" (EZLN). MdM members looked to the Zapatistas, and especially the Zapatista women, who played critical leadership roles in the uprising, for inspiration to resolve gender disparities in their community.

Inspired by their recent participation in the Xicano-Zapatista Encuentro, MdM produced four Live Art Shows organized around the changing seasons, three zines, and one documentary in their first year together. The second Live Art Show and zine release, *Seeds of Resistance*, coincided with Día de los Muertos and was held November 9, 1997, at the Community Service Organization (CSO) in Boyle Heights and was held in honor of "women in spirit." MdM produced the third zine and show *Of Mixed Waters* on March 8, 1998, at the CSO. This was the first show held in honor of International Women's Day, Women's Herstory Month, spring equinox, and Mexica new year, which set the precedent for scheduling future shows on an annual basis around these observances.[13] The fourth show *Mujeres de Maiz: The Roots of Herstory* went back to the PRC on August 7, 1998. Like the first three shows, MdM organized an art exhibit, but rather than releasing a zine, Claudia and Felicia directed and produced a documentary that chronicled the first four years of the collective. In remembering the first Live Art Shows, Rachel recalls, "The first MDM show was magic. It was long and unorganized and the lights and settings were anything we could get our hands on. But it was packed and people loved it. I was an MC that night and I was young and so scared and I made so many mistakes, but I had this feeling that I was participating in something monumentally important and it was exhilarating. It was one of the best times of my life."[14] Marisol describes the first shows as "experimental" and "healing":

> Artists of different backgrounds and across disciplines came together to create new works. Imagine poets, filmmakers, singers, musicians, visual artists, MCs, classically trained dancers, and flamenco dancers creating work together to be showcased in front of an audience/community—this was our first year. Visual artists created new work and exhibits for each new live show. We invited artists to meet to dialogue at different homes and venues in an attempt to build a vision for this brand new collective/network. The vibe at the shows was always positive and inspiring. Giving the microphone to young women to share was a powerful experience for both the person on the stage and the person in the audience. Audiences lined up out into the street to get into the show and gave the performers and artists a lot of love and encouragement. It felt like community. We had many courageous performers and artists who had common and sometimes similar tragic experiences that were shared through song, poetry, and paintings. This was a very healing experience for so many of us.[15]

Since 1997, MdM has produced more than twenty Live Art Shows and art exhibits and published fifteen issues of *Flor y Canto*.[16] Collaboration is a distinct and intentional feature of the Live Art Show. Mujeres de Maiz functions as an umbrella collective that brings together established groups and individual artists who then become a part of the MdM extended network. More experienced creators are often paired with younger or emerging visual and performance artists and musicians to guide them in the development of their craft through direct intergenerational mentorship. This practice not only fortifies the extended spiritual artivist feminist network established in 1997 but also ensures its continuation. Cross-genre, interdisciplinary, interethnic, and intergenerational collaborations are reinforced in and through MdM, with some of these relationships continuing well after the Live Art Show. Women members of the Balagtasan Collective, Pinay spoken word artists, came together for the first time and Las Ramonas, a three-member Xicana comedy and guerilla theater troupe formed and stayed together as a result of their participation in a Live Art Show.

Over the years, we have expanded our programming and the Live Art Show has become the kickoff for a month-long series of community events including a Mujer Mercado, poetry night/procession, film screenings, women's gatherings such as the monthly Coyolxauhqui full moon circle, and workshops with topics ranging from art making, creative writing, gardening, self-defense, and women's health, often in collaboration with other feminist of color organizations and groups from the Eastside including Justice for my Sister, AF3IRM, Hood Herbalism, and WE RISE LA, to name a few. We have also presented and performed at numerous academic conferences, in college classes, and at high school assemblies. In 2017 MdM celebrated its twentieth anniversary with the exhibition *Mujeres de Maiz: Twenty Years of ARTivism & Herstory en LA*, which ran from March 4 to May 29 at LA Plaza de Cultura y Artes in Downtown Los Angeles. That same year, we became a nonprofit organization and began offering online programming, relying on social media to connect with a wider audience, which increased significantly in 2020 as a result of the COVID-19 pandemic.

While a central intention of MdM is to empower women and girls of color, the events are designed so that all in attendance can find resonance with MdM's feminist of color politics, spirituality, and aesthetics grounded in a Xicana Indígena sensibility. People of varied ethnic, racial, gender, sexual, educational, and linguistic identities and ages are encouraged, through witnessing the collaborative and innovative performances, to define themselves in relation to others in ways that do not hierarchize difference. Audience members are thus also purposefully included in the phrase "Todos somos Mujeres de Maiz!" Due to the carefully procured method of organizing the content of the Live Art Show and other events, individuals are able to connect with the various aspects that matter to them. Claudia succinctly explains:

> Mujeres de Maiz provides a space, an outlet of voices that speak of something [the audience] cannot find in popular culture. [MdM artists and performers] speak about alternative health, they speak about spirituality, we speak about connection to nature, we speak about connection to cultura, we speak about community and family. We provide a space that puts values on the forefront of how to be a better human being, or how to become a better person. Reaching, targeting, primarily women. It's giving women a space to talk about their issues. To talk, see, or to hear these voices where nowhere else is being heard. There's no space for them. So, I think some people are attracted to [the Live Art Show] because it's about cultura. Some people are attracted to it because it's about spirituality. People are attracted to it for different reasons.[17]

The audience comes to the Live Art Show to share the energy put in motion by MdM, and to participate in an urban women of color–centered healing ceremony spearheaded by Indigenous Xicanas. As a result, MdM functions as an extended support network—a circle of belonging—one that does not seek utopia, but one that centers hope, affirmation, and dignity. It is a space of possibility to envision another city and another world and to enact that vision. We share our vision with you in *Mujeres de Maiz en Movimiento: Spiritual ARTivism, Healing Justice, and Feminist Praxis*.

STRUCTURE OF THE BOOK

The editors embarked on this journey by inviting founding MdM members, integral organizers, and artistic-spiritual femtors to submit a written testimonio, short story, prose, or other mixed-genre piece about their experiences with Mujeres de Maiz. The anthology prioritizes these testimonios, each contributor accounting for their unique subjectivity, memories, experiences, and personal relationship to MdM. We intentionally placed the testimonios in dialogue with academic-oriented essays, many of which are written in first-person voice blending autobiography, prose, and theory, similar to an "artist-meets-critic" format. We have also included previously published poems and visual artwork selected from past zine issues that reflect a wide array of social issues, topics, and images important to the organization. The contributors include emerging and professional writers, scholars, visual and performance artists, and community organizers. While primarily written in English, many authors weave Spanish, Nahuatl, Tagalog, and other heritage languages into their stories, reflecting their natural inclination to codeswitch. In order to preserve the authenticity of each author's voice, we retained the stylistic preferences employed by each contributor. This includes the usage of accents, the choice of italicizing non-English words (or not), and other deliberate grammatical decisions.

Our story opens with "Mujeres de Maiz: Seed to Spiritual Artivism—An L.A. Herstory," by Felicia 'Fe' Montes, which she describes as an "offering to a sacred fire—the fuego of Mujeres de Maiz" and "an ode to my greatest love, a testament to my life's work, vision, and my ultimate creation." The essay offers a window into the genesis and evolution of the collective, as seen through the eyes of a principal member, artist, performer, activist, and organizer deeply rooted in the community.

The book is organized into four thematic sections, honoring the traditional four-part structure of many Indigenous ceremonies that various contributors participate in. While much of the content overlaps and many entries could be included in any one of the sections, we provide a starting point from which readers can begin to understand MdM's organizing principles. The initial structure can then be reconfigured to generate fresh dialogues. This flexibility proves particularly valuable for educators, artists, and community organizers who wish to experiment with applying different readings within their particular context.

ROUND 1. EMERGENT SPIRITUAL JOURNEYS AND HEALING SPACES

Drawing on lessons from the likes of Ella Baker and Grace Lee Boggs, adrienne maree brown defines emergence as emphasizing "critical connections over critical mass, building authentic relationships, listening with all the senses of the body and the mind" and emergent strategy as "how we intentionally change in ways that grow our capacity to embody the just and liberated worlds we long for."[18] Accordingly, emergent spiritual journeys and healing spaces are pathways and locations that can lead us toward liberation through an embodied spiritualized praxis. Collectively, the essays and poems in this section tell a story of the blossoming of Mujeres de Maiz, emphasizing accounts of spiritual artivism and radical interconnectedness, or In Lak'ech.[19]

Round 1 opens with "Danzando con el Fuego," by MdM co-founder and filmmaker Claudia Mercado, who blends prose and poetry in an homage to Los Angeles, narrating rare stories about Xican/x landmarks, radical queer collectives, and salient events including the Popular Resource Center (PRC), the pirate radio station *Radio Clandestina*, MdM's annual Live Art Shows, and In Lak Ech, an Indigenous Xicana spoken word, drum, and song collective who would become a quintessential element of Mujeres de Maiz. Mercado infuses her testimonio with vivid imagery and powerful storytelling, inviting the reader into the MdM circle.

"Magandang Misteryo (Beautiful Mystery)" is a testimonio by Liza Cohen Hita, who with Filipina-Jewish heritage summons fundamental understandings of Chicana as a chosen political standpoint and identity, not a biologically determined one. Cohen Hita recalls developing an anti-imperialist transnational feminist consciousness in college, alongside other MdM organizers and artists. Their praxis collectively deepened as a result of their participation in the Xican/x-Zapatista Encuentro. In her essay "Reflections on Mujeres de Maiz," Chicana theologian and MdM spiritual mentor Lara Medina provides an overview of MdM's spiritual traditions, tracing their lineage to the "foremothers of the 1970s who bravely initiated reclamations of Indigenous identity and cultural practices."

"Coyolxauhqui Full Moon Circle: Self-Care as Community Care" is a critical essay by Nadia Zepeda that explores the significance of the monthly outdoor women's gathering and talking circle in East Los Angeles hosted by Mujeres de Maiz since 2010. Drawing from oral histories of three circle keepers and healing collective participants, Zepeda demonstrates the ways Chicanas are finding and reconnecting with Indigeneity through an ancestral spiritual practice in the present, both individually and collectively.

"Mujeres de Maiz Arising: Shifts and Movement of Positioning Xicana-driven Indigenous Spirituality" is a blend of critical essay, testimonio, and storytelling by Angela Mictlanxochitl Anderson Guerrero. The chapter explores what it means to be a "transterritorial de-Indigenized scholar-practitioner" and how decolonial spirituality serves as a foundation to this critical work. By drawing inspiration from the past and present, while casting an anticipatory eye to the future, the chapter navigates the terrain of this journey. Round 1 closes with poems that touch on embodied spiritualized praxis through radical self-love, the intimate connection between sisters, and the healing magic conjured through dance.

ROUND 2. MOVIMIENTOS DE REBELDÍA

I want the freedom to carve and chisel my own face, to staunch the bleeding with ashes, to fashion my own gods out of my entrails. And if going home is denied me then I will have to stand and claim my space, making a new culture—una cultura mestiza—with my own lumber, my own bricks and mortar and my own feminist architecture.[20]
—GLORIA ANZALDÚA, "MOVIMIENTOS DE REBELDÍA Y LAS CULTURAS QUE TRAICIONAN," P. 44

In "Movimientos de rebeldía y las culturas que traicionan," Gloria Anzaldá theorizes the arduous task of negotiating the contradictions between loving and defending our cultures to outsiders while simultaneously challenging oppressive norms, traditions, and expectations, especially for Indigenous women and queer people. Contributors in Round 2 fuse stories of love, transformation, and spirit-work with an incisive critique of interlocking oppressions, both intimate and structural, encouraging movement toward liberatory otherwise worlds, what the Zapatistas envision as "a world where many worlds fit." Round 2 opens with Felicia's poem "I am International Woman," highlighting the relationality between Indigenous Xicanas and women of the Global South and their sacred role as "mujeres en ceremonia."

Round 2 unfolds with a dynamic trio of testimonios by three inspiring MdM members. "Re-Collecting" by D'Lo, a "male-pronoun using, woman and femme-loving, trans masculine Tamil Sri Lankan American," poetically recites his transformative journey alongside MdM. "Recollections: My Journey with MdM" by Skryb Anu, recalls memories of personal loss and healing through the creation of and performances with queer women of color multimedia poetry groups and their participation in MdM spaces. Lastly, in "The Will of the Water," Marisol

Lydia Torres details her participation with In Lak Ech, MdM Live Art Shows, her love of political theater, and the formation of Las Ramonas with two other longtime members of MdM. The section comes to a close with "The Spiritual Activism of Mujeres de Maiz: Queering the Boundaries of Art and Action" by Karen Mary Davalos. The chapter provides an illuminating examination of MdM's myriad activities and orientations and situates them within an Indigenous Xicana spiritual activist lineage.

Defying simple classification, Mujeres de Maiz is part of a long tradition of Chican/x feminist thought and arts. Since the late 1960s, Chican/x feminists have constructed their multiple subjectivities not only in resistance to Chicano nationalism and U.S. hegemonic feminism, but also in solidarity with an emerging U.S. Third World feminist consciousness informed by decolonial and anticolonial movements worldwide. As they critiqued white supremacy, heteropatriarchy, capitalism, and imperialism, feminists of color in the United States created a new crossracial political subjectivity that linked various struggles for social justice and much of this occurred through spiritualized practice. This political solidarity is evidenced in the cultural production of many feminists of color, including Mujeres de Maiz and the poetry in this section.

ROUND 3. LA CULTURA CURA: ARTIVIST AESTHETICS

While the chapters in the previous section grapple with confronting and repurposing harmful cultural norms, the contributors in Round 3 explore the ways *la cultura cura*, or culture heals. We intentionally placed artist's testimonios in dialogue with academic essays that consider the work of the artist, similar to an "artist-meets-critic" format. Round 3 opens with "Art is Ceremony," a testimonio by queer Xicana multidisciplinary artist Gina Aparicio. In this piece, Aparicio reflects on her participation in MdM as one of the original core members and shares memorable stories as one of the group's photographers, zine co-editors, and art exhibit co-curators. In the chapter "Queer Xicana Indígena Cultural Production: Remembering Through Oral and Visual Storytelling," Susy Zepeda traces oral and visual stories of queer Xicana Indígena artists, including the work of Gina Aparicio and Claudia Mercado, to address colonial forms of epistemic violence. By focusing on queer Indigenous artists' and cultural producers' visions of transformation, Zepeda demonstrates how they construct decolonized knowledge that simultaneously reconceptualizes the past, present, and future for Xican/xs and Latin/xs. Significantly, the historical memory constructed by these cultural producers offers critiques of United States and transnational systems of domination that are ultimately expressed in their writing, sculptures, films, and spiritual practices.

"Bringing Art to the People: Decolonizing Art Spaces and Exhibitions" by Michelle L. Lopez delves into the content and symbolism found in artworks that have been presented at MdM exhibitions. These exhibitions challenge conventional art norms by taking place in non-traditional settings, breaking down elitist notions in art presentation. Lopez meticulously catalogs MdM's extensive legacy of using art as as a means for catalyzing social change and contributions to the Los Angeles Artscape.

In the chapter "Femzines, Artivism, and Altar Aesthetics: Third Wave Feminism Chicana Style," Norell Martínez guides us through the world of MdM zines. MdM adopts a politicized spirituality influenced by Mesoamerican conceptions of art and poetry that understands these art forms as healing, transformative, and connected to the divine. Martínez argues that MdM employs this framework within the zines to make a larger critique of patriarchy and gender violence, ultimately seeking healing from these traumas. Poems were selected for this section that illustrate Martínez's claims.

ROUND 4. MDM EPISTEMOLOGIES AND PEDAGOGIES

The fourth and final round explores MdM ways of knowing, learning, and teaching, whether that be through song, oral traditions, activist research, social media, or dreams. Many of the contributors in this section, including the poets, ruminate on their roles as mothers, teachers, and guides to younger generations. We open with "In the Spirit of the Voluta," by Cristina Gorocica, who recounts the origin story of In Lak Ech, weaving together prose and song illuminating her roles as a community organizer, artivist, and mother and her responsibility to pass on her legacy to her daughters.

Gabriela Martinez, Pedro Martinez, Megan Pennings, and Dionne Espinoza formed a research team that gathered oral herstories of seven MdM members in anticipation of the collective's twenty-year anniversary.

Their chapter "Conocimientos from the Mujeres de Maiz Oral Herstory Project" explores the multiple levels of *conocimiento* embedded in the research process and highlights the knowledge that can emerge at the intersection of community engagement, academic research, and social justice. The authors frame the Mujeres de Maiz Oral Herstory project not only as research about activists, but also as spiritually transformative activist research.

In "Becoming an Activist-Scholar-Organizer with Mujeres de Maiz," I weave personal narratives with ethnographic field notes to chronicle pivotal moments and experiences during my dissertation research where I sought to document the creative, political, and spiritual practices of Mujeres de Maiz from 2011 to 2014. Written from the perspective of an insider-outsider Indigenous Xicana feminist researcher and community organizer, the chapter seeks to provide a useful account of the joys, struggles, and opportunities that can arise in community-engaged ethnographic research. It serves as a guide that activist-scholars can look to for insights as they embark on their own research projects.

Megan Pennings examines how MdM engages spiritual artivism on social media to attract women of color audiences and raise the consciousness of their followers. Her chapter "Restoring the Mind, Body, and Spirit: Mujeres de Maiz and Social Media as a Tool of Spiritual Artivism and Education" focuses on the ways MdM deploys a feminist of color praxis on social media and argues that through their Instagram platform, they have created a virtual space for their followers to deepen reconnections to their mind-body-spirit and become informed about ancestral healing practices.

"The Bees. The Honey. The Humanity." is a testimonio by Martha Gonzalez, who looks back on her experience at the first Live Art Show, centering her reflections on the emotions evoked on that special night. Gonzalez points to the importance of the MdM stage and how it has provided a space for countless artivists to come of age. We arrive full circle with "dreamseeds of the women of the corn," where Iris De Anda shares a captivating story of the prophetic dream that led her to MdM and how her connection to the collective was cemented through poetry, creative writing, and the zine. Finally, Iris's "Makeover Manifesto," which can be read as part mantra, part invitation, encourages readers to love yourself, reclaim your power, and see yourself as a mujer de maiz.

Taken together, the critical and creative pieces reveal MdM's framework and exemplify the issues and causes the collective has prioritized over the years. MdM's political-ethical-spiritual commitments, cultural production, and everyday practices are informed by Indigenous and transnational feminist of color artistic, spiritual, activist, and intellectual legacies representing a convergence of various political projects, social movements, and ceremonial circles that members are involved in. MdM is a contemporary grassroots radical women of color organization that works at the interstices of traditionally defined social movements. Activist-historian Maylei Blackwell notes that as political subjects with multiple identities, women of color organizing often takes on the following features: "(1) multiple issues in one movement, (2) an intersectional understanding of power and oppression, and (3) the tendency to work in and between movements."[21]

Mujeres de Maiz en Movimiento contributes to the legacy of radical women of color who use art and writing to theorize their lives and to tell their individual and community stories, simultaneously constructing and transmitting knowledge by "walking in the histories of their people."[22] Chicanas in particular have built an impressive archive of community-based feminist and queer publications.[23] In her seminal study of Chicanas in the Chicano movement, Blackwell uncovers the ways Chicanas have historically bridged geographic, political, generational, and ideological distances among one another through "print-mediated exchange."[24] For example, Chicanas deliberated at campus and community meetings and conferences and subsequently circulated their ideas in newspapers, journals, pamphlets, and magazines, which were often republished and widely circulated. Blackwell argues that these "print mediated discussions not only built new critical interpretive communities; they, along with caucuses and conferences, constituted a Chicana counterpublic."[25] She defines counterpublics as "parallel discursive arenas where those excluded from dominant discourses 'invent and circulate counter discourses, so as to formulate oppositional interpretations of their identities, interests and needs.'"[26] Historically zines and anthologies have served as a print mediated space for radical feminists of color to create and legitimate "counterpublics," which now includes *Mujeres de Maiz en Movimiento*.

THIS BOOK IS FOR YOU: ¡TODOS SOMOS MUJERES DE MAÍZ!

The book project emerges from and contributes to knowledge at the intersection of artivism, cultural criticism, healing justice, and feminist of color spiritual praxis. As editors, our intention was to produce a multidimensional text that is both accessible and appealing to a general readership and that can also be taught in advanced high school classrooms, introductory community college courses, and upper-division undergraduate seminars at colleges and universities. Given the recent legislation mandating ethnic studies graduation requirements in California high schools, California Community Colleges, the California State University, and the University of California, the book is a timely resource. We have created a recommended reading and resources list, assignments, and other activities that make the book uniquely desirable to a wide array of educators and students.[27] Furthermore, for artists, community organizers, and activist-scholars invested in social justice and liberation, it is imperative to look to the change-makers and cultural shifters who have successfully engaged in this work for decades, not merely for inspiration, but to learn from their ethos, ideologies, frameworks, and practices, and to experiment with applying these across different contexts. Consequential lessons emerge from studying long-standing grassroots and community-based organizations such as Mujeres de Maiz who have weathered shifting political climates and created apertures to challenge oppressive apparatuses and build life anew again and again. The book will especially resonate with youth of color who seek accessible in-depth studies of sustainable feminist organizing, for which there is a dearth of published material. Thus the text functions as an important pedagogical tool in diverse settings and can act as a guidebook for critical self-exploration and collective organizing, what Gloria E. Anzaldúa has termed "inner work, public acts."[28] We hope our twenty-first century Xicana codex inspires you to begin—or continue—on your transformative and healing path.

NOTES

1. In English, *Mujeres de Maiz* translates to "Women of the Corn." I don't put an accent on the *i* in *maiz* to honor the way it's typically spelled in print, which

reflects a X/Chican/x Spanglish usage. Mujeres de Maiz will also be referred to as MdM, which is a commonly used acronym among its members. Yaanga is the name of the Tongva-Gabrielino village site in what is now known as Downtown Los Angeles. "Mapping the Tongva Villages of L.A.'s Past," *Los Angeles Times*, May 9, 2019, https://www.latimes.com/projects/la-me-tongva-map/.

2. *"Not a Cornfield* transformed an abandoned rail yard in Downtown Los Angeles into a thirty-two-acre cornfield for one agricultural cycle in 2005–6. The work began nearly a decade of remediation of this iconic yet neglected site, the last remaining undeveloped land of the native Tongva and Gabrieleno people, and the site of the Zanja Madre—or 'mother ditch'—that linked the LA River to the first Spanish settlement in Los Angeles." "Not a Cornfield," Metabolic Studio, May 22, 2017, https://www.metabolicstudio.org/tags/not-a-cornfield. It is now known as Los Angeles State Historic Park.

3. Alicia Gaspar de Alba coined the term *alter-Native* to describe an approach that "contests the ethnocentric academic practice of categorizing marginalized indigenous cultures as 'subcultures' or objects of discovery" (10). Specifically speaking of Chicanxs, Gaspar de Alba asserts, "Chicano/a culture is not only an 'alter-culture' that simultaneously differs from, is changed by, and changes the dominant culture. It is also an alter-Native culture—an Other culture native" to this particular geohistorical location that was "once called an outpost of New Spain, then the Mexican North, then the American Southwest, and most contemporarily the Chicano/a homeland of Aztlán" (17). It is important to note that each one of these localized geographical namings are colonial and colonizing *and* as a reconnecting detribalized Apache/Xicana and fourth-generation Angeleno, I find resonance with the act of claiming a space of belonging alongside other urban Indian, Xican/xs, and people of color in L.A. Alicia Gaspar de Alba, *Chicano Art Inside Outside the Master's House: Cultural Politics and the CARA Exhibition* (Austin: University of Texas Press, 1998). Gloria Anzaldúa, "Speaking Across the Divide," in *The Gloria Anzaldúa Reader*, ed. AnaLouise Keating (Durham, N.C.: Duke University Press), 282–94, for her perspective on Ch/Xicana detribalization.

4. A baktun is twenty katun cycles of the ancient Maya Long Count Calendar. The 2010 Gregorian calendar year fell within the thirteenth baktun, which was completed on December 21, 2012. This date marked the beginning of the fourteenth baktun, also known as Sexto Sol or Sixth Sun in Nahua cultures.

5. Martha Gonzalez, lead singer, percussionist, and songwriter of the band Quetzal, is the founder and leader of Entre Mujeres. The members are Claudia González-Tenorio (CAVA), Tylana Enomoto (Quetzal), La Marisoul and Gloria Estrada (La Santa Cecilia), and dancers Xochi Flores (Cambalache) and Carolina Sarmiento (Son del Centro). Gonzalez has participated in Mujeres de Maiz as a performer and mentor since it was created in 1997. Her testimonio "The Bees. The Honey. The Humanity." can be found in chapter 35 in round 4.

6. Zines, short for fanzine, are do-it-yourself small-scale publications that emerged in the 1990s punk and feminist activist scenes, often produced on a shoestring

budget by an individual or a collective. Zines are noncommercial independent media that circulate information and communicate personal stories that are often devalued in popular culture, public discourse, and mainstream politics. In her study of third-space queer and feminist of color zines, Adela C. Licona argues that these action-oriented, multiply voiced, coalitional publications work to raise consciousness, reeducate and redefine community, and mobilize social justice and transformation. "By challenging, reimagining, and replacing exclusionary and oppressive discursive practices," she contends, "zines perform new expressions of subjectivity." Adela C. Licona, *Zines in Third Space: Radical Cooperation and Borderlands Rhetoric* (Albany: State University of New York Press, 2012), 2. Thus zines produced by feminists and queer people of color can be important sites of cultural intervention and disruption of the status quo.

7. Ramon Grosfoguel, Nelson Maldonado-Torres, and Jose David Saldivar, eds., *Latino/as in the World-System Decolonization Struggles in the 21st Century U.S. Empire* (London: Routledge, 2005), 16–17.

8. *Chican/x* is a politicized term associated with a collective history of oppression and resistance connected to a political consciousness with its origins in the Chicano movement of the 1960s and 1970s. Despite the fact that Filipinxs, Mexican immigrants, and Indigenous- and Afro-Latinxs with origins across the hemisphere have identified with the term Chican/x since its emergence, dominant constructions often erroneously subsume this diversity under the banner "Mexican American." An *X* was first used in place of the *Ch* in the 1990s by a cohort of Xican/xs and Xican/x-Indígenas who identified with contemporary hemispheric Indigenous political projects of sovereignty, liberation, and decolonization, emphasizing their Indigenous heritages as integral to their lives. For an examination of the evolving nature of Xicanidad and Xicanisma, review Ana Castillo, *Massacre of the Dreamers: Essays on Xicanisma* (New York: Plume, 1994); Roberto Hernández, "Running for Peace and Dignity: From Traditionally Radical Chicanos/as to Radically Traditional Xicanas/os," in *Latin@s in the World System: Decolonization Struggles in the 21st Century U.S. Empire*, eds. Ramon Grosfoguel, Nelson Maldonado-Torres, and Jose David Saldivar (Boulder, Colo.: Paradigm, 2005), 129–44; Cherríe Moraga, *A Xicana Codex of Changing Consciousness: Writings, 2000–2010* (Durham, N.C.: Duke University Press, 2011); and Elisa Facio and Irene Lara, eds., *Fleshing the Spirit: Spirituality and Activism in Chicana, Latina, and Indigenous Women's Lives* (Tucson: University of Arizona Press, 2014). *Mujeres de Maiz en Movimiento* extends the work of these scholar-activists to further understandings of Xicanisma by examining its usage among feminist artivists in Los Angeles since 1997.

9. This naming of the MdM zine hearkens to the Chicano literary events held across the Southwest from 1973 to 1978, called the Festivales de Flor y Canto, named for the Mesoamerican vision of poetry as *in xochitl, in cuicatl,* or flower and song. These festivals featured Chicano movement poets, playwrights, performance artists, visual artists, and musicians. Alurista, *Festival de Flor y Canto:*

An Anthology of Chicano Literature (Los Angeles: University of Southern California Press, 1976).

10. The first recorded academic citations of the words "artivist" and "artivism" are found in Chela Sandoval and Guisela Latorre, "Chicana/o Artivism: Judy Baca's Digital Work with Youth of Color," in *Learning Race and Ethnicity: Youth and Digital Media*, ed. Anna Everett (Cambridge, Mass.: MIT Press, 2008), 81–108, and M. K. Asante Jr., "By Any Medium Necessary," in *It's Bigger Than Hip Hop: The Rise of the Post-Hip-Hop Generation* (New York: St. Martin's Press, 2008), 199–210. However, Xican/xs have used the term in the East L.A. scene since the 1990s. Victor Hugo Viesca, "The Battle of Los Angeles: The Cultural Politics of Chicana/o Music in the Greater Eastside," *American Quarterly* 56, no. 3 (2004): 719–39; and Martha Gonzalez, *Chican@ Artivistas: Music, Community, and Transborder Tactics in East Los Angeles* (Austin: University of Texas Press, 2020).

11. Amber Rose González, Martha Gonzalez, and Felicia 'Fe' Montes, "Mujeres de Maiz: Talking and Walking L.A.'s Otr@ ARTivism," Mujeres Activas en Letras y Cambio Social (MALCS) panel, California State University, Los Angeles, July 20, 2011.

12. Felicia 'Fe' Montes, "Mujeres de Maiz: Seeds to Spiritual ARTivism—A L.A. Art Herstory" (master's thesis, California State University, Northridge, 2009), 79.

13. Montes, "Mujeres de Maiz," 32–33.

14. Rachel Negrete Thorson, email message to author, December 7, 2014.

15. Marisol Lydia Torres, email message to author, December 7, 2014.

16. Fifteen zine issues have been published between 1997 and 2018. Three issues were published in 1997–98 around the seasons, one issue was published annually between 2006 and 2016, and the latest issue was published in 2018. No issues were produced between 1999 and 2005, in 2017, or between 2019 and 2023.

17. Claudia Mercado. Interview with the author. May 19, 2011.

18. adrienne maree brown, *Emergent Strategy: Shaping Change, Changing Worlds* (Chico, Calif.: AK Press, 2017), 3.

19. The Maya living philosophy In Lak'ech, translated as "I am another yourself" or "You are my other me," was polularized in Chican/x communities by Chicano playwright and poet Luis Valdez in his 1971 poem "Pensamiento Serpentino." Valdez delineated a Chicano identity beyond ethnic and racial heritage, instead advocating for Indigenous spiritualized knowledge as a path toward freedom. He called for anchoring Chicano identity politics in a metaphysics of interconnectedness. Luis Valdez, *Luis Valdez Early Works: Actos, Bernabe and Pensamiento Serpentino* (Houston: Arte Público Press, 1990), 173. Chela Sandoval has called In Lak'ech a "method" and a "political system of recognition" deployed by radical women of color in the 1970s and 1980s. Chela Sandoval, "Foreword: AfterBridge: Technologies of Crossing," in *This Bridge We*

20. *Call Home: Radical Visions for Transformation*, eds. Gloria E. Anzaldúa and AnaLouise Keating (London and New York: Routledge, 2002), 23.
20. Gloria Anzaldúa, "Movimientos de rebeldía y las culturas que traicionan," in *Borderlands / La Frontera: The New Mestiza*, 3rd ed. (San Francisco: Aunt Lute Books, 2007), 44.
21. Maylei Blackwell, *¡Chicana Power!: Contested Histories of Feminism in the Chicano Movement* (Austin: University of Texas Press, 2011), 27.
22. Chrystos, "I Walk in the History of My People," in *This Bridge Called My Back: Writings by Radical Women of Color*, eds. Cherríe Moraga and Gloria Anzaldúa, 2nd ed. (New York: Kitchen Table: Women of Color Press, 1983), 57.
23. Examples include *Mango*, a community journal edited by Chicana feminist poet Lorna Dee Cervantes, and "la mujer" special edition of *Chisme Arte*, a publication of the Concilio de Arte Popular, a statewide Chicano arts advocacy group in California. Other examples include *Tongues Magazine*, an online zine published by and for queer women of color in Los Angeles; *malintZINE*, an online zine by radical/women/queer/people of color based in Tucson; and *Muchacha fanzine*, a radically intersectional decolonial publication. Additionally, grassroots student-generated publications like the newspaper published by Las Hijas de Cuauhtémoc at California State University, Long Beach, was the impetus for the journal *Encuentro Femenil* and *Coyolxauhqui Remembered: A Journal of Latina Voices* out of San Francisco State University.
24. Blackwell, *¡Chicana Power!*, 133.
25. Blackwell, *¡Chicana Power!*, 134.
26. Blackwell, *¡Chicana Power!*, 134. Blackwell's definition of counterpublics builds on feminist philosopher Nancy Fraser's interpretation of the work of Jürgen Habermas.
27. These materials can be found on our website, https://www.mujeresdemaiz.com/. There you will also find a section to submit your own MdM story. ¡Porque todos somos Mujeres de Maiz!
28. Gloria E. Anzaldúa, "now let us shift . . . the path of conocimiento . . . inner work, public acts," in *This Bridge We Call Home: Radical Visions for Transformation*, ed. Gloria E. Anzaldúa and AnaLouise Keating (London and New York: Routledge, 2002), 540–79.

Mujeres de Maíz

Seeds to Spiritual Artivism—An L.A. Herstory

FELICIA 'FE' MONTES

PART I: MUJER DE MAÍZ

THIS WRITING is a choice, an offering, and a labor of love—as is the collective it is honoring, Mujeres de Maiz. The purpose of this creative herstory is to describe, document, understand, and validate the creation and necessity for creative women's collectives, specifically the Los Angeles–based women of color art collective, now organization, Mujeres de Maíz. This is an effort to "document the undocumented" women of the Chicana/o art movement in Los Angeles during the late 1990s and early twenty-first century who have had difficulty finding access, space, and acceptance from both within and outside the Chicano art movement, the art world in general, as well as other spaces such as academia, spiritual, and wellness worlds. Our work, as well as this writing, challenges dominant Western art to create space for a transformative art that is by, of, and for women of color.[1]

As a Xicana Indigenous artist, activist, community and event organizer, educator, emcee, designer, poet, performer, professor, and wellness practitioner living and working across East Los Angeles, I believe art is a tool for education, empowerment, and transformation, and I have translated my passion for art and social justice as the co-founder and coordinating member of two groundbreaking creative women's groups—Mujeres de Maiz (MdM) and In Lak Ech, a Xicana Indigenous drum and song group named after a Mayan phrase meaning "You are my other me," as well as the online one-stop cultura shop El MERCADO y Mas (formerly Urban Xic).

I see my organizing, curating, and creation of spaces, whether on the wall, stage, or page as art. It is social practice (or public practice)—community-based and engaged art. This is the work of our artistic and cultural foremothers and forefathers, the veterans of the movements who paved the way and inspired us to also create. It is a way of life. Artist and curator Gilda Posada writes about this in her article "Mujeres de Maiz: A Lifetime of Social Praxis":

> Examining the role and erasure of the Chicanx and Indigenous artists in the U.S. who have long been engaging in social practice to achieve social change, I look to the collective Mujeres de Maiz, whose artists and projects challenge European and U.S. Western academic concepts of a "participatory aesthetic" and take on social practice as a praxis (a reflection and action directed at the structures to be transformed) and way of life, rather than a one-time event or project. Not only does the work of Mujeres de Maiz allow for a decolonization of the white/Western art world, which has historically promoted oppressive, xenophobic, and primitive notions of Indigenous peoples; it also allows for a recovery of pre-colonial knowledges that have been lost through the ongoing process of colonialism. Mujeres de Maiz's social practice, or rather social praxis, therefore accounts for the past, present, and future of Indigenous womxn and womxn of color at large, by centering pathways towards survival and the healing of mind, body, and spirit.[2]

As a fellow artivist and cultural worker she understands the work and its lineage, place, and importance.

I share about myself, my work, and my upbringing here as a testimony to the work, people, family, ancestors, and so much more that have been a part of the seeds to harvest what is and has grown to be Mujeres de Maiz. I am both second- and third-generation Mexican, with my families having migrated at different times from Chihuahua, Mexico. My grandparents raised their families in East Los Angeles, California, so it has been my home for generations. I feel it is one of the reasons I am so deeply connected and dedicated to the area and community. I am also a movimiento seed of resistance, an artist and activist who began my journey in the womb of my mother. Born in November of 1975 into my parents Carlos and Olivia Montes's deep involvement in the Chicana/o movement and East LA, I am a product of the rhetoric, art, protest, activism, energy, and spirituality of the late 1960s and 1970s. Growing up, I frequented marches, organizing meetings, cultural celebrations, and fundraisers for many causes. I was an activist, artist, and organizer in training who would later attempt to hone my crafts within academia, the Chicana/o art world, a myriad of meetings, and eventually ceremonies. I am a self-proclaimed recovering "Overcompensating Xicana," who works for community empowerment and social justice through my work, from the classroom to the community, from the streets to the stage.[3]

My artistic creations are based on social and spiritual change and work on the front lines of activism and organizing. My creation of visual and multimedia art and performances include silkscreen, installation, performance art, and exhibitions both individual and collective. The work, whether performance, 2D, sculpture, or a combination, focuses on spirituality, gender, culture, access, and ritual, and is always based in community. Because of the decades of work, I am connected throughout the Southwest as an established Xicana cultural worker and social practitioner of a new generation, and have worked with most of the key arts and cultural centers and social service agencies in East Los Angeles. I have also worked in the Los Angeles transnational art and organizing efforts and organized and performed in hundreds of cultural events, conferences, classrooms, and protests for many arts and social justice causes since 1997 across the Southwest, Colombia, and Mexico including Chiapas, Mexico City, and Oaxaca.

As a healing arts practitioner, I am an apprentice of Western Herbalism and study and practice Mexican Traditional Medicine and Aztec/Mexica and other Indigenous dance, song, and traditions. Since 1997, I have continued my soul searching, self-knowledge, and transformation through Indigenous traditional ways and ceremonies, which I have been blessed to be a part of. This path has included both Northern and Southern traditions including participation and support of sweat lodges, medicine and sun and moon circles, women's circles, Aztec dance, and spiritual prayer runs including the Peace and Dignity Journeys, which prophesizes the unification of the Eagle (North) and Condor (South). I share these not as a list or badge, but to show the deep work that decades of intertribal prayers, political organizing, and solidarity have birthed. The deep spirituality and solidarity or "spirit-darity" among communities of color especially brown, red, and black during the civil rights movement birthed connections, organizations, and deep ties that have continued for decades. These spaces have allowed others and myself to look into ourselves, our present, past, and future and reconnect with Indigenous ways of praying and giving thanks. This is the basis for the prayer, protest, performance, and project that is Mujeres de Maiz. I am forever indebted to my guides and companera/o/xs along the red road who have taught, enlightened, and humbled me along the way, from the Southwest's beloved ancestor Gustavo Gutierrez, as well as maestras Cherríe Moraga and Celia Herrera Rodríguez to Los Angeles's own Xochimilco and Antonio Portillo, and Linda Vallejo who have led me in prayer and reflection.[4] Many of these elders, or veterana/os, have reminded us of the importance of the future generations or those who could be seen as "elders in training." All of them are also artists and creators who honor tradition.

Some have seen the work of Mujeres de Maiz coming from the same root and from these future guides. With the degrees, performances, prayer, mercado, and decades of work, I/we have reached many communities and circles with a message of women and Indigenous empowerment through art and activism.

PART II: MUJERES DE MAÍZ HERSTORY

It is high art, raza specific, and international in scope. It is humanistic. The sensibility is global. It is contemporary and diverse, rich, creative, far-reaching, Indigenous, and its time is now.
—FRANCES SALOME ESPANA

For Mujeres de Maiz, art has a purpose—it is not simply always art for art's sake—but it is also a tool for transformation and social change. Our events, publications, and projects are organized and promoted through grassroots strategies, with often little to no funding, and mostly donations of time and money. For these and other reasons they often have a homemade rasquache aesthetic, making the most from the least, "which combines inventiveness with a survivalist attitude" (Mesa-Bains, 12). To audiences, Mujeres de Maiz has been many things. It has been a class lecture, a self-help book, and even a mirror to help both its members and the audience reflect on themselves and the world around them. In this way, the group creates while also doing outreach to women across Los Angeles. The women also seek to spread this vital energy to other women who are in need of sisterhood and a creative outlet.

Mujeres de Maiz acknowledges the work and struggle of their predecessors in the Chicana/o art movement and beyond. In addition, we recognize there are many women doing important and groundbreaking work. Some see "the Chicano art canon" as gendered in that much of the studied performance work prior to more recent years was often limited to the founding fathers of the Chicano art world, for example, ASCO and El Teatro Campesino.[5] The women of Mujeres de Maiz have attempted to search for and honor their predecessors, specifically women's energy and creations. California artists including the amazing work of Bay Area visual artists Yolanda López and Ester Hernandez and Los Angeles artists Yreina Cervántez and Judy Baca, among others, have inspired Mujeres de Maiz. There were also performing artists, teatristas, and poets who paved the way and are the "foremothers" of Mujeres de Maiz. These include Gloria Endiña Álvarez, Raquel Salinas, and Flores de Aztlan, among others. These artists all had a Xicana Indigena aesthetic and agenda in their work, sharing the personal and political and pushing the work to be empowering, activist, and spiritual. So, then, where were the rest of the artists? Where were the other women? The gay? The activists? And more poignant for our generation, where were the young people, the new generation? This section follows suit with what Guillermo Gómez-Peña and Cherríe Moraga achieved through their work—to "document the undocumented," one of Los Angeles' most active women's arts groups of the late 1990s and early twenty-first century, Mujeres de Maiz, and speak to its longevity.

It is important to note that when Mujeres de Maiz started there were not many young culturally and politically, much less spiritually conscious women performers in the East Los Angeles art scene that were accessible to young people and performing on a regular basis. At that time the woman we saw on stage and in an empowering manner was Martha Gonzalez, lead singer and conga player from the band Quetzal who sang songs like "Chicana Skies" and talked about Coyolxauhqui. For most, this was the first time we heard Chicana spiritual-political lyrics. She was and still is a huge influence on the Chicana art scene today.

Although there were those who paved the way, it was not the norm for individuals, specifically women, to work collectively and consider themselves part of an organized group or movement. However, there are examples of all-women groups like Las Mujeres Muralistas (the woman muralists) who organized in the early 1970s and pushed boundaries by painting murals with and by women—where women had central roles not only in the creation of the work but in the work's content. Las Muralistas, along with their cultural counterparts have "projected a feminist statement in their art as well as through their public actions," as do the women of Mujeres de Maiz (Davalos, 64–65). In "Being the Subject of Art," bell hooks reminds us that "consciousness raising groups, gatherings, and public meetings need to become a central aspect of feminist practice again," and so is the work of MdM (Brown, ix).

THE ROOTS

Mujeres de Maiz was formed to proactively create positive work for, by, and about women and femmes. The women of Mujeres de Maiz came together organically as women who were involved in the Los Angeles and specifically East Los Angeles social justice movement and its organizing projects and events. Many women felt that they were not part of an artistic community, feeling isolated in their work, and wanting to share with others.

Mujeres de Maiz would not exist without its founding group In Lak Ech, who formed after activist women, Marisol Lydia Torres, Claudia Mercado, Cristina Gorocica, Liza Cohen Hita, Rachel Negrete Thorson, and myself came together and started sharing their words and poetry. Some of us did not even call it poetry and we did not identify as poets. It was just something we did sometimes to release. When we shared, our emotions came out and so did tears and laughter. It was magical and the women kept sharing and soon after we realized that this was medicine for us. I remember trying to think of a name for the group. I was hoping for Aztlan Angels as I loved the mix of street and culture. But as was in prophecy and probably in the stars that the women determined our destiny and decided on In Lak Ech, a Mayan phrase loosely meaning you are my other me—we are all reflections of each other and interdependent. It can be connected to the proverb "Do unto others as you would have them do unto you." Very quickly I realized how key sharing was for the women of In Lak Ech—how this was not just about sharing poetry, but that this was healing, it was medicine and it was helping all those involved. It allowed us to share our feelings and experiences and process them artistically. This was healing for us and by sharing it became healing for others.

Soon after, maybe a few months, some of us decided it was time to open up the group and make In Lak Ech available to others. And so the idea of Mujeres de Maiz was born (though we did not have the name yet). We put out the word, set a meeting time, and called upon those who had done this type of work before. The very first meeting took place in the spring of 1997 at the Aztlan Cultural Arts Foundation, which was a converted old jail turned cultural center in Lincoln Heights / North East Los Angeles surrounded by warehouses in an industrial area near the Los Angeles River. Those present at the first meeting were visual artist Lilia Ramirez, jeweler and visual artist Lisa Rocha, singer and writer Liza Cohen Hita, queer women singers, poets, and filmmakers Skryb and Sphear, as well as Aida Salazar and Victoria Delgadillo, organizers of a previous all women's art event that inspired me to do similar events. That event titled "Caught Between a Whore and an Angel" was very key to me and eventually to how Mujeres de Maiz events would be organized. We decided to host a "Live Art Show," not just a festival, but an exhibit, performance, event, festival, concert, and ceremony all in one. And this has been the signature style of Mujeres de Maiz ever since then.

As young artists at the time with no formal training and a whole lot of ganas and what we felt was an urgency to do the work—we did everything a la brava and rasquache style. Organize an event? Sure, let's do it! Create a zine without knowing much about how to, why not? Produce a concert and one-day pop-up exhibition, yes! We said yes to everything and simply figured it out. With little to no budget we created. To this day when we get ideas or want to do something new, we just figure it out and call on a friend. Friends and femntors have been key to teaching us and guiding us.[6]

FIRST GATHERINGS

Mujeres de Maiz was born in the spring of 1997 simply as an idea to form some kind of bond or connection among creative women of color. Though it has always been grassroots and very community based, another impetus for its start and structure began in my Chicana/o Studies classroom at the University of California, Los Angeles, in a course taught by Max Benavidez titled "Urban Exiles: Chicano Arts In Los Angeles." Mr. Benavidez would bring in guest speakers almost every other week who were key figures in the Los Angeles Chicano art world. These were people I already knew by name, though not always personally, having grown up in East Los Angeles and its bustling artistic and activist scenes, specifically spending a summer at fifteen years old volunteering at Self Help Graphics & Art (SHG), the renowned Chicana/o cultural art center.

I loved and honored the work of those we were studying. I was inspired, I learned from them, and still, I was searching for more. I wanted to hear of the people doing work in the present, those closer to my generation and closer to my understanding and style or "stilo" of Chicanidad and Xicanisma.[7] For my final project for that class, I decided to organize an event showcasing the Los Angeles artistas and activist women I knew and would soon find. And so began the writing and formal documentation of Mujeres de Maiz as I was to write an accompanying paper to the creative project of producing an event. It was evident from the start of my idea that there were many others with the same hopes. There were artists who wanted to create and activists who wanted to move people to action. Our first steps were to talk to each other and then get others involved. The women artists and activists who were closest to me at that time were the members of the group In Lak Ech, which had just formed months before. I turned to them and we spoke of the vision and the possibilities. We met and planned when the first event would happen and how to get everyone together and who could help with what. A flyer was made asking for women artists of all kinds to contact us (figure I.2). Many calls were made and outreach was done to connect with women artists from all over Los Angeles.

The need for this kind of sisterhood and woman-centered circle was expressed repeatedly in the first few meetings of the group. All involved were very excited about the collective and anxious to see where it would lead those involved. Our first meetings were similar to talking circles

who's that grrrl?

that grrrl is you!

Come express what you do best and
share it with the rest.
Creatively work it *grrrl*,
'cuz it's all about you!
art······· dance·········poetry·······video
music·····performance····y······mas
To share/help with this event featuring women o' color
Call us @
818.309.2210 or 310.585.4019

FIGURE I.2 "Who's That Grrrl?" Callout flyer, 1997. Felicia 'Fe' Montes.

rather than planning meetings. At that time, the intense need for women to come together to talk, share, express, and of course create was evident. Many of the mujeres expressed that this was the only time they have been together with such a group of outspoken, conscious, and creative women who accepted the journey to consciousness and awareness. The birth of the group was definitely an organic process. Each meeting was a learning experience for all those involved.

In the beginning, we decided to focus on planning and logistics. However, realizing the importance of talking circles and sharing time, the group also chose full moons to be the time when the group would meet as a talking circle and gain strength from each others' stories and energies. Weekly meetings were also decided against from early on, as all realized that most were involved in many other things, including family life, school, work, activism, and other projects and organizations, and had limited time. In the end, the group met for talking circles and sharing more sporadically and then met on a weekly basis right before the event and publication. In future years, this would continue, as the group would meet only seasonally around the large event happenings and publications, including the anniversary.

At one of the first meetings, conversations surrounding what the name of the group would be came up. What could represent all these women coming together? What would represent their creativity and their cultures? One artist and poet in attendance, Lilia Ramirez, a founding member of Los Angeles' Peace and Justice Center, a youth-led multimedia cultural arts center, mentioned "maiz, Mujeres de Maiz," and that was it. There was discussion after about the name being in Spanish, and how it was very culturally specific, but the name stuck and became very symbolic for the women. Even those who did not speak Spanish connected to the name, understanding corn is connected to the land. It has held and been very popular ever since. Ramirez also mentioned that she believed the name had history, as there might have been a group of women with a similar name during the Teatro movement of the 1970s. The women of Mujeres de Maiz chose the name because, like corn, they also come in many colors, shapes, and sizes, and believe as women that they are the base and sustenance of their culture and families and that both are important and sacred. A key connection was also made to the Zapatista women of Chiapas, Mexico, and their struggle as oppressed peoples in their own land. The group learned later that the new name for the collective was also the title of a book about the Zapatista women by Spanish writer Guiomar Rovira (2000). Since then we have had the name show us that it too was destined, is medicine for many, and has called various artists to find a home with us.

Chicana artists and writers have a long history of reworking ancient Mesoamerican images and icons such as Tonantzin (Virgen de Guadalupe), Coyolxauhqui, Coatlicue, and maiz, something very prevalent in the work of many of the Mujeres de Maiz. Recent art critiques and "cutting-edge" artist circles often push new Chicana/o artwork to be free of these so-called repetitive icons even though they are deeply connected to spirituality and Indigenous cultural traditions. New generations of artists are discovering these images on their own and in my opinion, this cannot be called trite or redundant. The use of corn and the idea and name of Mujeres de Maiz could be looked at as evoking Chicano cultural nationalism, which in part it is, and perhaps even seen as corny (pun intended). However, for many of the artists, it is also speaking to the sacredness of corn and the centrality of women in Indigenous cultures and creation stories in the Americas. The use of corn imagery can also be about a specific political message against genetically modified corn and the deep political roots of corn and the land. These same critics are also making certain Chicana/o art marginalized by isolating Xicana/o and Indigenous artists whose work has profound meanings that are deeply layered works of art with political, spiritual, and human importance. Yreina Cervántez notes this work is "not simply regurgitated stereotypes but actually archetypes in cultural and genetic memory, which when reclaimed and transformed by these new generations become symbols of empowerment."[8] Similarly, Amalia Mesa-Bains writes that spiritual art is an act of resistance toward domination. I would add that this art carries knowledge, power, and prayer and is one of the ways they share history, worldviews, and creation stories using oral history and images. A few of the artists have also had dreams of women and corn or synchronicities that called them to our group.[9] We believe this is not a coincidence and is part of the prayer work that has been done seven generations before for us to be here today and part of what our work continues.

SAFE SPACES

The women of Mujeres de Maiz have come together to heal in mind, body, and spirit through the arts. They have decided to do it collectively for many reasons including support, access, safe space, and expression of shared experiences. The collective came about because of this need for a space for women of color artists, especially Xicana political artists, to create and offer their counter-hegemonic theories in the flesh. They create art for resistance, affirmation, and ultimately healing. The group believes this kind of intergenerational, crosscultural, and interdisciplinary work is essential for the transformation and healing of the self, community, and world.

Women of the city came together in abandoned halls and warehouses of East Los Angeles to tell their stories, to see their reflection on stage and in the arts, and to give back and to share their gifts and energy. Part of the early MdM vision was for grassroots events to occur in spaces in the community, specifically community cultural centers. The first Live Art Show and every event since then have been planned and presented in community centers or event, boda, and quinceañera halls—a direct political decision to bring art into nontraditional, nonacademic, and non-institutionalized venues. It is also with an intent to bring critical art to the community and to masses of young people of color throughout Southern California who often do not have access to art or who come from different points of view. This decision is also a result of not having access to other mainstream venues such as performance theaters and museums, both private and within universities.[10] Smaller community venues tend to be the ones that recognize people of color and women's creative work in Los Angeles and have been providing spaces for small group exhibitions and performances like Self Help Graphics, Tropico de Nopal, and Avenue 50 Studios.

From Mujeres de Maiz's inception, the events organized have always been multimedia, using whatever medium is available to discuss important issues or create an image. This included films, visual art, exhibitions, installations, dance, poetry, performance art, music, and other mediums. Individuals were always welcome to participate, and collaboration and collective work was especially encouraged. In fact, MdM became a larger collective that encompasses other collaborative groups and collectives. There are many collectives and individuals who are a part of the larger umbrella group and therefore it has been a clearinghouse for women of color in Los Angeles and can be seen as a model for intercultural creativity.

Mujeres de Maiz has been a place of support and refuge for many women of color artists. It is a safe space and a place where all are welcome and where people put their words into action. This kind of space is very important to women artists. It is time dedicated to creation, not of dinner, the household, or the family, but of creating ourselves and our art. I believe this is why the group is still going, celebrating over twenty-five years in 2022. It is really about this immense need for a women's space to share experiences and creations, specifically around education and empowerment. I helped to create this space because I too wanted that space. MdM is not only about the amazing art or poetry—although it is always amazing! It is about having the space to share, the support from others, the sisterhood, and the spirituality. It is a place where I can be all of the different me's and share all my different passions and interests. I believe that is why it is so beloved by me and why I continue to move it forward.

The collective started as that safe space where beginning, emerging, and perhaps even timid artists could share their work from pen to paper to performance. A place that was nonjudgmental to these other voices not yet seen or rarely heard. Many of the women say they felt isolated because of the worldview, philosophy, and content of their work. The more political and spiritual the work, the more distance and space was felt between them and the mainstream and Chicano art worlds. The artists, if trained in the academy, often had a hard time relating to other students and faculty who could not understand or even discuss their work in an informed way regarding anything more than technique.

Women of the collective had a vision of a safe space for them to discuss, create, and share their creative works. Mujeres de Maiz evolved as an open collective of creative women of color with no membership, no fee, and no initiation. It is a women's circle, an organizing collective, an activist and wellness group, and a support network of creative women in pursuit of work opportunities as artists.

TODOS SOMOS MUJERES DE MAIZ

The year 1997 was an important year for Los Angeles Xicana/os and my own activist development. It was the founding year of In Lak Ech and Mujeres de Maiz and of the annual "Farce of July" event put on by Xican@ Records and Film as an alternative July 4th event. That year was also when many different individual and group artists came together to organize the Encuentro Cultural Intercontinental por la Humanidad y Contra el Neoliberalismo, a cultural gathering of Chican@s and Chiapanec@s along with the Zapatistas, in the Zapatista autonomous center of resistance of Oventic in August of 1997. That conference of sorts was a very influential event that shaped that generation of Los Angeles artists and activists. All were heavily influenced by the months of meetings before the event attempting to collectively organize the gathering and base it in art and women's voices. Each of us who was a part of the gathering and a part of the energy and organizing in 1997 was forever changed. It was the connection of so many issues, developments, opportunities, and possibilities all at once—and we all took chances.

The structure of the encuentro had dialogue every morning and art-making in the afternoon. Collectively crafted creations were made every afternoon including murals, poetry, teatro, dance and movement, and music and songwriting conducted by members of the music groups Quetzal, Aztlan Underground, Teatro ChUSMA, and poetry group In

Lak Ech, as well as individual artists in various mediums. Dr. Martha Gonzalez of the band Quetzal, a good friend and also a participant and organizer of the encuentro, writes about the gathering in her book *Chican@ Artivistas*.[11] She recalls, "Experiencing con-vivencia, or the praxis of conviviality, through music, art, poetry, and *teatro* in this encuentro was a step toward building both individual and collective critical consciousness" (69). And that was a solid base of politics and amor (incidentally a song title by Gonzalez). This base was a seed that many artists sowed in the fields of East Los Angeles, including Mujeres de Maiz.

The importance of dialogue and working in a collective for the betterment of all was the basis for all the work and has had lasting effects across the collective and among other artists of the time. After the 1994 uprising and especially after the Gathering, Zapatista imagery, *dichos*, and philosophy have become part of the Los Angeles Chicana/o artistic and political vernacular. The ideas of "For everyone everything" and "We are all Marcos/Ramona (Todos Somos Marcos/Ramona)" penetrated the psyche of the group. The artists that went to Chiapas became deeply involved in not only the artistic movement in support of the Zapatistas but in fact began to organize themselves and become involved in community actions and events in support and solidarity with the Zapatistas.

The connection and work with the Zapatistas as well as the participation in Indigenous ceremonies and cultural restoration projects led Las Mujeres de Maiz to be deeply rooted in political and spiritual activism and practice. All their work is centered around this. Many of the women identify as Indigenous connecting to their specific nation/tribe through traditions, lands, and practices. One term that is used for those with ancestors from Mexico can be called Xicana Indigena, an identity that honors the tenets of the Declaration on the Rights of Indigenous Peoples and recognizes the violent history leaving most migrants in cultural, spiritual, and physical diaspora.[12] Their work not only calls attention to issues such as racism, sexism, and specific community issues like police brutality and immigration, but it also pushes people to act and organize for change. It is a voice of dissent to the oppression and repression of the day and also an important way to heal and maintain balance and sanity and "get well" through art. The artists, like the collective's founders, are not only artists but also organizers, activists, educators, and healers in their community making both artistic and political change while keeping grounded and balanced through their quest and relearning of their Indigenous spiritual traditions. As Xicanas, we are at the crossroads realizing the intersection of our cultures, traditions, genres, and politics, and how within us they are whole.

This type of work can be seen as inhabiting what Gloria Anzaldúa calls "El Mundo Zurdo" (the left-hand world) where people from diverse areas, backgrounds, and so forth come together based on their commonalities and shared vision (Keating, 9). I believe it is also what the Zapatistas state as "un mundo donde quepan muchos mundos" (one world, where many worlds fit). Most importantly, the differences among people have the potential to bring about important alliances that can change the world. Subcomandante Marcos talks about the various people who feel oppression and how they are all connected because of that oppression when he states, "Marcos is Gay in San Francisco, black in South Africa, an Asian in Europe, Chicano in San Ysidro . . . all the exploited, marginalized and oppressed minorities resisting and saying, 'Enough'!" (EZLN, 1994). When people come together groundbreaking things can happen. In the work of Mujeres de Maiz, they build solidarity and connections and through their art, and they speak, heal, and change themselves and their communities. It is what we as MdM call spiritual *artivism* or what Gloria Anzaldúa and Chela Sandoval have termed "spiritual activism," the "theoretical-ethical-moral-emotional-intellectual work" that feministas of color do.[13]

FLOR Y CANTO

Mujeres de Maiz, as an organization, engages in the ancient tradition of "teaching and healing" . . . by offering "flower and song," which, according to Miguel León-Portilla, "is an affirmation of the lasting quality of poetry. In some mysterious way, it is perennial and indestructible. Although flowers, considered the symbol of beauty, perish, when they are related to song, they represent poetry and are everlasting" (Leon Portillo, 78). In the late 1960s and early 1970s, Chicano poets and cultural workers such as Alurista revived this ancient tradition of sharing flowering words (poetry and song) for healing and change. Flor y cantos were events organized for people to share their creations from poetry, song, and even dance and *teatro* in various mediums from community centers, schools, and political rallies. The women of Mujeres de Maiz carry on these ancient and more recent traditions of flor y canto in many spaces and manifestations. They share them as offerings or ofrendas to the people. They are leaders, educators, and activists using art as a tool for social change and transformation, connecting issues from local to global, personal to political. The group is bound together by their creative spirit and by their interest in using art as a tool for healing and change.

Those involved often have had the privilege and access to these various artistic mediums, and in most cases have experiences or formal training in these fields. If not, they have an interest and a desire . . . and with motivated mujeres like those involved in MdM, that is all it takes. Access has come mainly through higher education as many of the mujeres met and began to create while in college and have since received bachelor's degrees and graduate degrees, now most with masters and some with doctorates. The work within this book is a testament to their work in higher education as many of the essays come from the participants documenting parts of their work within academia.

The artists of Mujeres de Maiz create art for a purpose and not just for art's sake. They are the theorists, practitioners, and critics of their own work, seeing quality and effectiveness not only perhaps in the line quality of the brush stroke or film, but the outcome and transformation of the audience member viewing it. This is in extraordinary opposition to Western thought and its idea of quality and success. Skryb describes the ultimate success of the work is "if it reaches just that one [woman]" (Mercado and Montes, 1999).

QUIENES SOMOS

Integral to the conceptualization of Mujeres de Maiz was to have a collective that represented a diverse group of women in culture, age, perspective, sexuality, and so forth. At its start, the women's ages ranged from eighteen to thirty years old (with some exceptions). By the twenty-fifth anniversary in 2022, key members are now mainly in their forties. Some more recognized and experienced writers and artists and even high school students have participated, but the majority at the start were college-age Chicanas and women of color in their late twenties and thirties who wanted to express themselves creatively and share it with others. The majority of MdM are from the greater Los Angeles area, specifically East Los Angeles and the vicinity. Some have come to L.A. from the surrounding regions of Southern California for school, artistic, or organizing purposes, and have come to MdM in this way. The group is definitely influenced by American popular culture, their lives as urban city dwellers, and their familial cultural traditions. Most were born in the United States and are daughters of immigrant mothers and countries. Sometimes they are also immigrants themselves, with varied experiences. They are daughters of the struggle and some are also mothers.

Their thoughts and creations are specific to their age, character, personality, interests, style, views, and neighborhoods. Advertisers call them Generation X. Lalo Alcaraz Lopez, Chicano political artist and cultural critic, calls them "Generation MEX," referring to the cultural mix of First and Third World thoughts and experiences, of being bi- or even tricultural, and able to move between class, cultural, and religious divides (Alcaraz, 1994). These women are often targets of much negativity. Still, from all these experiences they create art, becoming the producers of much creativity. Their experiences include being poor, from inner cities, and growing up within disenfranchised school systems with uneven playing fields, not to mention the feelings of being "la otra" (the other), perhaps short, dark, Spanish-speaking, part of a subculture, and perhaps questioning her sexuality. The recipient of multiple oppressions, a Mujer de Maiz turns these into her muse, her gifts, and blessings—in fact, something to create beautiful art about. They know, understand, and appreciate everything from Barbie, McDonald's, graffiti, and *West Side Story*, to rancheras, carne asadas, and La Virgen de Guadalupe. As women involved in Mujeres de Maiz, the Generation Mex'ers (re)learn, teach, and share Aztec dances and ancient prophecies while discussing the effects of postmodern thought and neoliberalism. They are twenty-first-century Xicanas, AzTechas, cyber-toltecas, organizing actions and writing abstracts through talking white screens. In her essay "Border Arte," Gloria Anzaldúa calls this nepantla an in-between borderland state, where pain and angst can be beautifully transformed.

The women of Mujeres de Maiz, as most women of color artists, do art to survive ... literally. Some say it keeps them sane and whole. It keeps them envisioning another world, free of violence, of pain, of poverty. The majority of the women are not able to live off their art, instead in order to be able to keep creating, they teach art, they document art, they study it, and sell it at accessible prices for all. They make posters of their art, they paint poetry on purses, and create chapbooks, CDs, and recordings for other women to be able to live too. They also share their art with others as a gift and tool through workshops and classes showing young people, elders, and everybody in between that they too have a gift or story that can heal them and others. The women also hold "regular" day jobs as educators, teachers, community organizers, and program administrators in order to pay the bills and continue their passion.

Though there is a committed core group of Mujeres de Maiz, many of the women have found it hard to balance time and energies between their own creative work, families and children, and the work of organizing for other artists through Mujeres de Maiz. It's important to note that many of the core members are not married nor have children and many are queer. Not having children, familial commitments, or dependents has been a reason why some of the women have time and energy to create art and also create spaces for others to share their work. Also, some of the women were not in higher learning or working on large projects that perhaps allowed them more availability to be core members and organizers. Still, it is a constant push and pull for some of the core members to take the time to create their own work. I specifically have always put the organizing of Mujeres de Maiz, In Lak Ech, and other political organizing work before my own creativity . . . something that I realize I need to change to keep myself balanced and healthy.

The group has tried to connect with some of the younger generation and other interested organizers and artists in order to have support for the events and also to share with others what we have been doing. These mentees of sorts have become the next generation of Mujeres de Maiz and the group is actively looking for women who are interested in learning the different roles of what it takes to put together the annual event and zine. MdM has been fortunate to have college interns through various local college service learning programs from Chicana/o/x Latina/o/x Studies departments, most notably at the University of California, Los Angeles (UCLA), where we have continually worked with students since 2015. The possibilities are endless with the dedication and time of the women.

Integral to the current framework and future longevity of the group are women with time and energy to continue the vision and mission of empowering women of color artists and the local community. With this goal, MdM will always continue to do the work that needs to be done, perhaps even in other manifestations or, as we often say, femmifestations, but it will be done.

TRANSNATIONAL MEMBERSHIP: A GLOBAL HARVEST

The group encourages participation of the peoples of the four directions, black, red, yellow, white, and everything in between. Women involved in MdM include African, Central, South, and Native American, Filipina, Chinese, Sri Lankan, and Chicana/o Mexicana/o. They also recognize the need for and power of solidarity and sisterhood across lines of race, class, gender, age, and sexuality and have actively encouraged and sought this bond.

The women of color who have performed at the collective's events do so because of the solidarity and sisterhood they feel with the other members. They work against global injustices across the world and not only do solidarity and activist work but create artwork speaking to the interconnectedness of their beings as women of color. The group has met mainly in educational and political settings, from marches to workshops, presentations, and through social settings of people of like-minded political and world views. Liza Cohen Hita and Alejandra Sanchez, two members of Mujeres de Maiz in its formative years, are important individuals who made connections and bridges between the Filipina and Chicana activist communities, each being culturally a part of both. Higher learning institutions that we attended and protested at also brought many of the MdMers together, specifically D'Lo, Sarah Rosencrantz, and most of the members of In Lak Ech attended UCLA. The other unifying factor was our politics, from the campus to the community, to the streets, and internationally. Many of the mujeres were involved in student organizations dedicated to representing their culture or rallying for a cause. In 1996 one such cause was stopping the dismantling of affirmative action with California's Proposition 209.

Various members were also involved in the community doing research and solidarity work with Indigenous political movements in Chiapas, Mexico, and the Philippines including Pinay poets Liza Cohen Hita and Faith Santilla. Their work intertwines the harsh realities of urban jungle street life in Los Angeles with that of the realities of their families and communities in the Philippines. Both refer to the Indigenous struggles in their mother country and make connections to the land and against global capitalism with their anti-imperialist political poetry. For example, women of Balagtasan Collective have become a traditional part of Mujeres de Maiz, offering up intercultural political poetry on a Pinay (Filipina) tip. Santilla, while performing at Mujeres de Maiz's International Women's Day event in 1998, surrounded by a group of Chicana and Pinay women with guitars, flamenco shoes, and traditional Pinay and gitana clothing, touched on the interconnectedness of women's work and being, while shouting her poem to the audience and those neighbors who could hear: "She is in the Comandante Ramona, she is the peasant woman whose basic rights have been unmet . . . she is down the street from here celebrating her quinceanera. . . . She is organizing strawberry workers in Watsonville. She works in factories and sugar mills for below minimum wage, she is sitting in the audience, she's performing up here on stage and she's forwarding the revolution, breastfeeding two babies and still holding up half the sky" (Mercado and Montes, 1999). Santilla's work received a standing ovation, tears, and joyful applause as women, men, and children throughout the hall, shouted "Que Viva La Mujer (Long Live Women)!," and reveled in the energy and inspiration of her words.

Other members refer to their "sisters in the struggle" across the world in paintings, films, dances, and more. The resistant women of Chiapas are referred to in much of the visual artwork and poetry, as are sweatshop workers in Thailand, Juárez, and Downtown L.A., and the list goes on. The work aims to connect all the struggles and call audience members to action or at least consciousness. This is women of color feminism and cultural activism accountable not to theorists and critics, but to the community it documents and serves.

Women from mixed backgrounds have also used the stage and their creativity to not only discuss their radical politics and position, but also to honor their varied heritages. Ymasumac Maranon of Quechua Indian and European descent honors all sides of her multiracial identity by documenting the traditional ways of her Quechua culture through poetry by using Quechua words and beliefs. Also, various films and videos by Womyn Image Makers (WIM), a Xicana and Native American group of filmmakers, were screened at MdM performances. All the women are nepantleras, border crossers, and intermediaries, moving through different tongues, cultures, traditions, educations, and roots, and through their art, they show their reality. Overall, MDM participants create what Maria Elena Fernandez, performer and professor, sees as a "foundation of social consciousness and a vision for liberation and equality" (Mercado and Montes, 1999).

ALL OUR RELATIONS

Many of the shows have celebrated International Women's Day and are always herstoric gatherings that include some emerging poets from different communities. Various groups that have shared at MdM events include In Lak Ech, Sunrise Child, and Wadda G (Women Aware, Deep, Dark, and Gay), made up of D'Lo, a Sri Lankan poet and two African American women, Skryb and Sphear.[14] Other collectives participating in Mujeres de Maiz's various organized performance spaces include Cihuatl Tonali (Nahuatl for women's energy or destiny) and Chomiha (Mayan women energy). The groups play various Indigenous instruments to accompany their poetry and song, including drums, rattles, and flutes, as well as the African djembe, Aztec huehuetl, and others. The groups talk and sing of women's oppression and privileges and refer to a line of ancient spirits and deities that guide them, including the Aztec moon goddess Coyolxauhqui. All the groups use names that show with pride who they are and what they are about and align with MdM's overall vision.

Also important to note are the responses from the men in attendance at the events. Claudia Mercado mentions that when a group of women comes together to express themselves creatively, they are often called lesbians or man-haters. The women of the group took on these labels and also rejected them, along with many others, but they continued their vision for the group and for a better community and world. MdM would say, we might be both of those, or we might be none of those . . . but our work and art will continue. Some of the men have been especially supportive, even helping document, work at, and volunteer at events. They also see the events as transformative to themselves and those around them. Antonio Mejia, a tattoo artist and painter who attended an event in 1997, says it "inspires everyone—especially me and then I can turn around and take this and pass it on to my sister or other women in my life." Rick Chavez, hip hop artist and son of Dolores Huerta of the United Farm Workers, states, "Everytime I come to this it points out a lot of my shit . . . the way I think, the way I act. . . . This is like my class. I'm learning and keep it up cuz we need help." Both speak to the need for men to hear, see, and feel the experiences of women, both good and bad. The women of Mujeres de Maiz educate and empower audiences through their creations as dedicated cultural workers with a mission and vision to help themselves and their communities.

THE HARVEST: BRINGING ART AND HEALING TO THE COMMUNITY

The individuals of the larger collective are committed to making art accessible through performing or sharing their work in non-traditional venues and sites from school quads and classrooms to warehouses, marches, and streets. In this section, I focus on three sites important for MdM to bring art and healing. Each was organized with different audiences in mind, without changing the integrity of the work and art forms.

HIGH SCHOOL ASSEMBLIES AND COLLEGE CAMPUSES

MdM has taken their message and art to high school assemblies and college campuses for workshops, conference presentations, and special events, mostly in Southern California, but also across the country. The main goal of the assembly was to expose young people to empowering women role models and artists and to educate them on the existence of Women's History Month, International Women's Day, and the many contributions of women in their lives and across the world.

Women were the main focus and the content of their work was empowering and politically uplifting, something not usually shared with these young audiences but very well received. Over the decades, various assemblies were organized with this intent and vision. Mujeres de Maiz would go on to curate other high school assemblies, women's conferences, and workshops focused on youth. This is a key component and interest for our work as this is where many of us began to feel disempowered or realize our place in the world and if we could change some of the narratives and experiences of young women, so much could change.

MdM also regularly participates in college events, workshops, and conferences. One example is an interactive multimedia Live Art Show titled "The Red Road to the Xicana Kalli" at the Chicano House at California State University, Northridge. This was organized as part of my Master's thesis about Mujeres de Maiz. The space was different in that the audience was asked to make their own path through the rooms of the house to have their own creative experience and interact with the artists and displays according to their interests. This was definitely something different for the guests, participants, professors, and students in attendance, and even for the performers. The idea was to show various artists of different genres and backgrounds in one space, to do something different from the usual stage performance and to challenge both the performers' and audiences' understanding of "performance" and each other's roles and boundaries, thereby pushing the audience/performer dichotomy and separation of the fourth wall.

The afternoon event was an important showing of women's creative work in various formats, specific to the style and energy of the new generation of Xicana Indigena artists involved in Mujeres de Maiz. Mujeres de Maiz and In Lak Ech for some time have shared on college campuses. We have been invited by student groups, cultural centers, and professors to share our specific brand of Indigenous feminism, spirit, song, and poetry. It has been an important way to connect with generation after generation of young activists and especially young women of color on an identity journey. In addition, it has supported us in our own journey as it is one of if not the only venues that support monetarily.

MUJERES CON PALABRA—PROYECTO IN LAK ECH

I am impressed at a heart level with the work of In Lak Ech because it responds to a Xicana-Indígenismo thirty-five years in the making. Blending Northern Native musical influences with Southern Indígena filosofía, the CD celebrates the myriad spiritual and political roads Xicanas have walked to acquire a living uncompromised identity and cultural practice in the United States. Here Medicine Songs are spoken hip hop style and a few tracks later, sung with tambor as a prayer in Ceremony. Here the Pre-Columbian flauta poeticizes the natural lyricism of an honoring poem en Español, and another poet employs her best Chicano English as the fierce language

> *of revolution. . . . At its heart, In Lak Ech reflects all of what it means to be us in 21st century Aztlán: mujer, madre, artista-activista, meXicana—humilde ante de dios y brava ante la cara del "patrón." Gracias for the great esfuerzo, hermanitas.*
> —CHERRÍE MORAGA'S LINER NOTES ON THE IN LAK ECH MUJERES CON PALABRA CD (2007)

In Lak Ech is key as the founding group of Mujeres de Maiz and the spiritual base as well. We met in activism and in sharing poetry and art, but we learned about each other through sharing words and palabras. We grew closer through road trips, ceremonies, and conferences. We met each other's families and became relatives through spirit and sweat. I will forever be indebted to the women of In Lak Ech. I even get emotional writing this now as I feel intense love realizing the impact a few women coming together can have.

Music is an important tool to educate and empower, to transform moods, energies, and even lives. A compact disc (CD) of In Lak Ech's work was another site to honor and document the women's work and make it accessible to a wider audience. The CD was meant to document the formative first years of the collective's creative work, which consisted of performance poetry and Indigenous spirit-focused songs and was produced by Martha Gonzalez.[15] "Mujeres Con Palabra" is In Lak Ech's first album and was released on Sunday August 19, 2007.

The project was Chicana feminism in action—women of color documenting themselves, their truths, and experiences in an accessible format for other women, young and old to learn from. The content and themes of the poetry and ceremonial and Indigenous songs are Xicanista-infused, a Chicana feminist Indigena experience and lens throughout the poems and songs, hoping to empower and educate women of color. It is important to note how the women of In Lak Ech came to sing these types of songs.

The women connected with Northern Native American and Southern-style Indigenous circles and began to learn songs in ceremony and through traditional Native practices.[16] At the same time, we were creating and performing poetry in many different settings. There was no training or schools for this—it was a natural progression of learning the styles, tempos, tones, and Indigenous language of these songs by being participants in the circles, spaces, and ceremonies. Cristina Gorocica and Marisol Lydia Torres began creating songs that they felt were important to share with the group and with the public like "I Live," "Wombyn," and others, which have become favorites for In Lak Ech. The women began using rattles and hand drums and even moved to the Aztec drum, the huehuetl and chachayotes, as most of the women are Aztec dancers. Many of the songs came to the women in their dreams or, as they say, were "gifted" to them by the creator. In Lak Ech has continued to share various styles of drumming and has gained respect from drummers, elders, and people from all walks of life, for offering our truth, through songs and prayers. The women of In Lak Ech were called to the drum and to sing prayer songs through ceremony, through prayer, and through their love for the people. We understand that drums across the world are seen as the heartbeat of nations, that connecting with it can heal, and it is a way to honor ancestors and all relations. The album has twenty tracks, with twelve poems and six songs. The CD packet has a sleeve, which carries a fourteen-page full-color booklet in an accordion-style fold in the ancient tradition of the Aztec codex (amoxtlis).[17] Each poet of the group has one or two pages with the text of their poem on it, as well as art or images that they created or designed. These are contemporary Xicana codices, making personal experiences and feelings available in print for all to see.

The album documents the undocumented of the Los Angeles Chicana/o art world, this new generation's women's work, through what Cherríe Moraga sums up in her review as "Southern Native philosophy in Northern Native sounds," therefore creating Xicana traditions and sounds. The group is often told how the songs are loved by children, teenagers, and adults alike, especially by young women. Because of the CD, these songs now stream online. They are music for TikToks and have been heard across the continent in ceremonies and spaces as the songs have traveled mainly through the Peace and Dignity Journeys, which I ran in 2000. The songs travel as do the sentiments and spirituality. Traveling is key when speaking about Northern and Southern traditions and the mixing of ways. Sharing and connecting have been part of Indigenous ways since time immemorial. Trade routes and travels have allowed for customs, clothing, songs, goods, and traditions to travel. This, along with the Native American activism of the 1960s and 1970s and the work of the

American Indian Movement, including the occupation of Alcatraz and Wounded Knee, have fostered this intertribal and continental Indigenous connection. Mujeres de Maiz and In Lak Ech are the harvest of the spirit-darity work of the civil rights movement and we continue the struggle with our hearts in our hands. For the women of In Lak Ech, this is why we share our art . . . so that others may feel and heal, whether it be empowerment, healing, or connection to their culture and families.

TRANSFORMATIONS

Much of the work of Mujeres de Maiz shifted from solely artistic and performance-based to holistic and wellness work beginning in 2008 and more visibly since 2017 when we collaborated with other Eastside women's organizations to create the Four Directions Wellness Clinic, a pop-up event focused on holistic healing based in culture and consciousness. Here the women found healing not only for themselves but also for their peers and community. Organizing these types of events was a key transition for MdM as the work looked inward as well as outward. Since then, much of our work is centered around wellness. We realize how much we need it and the community responds immensely by showing up to these events in large numbers and supporting and requesting more.[18]

The group, since its inception, has run on its own resources with no grant money or outside funding other than the funds brought in through the annual event. The group was not an official non-profit organization for almost twenty years. It was and is collectively run and entirely grassroots, "con ganas and amor," as we would say, relying on organizations and artists to donate funds or in-kind or reduce their time and/or costs.[19] Only a few times in the group's history has it received grant funds and this has happened since receiving non-profit status in 2017. When we have received funds, we are excited to support artists with honorariums and organizers with stipends because their work as women of color curators, producers, and performers is so valuable.

FOR THE FUTURE GENERATIONS

The hope for Mujeres de Maiz is to continue dialogues on issues relevant to women of color. The group believes that this kind of intergenerational, crosscultural, and interdisciplinary work is essential, not only because of the need for understanding among various groups and community building, but also because of the harsh realities of ignorance, and the lack of funds and support for this type of cultural work.

Mujeres de Maiz plans to maintain the vision and integrity of its work for years to come. Most involved believe that their work is not for them but to honor and share with those that came before and those yet to come. It is for the future and current generations to heal and to transform themselves and the world around them. Because it has these deep-seated beliefs it will be forever alive in the hearts of women of the greater East Los Angeles community. Nearly three decades since its founding, the group remains a powerful force for change, maintaining a strong presence in many spaces, continuing to grow its offerings. It is especially noteworthy that a grassroots volunteer-run activist women's group such as Mujeres de Maiz has been able to maintain its workload and its impact on generations of women artists. Through changes such as school, family, and new members—it takes just a few to pull things together and get the ball rolling. It is from our deep commitment to the work that MdM connects art, activism, and spirituality. It represents all of who we are.

Creating projects that speak to many, while speaking to one, is not only useful and creative, but it is real and necessary. The group realizes that "what [they] are capable of producing . . . could make a profound contribution to the social transformation of these Americas" (Moraga 1993, 59), and bring about a re-evolution of change in the home, streets, community, and beyond. Gracias to Mujeres de Maiz and *all my relations*.

NOTES

The majority of this writing was done in the early 2000s and submitted as my thesis in 2009. This chapter is a revised version of my master's thesis: Felicia Montes, "Mujeres de Maiz: Seeds to Spiritual Artivism—An L.A. Herstory" (master's thesis, California State University, Northridge, 2009). This writing and herstory is my offering to a sacred fire—the fuego of Mujeres de Maiz. This is also an ode to my greatest love, a testament to my life's work, vision, and my ultimate creation: Mujeres de Maiz. I have literally birthed and nurtured Mujeres de Maiz as it has to me. I have grown up within Mujeres de Maiz, found my way, lifelong friends, literal comadres, and built familia. For these reasons, and because I am an artist and performer, I chose to write this chapter by weaving together primary sources, research inquiries, interviews, the creative work of the artists, and critiques or discussion of the art to create a more comprehensive documentation of the work of Mujeres de Maiz. The primary sources include the individual and collective artistic creations of MdM, such as poetry, live and recorded performances, paintings, and self-published zines, as well as flyers, announcements, and statements. My work and documentation of MdM is based on participant observation as the group's co-founder, coordinator, and current director. As an insider, I have the advantage of access to the members and their work to gain a multileveled understanding of the collective. The interviews and personal testimonies of the women involved, as well as performers and audience members, have allowed me to get an in-depth view and understanding of the group and its importance in the Los Angeles and Chicana/o art world, wellness and social justice circles, and other areas where it has made an impact.

1. My pursuit of this knowledge takes an interdisciplinary approach, pulling from various fields such as Chicana/o/x studies, art history, and women's studies. MdM and this writing are influenced by Cherríe Moraga's groundbreaking essays "Queer Aztlán" and "Art in America con Acento," which poetically call for radical changes in thought and creativity for those within social justice circles and society in general. *The Last Generation* had profound effects on the artists of Mujeres de Maiz and was essential to many of the women's politicization. Gloria Anzaldúa and Moraga introduced MdM to spiritually and culturally based feminism. We feel that we are following in the footsteps of Moraga and Anzaldúa and other Xicana Indígena women's work, which identifies, describes, and questions the status quo and is seen as a prayer for the present, past, and future generations. Like our predecessors, MdM artistas have no boundaries on our work.

2. Gilda Posada, "Mujeres de Maiz: A Lifetime of Social Practice," *Art Practical*, 2017, https://wayback.archive-it.org/15633/20210124043400/https://www.artpractical.com/feature/mujeres-de-maiz-a-lifetime-of-social-praxis/.

3. Felicia 'Fe' Montes, "Overcompensating Xicana Complex," in *Ten Fe Poetry* (Mujeres de Maiz Press, 2011).

4. The *red road* is a term used to speak of the Indigenous ceremonial journey. There is no one red road, but it is generally seen as the path, the various ceremonies, and the roads one takes to find oneself and for self and community healing. MdM intentionally works to honor embodied knowledge within the mind, body, and spirit because there is an intense connection with the spirit *and* the work—the spirit of the work. *Spirit* here refers to the guides and ancestors and the artists' own beliefs and spiritual practices as practitioners of the red road (or Native American and Indigenous philosophies). On another note, some women within the group may be practicing Yoruba traditions and/or strains of Catholicism. Chicanas, usually of mixed cultural and regional experiences oftentimes practice a mix of various traditions from their upbringing and lived experiences—what Dr. Lara Medina calls "nepantla spirituality," or the unique

mix of traditions and spiritualities that each woman creates for her own healing and growth.

5. Some of those who discuss and critique the Chicano canon are writers and theorists such as Yolanda Broyles-González, Karen Mary Davalos, and Alicia Gaspar de Alba.
6. *Femntor* is a femme mentor, a guide, a teacher or maestra.
7. *Chicanidad* here refers to the style, culture, community, and connections based in social justice and Chicano/a culture. *Xicanisma* is Xicana feminism, a culturally and spiritually based feminism focused on women of color, on Chicanas.
8. This lesson came from a conversation with Yreina Cervántez in 2017.
9. Find the testimonio by Iris De Anda in chapter 39 in round 4.
10. This is a historical issue, dating back to at least when ASCO tagged on the walls of the Los Angeles Contemporary Museum of Art. This is a long story for most Chicana artists, though in recent years those once-closed doors have been cracking open.
11. To learn more about the encunetro and artivismo, review the book *Chican@ Artivistas* by Martha Gonzalez.
12. Many of the chapters in this book explore this topic further.
13. Sandoval and Latorre, "Chicana/o Artivism," xv.
14. Review chapter 11 by D'Lo and chapter 12 by Skryb in this collection.
15. An ethnomusicology major at the time, and a community artist and seasoned musician, Martha guided us through what ended up being a four- or five-year road to complete the album. This was mainly because of time and trying to sync all of our schedules to be able to meet, discuss the project, rehearse, record, and then plan, edit, revise, and finalize what was to be a collective project representing six different women's poetry and songs.
16. Most Mexican and Central American people come from Indigenous lineage. On this side of the imposed U.S. border, they are often not recognized as Indigenous by either the U.S. government or northern Native nations. As Xicanas with Mexican ancestry and ancestry from various Native nations across Mexico, our Indigenous ancestry is usually not recognized. We do not have official Bureau of Indian Affairs cards to prove our blood percentage, and so we are not thought of as "real" or "true" Indians. For this reason, some are not welcomed within Native circles and ceremonies. This view is not held by all, but it does have a strong sentiment within Native America.
17. Graphic design, consulting, recording, and promotion were mostly all done pro-bono by Joel Garcia of Nomadic Sound System. All was done at no or very limited cost, except for the printing, which, because it was on recycled paper and has special instructions for the folding (as a codex), it was thousands more than the usual cost for a basic CD in a jewel case. In Lak Ech fundraised over the years and saved up in order to be able to pay for the costs of not only recording and production, but also the printing of the CD. Many gave of their time, we put away money from the seasonal university honorariums, and we also organized

a community cultural fundraiser in order to cover the costs. The group did not receive any grant or funds other than these small self-organized events and our occasional payments for performing. This do-it-yourself (DIY) and "Si Se Puede" (Yes We Can) attitude has guided In Lak Ech and many of our artist/activist peers and is a staple component of Mujeres de Maiz.

18. MdM's healing justice work is discussed in Nadia Zepeda's essay "Coyolxauhqui Full Moon Circle: Self-Care as Community Care" in this collection.
19. The costliest part of the events include the rental of the space, sound, printing of fliers, supplies for stage/production needs, copies of program/schedule, and art exhibition and installation needs. The largest expense of the year often is the annual zine publication.

BIBLIOGRAPHY

Alcaraz, Lalo. "Generation X & Generation Mex" comic in *Migra Mouse: Political Cartoons on Immigration*. Canada: RDV Books/Akashic Books, 2004.

Anzaldúa, Gloria. "Border Arte: Nepantla, El Lugar De La Frontera." In *La Frontera/The Border: Art about the Mexico/United States Border Experience*. Ed. Natasha Bonilla Martinez. Trans. Gwendolyn Gomez. San Diego: Centro Cultural de la Raza and Museum of Contemporary Art, 1993.

———. *Borderlands / La Frontera: The New Mestiza*. San Francisco: Spinster/Aunt Lute, 1987.

Broyles-González, Yolanda. *El Teatro Campesino: Theater in the Chicano Movement*. Austin: University of Texas Press, 1994.

Champagne, Lenora. *Out From Under: Texts by Woman Performance Artists*. New York: Theatre Communications Group, 1990.

Davalos, Karen Mary. *Exhibiting Mestizaje: Mexican (American) Museums in the Diaspora*. Albuquerque: University of New Mexico Press, 2001.

Espana, Frances Salome. "On Filmmaking: A Personal Odyssey." *Chicana (W)rites on Word and Film*. Ed. Maria Herrera-Sobek and Helena Maria Viramontes. Berkeley: Third Woman Press, 1995.

Facio, Elisa, and Irene Lara. *Fleshing the Spirit: Spirituality and Activism in Chicana, Latina, and Indigenous Women's Lives*. Tucson: University of Arizona Press, 2014.

Fusco, Coco. *English Is Broken Here: Notes on Cultural Fusion in the Americas*. New York City: The New Press, 1995.

Gaspar de Alba, Alicia. *Chicano Art Inside/Outside the Master's House, Cultural Politics and the CARA Exhibition*. Austin: University of Texas Press, 1997.

Gonzalez, Martha. *Chican@ Artivistas: Music, Community, and Transborder Tactics in East Los Angeles*. Austin: University of Texas Press, 2020.

Gorocica, Cristina. "Bus Stop." Los Angeles: Unpublished Poem, 1998.

Hurtado, Aída, and Norma E. Cantú. *MeXicana Fashions: Politics, Self-Adornment, and Identity Construction*. Ed. Aída Hurtado and Norma E. Cantú. 1st ed. Austin: University of Texas Press, 2020.

hooks, bell. "Being The Subject of Art." *Expanding Circles: Women, Art, and Community*. New York: Midmarch Art Books, 1996.

In Lak Ech. "Mujeres con Palabra." Xicano Records & Film, 2007, CD.

Keating, AnaLouise. *Entre Mundos/Among Worlds: New Perspectives on Gloria Anzaldúa*. New York: Palgrave Macmillan, 2005.

León-Portilla, Miguel. *Aztec Thought and Culture: A Study of the Ancient Nahuatl Mind*. Translated by Jack Emory Davis. Tulsa: University of Oklahoma, 1978.

Lippard, Lucy. *Mixed Blessings: New Art in a Multicultural America*. New York: Pantheon Books, 1990.

Mankiller Drum Group Website. April 2009. http://www.geocities.com/wellesley/9574/page2.html.

Martinez, Elizabeth. *De Colores Means All of Us: Latina Views For A Multicolored Century*. Boston: South End Press, 1998.

Mercado, Claudia, and Felicia Montes, dir. and prod. *Mujeres de Maiz: The Roots of Herstory*. Blood Red Road Journey, 1999.

Mesa-Bains, Amalia. "El Mundo Feminino: Chicana Artists of the Movement—A Commentary on Development and Production." *Chicano Art: Resistance and Affirmation, 1965–1995*, ed. Richard Griswold del Castillo. Albuquerque: University of New Mexico Press, 1990 (Wight Art Gallery, UCLA).

———. "Curatorial Statement," in *Ceremony of Spirit: Nature and Memory in Contemporary Latino Art*. San Francisco: The Mexican Museum, 1993.

Montes, Felicia "Fe." "Lotería Xicana." *Aztlán* 45, no. 1 (2020).

———. *Ten Fe Poetry*. Los Angeles: Mujeres de Maiz Press, 2011.

Moraga, Cherríe. *The Last Generation*. Boston: South End Press, 1993.

———. *Loving in the War Years: Lo Que Nunca Pasó Por Sus Labios*. Boston: South End Press, 1983.

Mujeres de Maiz. "El Nacimiento del Dios del Maiz." *Flor y Canto*, vol. 1. Los Angeles, 1997.

———. "Seeds of Resistance." *Flor y Canto*, vol. 2. Los Angeles, 1997.

———. "Of Mixed Waters." *Flor y Canto*, vol. 3. Los Angeles, 1998.

———. "Toltecayotl Cihuatl." *Flor y Canto*, vol. 4. Los Angeles, 2006.

———. "Cantando Al Amanecer." *Flor y Canto*, vol. 5. Los Angeles, 2007.

———. "Somos Medicina." *Flor y Canto*, vol. 6. Los Angeles, 2008.

Ochoa, Maria. *Creative Collectives: Chicana Painters in Community*. Albuquerque: University of New Mexico Press, 2003.

O'Grady, Lorraine. "Olympia's Maid: Reclaiming Black Female Subjectivity," in *Art, Activism, and Oppositionality: Essays from Afterimage*, ed. Grant H. Kester. Durham, N.C.: Duke University Press, 1998.

Pérez, Laura E. "Spirit Glyphs: Reimagining Art and Artist in the Work of Chicana Tlamatinime." *MFS Modern Fiction Studies* 44, no. 1 (Spring 1998).

———. "Chicana Art: The Politics of Spiritual and Aesthetic Alarities." Durham, N.C.: Duke University Press, 2007.

Posada, Gilda. "Mujeres de Maiz A Lifetime of Social Practice." Art Practical, 2017. https://wayback.archiveit.org/15633/20210124043400/https://www.artpractical.com/feature/mujeres-de-maiz-a-lifetime-of-social-praxis/.

Prado Saldivar, Reina. "Goddesses, Sirenas, Lupes y Angel Cholas—The Work of Alma Lopez." *Aztlán* 25 (Spring 2000).

Quiñonez, Juanita Naomi. *The Smoking Mirror*. Albuquerque: West End Press, 1998.

Saldivar-Hull, Sonia. "Mestiza Consciousness on the Border." *Feminism on the Border: Chicana Gender Politics and Literature*. Berkeley: University of California Press, 2000.

Sandoval, Chela. "Foreword: Unfinished Words." *Entre Mundos/Among Worlds*, ed. AnaLouise Keating. New York: Palgrave Macmillan, 2005.

Sandoval, Chela, and Angela Y. Davis. "U.S. Third World Feminism." *Methodology of the Oppressed*. Minneapolis: University of Minnesota Press, 2000.

Sandoval, Denise, and Luis Rodriguez. *Rushing Waters, Rising Dreams How the Arts Are Transforming a Community*. Evanston, Ill.: Northwestern University Press, 2012.

Subcomandante Marcos. Speech from 28 de mayo de 1994. February 24, 2009. http://palabra.ezln.org.mx/.

Venegas, Sybil. "Conditions for Producing Chicana Art." *ChismeArte/Xicanarte*. Los Angeles, 1977–78.

MIS MANOS SOLO ESCRIBEN

MARILYNN MONTAÑO

Sol de día
Lunita por noche
Soñadora por Vida
Luchadora Y Xingona en la sangre

Pueblana
Mexicana
Xicana
Storyteller
Escritora
Pero sobre todo, Womyn
Sí, Muxer

No need to be told of my beauty because no mirror can see what I am

I

Sacrifice my sleep
Velando las noches por el amor a mi historia
Writing my HERSTORY
Savoring my words and blending them into the blue margin lines of my paper

Pouring down the warmth of canela into my señorita lips
Dipping down my salsa verde onto my pepperjack quesadillas
Swimming into the tunnels of my hips

Unstrapping my liga from my pelo
My hair tumbles down reaching to the tips of my breasts suaved back to my tracero

I see my feet

Standing, pushing out these wrecked walls

Paving my own HERSTORY onto the semillitas that have branched out beyond these wrecked walls

I am the her behind the story

Santa Ana, Calif.

Mujeres de Maiz, Flor y Canto: Identity Blinging, no. 11 (2013): 34

ROUND I

EMERGENT SPIRITUAL JOURNEYS AND HEALING SPACES

1
Danzando con el Fuego

CLAUDIA MERCADO

When I returned to what was once my home in LA 1996
I
didn't fit inside
I was like that 50-foot woman from the 1950s horror film
A threat
for holding a piece of gold
Mi voz
My truth
Scaring my mother with my wild tongue
Assaulting the aesthetics of beauty for not shaving or wearing a bra
Squashing my family's american dream with my fist up in the air
Steps cracking concrete like old patriarchal traditions
I
A newcomer in my own neighborhood
Searching for mi gente with ma hawk-eye view
Yes
A raw free spirit
Dusting off
Clinging remnants of previous deaths
Navigating interior landscapes amidst darts of expectations
I
found my other me

In Lak Ech
hermanas de flor y canto
a Diosa masa blend of
poetry, animated resistant brown women's bodies, drumming, singing
canciones de corazónes
Reclaiming la Madre
de vida y muerte
Coatlicue
mi kalli antigua
I
We
Embarked on a journey of the unfolding core
Initiations in the urban alley of my subconscious
I looked into the obsidian mirror
and became
a Mujer de Maiz[1]

As I reflect on my collaborative journey with Mujeres de Maiz, I am overwhelmed with the spirals of visions, activism, beauty, knowledge, love, pain, and sacrifice it has manifested for me. I am very grateful to have been part of this transformational circle of women who continue to be an inspiration and pillars of strength. However, like all things in life, Mujeres de Maiz would not have been born without certain things in place. Thus, I am also grateful to all those who have dreamed and toiled for a better world, that movimiento of many words, actions, and spaces that provided the necessary elements for Mujeres de Maiz to be born. To All My Relations, Tlazocamati.

    In 1997 I returned to what was once my home in Northeast Los Angeles, my communities of Lincoln Heights, Cypress Park, Highland Park, and Eagle Rock. I had left L.A. straight out of high school. With twelve years of Catholic education and a traditional Mexican upbringing, I left to pursue my education at the University of California at Berkeley and returned home a changed woman with a film studies degree in hand. Armed with some fierce women of color and Xicana feminism, coupled with my twenty-five-year-old optimism and a deep desire to connect with the L.A. art community, the universe pushed me straight into the heart of *La Chicanada*—Centro Regeneración or the Popular Resource Center—in the community of Highland Park, Los Angeles, California.[2]

It looked like an abandoned warehouse, but to the local politicized Angelino artists of Mexican, Central, and South American descent, it was prime real estate for their artistic collaborations and political expressions. It was in this fertile ground in 1997 at the PRC in Highland Park, California, where I would collaborate in the creation and begin the documentation of Mujeres de Maiz, which has and continues to create *herstory* in Los Angeles.

I
I am the woman who creates herself
and digs deep into the unknown
searching for herstory
rooting my presence at home
at the meeting
and in bed
voicing our struggles
reclaiming my grandmother's knowledge
Soy
Soy la mujer despierta
la privilegiada desconocida
la afortunada pero con pesas
Soy la Mestiza sin fronteras
la Xicana con fronteras
la india violada
la activista temida
la feminist ardiente
la
Mujer
Que
Tiene
Voz[3]

When your spirit wants something bad enough and you listen and ask, things fall into place, if it is meant to be. Before I knew it, I had arrived with *communidad*. I remember asking if there was a show dedicated to women, specifically Xicanas or women of color on Radio Clandestina, and after being told there wasn't, I asked if I could create one. Without hesitation, they said yes, and there I was hosting *Lucha Por Tu Voz* (Fight for Your Voice) with no experience in radio programming *pero con muchas ganas* to get involved.

Volunteering from that creative space, I encountered other female artists and organizers who, like me, wanted to create, empower ourselves, our communities, and ultimately inspire social change in the world. It was clear to us that it had been over thirty years since the height of the civil rights and feminist movements, and yet women's voices were continually absent from the established platforms of representation. This is not to say things are very different today.

Nonetheless, in an effort to unite women and provide a space for our voices, I invited Felicia 'Fe' Montes to co-host "Lucha Por Tu Voz" with me. The show was short-lived because I think what we really desired was sisterhood, to come out as artists, and ultimately empower and unite women of color. And so we invited Marisol Lydia Torres, Cristina Gorocica, Rachel Negrete Thorson, and Liza Cohen Hita to share their writings among us. Little did we know we would become the poetry and song group, In Lak Ech—the seed that sprouted Mujeres de Maiz (figure 1.1).

In Lak Ech is a Maya concept that translates to "You Are My Other Me." I first came across this concept at UC Berkeley when I participated in a Chicana-Latina retreat organized by a campus group called Mujeres en Marcha. As the theme of the retreat, I realized it was a powerful concept to honor the self and the other. It acknowledges an Indigenous world-view on the one hand, and yet, its essence is universal. For me this concept hit me at my core, it liberated my spirit, and reminded me of the profound humanitarian wisdom of my Indigenous ancestors. This name definitely resonated amongst the women of In Lak Ech, despite the fact some of the women have ancestral roots outside of the Americas. I am forever grateful for these sisters of *flor y canto*, who inspired me to come out as an artist and gave me the beautiful healing experience of singing and drumming in unison.

With the desire to support and push for more women of color artist representation, a callout was made by Felicia Montes and myself to all women to share their art, be it visual art, music, theater, poetry, or filmmaking, regardless of age, ethnicity, or level of training. And like a

FIGURE 1.1 *In Lak Ech*. Photo by Aurelio Jose Barrera.

spark of light, on June 29, 1997, at the PRC, Mujeres de Maiz was born as an all-women multimedia performance show, a one-night exhibit, and a self-published zine. It was and continues to be such an empowering feeling to witness the organizing effort and the coming together of many women sharing their art and proclaiming their voice. The synchronicity, unity, and feminine energy of women of color in all its forms feels truly extraordinary, otherworldly, and simply magical.

For example, before our first Live Art Show, I remember Felicia kept talking about how we needed artwork and writings for a zine and how someone was giving a Photoshop workshop that would help us create our zine. "Not a magazine, but a zine?" I asked, somewhat puzzled at first because my punk rock days had peaked in the eighties. Somehow Bikini Kill and the nineties zine movement had escaped my radar. In the hustle of acquiring artwork for the zine, I was "coincidently" introduced to my Aunt Virgie's neighbor Maria, who had just finished a painting of the God of Corn being birthed. With Maria's permission, her painting became the front cover of our first zine, which we titled *The Birth of la Diosa de Maiz* (figure 1.2). Interestingly, many years later, I realized that corn is a plantcestor that is both male and female in nature, a fact I was not aware of when Felicia and I decided to change the painting's title.

FIGURE 1.2 Front cover, 1997 zine. Mujeres de Maiz.

FIGURE 1.3 MdM early days. Mujeres de Maiz.

Another interesting fact I find unique to Mujeres de Maiz's herstory is how MdM has been a leading voice in promoting the honoring of International Women's Day in Los Angeles. After our first Live Art Show, I was approached by an African American woman in the PRC's parking lot, who suggested that MdM consider honoring International Women's Day for our next event. "*Of course!*" I thought. This was the missing link that was needed to truly reflect the vision of Mujeres de Maiz, which was to unite and empower culturally diverse, politicized, and spiritually inclined women of color artists and activists. The raw social justice voices echoing throughout our first Live Art Show resonated with the essence of International Women's Day as it emerged amidst the social justice, labor, and feminist movements of the early twentieth century.

For over a decade, MdM was one of a few, if not the only collective in downtown and its surrounding communities of Lincoln Heights, Highland Park, Boyle Heights, East Los Angeles, El Sereno, and South Central L.A. that consistently honored International Women's Day in March. All our annual multimedia Live Art Shows, with the the exception of the first one, have been in honor of International Women's Day. Today, schools, cafes, galleries, community and city events, and public institutions throughout Los Angeles celebrate International Women's Day.

Thanks to this African American sister, Mujeres de Maiz has definitely played an influential role in establishing an awareness of International Women's Day in Los Angeles.

Glide with la culebra she whispers
intoxicated by her sweetgrass scent
I follow
her leather serpent scales glide past my thighs
disappearing
beyond the black velvet L.A. night sky
leaving me
con la luna llena
full moon
Coyolxauhqui
and the end of my moon
I fall in her arms
staring into my eyes
full moon asks me to kiss her
wind chimes
awaken the rivers of my veins
pumping the heart of my real self
her eagle penacho feathers
caress and fan my animal heat
soothing hardened nipples
birthing a new heartbeat
between la naturaleza and me
piercing into the darkness
like the bells on her face[4]

For me, the importance of advocating for racial and cultural inclusivity also meant making room for representations of sexuality and gender diversity. At our first show, it was interesting to see the reactions of people who entered a semi-closed-off installation in the back of the PRC that was showing an erotic safe sex video for and by queer Latinas that I had shot. Not surprisingly, most bewildered comments were from men. Regardless, Mujeres de Maiz cultivated a safe space for LGBTQ and nonbinary voices, many who have continually shared their art and stories over the years, such as Womyn Image Makers, Tongues, Butchlalis de Panochtitlan, D'Lo, Gina Aparicio, Skim, Medusa, Skryb Anu, and Celia Herrera Rodríguez, to name a few (figures 1.4–1.5). As a key organizer of the sixth Mujeres de Maiz Live Art Show in 2004, I offered the title "Danzando con el Fuego," because I truly felt this Live Art Show at Self Help Graphics established MdM as a committed open space for queer folks.[5] While designing the flyer with Margaret 'Quica' Alarcón and Gina Aparicio, I suggested adding a line that read "A Night of Mujeres de Maiz a la Tongues Flava," to acknowledge the unique collaboration between MdM and several queer-identified collectives, such as Tongues and Womyn Image Makers who helped sponsor the event that year.[6]

FIGURE 1.4 Butchlalis de Panochtitlan. Video still. Claudia Mercado.

FIGURE 1.5 Womyn Image Makers. Womyn Image Makers.

This is not to say there weren't queer folks representing at MdM before, because there definitely were, including me. However, Tongues and Womyn Image Makers were other women of color collectives actively working with the community who helped organize, participate, and promote Mujeres de Maiz that year and afterward.

> Starving like a dried-up river, Juana Gallo has been coming out full force lately. After years of hiding and forced silence, she escaped my repressive censorship and denying grasp. She felt the gravitational pull of the warm bright life-giving rays of Tonatiuh reeling her out of the darkness. She did not fear the fire for she had sung to that sacred element many times before. But unfamiliar with the licks of its flames, Juana caught on fire. Her mind on fire, her body on fire, her spirit on fire. Consumed by the passion, she burned. Stunned at the charred remnants of her broken hungry living shell, I picked up the broken pieces, mended her wounds, swept the ashes and set her free to fly. Each remnant a lesson learned. Each remnant unifying us. Each remnant a step closer to becoming.[7]

Little did I know that by suggesting "Danzando con el Fuego" as the 2004 theme, I had invoked the sacredness of fire and I would consequently be consumed by fire over the next six years.

The proceeds of that year's Live Art Show allowed me to participate as a delegate observer and video documenter of La Red Xicana Indigena's work at the United Nations Permanent Forum on Indigenous Issues in New York.[8] Several of the core organizers of Mujeres de Maiz, including Gina Aparicio, Maritza Alvarez, Margaret 'Quica' Alarcón, Felicia 'Fe' Montes, Martha Gonzalez, and myself had been organizing with La Red Xicana Indigena collective to put forth Xicana Indigena gatherings since the early 2000s. Our collaborations led to the 2003 MdM Live Art Show "Red," which served as a fundraiser for our second national gathering of Xicana Indigenas, which took place in the Angeles Crest mountains. The first gathering, "Cihuatlatokan," was in 1999 and was spearheaded by Sara Mendoza of LAIPA (Los Angeles Indigenous Peoples' Alliance), Rosalia Gonzalez, and some Mujeres de Maiz.

My participation in La Red exposed me to a wider intercontinental understanding of "indigenismo." This desire to explore and learn about "indigenismo" led me to work and document diverse Indigenous women

FIGURE 1.6 South Central Farmers 2006. Gina Aparicio.

and organizations, such as the International Indigenous Grandmother's Gatherings organized by Morning Star Foundation, the Acjachemen-Juaneño struggle to save their sacred site of Panhe in San Clemente, California, and the South Central Farmers' fourteen-acre community garden struggle in Los Angeles. Without a doubt, my exposure and video documentation of diverse Indigenous women, struggles, and organizations, influenced the Live Art Shows "Somos Medicina" (2008), "La Sagrada" (2009), and "13 Baktun" (2010).

Que queremos compañeros?
Justicia!
Cuando?
Ahora!
Taking a place away like this is just like cutting down another rainforest.[9]

For thirteen years, 350 families planted food and medicinal plants on a fourteen-acre urban farm in the middle of South Central Los Angeles.

After years of protesting the sale of this safe haven and raising the necessary funds to purchase the land from the developer whom the city of Los Angeles had made a backroom deal with, I witnessed and documented the destruction of this communal oasis. The documentary short *Aquí Estamos Y No Nos Vamos* would not have been possible without *el pueblo*, the youth, environmentalists, and my sisters in the struggle, especially Maritza Alvarez and Gina Aparicio, as well as Rufina Juarez of La Red Xicana Indigena (figure 1.6).

The words of the International Indigenous Grandmothers and those of many at the UN clearly confirmed for me what I already knew—an Indigenous worldview is medicine to the people and to our Earth Mother. Consequently, I suggested the themes "Somos Medicina" and "La Sagrada" for the MdM Live Art Shows. In fact, in 2008, Self Help Graphics was undergoing a shift in administration and was on the brink of closing when Mujeres de Maiz went in and gave it a much-needed limpia, literally and spiritually. Mujeres de Maiz cleaned, mopped, painted, and transformed that space not only for our event but in gratitude for all the years it had its doors open to us and the overall artist community.

That year, Mujeres de Maiz not only gave SHG a physical facelift and energetic cleanse, but the theme "Somos Medicina" also enabled MdM to manifest our vision for a month-long exhibition and additional event programming, rather than just a one-night experience. Gina Aparicio and Marisol Lydia Torres curated the exhibit, Felicia 'Fe' Montes spearheaded the programming, and Maritza Alvarez, Martha Gonzalez, and myself constructed a mini film theater inside the SHG gallery as part of the exhibit and for a film night. This year is also inscribed in my memory because it was important for me to have a sacred fire present in honor of our work, vision, and spirit.

The location of the 2009 Live Art Show "La Sagrada—She, the Sacred" could not have captured the sacredness of land better than what today is called the Los Angeles State Historic Park, home of Lauren Bon's 2005 *Not a Cornfield* living sculpture.[10] Thanks to Olivia Chumacero's support and working relationship with Bon's Metabolic Studio as consultant and caretaker of the native fauna and flora, MdM was able to utilize both the creative art space of Metabolic Studio and the park (figure 1.7).

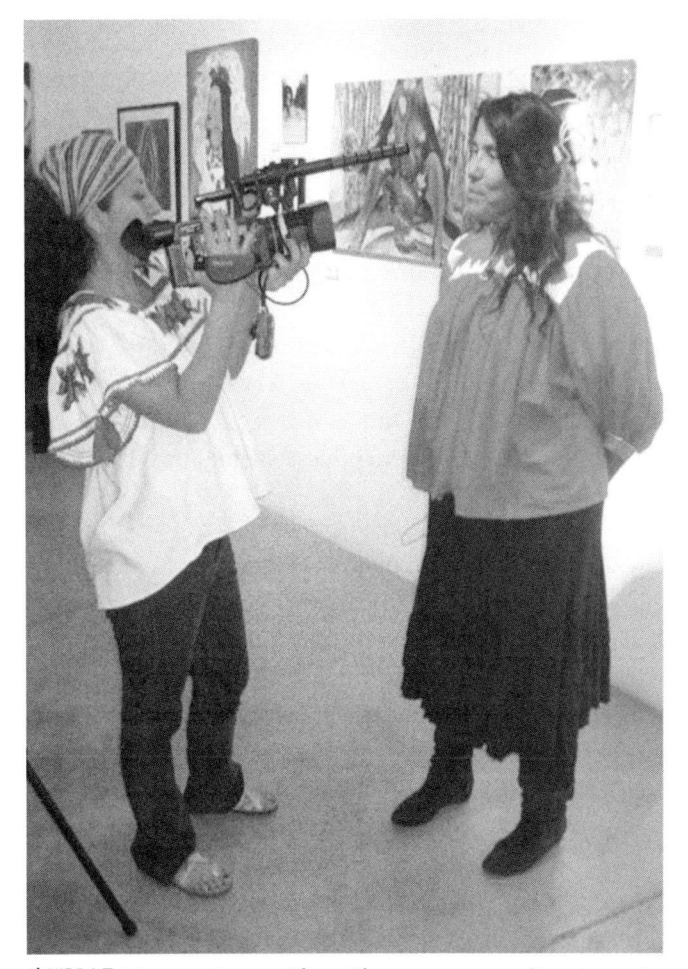

FIGURE I.7 Me interviewing Olivia Chumacero 2009. Gina Aparicio.

Although it is customary for MdM Live Art Shows to begin with a spiritual meditation/prayer, it was an amazing feeling to open "La Sagrada— She the Sacred" with an outdoor collective prayer amidst a flourishing California native garden, acknowledging the Tongva original people of that land while having the beauty of the downtown LA skyscrapers in the background. Growing up just over the Broadway bridge from where the park is located, I had witnessed the transformation of this land from being an abandoned railroad junkyard for years to a lush, green haven, especially one that was redefining the history of that specific land. I felt empowered to be part of this moment and proud Mujeres de Maiz was helping to honor this land's history.

Other memorable moments of this Live Art Show were the intergenerational live mural making that Lilia Ramirez organized, as well as her beautiful installation of the young corn goddess, Xilonen (plate 9). What a comical coincidence that a short film about sexual self-pleasure, part of a reel of short films I curated for the show, kept getting stuck on repeat! I can only speculate what folks might have thought as they walked by the screening room and repeatedly kept seeing the same self-gratifying images over and over again. Lorne Dee Cervantes and Josefina Lopez's spitfire *palabras*, Maya Jupiter and Aloe Blacc singing their hearts out to each other, Medusa the gangster goddess calling forth Harriet Tubman, and oh so many more . . .

Like many
puro Michoacano
taking the train up North
he the 49th bracero
knew the U.S. game
Sunkist fields
railroad deals
folding boxes year after year
yes
he escaped Mexico's colonial shields
maybe even running away from his own fears
but became godfather-like to those
crossing over hear
un tamal oaxaqueno
my grandfather smiled at me to bring
cracking like old paint on wood
sitting hours with his blasting headphones
in the warm sun
sleeping
sinking without drowning
life in one hand
death in the other
a dying wish unforeseen[11]

FIGURE 1.8 Susana Baca collage. Video stills. Claudia Mercado.

In 2009 Maritza Alvarez and I documented the fourth International Grandmother's Gathering in Hawai'i. It was Maritza who suggested the theme for MdM's eleventh Live Art Show, "13 Baktun, Return of the Wisdom of Elders," based on a teaching of an Indigenous Maya grandmother from the gathering. Again, like magic, as we prepared to honor our ancestors, those who have paved the path for us, I was able to confirm the musical guest appearance of Susana Baca whose career began "coincidently" on International Women's Day and whose life's work has been dedicated to giving voice to her ancestors—the Indigenous Black soul of Peru (figure 1.8).

It was a huge undertaking and an honor to host Grammy Award–winning songstress Susana Baca, who came from Peru to collaborate with some of the Mujeres de Maiz musicians, a feat that would not have been possible without the support of MdM's circle of university professors, such as Maylei Blackwell, Lara Medina, Yreina Cervántez, and Dionne Espinoza. The opportunity to organize and document this musical collaboration between Susana Baca and Martha Gonzalez of Quetzal, La Marisoul Hernandez, Gloria Estrada, Tylana Enomoto, Nikki Campbell, Marisa Ronstadt, Maya Jupiter, and others was a gift and impressively herstorical.

Needless to say, there are many stories, special moments, and some amazing women who have inspired my journey with Mujeres de Maiz as I weaved in and out as an organizer, artist, and documenter—or all of the above. For twenty-five years I have had a space for sisterhood to dream, create, heal, explore, learn, and work. It hasn't always been fun and easy, and there have been sacrifices involved. Nonetheless, like Chicomecoatl—Seven Serpents, the female deity of Corn—Mujeres de Maiz has nourished my mind, body, and spirit, and I in turn have offered my time, dreams, sweat and tears to this home.

Although it was in the PRC's physical space where Mujeres de Maiz was born, for me, the seeds of inspiration that informed my vision toward Mujeres de Maiz first began with my grandmother Maria Camacho Quintero's humanitarian fire and spiritual worldview. She was a strong wise heartfelt creative woman connected to land who created community in her home. With my grandmother Maria's passing at age eight, along with the colonization that comes with living in a patriarchal imperialist nation, remembering this part of myself became dormant.

It was not until I was in college when I came across the activism, artwork, and writings of women of color feminists of the seventies, eighties and nineties that I began to reconnect with my fire.

It is new for many women
even for the old
who once bled
a celebration in ruins
no longer
a moon ceremony
honoring our umbilical cord
with time and space
A moon ceremony for
Pink Orquídeas
a rite of passage
the right to know
she
is blooming fuchsia spring
powerful like the rays of the summer sun
tenderly plump on the vine
eagerly awaiting life[12]

Going beyond my own life experience, Mujeres de Maiz is a product of the work of all our ancestors, social justice uprisings, revolutions, civil rights movements, and women of color feminist leadership who, like us, had awakened to their desires and visions for a better world and were willing to do something about it. It is that fire we all carry and is manifested in different ways. For me, it has revealed itself through my community activism, filmmaking, flor y canto, and my hands in the land. It is the collective vision and energy of love that has and continues to impact and empower people, a bridge back to home to self, family, community, land, and spirit. Mujeres de Maiz has provided me with a home to dream, collaborate, manifest, perform, heal, explore, resist, decolonize, pray, and remember my higher self. As one of the co-founders and the primary video documenter of Mujeres de Maiz, I feel truly blessed to have experienced and shared this journey with so many beautiful people and give thanks for all the fire it has given me.

NOTES

1. Inspired after reviewing my short film *Obsidian Mirror* (1997–98) in collaboration with Lilia Ramirez and Evelyn Montes that was created shortly after the first Mujeres de Maiz Live Art Show.
2. The PRC, Popular Resource Center, also known as Centro Regeneración or Regeneration, was founded by Rage Against the Machine's lead vocalist Zack de la Rocha in the early 1990s.
3. Excerpt from Claudia Mercado, "The Connection," *Mujeres de Maiz, Flor y Canto: The Birth of la Diosa de Maiz*, no. 1 (1997). This was also my first poem with In Lak Ech, performed at the first Mujeres de Maiz Live Art Show in 1997.
4. Excerpt from Claudia Mercado, "Lovermoon," *Mujeres de Maiz, Flor y Canto: Of Mixed Waters*, no. 3 (1999).
5. Self Help Graphics & Art (SHG) is a community arts center that was originally located in East Los Angeles but today is located in the community of Boyle Heights, Los Angeles. SHG has always welcomed and supported the work of Mujeres de Maiz, https://www.selfhelpgraphics.com.
6. Womyn Image Makers was a queer Indigenous identified women's filmmaking collective composed of Maritza Alvarez, Aurora Guerrero, Dalila Mendez, and Claudia Mercado. *Tongues* was a "magazine envisioned, produced, and suffused by Queer womyn of color" (no. 3, 2003). These two artistic and creative groups were leading queer voices in Los Angeles during the early 2000s.
7. Excerpt from Claudia Mercado, "Juana Gallo y el Fuego," *Mujeres de Maiz, Flor y Canto: Toltecayotl Cihuatl*, no. 4 (2006).
8. "La Red is a network of Xicanas indígenas based in Arizona, New Mexico, and California, who are actively involved in political, educational, and cultural

work that serves to raise Indigenous consciousness among our communities and supports the social justice struggles of people of indigenous American origins North and South." https://cherriemoraga.com/index.php/la-comunidad-y-politica/14-la-red.

9. Dialogue from my documentary on the South Central Farmers struggle. *Aquí Estamos y No Nos Vamos!*, directed and produced by Claudia Mercado (2006), Los Angeles, Calif., https://vimeo.com/35181322.
10. Visit http://notacornfield.com for more information.
11. Excerpt from Claudia Mercado, "Aliento Alimento," *Mujeres de Maiz, Flor y Canto: 13 Baktun Return of the Wisdom of Elders*, no. 8 (2010).
12. Excerpt from Claudia Mercado, "Pink Orquidias," *Mujeres de Maiz, Flor y Canto: Soldadera de Amor*, no. 9 (2011).

2
Magandang Misteryo (Beautiful Mystery)

LIZA COHEN HITA

I CLOSED MY eyes, tight, tight, tight, until my eyeballs ached and my cheeks hurt. The young age when my uniform changed from plaid to blue pleated skirts and white sailor tops, but old enough to revel in the sheer, honest rawness of rebellion. My emotions pounding through my body, anger pulsing through every smooth and textured highway of my veins, my blood on fire. Somewhere in the grainy darkness of the insides of my lids, something was there. Quiet and old and present. If I could focus on it long enough, I would get tired, and my breathing would finally slow, my face would relax. My tears, a salty residue, resting at the corners of my eyes, opening slowly. Sighing deeply, inhaling the scent of my ancestors, coming again from deep in the cosmos to soothe me, reminding me. And then came the strong tide, the words pouring into the cove of my writing. Pouring all the lava onto those pages and dreaming distant lucid dreams of something at the intersection of righteous and crazy, comforting and patient. Seeing myself amongst the sleek silhouettes of my old ones, the beautiful mystery of all my ancient relations, against the black earth and a sky vibrant with a spectrum of hope. Women of all generations praying at sunset.

Fast forward past deep talks, whispers and secrets and pacts to the death; loud laughter and even louder arguments, and hazy clouds of forgettable fun. UCLA, 1997. That old trash of privilege and wannabe-something-other-than-me, soaked in accelerant lust for revolution. Light the match.

This fire carried me into a labor organizing course with a strong Xicana with pecas like myself and a stare that could make me feel to the marrow of my bones, an intense personal knowing, grounded in cornmeal and old stories of transformation. Her ancestors were always close around her. I could smell their scent. Our friendship and desire to help The People linked me to a necklace of beautiful women, islands of eccentric creative passion strung along the warm tropical waters of this serene time and place. From the tremors of my own childhood discontent to rooftops and East L.A. lomas and Chiapas and ceremony and medicines of introspection, there I was praying, basking in that light, next to that fire, smoking tobacco.

Highland Park, spring 1997. Something special was happening in LA. And in me. The words that had filled up countless notebooks were now coming to life. This was an easy birth. Five sisters as midwives. I remember the day In Lak Ech was named. There is no point in painting an exact portrait here, as there are probably five stories of that birthday. But from those initial conversations came this immaculate conception, this seed. No one of us is directly responsible—it was created from the ancestral knowledge of women who wrote and sang and danced their prayers for all our relations, a mandate from the Great Mystery. Childhood dreams rip into life from that place in between being born and almost dying, where you can't breathe and then you come into this world screaming, singing to the beat of a big drum.

MdM, 1997, feels like a private memory because the origins were intimate, complex, rich, and painful. But a good pain, like that of your second birth. You know the feeling is coming but that knowledge doesn't diminish it and you surely can't wish it away. My experience was of watching a dedicated maverick, a prodigy of sorts in this world of art and activism, with soft curly hair and deep red lips, head always held high, higher than was comfortable for my own head, the kind of stance we see in archives of old pictures with fists pumping in the air. Ficha. La Fe. That first zine was a twilight moon child, literally cut with scissors and pasted with glue, just so, just right, it's good to go, printed at the copy shop as the midnight oil burned low. Nothing could stop it. Just a few of us, both men and women, worked tirelessly during the days before that first show. All that time, I felt like I was watching something much larger than myself, almost from a distance, from the outside looking in. I was learning from the intensity of Fe's commitment, the type of *ganas* that knows its purpose to the core, a mandate of love. She had such enduring faith in the beautiful mystery that was to come that beyond the confusions and apprehensions and endless discussions, this intention survived the tread. Looking back, I feel like a real novice. I didn't have the words to describe this process, this creative sovereignty. While this was always a collective vision, both the tangible and intangible, there was a seed that was planted with that very first MdM experience and no matter how many people are involved in the creation of something so sincere and dedicated, only one hand can drop that seed into the earth.

What an honor it was to be part of the first MdMs. The first cycle of shows and the planning and the newness of something so magnetic just drew droves of all kinds of people. It really was amazing. Wow. That's how I remember it, like a sound wave bustling through a new dimension, something cosmic and magical. So, I was like a magician. On stage, in the audience, behind the scenes, immersed in the pages of my books, absorbing that light exuding from the pages, the crowd dark and silent, the smell of my ancestors near.

My elders were smoky mixcoatl trails in and out of my childhood dreams and then they would retreat into the caverns in the edges of the expansive uncharted universe. They came again at night in a time of deep crisis, with a rumbling guttural roar, marching toward me in translucent plumes of ancestral magnitude to remind me of who I am. Not in human likeness, but in the forms of different elements—smoke, wind, water, fire—in the language of the holy ones without faces.

My mother's maiden name is Macahilig. It means "the one of art and music." In the thick lush Filipino landscape of eight hundred years of resistance, the giants roamed our village and the dreamweavers guided us through the spirit world—all recollections on a monsoon-soaked June afternoon. The performance space gave me the courage to ask my old ones for permission to share our stories. I didn't know that I was actually talking to my old relations at the time, but as I pieced the sequence of very carefully defined events together, they could have only led to a spiritual conversation with the elements, the animas, and my ancestors.

I needed their direction. My ancient ones that trekked through the exodus of the twelve tribes of Israel, three tribes in each direction with the Cohanim in the middle—my people, the Cohens—continued to nourish my spiritual expression, reminding me that before any state was up for debate, there was only holy land there and nothing else and that we are all holy beings.

My Jewish lineage stayed quiet and loyal cloaked in the protection of being a Chicana, as deep anti-Semitism lurked behind mosh-pit-worthy anthems and the not-so-low-key or quiet rhetoric of some of my so-called friends and *comaradas*. The same ol' mantra is to create a common enemy so we can feel solidarity in our disgust. I've heard so many versions of this that are rooted in fear and inexperience. Guarded from true acceptance and radical empathy. When they say "All My Relations" in our sacred circles, they don't really mean *all* our relations, just some, just the ones that they like best. After all, this isn't the *White Roots of Peace*, right? The old stories of our ancient ones in living testimony in our medicine wheels are just whispers now, something archaic and unuseful to those who live in perpetual division, even in our shared brown skin. Us. Them. You. *Feel it, be it, breathe it all in*. Take in all the displaced rage. I didn't know the bitter shame I had harbored until I planted my feet in the lands and waters of my generations thousands of years old and made peace with not acknowledging them. And cried.

Being a Filipinx-Ukrainian Jew, baptized Catholic, raised in secular society, hiding somewhere in those baggy clothes, I blended into the camouflage of the urban activist landscape. Mainly, I looked like my sisters from the South, whose landscapes mirrored the big tropical leaves of my own homelands with deep chola-lined eyes and lips. We understood each other. Sometimes this was comforting, and sometimes this was isolating. Being a Chicana meant being exactly where I found myself. It was a sliver of quantum time, dispersed infinitely amongst the fractals of my earthly and divine identities. In between worlds, but just where I needed to be. Even when people would discover who I was, where my family was from, where I was raised, mostly through my own disclosure in very public moments of performance art, I was always a Chicana—people could not extract it from their mind—the unwavering bond, intangible belonging, mothering, nurturing, warrior that is Chicanisma. It was all-embracing and took what could have been seen as cultural ambiguity or denial and sang a soft song to the girl who missed her people, and sometimes her hard-working parents, and sometimes her own childhood, and sometimes her own peace of mind.

Within less than a year of our first meeting in that labor organizing class, I was in Oventic, Chiapas sharing art and freestyling with the Zapatistas, which led me to my first medicine ceremony where I met my husband and picked up my own seed from the dusty desert valley. Within the mayhem that occurs during organized chaos, I listened closely to these places that my journey had taken me. Ear to the ground to the heartbeat of the earth. Within the spheres of sacred spaces, ceremonial and otherwise, there are holy orders that encourage people to pay attention to natural law and embrace an old Way of Life. A city girl is not well versed in the art of simplicity, but I was fortunate that it reached its arms out to me first and called me to service. Took my casual dreams and made me a serious woman. I made promises. And all the days of my life from that point on have just been an attempt to be good on my word. From poetic words, to healing words, to prayer words, to songs, to just my breath. Slow and steady in the depth of night.

The interconnected atomic blast of those early years changed the atmosphere of my life forever. It inspired a deep piece of me that all the challenges after those years could not rob. The foundation that MdM created, the dedicated sisterhood and tenacity of spirit, helped me survive a series of devastating losses, mostly of dreams I had that life stripped bare.

To cope with the crumbling remnants, I decided on the third day of our Sundance ceremony during my first year dancing that I would get a PhD. I didn't really know that's what I had asked for at the time. It was just a fleeting, third-day, tired, random thought. That's what it felt like. Was it the hunger? No, maybe the thirst. Our elders kept saying, "Dancers, remember to pray for yourselves! Love yourself as you do the people." Three days later, I hadn't spent even one beat of the drum thinking about the remote enigma of me. In the early, barefooted, cold misty morning, even before entering the arbor, I honestly just wanted to get these prayers for this Liza person out of the way. So, in my obsession with proof, I whispered the words to Creator. Quiet and simple. And quick. Not to have this degree, but to explore the possibilities of my potential, my untapped sap, my unseen callings, and my diverse voice—guide me to where I should be. Utilize me. And after that fleeting moment, every time I wanted to quit, when my eyes would burn with flashes of angst and desperation and regret, I would remember that sacred Tree of Life and God's generous and loving torch during my dark night of the soul. No Queen Bee, no sleepless nights, no crying children missing their father, no racist undertone, no undermining, patronizing woo of deflated support and doubtful echoes—nothing could stop me from getting this PhD because it was a prayer. Even if it was just a piece of paper—it was mine. And honestly, in your loneliest moments, when the world grows tired of your sorrow, you can hold out just one hand that holds everything in your existence that is truly yours, that no one can ever take away. And this was one of them. Not because it was knowledge, but because it was my energy, my fortitude, and commitment. I learned what I was made of. I learned to love my grit.

The essence of the me that is part of this MdM collective is buried in my bones, part and parcel of the way I walk in this world because it led me down this path. It reminded me of my powerful womanhood. I'm called mama, sister, professor, doctor, friend, and helper, and as I walk through life, each step is a motion to the cosmos that I'm still present—thank you for my life! Each movement generating a further bond with my authentic self. Its meaning is cradled in the tenderness of its history. A sacred time all its own, lush with iridescent shimmer.

When I dreamt as a child and saw that beautiful mystery, those women at sunset, I never thought of feminism as something separate from myself. It was never a choice because I was always standing amongst them. If I love myself or not, I will love and respect and stand in solidarity with other reflections of my womanhood, my personhood, the feminine within me that is also within each of my sisters and all of my brothers. Sometimes I didn't love myself, and sometimes I still don't, with sickness engulfing me at vulnerable moments, but my sisters lift me up, they remind me of the middle ground. Not in the form of compromise but in the sanctuary of comadrismo, the friendship that endures through the harsh winter and blistering summer. Something timeless. A certain kind of healing.

At the heart of MdM is a memory. The memory itself is medicine. The memory pushes me to write when the ember seems dark and cold. It turns the coal to reveal the warm, fiery underbelly, burning with life. It reminds me. This memory is fleshy, rippled green silk, leaves from the branches of this universal form—it is alive with energy, feelings, dreams, and a spirit expansive through limitless possibilities. All from that seed. It brings sisters together, it provokes a warm feeling thinking about dynamic expressions and experiences, walking through the galleries, seeing the dancing, feeling the vibration of the floor, the echo of the walls, the sound dissipating through the thick night of the old city, where our old ones gather to listen along. I close my eyes and I'm there. Even from here in Arizona, even though I haven't been to a MdM show in years. I remember. I have that feeling. I honor the journey MdM has taken me on and how it has woven countless monumental experiences together by its sheer will. I take a deep breath and open my eyes, gentle and forward gaze, smiling.

3
Know Your Enemy

The Sham of Filipino Independence

LIZA COHEN HITA

Do you know who I am?
One of mixed descent
Of milky white European exile
And deep molasses Island poverty
Born from a typical military love affair
You know—The ones that seem so prevalent
On army bases throughout the South Pacific
And all along the West Coast of the United States
Spawned from a family forced to *be-all-they-could-be*
Because everyday reality wasn't
Paying their bills or feeding their children
So brought into the colonized world of military intrusiveness
And reared in the urban jungles of California

I was introduced to the perils of my history one day
By my adult discontent
With capitalist America
So you know who that country is?
Your liberator?
Co-conspirator in the rape of a nation?
The loving motherland
that sent 126,000 soldiers to help the Spanish
Fuck your mother, kill your brother
Destroy the future your children cried hungry for
Made your homeland a whore
The land of the free
That took your freedom
And made you a token of
an upwardly mobile minority
Made you use your seniority
On other people with brown skin

Colonized by the same deep-cover
    lover
Lover of material wealth
Stealth bombers
And a poor, disenfranchised feudal
    system
So, bon appétit
Eat up the fruits of my mother's labor
The soft, boiled pieces of white rice
Her small, strong hands picked
Stooped over, on her knees
Feeding the pockets of some
international imperialist
Pimping her hopes for a better life
When all she has to say is:
Where there's a will there's a way
But the American dream led her astray
So on this June 12th
Do you know what this day is?
The day when we as pinay and pinoy
Toys of some higher power
Celebrate the liberation from one
    oppressor
And the rejuvenation of
Modern-day crusades
Crusades for paydays
And all shades of workers
Willing to fiend for the green
The empire of the modern era
Trying to convert dirt into computer
    chips
Wining and dining Ramos
Over sips of Indigenous blood
Telling him that to survive
In this New World Order
One must sell one's soul
On a devalued peso

In the free market economy
So you wanna-be exploiter of the
Third World,
You must bow down to
Globalization, Taxation
Liberalization, Privatization
IMF regulations and
The United Nations
To earn your freedom
And then WE'LL tell you
when and where that is,
thank you
All at the expense of your
people, okay?
Like Catholic steeples
Pay homage to the all
mighty dollar
Yeah, you hear me hollering
Over the sour grapes of
your rule
But too bad for you I went—
back to school
To learn
Who am I?
Who is this country?
What is this day?
And don't get played out by
all the garbage the media tries to feed
    you
Just trust that innate,
anxious feeling inside
That tells you that something here is
    very, very
Very, very wrong
So don't tell me my intuition
is a lie
And don't stifle my ambition

Because to rebel is justified
So I won't pledge allegiance
To a country that's never been a friend to me
And some advice to my brothers and sisters—
    Know your enemy

Mujeres de Maiz, Flor y Canto: Birth of La Diosa de Maiz, no. 1 (1997): n.p.

4
Reflections on Mujeres de Maiz

LARA MEDINA

WHILE THE majority of Chicanas and Latinas participate in religious traditions that continue to attempt a male monopoly over the sacred, many others turn to traditional Indigenous ways that honor the sacredness of the universe, of women, and the ancient Mesoamerican tradition of communicating with the divine through the arts and through community. But while these women are returning to a traditional path, they are also creating a new one in response to societal marginalization, neocolonialism, and ongoing racial, gender, and sexual oppressions in and beyond our communities. Mujeres de Maiz, now a twenty-five-year collective of women of color artists, carries on the legacy of Native women who create autonomous sacred space to share their arts, words, music, and wisdom. Their actions strive to maintain balance in themselves, our communities, and our universe and reflect what Native scholar Gerald Vizenor calls "survivance," or "the state of being that encompasses more than physical survival but an active sense of presence, the continuance of native stories, not a mere reaction. . . . Native survivance stories are the renunciation of dominance, tragedy, and victimry."[1] Mujeres de Maiz tells the stories of Indigenous-identified Xicanas/x and their allies by drawing from ancient knowledges put through the sounds, symbols, and colors of twenty-first-century urban life. In doing so, they offer us a powerful message: We are strong women of color building strong communities and shaping our next generation to resist the consequences of neocolonialism through creativity, organizing, and a reclamation of our Indigenous knowledges.

Their identity as "urban Native spiritual/cultural/political women artists" committed to sociopolitical justice and self and community empowerment first emerged from the marginalization they experience as brown women in white America and the repression of Native peoples globally. Inspired by the 1994 Zapatista uprisings and equipped with their own community organizing experience, two young urban Xicanas in Los Angeles, Felicia 'Fe' Montes and Claudia Mercado, decided to create a space where women of color poets, painters, and performers could express themselves and share their works privately and publicly. "If they didn't tell their stories, who would?"[2] Other mujeres shared their vision and in 1997, Mujeres de Maiz self-published a grassroots zine and produced a one-night multimedia performance titled "Birth of La Diosa de Maiz." Since then, women of African, Asian, Arabic, and Latina bloodlines have joined with Xicanas to express what art historian Sybil Venegas calls a "sacred right of self-preservation."[3] These women are linked by a commitment to use "art as an educational tool for resistance, healing and change."[4] Since its founding, Mujeres de Maiz has produced fifteen zines, more than twenty multimedia Live Art Shows, and several community conferences reaching out to intergenerations of young women and their mothers around topics related to physical health and emotional well-being. They have touched and healed the hearts, minds, and souls of thousands of Xicanas/x/os and their allies. After attending a Mujeres de Maiz event, one leaves not just having been entertained, but rather having been touched deeply in one's being, affirmed in one's feminist, cultural, and political identity, and healed from the pain of not seeing oneself on stage in the public arena. Mujeres de Maiz represents all of us: *Tu eres mi otro yo, In Lak' ech*.

Their identity as urban Native women, straight and queer, grounded in Indigenous values, epistemologies, ceremony, and belief in the ancient goddesses, makes public a cultural and spiritual identity that was meant to disappear under colonialism. Internalized racism among communities of color has made it disadvantageous to be *una india/un indio*. The women of Mujeres de Maiz, many who are now mothers of young children, are committed to raising the young ones according to Indigenous values of self-respect, self-determination, interdependency, reciprocity, the centrality of women, the ancestors, and honoring the cosmic forces. The phenomenal community response to their performances, art exhibitions, writings, and workshops reflects a surviving Indigenous identity thirsty for the soul-healing work offered by Mujeres de Maiz. In their own words, "What we are doing is transforming, healing ourselves, our communities and the world one poem, one painting, one performance at a time."[5] Through the use of drama, humor, dance, music, poetry, and visual art, Mujeres de Maiz offers a spiritual practice rooted in the ancient Mesoamerican tradition of communicating with the divine through the creative arts. For Mujeres de Maiz, it is through the arts that the healing of psychic, physical, and spiritual wounds take place. As one observer comments in zine no. 4, these women "are our scribes, unearthing a different way of seeing, a different way of walking in this world." Within their work, "the sacred and divine are incarnate . . . a seed in our struggle to remain human."

In recent years, Mujeres de Maiz has expanded their work to include the sponsoring of community workshops on a variety of decolonizing health and spiritual practices. Topics range from preparing Indigenous foods, to traditional birthing techniques, to reconnecting with the feminine energies of the universe. Their commitment to gather women together monthly to honor the full moon offers a collective ritual that reinstates women's relationship to the sacred lunar cycle.[6] Inviting community healers who are trained in specific healing modalities and making the workshops accessible to working-class communities is a tremendous gift from Mujeres de Maiz. They are offering a pathway for individual women across generations to join a collective effort to truly decolonize how we live our everyday lives. Their commitment to transform and heal our communities expands as they themselves grow in healing knowledges.

My participation in Mujeres de Maiz events and workshops affirms the spiritual path I and many of my peers from the first Chicana movement generation began to walk on many years ago. Seeing myself reflected in the artistic representations gathered by Mujeres de Maiz provides a level of affirmation I could not conceive of as a much younger Chicana. Mujeres de Maiz has grasped the teachings of the ancient ones and the foremothers who in the 1970s began the arduous task of reclaiming our Indigenous selves, and they have carried it forward to a profound level of engagement. Their work affirms what me and my peers knew was the right path to travel back to ourselves. I am extremely grateful for the work of Mujeres de Maiz, for their learning traditional ways of healing, for bringing them to our youth and our communities, and to their commitment to the ongoing challenge of "decolonizing everything." I have brought the work of Mujeres de Maiz into my classes frequently either through digital representation or inviting representatives to speak to my students. It has been an honor and a privilege over the years to offer my full support to Mujeres de Maiz.

Adelante!

NOTES

1. Gerald Vizenor and A. Robert Lee, *PostIndian Conversations* (Lincoln: University of Nebraska Press, 1999), 93.
2. *Mujeres de Maiz, Flor y Canto: Toltecayotl Cihuatl*, no. 4 (2006): 2.
3. Sybil Venegas, *The Day of the Dead in Aztlán: Chicano Variations on the Theme of Life, Death and Self Preservation* (Los Angeles: University of California, Los Angeles, 1993).
4. *Mujeres de Maiz, Flor y Canto: Toltecayotl Cihuatl*, no. 4 (2006): 3.
5. Felicia 'Fe' Montes, interview with the author, September 2008.
6. Review chapter 5, "Coyolxauhqui Full Moon Circle" by Nadia Zepeda in this section.

5

Coyolxauhqui Full Moon Circle

Self-Care as Community Care

NADIA ZEPEDA

IN APRIL of 2013, the smell of *copal*[1] immediately told me I was where I needed to be.

The smoke that came from the center, the *ombligo*,[2] of the circle was so inviting. As I looked around, I saw Gaby, the fire keeper, smudging all who were joining the circle with copal. She noted in her introduction to the space that she learned how to keep fire by having participated in Danza Azteca.[3] Michelle, the circle keeper of Omecihuatl, welcomed everyone and let folks know that we were gathered here to honor our ancestors.[4] She shared that she was Native and Chicana, and that her grandma taught her how to tend to the altar as if it were an elder. She encouraged those who had not put anything on the altar to add something in honor of the space, as it will charge their belongings with the energy from the circle. I was nervous to go to my first circle because I was not sure what to expect, but something called me to go—I knew I needed this. The day of the full moon, I took some fruit and a blanket and made my way to the circle, which was inside La Colonia—a community center in a historically Native American and Mexican-American neighborhood in Orange County.

Michelle pointed to Iuri who started the full moon circle in Orange County and asked if she could open the circle up by honoring the four directions.[5] Iuri began the opening by honoring the East—where Life and masculine energy begins—and then she prayed before moving onto the other directions. We all stood and faced each direction with her and listened to her prayer. The women and I sat in a circle listening with our hearts—as we were encouraged to do—to women who were *desahogandose*[6] about things they were going through. None of us were listening to prepare a response, but instead, to empathize and to hold space.

As I got more involved with Omecihuatl, I realized that full moon circles were not unique to Orange County; they have been held all over Southern California. I started my doctoral program at the University of California, Los Angeles (UCLA), a year after I began going to Omecihuatl's circle, and at that point, going back to Orange County from West LA for monthly full moon circles was getting more difficult. I had *compañeras* tell me about full moon healing circles in the Inland Empire and Los Angeles. I saw on Facebook that Mujeres de Maiz hosted full moon circles as well. Coyolxauhqui Full Moon Circle has met every full moon since 2010 in City Terrace, an unincorporated area northeast of downtown Los Angeles, at the corner of two big intersections.

On a clear evening in February 2016, I parked in a *lavandería* parking lot waiting for 9:00 p.m. This parking lot in particular was next to a replica of the Coyolxauhqui stone, similar to the one found in el Templo Mayor in Mexico City.[7] As I walked toward the stone, Lorena, one of the circle keepers, smudged me with copal and welcomed me to the space.[8] In the invite, Mujeres de Maiz encouraged people to bring flowers and candles to place them on the community altar.[9] Fe, another circle keeper and co-founder of Mujeres de Maiz, welcomed everyone. Fe explained that the teachings of the circle were a beautiful blend of Northern and Southern teaching which she has been entrusted to carry. Before the circle began, we honored the four directions with a welcoming song. Marlene, the third circle keeper, let everyone know that they were going to pass around tobacco—an offering that initiates a check-in or a letting-go process—to let go of something negative or affirm something positive on top of the Coyolxauhqui stone. The couple of hours I spent with the people present were especially powerful because I was able to connect with them and could feel the power of ritual and prayer.

Attending talking circles, like Coyolxauhqui Full Moon Circle, for the past couple of years has allowed me to set out on my path to healing, rekindling my relationship with a spiritual practice that fits my queer Chicana feminist experience. These circles shift spirituality away from heteropatriarchal institutional practices sustained by my Mexican Catholic upbringing. Attending these circles also allowed me to participate in the healing of other womxn by holding space with and for them. The spaces for healing that Coyolxauhqui Full Moon Circle provides for the community motivated me to bridge practice and theory in my graduate work.[10]

In this essay, I focus on Coyolxauhqui Full Moon Circle to demonstrate the ways Chicanas are finding and reconnecting with indigeneity through an ancestral spiritual practice, both individually and collectively. I highlight the oral histories of three circle keepers[11] and healing of collective participants, which reveal the knowledge they used to guide their circle and the reasons they participate in the space. In this vein, I argue that part of the function of full moon circles is to inspire and allow participants to tap into their spirituality on their own terms, while seeking ancestral knowledge and moving toward healing from historical trauma. One of the insidious ways in which historical trauma occurs is through the deindianization/detribalization of many Chicanas.[12] This loss manifests in disconnection to their Indigenous ancestry, customs, and cosmologies. It is in the disconnect where the mourning begins, which I explain in the following section.[13]

Part of the intention of a full moon circle is to create a space for self-care and to develop methods of sustainability, in order to do transformative work in the community. Full moon circles might not seem political at first glance, but I found that these groups create sustainable wellness practices utilized by social justice activists. Many participants are activists, teachers, wellness *promotoras*, and mothers. For some, the full moon circles are the first time they gather in a collective space to intentionally heal. This is especially important because devising sustainable self- and community-care practices is a form of healing justice. Healing justice means creating methods to address the violence perpetrated in communities of color and also finding sustainable ways to avoid burnout.[14]

COYOLXAUHQUI MOURNING

For many Chicana/xs, the spirituality they grew up with was not sustainable for them, and instead, they found ways to practice spirituality on their own terms, in ways that reconnect them to an Indigenous spirituality that they no longer had ties with because of detribalization.[15] The disconnect faced by detribalized people has direct consequences of lost ancestry, history, knowledge, and memory. The theoretical framework that guides my examination of full moon circles relies heavily on the work that women of color feminists have laid out to center the lived experiences of marginalized peoples.[16] In their article, "Indigenous but not Indian? Chicana/os and the Politics of Indigeneity," authors María Cotera and María Josefina Saldaña-Portillo situate the detribalization of most Chicanas/o/xs in a historical context.[17] They note that colonization and state-sanctioned projects in Mexico aimed to incrementally eliminate Indigenous communities, cosmologies, languages, and practices through the nationalist project of *mestizaje*. They argue that *mestizaje* was designed as a eugenics project that labeled all Mexicans as a mixture of Indigenous and Spanish blood, situating their Indigenous roots as something of the past. Cotera and Saldaña-Portillo introduce the concept "mestizo mourning" to think about how some Chicana/o/xs can begin to interrogate the detribalization many have experienced as a result of these state-sanctioned projects. "Mestizo mourning" allows for an interrogation of the need to mourn the loss of ancestral knowledge, cosmologies, and practices. I seek to uncover how some Chicanas negotiate this loss and explore how some women reclaim and reconnect to Indigenous and ancestral spiritual practices. As I move forward in this work, I question if reconnection to ancestral and Indigenous practices can occur when hegemonic systems have done everything possible to remove those links.

In her book *Light in the Dark/Luz en Lo Oscuro*, Gloria Anzaldúa's work on Coyolxauhqui further examines Chicanas as remembering and reconnecting to indigeneity. She defines the "Coyolxauhqui imperative" as "a struggle to reconstruct oneself and heal the *susto* resulting from wounding traumas, racism, and other acts of violation que hechan pedazos nuestras almas, split us, scatter our energies, and haunt us.... [It is also] the act of calling back those pieces of the self/soul that have been dispersed or lost, the act of mourning the losses that haunt us."[18] Anzaldúa's "Coyolxauhqui imperative" can be used to articulate a loss Chicanas experience because of colonization and assimilation. In centering Coyolxauhqui in their reclamation, Chicanas articulate an Indigenous epistemology that centers wholeness and healing, but this also relies on the same indigenist iconographies that the Mexican state project used to detribalize many Chicana/xs.[19]

Inspired by Gloria Anzaldúa's "Coyolxauhqui imperative" and María Cotera and María Josefina Saldaña-Portillo's "mestizo mourning," I bring forward the concept "Coyolxauhqui mourning" to describe the condition many detribalized Chicanas experience in trying to reconnect with an Indigenous-based spiritual practice. Detribalized Chicana/x/os cannot fully reconnect to their direct Indigenous ancestry because of colonization and active state projects that seek the elimination of Indigenous communities by using mestizaje as forced assimilation. In attempting to reclaim or reconcile an Indigenous and ancestral spiritual practice, detribalized Chicana/xs realize that they are missing practices, knowledge, memories, and other links to their specific or family's Indigenous ancestry. Like the pieces of Coyolxauhqui that are lost in her dismemberment and cannot be recovered, many Chicanas are faced with the same dilemma—they can remember pieces, but something will be lost in their reconnection. In the case of detribalized Chicana/xs, they must mourn those lost pieces—for some Chicanas, this means grieving the loss of a direct tie to an Indigenous ancestry. However, Coyolxauhqui mourning also acknowledges a reconnection to an Indigenous identity and practice through honoring Native and Indigenous ceremonies and honoring elder and ancestor epistemologies in order to attain healing and wholeness.

Trying to understand how some Chicana/xs navigate their detribalization and negotiate Indigenous and ancestral spiritual practices is what prompted me to do this work. Even though many cannot trace their lineage because of the detribalization that occurred in Mexico, they found alternative ways of practicing their spirituality and reconnecting to their Indigenous descendants/roots.[20] The full moon talking circles become a space where women share the knowledges they have acquired and a space for reconnection to Indigenous spiritual practices.

The experiences of some Chicanas reconnecting with an ancestral and Indigenous-based spiritual and healing practice come from a longing to find what has been lost. In this quest, many Chicanas have navigated different ways to feel a connection to that loss. In what follows, I highlight profiles of individual and collective experiences in the Coyolxauhqui Full Moon Circle to arrive at an understanding of how these women are finding that connection. This process includes looking at what I call their "spiritual awakening," the knowledge that guides them and the circle—be it experiential or Indigenous from ceremonies they participate in—and, finally, how they are finding healing while participating in these spaces once a month.

INDIVIDUAL SPIRITUAL JOURNEY

A spiritual journey is as unique and diverse as the person who is engaging with it. This is no different for many Chicanas who are trying to find healing and spirituality in ancestral ways. There is no set journey that Chicanas take in when they move toward spirituality and healing. As demonstrated in this essay, many Chicanas take different paths to understanding their healing. Following the spiritual practices of Chicanas gives insight into who these women are and what knowledge guides their collective full moon healing circles. I understand that it is important to first understand the individual journeys some Chicanas face when finding their spiritual practice because it can inform how they heal collectively. This research provides a glimpse into three Chicanas' upbringing, how their spiritual practices are negotiated while growing up, and how their spiritual awakening led them to the spiritual path they are currently embarking on; this includes the full moon circles they participate in once a month. Also, by centering the lived experiences of these Chicanas—especially in their spiritual and healing practices—I am remembering the divides that occur between the body, mind, and spirit in hegemonic narratives that silence women by dismembering them. My intention is to find subtle moments of ancestral remembrances that occur during Coyolxauhqui mourning when Chicanas are reconnecting to an ancestral and Indigenous spiritual and healing practice while understanding that they are detribalized.

For the women I spoke to, early spiritual practices took many paths. Some grew up in Christian homes that instilled prayer, others did not grow up with a spiritual practice, while some experienced a mixture of Catholic and Indigenous teachings. The entanglement of colonization and patriarchal practices in Christianity often create an uninhabitable misogynist place for women. This is why many women move away from institutionalized practices in Christianity and begin a journey of spiritual self-discovery on their terms.

Coyolxauhqui Full Moon Circle keeper Lorena describes her upbringing as being very Catholic. She recalls going to church every Sunday, and feeling conflicted, as she got older: "I was always known as 'the rebel.' My mom is very Catholic, we grew up praying the rosary everyday.... We did not question it at the time. Now that I am older, I definitely question our beliefs. I think we have broken a barrier in our late twenties, my sister and I, we finally got to a point where my mom understands our perspective on spirituality is very different. Her perspective is like church and religion, but we are more spiritual."[21]

Part of the rift with Catholicism came from expectations that are often placed on women about their virginity. Losing her virginity at a young age and not being married brought a lot of guilt, which prompted Lorena to go "through a penitence, yo sola me puse en la penitencia for four years."[22] In *Borderlands/La Frontera*, Anzaldúa denotes that oftentimes Chicanas are put into two categories, the chaste image of the Virgen de Guadalupe or a betrayer like La Malinche and La Llorona; she calls this the *virgen/puta dichotomy*.[23] The rigid binary imposed on women by these institutions creates hostile environments in their daily lives. Often conflicted by these cultural and religious images, many Chicanas move away from heteropatriarchal practices and instead claim a spiritual practice that moves away from institutionalized forms of Christianity. This is the conflict that Lorena expresses in moving away from the Catholicism she grew up on and instead finding a form of spirituality that moves away from the judgment she often felt by her mom's belief system.

Lorena demonstrates how some Chicanas have a complicated relationship with institutionalized religion and often decide to move away from a practice they grew up with. Instead, they claim a connection to Catholicism through cultural means and create a spiritual path on their own terms. While it is common for some Chicanas to move away from a Christian practice, others vacillate between various Indigenous-based spiritual practices formed during their spiritual awakening.

Marlene, also a circle keeper for Coyolxauhqui Full Moon Circle, did not have a strong connection with Catholicism because of its views of purity and its involvement in colonization, but she was still connected to prayer. In college, she found a connection to spirituality through her participation in Danza Azteca. She explains:

> For me, Danza was my most important space because that was where I was able to explore my spirituality and it was something that I always wanted to do, even here pero me daba miedo aquí [but I was afraid]. [In Berkeley,] it was a cool space; we were all on the same page because we were all students. We definitely sought refuge in that space. It exposed me to a different cosmology. In terms of how we came up this road and how to connect to the world and the spirit world through dance. I'm a dancer, and it allowed me to understand my body and experience for the first time coming together of . . . it's hard to explain. So, it's a combination of that, different things coming together and warming the spirit. It exposed me to that. It exposed me to other spiritual processes because of Danza, I went to my first sweat lodge and sunrise ceremony and things like that. I learned about the copal and smudging and all these different rituals and protocols and stories, and that felt good. It reminded me of Michoacán and although that wasn't explained to me that way, that we're going back to the motherland and ancestors and all of that, but I connected to that.[24]

Marlene shares commonalities with the other women interviewed. College was a time when she, like others, found a connection to an Indigenous-based spiritual practice. Growing up in East Los Angeles, Danza was a big part of the community, but she did not feel encouraged to participate. It was in college, a time when many first-generation students feel far from home and isolated, when she decided to participate with many students who were also trying to find something familiar at UC Berkeley, which has historically been isolating to people of color. Marlene was exposed and impacted by the Aztec cosmologies that were incorporated in Danza. She describes a connection to the body, mind, and spirit that often gets separated because bodily and spiritual knowledge are not valued as much as the knowledge of the mind, which is equated to hegemonic knowledge production. Danza was also a catalyst for her participation in other ceremonies, which include sweat lodges and sunrise ceremonies led by Lakota leaders. Even though she is far from her ancestral homeland, these ceremonies became a reconnection to her Indigenous ways of knowing.

Unlike Lorena, Fe did not grow up with religion in their home, but they found spiritual awakening in the nineties, which led them on their journey toward an ancestral Indigenous spirituality. Fe's parents were part of the Chicano cultural nationalist movement of the late sixties and early seventies at a time when many people were critical of institutionalized religion and its involvement with colonization. Many folks, including Fe's parents, were critical of the institution of Catholicism and they did not introduce religion to their family practice. She recalls, "I was born into the movement, [my parents] were Chicanos who did away with Catholicism and the Catholic religion, so I wasn't baptized and we didn't practice religion on Sunday or any day, so I didn't grow up with that and didn't know traditional prayers, things that maybe family members did."[25] Fe was introduced to an Indigenous-based spirituality by being around people who lived ceremonial lives. Going to Chiapas to gather with the Zapatistas, being one of the founders of Mujeres de Maiz, her participation with Self Help Graphics & Art and their Day of the Dead traditions, and participating in the Peace and Dignity Journeys introduced her to different ceremonies and led her to a path of spirituality. She remembers one of those experiences this way:

> I went to the Peace and Dignity run in 2000, one of the main prayers for me was mainly for the community to have a place for women, Chicana women, in LA or the Southwest. For these kinds of traditions or these ways are more accessible and being able to come to these ways. So, for me I was still learning. I had learned a little bit but there was still a lot to learn that was definitely a ceremonial training of sorts being on the run, community-run, being with those prayer staffs, and all those communities. That I think [it] really shaped me discipline-wise a little bit and knowing that we all have to step up to learn certain things.[26]

Aware of the lack of access to ceremonies for Chicanas, Fe's prayer during the Peace and Dignity run was to open up spaces for Chicanas to find ceremony in Los Angeles. By setting the prayer she was being intentional about responding to the need for Chicana ceremonial spaces, but she also knew that learning Indigenous ceremonial ways was a tremendous responsibility. For Marlene, Peace and Dignity was also an opportunity to meet different folks from all over the continent and share space and knowledge with them. Many prayers have manifested since Peace and Dignity in 2000 and many of the women are still seeing the fruits of their intentions in the community.

While some of the women I interviewed claim direct ties to their ancestral connection through awareness of their Indigenous relations, those who have been detribalized only have relationships through everyday practices created by the women in their family. Oftentimes, these fractured practices are the only link to their mothers' and grandmothers' ancestral knowledges—this is their detribalized experience. These ways of knowing can be deepened through the information carried and shared by elders, so asking questions and picking up these lessons are key in reconnecting. For example, herbal remedies were discussed as being prevalent in the knowledge shared by these women's elders. Marlene and Lorena see remedies like teas and *aguas frescas* as a cultural/ancestral connection. They both talk about writing the recipes down, but their mothers were adamant about learning them orally *con los antepasados*, passed down by the women in their family. In discussing their spiritual upbringing, the women provided insights into how they grew up and how their Indigenous-based spirituality developed when they started going to college, by participating in Danza, or through a death in the family.

Some of the women interviewed felt a rejection of Catholicism because of the institution's relationship to colonization and misogyny, while others saw the importance of praying with their elders and they connected praying to both Catholicism and Indigenous spirituality. I focused on the women's individual spiritual journeys to have a better understanding of what knowledges they bring to the Coyolxauhqui Full Moon Circle. Understanding how they grew up spiritually also gave insight into how the women were able to negotiate their own spiritual practices either by understanding the complexities of merging Catholicism and an ancestral and Indigenous-based spirituality or by completely eliminating Catholicism and instead creating their own practice. Some of the women described their spiritual awakening as happening in college when they learned the histories of violence linked to institutionalized religion. In the following section, I demonstrate the collective healing the women engage in and how their spiritual foundation speaks to understanding their healing practice.

FULL MOON CIRCLES

Coyolxauhqui Circle has met every full moon monthly since 2010 in City Terrace around the local replica Coyolxauhqui stone. Once a month, about twenty (and sometimes up to forty or even 100 when held on special days and in other locations) women of color, queer, trans, and gender-expansive people come together to participate in a talking circle and accompany each other in individual and collective healing. In this section, I explore women's and gender-expansive peoples participation in the full moon circles to situate the knowledge that guides the circles and ceremonies and to uncover the direct moments of ancestral knowledge that arise and are shared. In other words, my intention is to highlight Chicana healing circles as a form of researching hidden ancestral knowledge through the experiences of Chicanas while exploring and interrogating decolonial spiritual practices.[27]

The full moon circle is a ritual many follow as a way to spiritually shed anything they have been carrying the previous month and to let new energy take its place. Some examples might be problems with partners, community conflicts, trauma they grew up with, and so forth. Many people with moon cycles gravitate to full moon ceremonies because they also experience this shedding when they bleed.[28] Fe shared that during her involvement in a moon circle in Mexico, the Coyolxauhqui Circle came to her as a vision for a future Mujeres de Maiz space. She shares, "Part of what I understood of the cargo coming back was to come and share or to make accessible some of the knowledge."[29] The moon ceremony in Mexico she participated in inspired her to hold these monthly circles. The reception the circles have received also shows a need and responsibility to make knowledge accessible to their community in Los Angeles.

When asked about the name Coyolxauhqui, Fe explained that they were influenced greatly by Chicana feminists who were reclaiming Aztec deities to theorize about their lived experience. Fe first heard about Coyolxauhqui in Cherríe Moraga's piece, "El Mito Azteca."[30] In Moraga's retelling of this myth, she gives a Xicana feminist interpretation of Coyolxauhqui where the goddess attempts to kill her mother Coatlicue so her brother, Huitzilopochtli, the god of war, does not introduce war and patriarchy to the world. In her account, instead of vilifying Coyolxauhqui, she becomes a Xicana feminist goddess and icon. Coyolxauhqui comes to represent how Xicana Indigenas have been impacted and "dismembered" through colonization and patriarchal violence as well as healing and wholeness through the process of "re-membering."[31] Similarly, scholar Gloria Anzaldúa also uses Coyolxauhqui as a way to describe "both the process of emotional and psychical dismemberment, splitting body/mind/spirit/soul, and the creative work of putting all the pieces together in a new form, a partially unconscious work done in the night by the light of the moon a labor of re-visioning and re-membering."[32] The women who participate in Coyolxauhqui Circle are engaging in this act of ceremonial reaching/remembering a kind of wholeness between their body, mind, spirit, and soul. With the intention of creating a space for healing and letting go put forth by the circle keepers, Coyolxauhqui Circle transforms into a ceremonial space. Fe gives insight on how the circle is run every month:

> It's usually getting there and set up. Starting the fire and smudging the stuff of the *altar*. When people come, smudging them and asking them to join the circle, and then we usually do an opening prayer to the four directions and a song, speak about what is the Coyolxauhqui circle—we say it started because of the women that went to a moon circle and wanted to come back and share and make this accessible. We also emphasize that it's a learning space and when I say it, I usually mention that it might not be their tradition. Some people might be long time sun dancers or *Danzantes*, and they might say "they are not doing it the way I know it," or "they are doing it differently." So, we usually mention it may not be your way. It's part of the north and south. You have Northern and other California ways and Southern Mexica *Danza* ways. Most of the people are beginners to newer people so that's mainly letting them know. And for those people asking, "why you are doing this?" Hopefully, we are not doing anything different than what they do. We just ask people to be patient and open because this is the way we do things.[33]

Collective meaning-making is an important intervention the circles are doing because they are directly countering heteropatriarchal knowledge productions that want to keep these ways of knowing out of the community. To manifest their collective making, Fe did the work of bringing women they knew together once a month during the full moon. She describes the uses of knowledges of both Northern Native and Southern Indigenous practice in conversation with their circle. Purification of the space by burning copal is medicine commonly used in the South and tobacco used in the North. Both practices are joined in the ritual. She also notes that Coyolxauhqui circle keepers are instructed by practices they participate in living alongside California Native communities, being a part of pan-Indigenous spaces like the Peace and Dignity Journeys and through Danza. This fusion allows the women to find the connection among the knowledges they have acquired through their participation in ceremonies both in the United States and in Mexico. The emphasis on the circle as a learning space also allows women who have not participated in any ceremony before to learn and connect in a respectful way. Because it is a learning space, Fe or any other facilitator will open up by describing their intention and the reasons why they use certain tools and where it comes from. These practices bring the women closer to a spiritual understanding of their ancestral past and to a collective spiritual understanding.

The experiences of the women who participate in the circle also give insight into the ways the circles are run and how they have been impacted by their participation in the circle. Marlene, for example, explains why she enjoys participating in Coyolxauhqui Circle as the circle keeper:

> I enjoy it because it's a learning space. We are taking all the different *enseñanzas*[34] we've learned along the way and trying to bring them together and create a space in very important times. I'm going to keep it real; I like it because it's a learning space, a sharing space. We definitely want to use what we have learned from *Danza* because that is our experience collectively. I like that it's not hardcore Mexica or hardcore Lakota because part of the other reason why I stay away from *Danza* or committing to the sun dance, because I've been invited, it's because I'm not any of those. Those aren't my traditions. I have the Mexica based on what my Nana says, but I feel my connections and my roots to Michoacán, *Purepecha*, and completely different things. For me, I can't, it's not betraying, but I feel like, let's keep it more universal.[35]

For Marlene, participating in the Coyolxauhqui circle allows her to use the knowledge she has gathered in her life and come together with the other women. She also notes the importance of creating a learning space for folks who are participating. While she acknowledges that both Northern and Southern Indigenous practices are embedded in the circle, she appreciates that space creates a new environment that represents the women who participate. Even though she has participated in Danza and has learned some traditional Native teachings, she also wants to honor the teachings that come from her *Purepecha* lineage. In Marlene's case, she is trying to navigate these moments of contention where she honors the practices that speak to the circle, but at the same time, longs for a need to reconnect to an ancestral lineage that was taken from her. The commonality she sees in all these teachings is the "universal" aspects of their ways that revere the Cosmos, the Universe, and the Earth. Her solution, like Anzaldúa's use of new tribalism, is to incorporate and to honor the universal.[36]

As one of the first people to join the circle, Lorena eventually became one of the circle keepers. She also shares insight about her participation in the full moon circle in Los Angeles: "I didn't know what to expect; it has been a learning circle. Through circulo we have learned how to drum, now the four of us get together to drum, that is so healing. Not having grown up with Indigenous traditions, *asi como* drumming, or pow wow. To hear the drum, it just calls you back. You know that it belongs to your people; the sound is your people calling you back. It's so powerful. That's how I want to feel like I belong. It's ancestral; I can feel it in my skin."[37]

At first, Lorena did not know what to expect from the circle, but shortly after joining, she was introduced to Indigenous ceremonial ways. She felt a visceral connection with the drum that took her back to an ancestral knowledge that was not known to her. In being called back, she felt like these were tools that belonged to her all along. The tools reappeared after being hidden/buried in a memory space. This subtle moment of Indianness flooded through her connection with the drum.

CONCLUSION

The women who participate in these full moon circles are finding wholeness in researching and reconnecting to an Indigenous and ancestral way of healing and praying. In *Light in the Dark,* Anzaldúa defines healing as "asking back the scattered energy and soul loss wrought by wounding. Healing means using the life force and strength that comes with el ánimo to act positively on one's own and on others' behalf. Often a wound provokes an urgent yearning for wholeness and provides grounding to achieve it."[38] The Coyolxauhqui Full Moon Circle, and others like it, are providing the women who participate with the grounding they need to heal. Meeting once a month to *desahogarse* allows these women to teach each other ways to cope with what they are dealing with in their lives. Using medicines that have been used by their ancestors to heal allows them to open themselves up to an experience some might not have access to without the healing in circles. Honoring the medicinal ways of the North and South, but also incorporating teachings and practices from their mothers and grandmothers, fills this circle with an extensive amount of knowledge. As the women find healing for themselves and their communities, the hope is that they will continue sharing and healing in the ways of their ancestors. The sites of possibility when honoring what has been lost and centering living Indigenous people, cosmologies, and ways of knowing can transform the ways Chicana/xs negotiate spirituality.

NOTES

1. Copal is dried tree resin used as medicine to cleanse an area. Copal is used in Indigenous ceremonies in Mexico.
2. Ombligo means naval or belly button in Spanish. Circle keepers for these two circles refer to the center of the altar as the ombligo. Placed at the center of the altar is the fire. Both Omecihuatl and Coyolxauhqui full moon circle have a community altar where anyone participating in the circle can place sacred things there.
3. Danza Azteca, also known as Aztec Dance, pre-Columbian Aztec history. Because of the Mexican state project after the revolution of 1821, the government made danza a part of an official historical narrative of Mexico. This ceremony was brought to the United States from Mexico City in the 1970s and has been popular among Chicana/os.
4. The description written by Iuri on the closed Facebook group defines Omecihuatl as the female duality of Ometecuhtli. Together they form "Ometeotl," which translates to "Two-Creator." Although there are controversies surrounding the root of this word in the Nahuatl language, many spiritual leaders say that Ometeotl is the name of the Great Spirit who created all living things. This (Great Spirit) is not male or female, but both. Omecihuatl is the female essence

of this Great Spirit, in other words "God in female form," or the Goddess of creation. https://www.facebook.com/search/top/?q=omecihuatl.

5. The full moon circle is a space that some women have created to meet once a month during the full moon to check in with each other in ceremony. By ceremony, I mean they are creating a space where they are tapping into ancestral knowledge and the spirit energy with an altar along with elements that represent the four directions—earth, wind, fire, and water.

6. The English translation to the verb desahogar is to vent. In Spanish, the word means getting well from a worry or concern by telling someone or a group of people about it.

7. For many Chicana feminists, the reclamation of the Coyolxauhqui stone disrupts the heteropatriarchal narrative in Aztec cosmology. Coyolxauhqui was the daughter of Coatlicue. After finding out that Coatlicue became pregnant by a feather and was going to give birth to Huitzilopochtli, the god of war, Coyolxauhqui along with her brothers and sister decided that this baby could not be born. When they were about to attack, Huitzilopochtli cut open his mother's womb and came out in full armor. He dismembered Coyolxauhqui and threw her into the sky. Many renditions of this story are misogynist, situating Coyolxauhqui as a traitor. Chicana feminist scholars have reappropriated the narrative reclaiming the image of Coyolxauhqui to represent the dismemberment that many Chicanas feel because of heteropatriarchy (Cherríe Moraga, *The Last Generation*; Gloria Anzaldúa, *Light in the Dark / Luz En Lo Oscuro*; Alicia Gaspar de Alba, *[Un]framing the "Bad Woman"*). Review Michelle L. Lopez's chapter 22, "Bringing Art to the People,'" for a discussion of Coyolxauhqui and her influence on Chicana art.

8. Native social worker Jean Stevenson describes her experience as a circle keeper in an Aboriginal community in Montreal, Canada. She writes, "The Circle is a safe place where the participants are able to work on their healing process. By doing so we help ourselves, which in turn has a ripple effect on our family and friends and eventually on our community. . . . Confidentiality is a very important part of the Circle" (Stevenson, "The Circle of Healing," 11).

9. Mujeres de Maiz centers healing and wellness through programming, publications, art, and education (http://www.mujeresdemaiz.com).

10. Please refer to my master's thesis, "Coyolxauhqui Mourning: Chicana Healing Practices Through Re-connecting and Re-membering Indigenous-based Spirituality," and my larger dissertation project, "Healing Justice in Chicana/x Feminist Organizing," for a glimpse of my research.

11. I am referencing "Circle Keeper" as defined by Native scholar Jean Stevenson. She describes the responsibility of Circle Keeper as "we are not above anyone else, as everyone is considered equal. We talk about our issues, our past, our present, and what we have learned. We cry and vent as much as anyone else in the Circle. . . . It is our responsibility to open and lock the doors, set out and

put away the items in the center of the Circle, take care of the Medicines and the items that we place at the center of the circle" (18).

12. In referring to concepts of deindianization and detribalization, refer to Susy Zepeda (2022), reprinted in this anthology and Patrisia Gonzales' (2012) work.

13. In *Decolonizing Trauma Work* Indigenous scholar Renee Link Water defines historical trauma as "Over 500 years of contact between the original peoples of the Americas and settler nations has produced extensive displacement and disconnection. Colonialism, manufactured by settlers, caused a great deal of damage to the spirit of Indigenous peoples. It is necessary to declare that the root of injury has been caused by colonial violence, which was significantly enforced by governments through legislation and institutions. We are now in a process of healing from historical trauma" (20).

14. My understanding of healing justice comes from the work of queer and trans activists of color, in particular the work of the National Queer and Trans Therapist Network. I am also informed by the book *Healing Justice: Holistic Self-Care for Change Makers* and Leah Lakshmi Piepzna-Samarasinha's piece, "A Not-So-Brief Personal History of the Healing Justice Movement 2010–2016."

15. To have a better understanding of Chicana feminist spiritual practices refer to Ana Castillo's *Massacre of Dreamers, Essays on Xicanisma*, Yolanda Broyles-González's "Indianizing Catholicism: My Path to the Source[s] of Healing," the recent compilation *Fleshing the Spirit* edited by Elisa Facio and Irene Lara, and *Voices from the Ancestors* edited by Lara Medina and Martha R. Gonzales.

16. The work of Linda Tuhiwai Smith, Cindy Cruz, and Cherríe Moraga are essential when thinking about the lived experience that women of color bring forward as a site of knowledge.

17. María Eugenia Cotera and María Josefina Saldaña-Portillo, "Indigenous but Not Indian? Chicana/os and the Politics of Indigeneity," *The World of Indigenous North America* (New York: Routledge, 2015), 549–67.

18. Anzaldúa, *Light in the Dark*, 2.

19. I also want to refer to *Blood Lines: Myth, Indigenism, and Chicana/o Literature* by Sheila E. Contreras to define *indigenismo* to understand how mestizaje, a postrevolutionary Mexican state project, sought to form a singular national identity. She states that *indigenismo* "often refers to public policy initiatives spearheaded by mestizo intellectuals, such as anthropologist Manuel Gamio that pursued the explicit objective of 'social realignment between the races'" (23–24). "Indigenismo also describes the stylistic appropriation of Indigenous cultural forms and traditions by non-Indigenous artists and intellectuals" (24). Ultimately, *indigenismo* highlighted Indigenous people in the past—the Aztec civilization—but failed to acknowledge and value living Indigenous people.

20. Scholars who have addressed this include Medina 1998; Gonzales, *Red Medicine*, 2012; and Facio and Lara, *Fleshing the Spirit*, 2014.

21. Lorena Santos, interview with the author, September 2015.

22. This translates from Spanish to "I put penitence on myself for four years." These interviews were conducted in English but when interviewing most of the women, especially when they described their upbringing, would often code switch between Spanish and English.
23. Gloria Anzaldúa, *Borderlands / La Frontera* (San Francisco: Aunt Lute Books, 1987), 31.
24. Marlene Aguilar, interview with the author, September 2015.
25. Felicia 'Fe' Montes, interview with the author, October 2015.
26. Felicia 'Fe' Montes, interview with the author, October 2015.
27. Inspired by the work of Gloria Anzaldúa and Cherríe Moraga, I look at their theorizing about Coyolxauhqui to mean a reconnection of lost ancestral connection and the act of healing. The compromiso then is to put themselves back together (healing) and reconnect to an ancestral spiritual practice.
28. Here, I have used *people* instead of *women* because not all that participate in monthly moon cycles are ciswomen and not all women have menstrual cycles, but may have a ritual to commemorate the full moon. As a ciswoman, I want to make sure that I honor gender nonconforming and trans folks in my work. A cisgender person is someone who identifies with the sex and gender presentation they were assigned at birth. Being cissexist is engaging in transphobic behavior when assuming that cisgender is "natural."
29. Felicia 'Fe' Montes, interview with the author, October 2015.
30. Cherríe Moraga, *The Last Generation* (Boston: South End Press, 1993), 73–74.
31. Moraga, *The Last Generation*, 73–74.
32. Anzaldúa, *Light in the Dark*, xxi.
33. Felicia 'Fe' Montes, interview with the author, October 2015.
34. Translates to *teachings* in Spanish.
35. Marlene Aguilar, interview with the author, September 2015.
36. In *Light in the Dark / Luz en lo Oscuro*, Anzaldúa defines new tribalism as "we are responsible participants in the ecosystems (complete set of interrelationships between a network of living organism and their physical habitats) in whose web we're individual strands" (67).
37. Lorena Santos, interview with the author, September 2015.
38. Anzaldúa, *Light in the Dark*, 90.

BIBLIOGRAPHY

Anzaldúa, Gloria. *Light in the Dark / Luz En Lo Oscuro: Rewriting Identity, Spirituality, Reality*. Edited by AnaLouise Keating. Durham, N.C.: Duke University Press, 2015.

———. *Borderlands / La Frontera: The New Mestiza*. San Francisco: Aunt Lute Books, 1987.

Contreras, Sheila Marie. *Blood Lines: Myth, Indigenism, and Chicana/o Literature*. Austin: University of Texas Press, 2008.

Cotera, María Eugenia, and María Josefina Saldaña-Portillo. "Indigenous but Not Indian? Chicana/os and the Politics of Indigeneity." *The World of Indigenous North America*, 549–67. New York: Routledge, 2015.

Cruz, Cindy. "Toward an Epistemology of a Brown Body." *International Journal of Qualitative Studies in Education* 14, no. 5 (2001): 657–69.

Facio, Elisa, and Irene Lara, eds. *Fleshing the Spirit: Spirituality and Activism in Chicana, Latina, and Indigenous Women's Lives*. Tucson: University of Arizona Press, 2014.

Gaspar, de Alba, Alicia. *[Un]framing the "Bad Woman": Sor Juana, Malinche, Coyolxauhqui, and Other Rebels with a Cause*. Austin: University of Texas Press, 2014.

Gonzales, Patrisia. *Red Medicine: Traditional Indigenous Rites of Birthing and Healing*. Tucson: University of Arizona Press, 2012.

Medina, Lara. "Los Espiritus Siguen Hablando: Chicana Spiritualities." In *Living Chicana Theory*, 189–213. Berkeley, Calif.: Third Woman Press, 1998.

——. "Nepantla Spirituality: My Path to the Source(s) of Healing." *Fleshing the Spirit: Spirituality and Activism in Chicana, Latina, and Indigenous Women's Lives* (2014): 167–85.

Moraga, Cherríe. *The Last Generation: Prose and Poetry*. Berkeley: University of California Press, 1993.

Smith, Linda Tuhiwai. *Decolonizing Methodologies: Research and Indigenous Peoples*. London: Zed Books, 1999.

Stevenson, Jean. "The Circle of Healing." *Native Social Work Journal* 2, no. 1 (1999): 8–20.

Zepeda, Nadia. "Healing Justice in Chicana/x Feminist Organizing." Berkeley: University of California, 2021.

——. "Coyolxauhqui Mourning: Chicana Healing Practices Through Re-Connecting and Re-Membering Indigenous-Based Spirituality," University of California, 2017.

Zepeda, Susy J. *Queering Mesoamerican Diasporas: Remembering Xicana Indígena Ancestries*. Urbana: University of Illinois Press, 2022.

6

Mujeres de Maiz Arising

Shifts and Movement of Positioning Xicana-Driven Indigenous Spirituality

ANGELA 'MICTLANXOCHITL' ANDERSON GUERRERO

Whispered Rezo
Si no creo en mí mismo, mi medicina no se vale.
If I do not believe in myself, my medicine has no value.
Believe in yourself—believe in your knowing.
Ometeotl.

MY PATH reclaiming Indigenous spirituality has been like opening my eyes to a beautiful stream and deciding to take off my shoes and walk barefoot. As soon as I entered, it felt different—maybe a little uncomfortable, but I settled my grounding and moved along. The walk through the stream was so nice; I started to see and feel so many new things. Especially things I had forgotten that I could no longer see from where I came from. And what lies ahead is calling, there was no reason to turn back.

Before I knew it, I noticed the water had risen and my next step took me tumbling down. I was at the mercy of the stream and my strength to stay afloat. I could have tried to scramble to the side to get out of the water and I actually did make a move, but then I felt the water calm and noticed I was being carried forward where I could walk again.

That is where I am at now . . . in the gentle waters where I can walk again, with a little more knowledge and confidence in what is out there and what I can do. As I walk on my spiritual path and reengage the "real" world, the metaphorical waters in life feel like I am going against the current. So, I make a writing offering to these waters, to all of you, in the hope of calming the water spirits of the "real" world.

I have a responsibility to share and to articulate what I am living. Because being accepting and happy with one's story is not enough in a world of histories that have misled and denied us opportunities of self-determination. Our senses to trust and to be open to generations before, now, and after from all the directions is difficult after so much trauma. For real, we are all related and by sharing we can understand the pain, the guilt, the anger, and the shaming we sometimes impose on one another as we take on these brave paths of ancestral healing.

WHO IS THE TRANSTERRITORAL DEINDIGENIZED SCHOLAR PRACTITIONER?

The scholar practitioner correlates a relationship between their academic and spiritual practice. The legacy of Gloria Anzaldúa, collectives such as Mujeres de Maiz, academic circles such as Mujeres Activas en Letras y Cambios Sociales (MALCS), and the anthology *Fleshing the Spirit*, have uplifted the Chicana/Latina/Indígena scholar practitioner. I'll never forget my first engagement with Mujeres de Maiz where I felt supported to offer and visibilize my palabra. With the encouragement of Ana Tlahuicoatl Lara and Felicia 'Fe' Montes, Mujeres de Maiz exhibited my first poem in their annual celebration and exhibition in 2015. That moment was pivotal to nourishing trust and hermandad con Felicia and so many others. Spaces such as this and other Chicana activations have cultivated spirituality in the personal and communal as a "conscious, self-reflective way of life and a way of relating to others, to ourselves, and to 's/Spirit' in a manner that honors all of life as an interconnected web" (Facio and Lara 2014).

The waters of the river have guided me to position myself as a "transterritorial deindigenized scholar practitioner." My doctoral work has been a quest of exploring how to integrate in life, the academy, and collective struggle, a ten-year journey within the Mexicayotl tradition in Mexico and Lakota healing circles in the United States. Although there is healing and affirmation of deindigenized peoples when acknowledged by Native peoples, this writing offering is not about defining or legitimizing our identities. Applying different lenses of Indigenous and Native studies, Chicana feminist studies, decolonization, grassroots postmodernism, and participatory theory, this conceptual ofrenda of palabras is seeking bridges of reflexivity and solidarity to resist the local and global neoliberal mechanisms inhibiting our abilities to be caretakers of the earth, to promote multiple ways of knowing, and to advance the interests of communities of struggle. In this chapter, I offer an approach to define and position the "transterritorial," "deindigenized," "scholar practitioner," via my experiences working with ceremonial circles within the Mexicayotl and a healing circle cared and guided by a Lakota family and their teachings. Hopefully it also serves as grounding on how we each tell our stories of Mujeres de Maiz rising from our Xicana-driven Indigenous spiritualities.

My Madrina and the Grandmother of the Danza de la Luna Huitzlimetzli in Austin, Texas, Rosa Tupina Yaotonalcuauhtli, tells women in her circle, "We have a computer in one arm and our baston in the other." Her words are carefully chosen to remind us of our cargos, our responsibilities, as scholar practitioners. The computer is a contemporary tool that gives us access not only to knowledge but also allows us to reproduce knowledge. The baston, two intertwined dried-out vines crafted into a walking stick, symbolically signifies our status as spiritual leaders and stresses that we are supported. It is borrowed from nature; it was a living organism stemming from the earth at one point. The baston reminds us that those who may seek our spiritual guidance will also be the ones who follow our example and teachings. The baston is a physical and spiritual tool that reminds us to practice with wisdom and love. The scholar practitioner must negotiate between their role in the academy and the responsibilities of their spiritual path.

The term *deindigenized* emphasizes the conflicted nature of our identity when navigating Indigenous terrains. It is not meant to devalue the lineages and indigeneity of Mexican and Mexican-American peoples. Roberto "Cintli" Rodríguez (2014) highlights this dynamic between indigeneity and deindigenization as he traces the cosmologies, traditions, and cultures of the signs, symbols, and stories of maiz (corn) pre- and postcolonization in the Americas. The project not only connects all people in the Americas to maiz but unfolds how deindigenized peoples "re-member" (Esteva and Prakash 1998) our overlapping histories to the land, language, culture, and lineages in resistant colonial narratives. This dynamic between deindigenized peoples and Indigenous/ancestral knowledge(s) activates the regeneration of our indigeneity.

In that spirit, I ask you to pause and lift up in your heart the regeneration of indigeneity planted by Dr. Cintli who passed July 31, 2023 during the final pasos of this publication. He said, "As someone who grew up deindigenized, the fact that I am able to partake in the writing of (creation) stories by itself also demonstrates that peoples who are deindigenized can be reconnected to ancient knowledges" (Rodríguez, 9). Reclaiming and re-membering our ancestral knowledges is our birth right and a path to liberation. Believe in your stories, Dr. Cintli believed in ours. ¡Nikan ká Dr. Cintli![1] ¡Ometeotl!

Through this framework, deindigeneity is utilized as an insurgent reframing that highlights a relational reciprocity with Indigenous lineages in the Americas. The dynamic activates what Indigenous dance scholars Jack Gray and Jacqueline Shea Murphy (2013) articulate as "the indigeneity lies in the doing of this repeating reciprocity, and in the acknowledgement of it; this is what dislodges the baleful colonial residue so it can transform into something else" (249). The deindigenized scholar becomes something else and moves us beyond the colonial subject. The "something else" are the possibilities of inquiry—such as, What agency do deindigenized peoples have in the process of "remembering" and regeneration?

Transterritoriality not only signifies the act of moving across territories over land but more importantly it uplifts territory as a "social relation." Raul Zibechi's (2012) observations of the territorialization of social movements in South America resonate with how I plant "transterritorial" movement and relationality of the deindigenized scholar practitioner. Zibechi outlines the "territorialization of the movement" as recuperating, reconfiguring, and relocating sites of practice and collective struggle. By traveling to ceremonies in Mexico and the United States, the community and I are consistently gathering on urban and rural territories. Our movement is reconfiguring the power and meaning of the land, our sacred sites. This marks a collective struggle for autonomous spiritual practice and hopes to uplift the discourse with the land and our relationship to it. Transterritoriality is an emancipatory "engaged participation" and "co-creative event" (Ferrer and Sherman 2008) that nestles knowledge production on a designated land and reconfigured sacred site of encounter.

I present myself as Angela Mictlanxochitl, the transterritorial deindigenized scholar practitioner moving to and from / from and to my spiritual and community relations in Mexico and the United States. My reflexive relationship with the academy and my practices within the Mexicayotl and Lakota spiritual lineages stress the delicate responsibilities of walking in both spaces of knowledge production.

BORDER THINKING AS SACRED TRANSIT AND DECOLONIAL SPIRITUALITY

Meaning along the Mexico and United States border, along the land, and among the histories of people becomes more invigorated with the growth of time. Contemporary Indigenous spirituality among Native Americans, American Indians, Pueblos Originarios, and deindigenized Mexican and Mexican Americans centering their practice around urban environments have demonstrated how spiritual practice and cultural traditions have always transgressed borders. Where there is land and space, there are possibilities to re-generate Indigenous knowledge(s) and epistemologies. However, inherent in the transit of people and practices is the "responsibility" to acknowledge, to ask permission, and to invite reciprocity and solidarity with the collective struggles of Native and Indigenous peoples from the local territories being engaged through contemporary Indigenous spiritual practices. How to practice and uphold this "responsibility" is very complex. My work explores the possibilities through the testimonios of Mexican and Mexican Americans reclaiming and creating meaning from their predominantly Mexica-centered spiritual practices.[2]

In the context of border thinking and decoloniality, my intervention hopes to broaden the conceptualization of "non-Eurocentric academia" by offering examples of how Mexican and Mexican American contemporary Mexica spiritual movement transpose the meanings of "borders" and "decoloniality." In the context of my work, I propose resituating border thinking in the context of sacred transit, and suggest positioning decoloniality as a spiritual movement that holds accountable, or at the least invites inquiry, into the actions and appropriation of Indigenous knowledge(s) and practices. Through these conceptualizations, non-Eurocentric academia may ask if its formation is best situated as an autonomous movement protecting, preserving, and sharing knowledge with other autonomous movements.

BORDER THINKING AS SACRED TRANSIT

Due in part to the United States Religious Freedom Restoration Act of 1993, today crossing borders as a Mexican and Mexican American Mexica Indigenous spiritual practitioner is less complicated by citizenship and visas. Our imaginations of the land and migrations of our ancestors in the north and the south can travel to sites and visit sources of ancestral knowledges and traditions. The growth of ceremonial circles throughout the Americas, such as Moon and Sun Ceremonies,[3] are a testimonio to sacred knowledge migration, which I offer as "sacred transit" for this discussion. Sacred transit is a growing number of Mexicans and Mexican Americans crossing significant distances to participate in ceremonies; to receive and to carry sacred objects; and to sustain relationships and collectives centered on contemporary Mexica spiritual practices. Sacred transit acknowledges the privileges of citizenship status, class, and social mobility, not typically bestowed among disenfranchised Indigenous peoples in the United States and Mexico. Such privilege casts a shadow on sacred transit as to whether contemporary Indigenous spiritual practitioners are appropriating ancestral knowledge sources and practices. When one has resources and freedom to travel across borders, they also have the freedom to transport traditions, sacred items, Indigenous artesania, and more. How does one hold such a responsibility in the spirit of sharing over appropriation for individual gain? How does sacred transit call into question the role and relationship to autonomous Indigenous populations and their collective struggles?

DECOLONIALITY AS SPIRITUALITY

Decoloniality is discussed in context of Tonawanda Seneca scholar Mishuana Goeman's approach to decolonizing spatial relationships (Goeman

2013) and how Guatemalan Maya Quiché scholar Gladys Tzul speaks to "webs of community and political forms" (Hernandez 2014). This approach to decoloniality is not comprehensive, but they are the most recent frameworks guiding the exploration of Mexican and Mexican American contemporary Mexica spirituality. Also, this is an attempt to be forthcoming by addressing the concerns of Native and Indigenous peoples and scholars with a cautious eye on what Jodi Byrd (2011) lists as the diaspora, migration, hybridity, and movement. By proposing decoloniality as spirituality, I ask if Mexican and Mexican American contemporary Mexica spiritual practitioners are working past the politicized context of contemporary colonialism. Decoloniality as spirituality questions the methods by which contemporary Mexica spiritual practitioners are self-reflective with their "reclaimed" practices. Decolonial spirituality asks how contemporary Mexica spiritual movements position and mobilize their agency and how/if it impacts autonomous Indigenous collective struggles.

Taking a step back, I offer a perspective of sovereignty by Harry Charger, a passed-on elder and Lakota spiritual leader, as a context to my proposition of decoloniality as spirituality:

> Without spirituality, there is no sovereignty. To us, sovereignty exists in spirituality. And spirituality is an expression of sovereignty, a god-given innate freedom, that feeling that you have that hey, I am a part of things, I am a part of something—but still a part of something, instead of wanting to be all of it. We pray as we do, being part of something. We were satisfied with that, you know.
>
> . . .
>
> And sovereignty is something you have to not just talk about, or read about, or write about, but you have to live it. And that is one of the big aspects of it, you have to live it. And if you don't, then you have got something else. You have another kind of control, or government, and it is not good. (Charger, Quigley, and Wiethaus 2007, 159–67)

If our sovereignty exists within a framework of decolonial spirituality, we are situating our ways of knowing and confronting the narratives and telling the stories of our remembered past. By doing so, a decolonial spirituality struggles with the task Jodi Byrd summarizes as centering Indigenous critical theory "within indigenous epistemologies and the specificities of the communities and cultures from which it emerges and then looks outward to engage European philosophical, legal, and cultural traditions in order to build upon all the allied tools available" (Byrd 2011, xxix–xxx). A decolonial spirituality is a reflexive way of building relationships and producing knowledge to help us live in a good way.

I offer an open-ended inquiry in the form of questions based on the decolonial strategies of Goeman on thinking through the ways Mexican and Mexican American contemporary Mexica spiritual practitioners activating sacred transit broaden approaches to border thinking and decoloniality. Goeman, in *Mark My Words*, proposes decolonizing spatial relationships by (re)mapping Native lands and bodies based on the stories by Native women authors. Their stories complicate the narrative and assumptions of "Indian," borders, and gender. Her goal is for Native nations to "rethink spatializing and organizing our communities around the heteropatriarchal structure of the nation-state model" (37).

QUESTIONS:

- How do Mexican and Mexican contemporary Mexica spiritual practitioners tell stories of the gendered and violent nature of their assumptions of "Indian," borders, and gender?
- Who are our storytellers?
- How do you conceptualize race and gender to disentangle Western geographical power and knowledge regimes?
- What are the intersections of the narrative, history, and memory of Mexican and Mexican American contemporary Mexica spiritual collectives?
- How does sacred transit exemplify a negotiation with ideas of politics and/or a release from politics?

COMING BACK TO THE WATERS OF LIFE...

So many questions... I have learned to be kind to myself. Stepping away from my career and entering a doctoral program was placing value on the time both my soul and body needed to travel back. How we nurture our thoughts and movement in our daily lives is so important. I have learned to be thoughtful about what and how I share my experience. Some of the messages, the teachings, I received are for me and others may not understand.

As an contemporary Mesoamerican spiritual practitioner, I consistently remind myself that the sacred tools[4] are an ancient relative and a precious newborn all at once. I must respect the time and the work—the practice—of getting to know them and learning the depth and vibration of their sacredness. There are lifetimes of knowledge I am holding and living; there is time and space for my responsibilities to grow and my circles to widen.

As a Madrina, a guide to beautiful souls in these waters of life, I ask my ahijadas to understand that I will always do my best as my perfect imperfect self to be of service and to share teachings. That being said, my counsel may sometimes fall hard and it may feel like I am not supportive. I hope in those moments that they know I am acting with integrity in light of the time and teachings I have received and how Spirit guides me. Regardless of our ebbs and flows, we are bonded. As an Abuela and as the guardian of the sacred tools, it's my responsibility to do my best to honor the "self" of each individual and the sacred tools. It's not a linear path; the caracol path is where the medicine is and a vision for the future.

With the permission of Great Spirit, all of the directions, the sacred elements, each of your hearts and the ancestral medicines, I offer my love and my palabra.

NOTES

This essay was submitted in 2017 and reflects the research and thinking from the "Non-Toward a Non-Eurocentric Academia: Border Thinking and Decoloniality" at UNC Chapel Hill and Duke Universities, in May of 2016, and her completed doctoral work, "Testimonio and Knowledge Production Among Transterritorial Mexican and Mexican American Indigenous Spiritual Practitioners: A Decolonial, Participatory, and Grassroots Postmodernist Inquiry."

1. Nahuatl saying honoring the immanence presence, spiritually and physically of those who have passed.
2. Angela D. Anderson, "Transterritorial Ancestral Spirituality: A Caracol Study of Mexican and Mexican American Mesoamerican Knowledges" (PhD diss., California Institute of Integral Studies, 2021).
3. Ceremonial names are removed to accommodate protocols.
4. Sacred tools refer to ceremonial objects that are not named to accommodate protocols.

BIBLIOGRAPHY

Anderson, Angela D. "Transterritorial Ancestral Spirituality: A Caracol Study of Mexican and Mexican American Mesoamerican Knowledges." PhD diss., California Institute of Integral Studies, 2021.

Byrd, Jodi A. *The Transit of Empire: Indigenous Critiques of Colonialism*. Minneapolis: University of Minnesota Press, 2011.

Charger, Harry. *The Seven Rites of the Lakota*, edited by Ulrike Wiethaus. United States: Yonno Press, 2013.

Esteva, Gustavo, and Madhu Suri Prakash. *Grassroots Post-Modernism: Remaking the Soil of Cultures*. London and New York: Zed Books, 1998.

Facio, Elisa, and Irene Lara. *Fleshing the Spirit: Spirituality and Activism in Chicana Latina and Indigenous Women's Lives*. Tucson: University of Arizona Press, 2014.

Ferrer, Jorge N., and Jacob H. Sherman. *The Participatory Turn: Spirituality Mysticism Religious Studies*. Albany: SUNY Press, 2008.

Goeman, Mishuana. *Mark My Words: Native Women Mapping Our Nations*. Minneapolis: University of Minnesota Press, 2013.

Hernández, Oswaldo J. "Confronting the Narrative: Gladys Tzul on Indigenous Governance and State Authority in Guatemala." Upside Down World. February 10, 2014. https://upsidedownworld.org/archives/guatemala/confronting-the-narrative-gladys-tzul-on-indigenous-governance-and-state-authority-in-guatemala/.

Rodríguez, Roberto Cintli. *Our Sacred Maíz Is Our Mother: Indigeneity and Belonging in the Americas*. Tucson: University of Arizona Press, 2014.

Murphy, Jacqueline, and Jack Gray. "'Manaakitanga' in Motion: Indigenous Choreographies of Possibility." *Biography* 36, no. 1 (2013): 242–78.

Zibechi, Raúl, and Ramor Ryan. *Territories in Resistance: A Cartography of Latin American Social Movements*. Oakland, Calif.: AK Press, 2012.

7
My Body is My Sanctuary

POVI-TAMU BRYANT

Loving my curves is not easy.
Loving my darker skin and kinky hair
is even more complex.
The body I move through the world in,
seems to be one that denies me access
    to respect.
I walk through the streets, of cities,
in these "united states"
bearing the body of the slave;
A body that is meant to be used
and discarded;

Darker skin, kinky hair, wealth
of curves speak of DNA that represents
    beings contending with death.
I am not suppose to want to BE;

Loving my body is tricky.
This "womanly" shape of mine is
constantly assaulted with sexual
attention: cat calls, groping, smacking.

These barrages of sexual desire
that I am not supposed to deny,
have created a body that walks
with fear.
A shape and form I love.
A body I can spend hoooours
    pleasuring.
A body I love to glimpse in any
reflective surface.
This same body clothed in dark skin,
with flowing curves is the thing that
    allows people to presume that they
    ought to have
access to me.
This same body is a physical
    representation of a being that is
open to attack and assault.
While my body is not the cause of my
    fear it has become a manifestation
of it.

Yet I am incapable of hating my body.
I know its secrets.
It has protected me.
It has shielded me from a society
that has no love lost for it, or us.

I understand my African phenotypes,
dark skin, wooly hair,
abundance of curves, as
    materializations of things this
    world
loves to hate and hates to love.
        Straightened hair
        Bleached skin
        Shame about my Hottentot ass.
These are supposed to be my history.
Self-love and self-care are not
supposed to be written into my herstory.
But due to my body's strength and
    nourishment, I have been allowed
    no other options.

Surviving so long in a world that is
    daily calling for its demise.
I worship at a temple that was
meant to be destroyed.
And I glory in it every day; for
its sheer daring.

My body is my sanctuary.

Los Angeles, Calif.
Mujeres de Maiz, Flor y Canto:
Soldadera de Amor, no. 9 (2011): 50.

8
For My Sister

NATALINA ROSS

We are brown grit angels,
Curbside-sitting, moonlight lusting,
for remedies for broken wings.
We are young mamitas
Slinging babies: Heartbreak, Perdida
   y Poesía
in our most intricate hand-me-down
   rebozos.
We are pinche escuincle mocosas
trudging our way through
youth like viejitas with our piernas
de madera.
We are the callejeras, putas,
   sinvergüenzas
Yelling into the night
on lava-licked full moons
"Y Que Güey?"
Next day,
sit in the purgatory
of our mother's living rooms,
underneath La Virgen de Guadalupe,
al lado de San Antonio,
hoping they won't exorcise todos de
   nuestros demonios.
We are the trabajadoras
that rise with the sun,
hair slicked back in tight
little buns, waiting
for paychecks to buy
Peace: velitas, flores, copal, a taquito
   with a single nopal.
We are the daughters who won't admit
we drink like our fathers,
pick unworthy lovers,
un huevón after huevón
who string out our hearts
like the lonely wail
de un accordión,
as we belt out rancheras
as strong as a South Texas flood

reminding each other
that nuestra lucha
is finding La Tierra
that matches the thickness
of our blood.

San Antonio, Tejaztlan
Mujeres de Maiz, Flor y Canto:
Identity Blinging, no. 11 (2013): 6.

9
Tamoanchan, Aztlan

LUISA LEIJA

release
release
release

dance to shake the loss from my limbs
dance to love her again
dance to all betrayal
dance to forgive him
dance to maintain unity
dance to remember the forgotten
dance to forget the forgetting
dance to uncover the myth
dance to reactivate dna memory
dance to recall voice from red earth
dance to be the love of my mother
dance to be the strength of my father
dance to believe the dusty dream
dance to reclaim the precious dirt
dance to listen from seven directions
dance for words

dance the drum beat beats our hearts
dance for jungles to keep breathing
dance for all children to be educated
dance because bombs kill without ever being deployed
dance for the grandmother holding on to meet her grandchild
dance because a mother lost a son
dance because a child is lost as he looks in the mirror
dance because she still smiles after a beating
dance because hope remains
dance because she keeps giving
dance for giving
for giving for giving for giving
dance to always find a way
dance to see light in the shadows
dance for the eagles' blessing
dance to be in collusion with the wind
dance to keep standing

release
release
release

to the Tree
we give
flesh and blood

Oakland, Calif.
Mujeres de Maiz, Flor y Canto: Soldadera de Amor, no. 9 (2011): 4.

ROUND II

MOVIMIENTOS DE REBELDÍA

10
I Am International Woman

FELICIA 'FE' MONTES

Soy una mujer de maiz
la madre tierra es mi pais
I am international woman.
representing from all four directions
I'm trying to make the connection
between dreams and reality
and the duality of my sexuality.
I am international woman.
After all womb-man we are the land
connected to the center,
the sacred circle,
the other world within ourselves
I am international woman.
From my body flows a constant
   stream of
truth marking the rebirth of
   consciousness,
of the re-evolution of el sexto sol
I am international woman.
the trembles are felt around the
   globe as
la madre tierra cries her tears
cleansing herself from the evil within,
her mijo, el hijo de la chingada,
the creation of destruction, given vida
   'cuz
"hell hath no fury like a woman
   scorned"
I am international woman.
Alone looking into the turquesa stone
   I see
the blood-red road ahead,
the rain and clouds bringing a
   storm . . .
tensions to my relations
I am international woman.
and as Getty banners speak of
   imagining in
hoods across L.A. I am reminded why
the world is still a ghetto, from the
   corner
Chinese Fashion land,

the vegetarian taco stand,
to the Vietnamese acrylic tips of the
   world
I am international woman.
my true roots weaved together
In trenzas, china curls, and blown-out
   frizz,
realizing that adornment can have
consequences whether xolotl blues,
or Nike shoes,
I keep strong with my Jordana hues
I am
international woman.
Living in the jungle, Chiapas, or L.A.,
we live to remember the pachamama's
   way

I am international woman.
Mujeres de Maiz,
M.C.'s, mujeres en ceremonia
with life juices that flow like water
from our bodies,
waves in tune with the moon,
seen at its fullest by the
eyes of those who look to the sky,
the land, and the
fire
to create sacreds from sacreds
and drink Of these Mixed Waters

Mujeres de Maiz, Flor y Canto Of Mixed Waters, no. 3 (1998): 7.

11
Re-Collecting

D'LO

MY QUEERSTORY THAT BROUGHT ME TO MDM

Backdrop: Lancaster, California, in the 90s
I am the child of Tamil-Sri Lankan Hindu immigrants, 2nd girlchild of a doctor and artist.
For all intents and purposes, I was a boy until the summer between 6th and 7th grade.
I was lousy at being a girl, but I was in fear of being found out. I managed to stay disguised up through high school.

Private Catholic High School was 95% white.
My homies were the other 5%
        WE were
Outcastes
        in a world of
        High Becky Hair
Privilege
        both wealthy and poor white kids some gone
                nose white
        the wealthy—bought fancy cars, crashed soon after
        they had the money
        wanted to be sneaky deviants

        maybe they had it bad at home
        maybe they had it too good
        Maybe
    everyone was escaping
        desperate for thrills in a land of tumbleweeds
    dry desert
    sandy air
    dusty shoes
    sleepy town
    wanna-be cool, like those guys over that Hollywood/Beverly Hill
        but it's hard when we come from the rigidity on this Quartz Hill
White teachers questioning their own happiness on this hill
White Priest keepin up in his red miata
White PE Teacher closeted
    But how US
    nonwhite
    were led to finding one another
Listening to Hip Hop, Freestyle, Killer Oldies
Sri Lankan, Latinx, Black, Asian whatever
Culture
    Wasn't permitted on school grounds.
We only shared with each other
Our families' richness
    and dysfunction
Learnt about coalition
    Accidentally and necessary
We didn't know how to romanticize struggle
    we had our own struggles,
    and didn't know we struggled.
We thought everywhere was Lancaster,
    We shrugged our way to college applications
    We did life the best way we knew how
Messy
I knew freedom to queerdom was outside, as close as the ocean.
Brown. Immigrant Family. Queer. Trans. I still have privilege.
UCLA

I felt the pressure of figuring out what it was that I wanted to do with my life very early, because as a closeted queer person, I was desperate for freedom. I may not have known exactly the medium, but I knew it was going to be art.

MY MDM STORY STARTS HERE

It was 1995; I stepped onto UCLA's campus as an ethnomusicology undergraduate. In my cohort was a young woman, Sarah Rosenkrantz a.k.a. Skinz (also a part of the the Mujeres de Maiz Sisterhood). My naïve desert-living self didn't know Skinz was white/Jewish until she told me, because her hip-hop swag looked nothing like the white I knew in the desert.

My Lancaster ass learned quickly that there were other white Jewish people like her who came from an odd place called the East Bay of NorCal.

Where though they were hella white, they were hella
cultured, hella down, hella politicized.

And though she is white, in retrospect, I can say that we were both outsiders who sought reflections of our social justice hip-hop-loving selves, outside of the ethnic communities in which we were raised.

We learned more about each other in the Ethnomusicology Department. I listened to hip hop and R&B; I played the vina, piano, drums, wearing whatever Mary J. Blige inspired me to wear. Skinz played congas and broke down her favorite MCs, tripped off jazz and tripped out just as much as me on all the new shit we learned about in our one hundred series classes: whether it be music and culture from the Middle East, India, Latin America, the Balkans, East Asia, Brazil. I was happy to find kindred in this department, someone who loved music and rhyming just as much as I did. Together we absorbed everything thrown at us that we could connect to.

ORANGE

Orange talked passionately about Revolution.
Berkeley commune chick
Of Jewish Hippy SNCC folk.
She walked, talked, dressed like she wasn't any of the above,
but a carrier of the civil rights torch.
Orange came to UCLA
I thought she was the me who hadn't given up on the human race.
I already knew the struggles around my identity
    Gay, Sri Lankan, Woman was I.
Orange inspired me to do the work,
    Student/ Womanist/ Activist/ Artist
Orange was my partner in crime as we performed all over L.A. with and for ALL our different communities.
Disturbing Silence we were named and we did Disturb Silence
People Pushed my Passion through the Porthole of Political Performance Poetry.

To our dismay, we learned that ethnomusicology was more of an anthropological study than for musical performance even if you learned how to contextualize it, and we also learned that we were musical people in love with performing, not studying. Skinz and I found ways to get involved in everything on campus that was art-related, while student organizations found ways to incorporate us into their programming— which meant that we, White/Jewish and Tamil Sri Lankan, spat spoken word for Raza Youth Conferences and anything MEChA related. Skinz accompanied me with drums at every queer Pinay/oy or queer Latinx/ Chicanx event, and we both played drums for the African Arts Ensemble.

And though Skinz and I dated men who were in our artist communities, I had finally just come out . . . but as bisexual (to shoulder the severity of my extreme queerness).

One early evening after rehearsal and finals, walking through the quiet campus, Skinz and I thought we'd take advantage of being the only souls on Bruin Walk. We posted up to smoke beedis and shoot the shit. About to enjoy this rare calm moment in nature in an usually bustling part of campus, we realized we didn't have a damn lighter. At the top of the Bruin Walk, I can see it still so clearly, the picture of a woman seated smack in the middle of one of the steps, like she owned UCLA, enjoying the sky as it turned its LA sunset colors into blue darkness. Skinz and I both walked up and apologetically asked, because we didn't want to assume that she was a smoker, if she had a lighter. But before we could even ask, she reached into her bag, asked us what it was that we were smoking. We sadly responded, "Beedis."

<u>And that moment is what I mark in my history of my involvement with Mujeres de Maiz.</u>

The young woman was Felicia 'Fe' Montes.

The next time I ran into her was at the bottom of Bruin Walk, when Fe and a bunch of other Mujeres brought Dolores Huerta to speak, and someone reppin EZLN.

Everything I remember is a blur of more political and cultural events that we shared with Felicia and the other women who were at UCLA who co-founded MdM. Rallies, walkouts, sit-ins, conferences on campus. The core group of MdM was at everything. My sisters were there—in protest and in performance. Outside of MdM, I was under the mentoring wing of Revolutionary Communist writer Michael Slate, organizing with the Artist Network of Refuse and Resist, on the "artSPEAK" events which were centered around police brutality. From these days, I cannot remember names sometimes, faces other times, but I will never forget the feeling.

IN THE BEGINNING, IT WAS NOTHING BUT FUN AND ART

As young women of color, we felt the magical power of our unity, while also feeling the seriousness of the climate in which we were functioning as young people of color. We wanted to create change in our communities that would resonate throughout the world. We had high hopes and ambitions and even though we may not have known how to connect to every international movement across the globe, we were definitely trying to, eyes open.

Performance: My memories of first performing at MdM were with Skinz, Martha Gonzalez, and Tylana Enemoto in a short piece where we did poetry and drumming. I think this was at the PRC. I remember in those times how every performance felt like an offering. I somehow lost that along the way to the person I am now, but I always had reminders, especially in places that were touched by MdM; because of the intentionality in making space for art, spirituality, and movement work to coexist.

I believe that our queer acronym LGBTQAIAQTSSGLNBGNC also deserves an additional C for College. It didn't hurt that it was a time to experiment. In most women circles, I was one of very few visibly queer folks. The rest were seemingly straight, curious, or closeted. It was a different era, but still love was made, our sexual bodies were experimented with, and deep connections still live on.

And for me—with every women's studies class, my hair was getting shorter. With every girl I dated, the clothes got baggier. Slowly the boy was starting to emerge again.

I think the women in Mujeres de Maiz have seen me expand/metamorphize throughout all my iterations of self and finally grow into the version of myself that was most authentic. In those college years, however, my journey to my trans identity took a pause at the place where I understood myself as being someone who was no longer *just* a woman of color, but as someone who is neither male nor female but a masculine genderless "Boi."

Performance: The next time I performed at MdM was with Skinz and Martha and Tylana again, and others I forget. I remember us meeting at Skinz's apartment and going over ideas of what we were going to do, we rehearsed at different places. The performance consisted of multiple pieces/poems/songs meshed together that honored our womanness. I think it might've been Skinz's idea at first, but we had decided that in the second half of our piece, we were going to be topless with body paint. Outside of Skinz who grew up in hippy-ass Berkeley, the rest of us came from immigrant families and were a bit nervous about being topless. We knew that the shame we had was rooted in patriarchy and that our bodies could be free. I don't think we were trying to be provocative actually; I think we were trying to reclaim our bodies as places that ultimate freedom and expression could be shown through. We had asked that no photos be taken, we had asked to be heard. And even if some of my homies said I had nice tetas, I knew we accomplished something powerful because of the response. Our bodies were beautiful. Different sizes and shapes and we were free young artists, free and passionate young women.

Other Performances: The time after that, I performed with Disturbing Silence and Angelik Vagrants, comprised of Alejandra and Penny with OB and Hugo. I remember also having the chance to work with my new group, Wadda G (Women Aware, Deep, Dark, and Gay). This was a mostly hip hop and experimental/theatrical group with the vocals of Skryb and Kimberly Calvert and the rhymes of Sphear and I. Wadda G represented where I was as an artist becoming more unapologetic about my queerness after the work I was doing with Skinz in Disturbing Silence. But it was soon after Wadda G disbanded that I went mostly into performing solo.

Coming Out to Family: The basic story without the frills is that I came out to my parents at the end of my college career, and it didn't go over so well—so, I moved to New York to work for the National Artist Network. It was a harder time in my life and with the cross-country move during a pre-cell-phone/Skype era, I deeply missed MdM and the other supportive artistic environments of Los Angeles. On the other hand, it was in adjusting to living in NYC, and being in creative communities with queer artists of color or, for the first time, organizing and performing within South Asian politicized arts circles, that I grew up and expanded artistically. I started to understand that I needed to delve deeper into who I was as a queer person in order to become a better artist. So instead of performing poems about larger world issues, I started writing monologues about my family, my queerness, my queer woes.

Performance: Until I left for New York in 1999, I performed at every MdM Live Art Show. I remember coming back to do the annual MdM day of art and performing one of the pieces I wrote in NYC—the piece in which I play my amma/mother as she vocalizes her efforts in coming to terms with the fact that her daughter "is a gay" and "felt like a boy trapped in a woman's body."

And it was doing this new style of art/writing in New York, where I started to slowly accept my transness. And as quick as I began investigating, was I immediately being tested on my feminism. With no surgeries and no hormone replacement therapy, what did this gender journey mean to my feminist identification if I wasn't a self-identified woman? Would I be seen as someone who could offer something to feminist conversations, or would I have to take a back seat and only be an "ally" merely because I was going by male pronouns? Was there a place for my herstory to mix in with my complex queerstory to allow for a feminist trans story? My feminism, queerness, and trans-ness came together easily for me in my head and my heart, but trying to explain it allowed for others to question me with ultimatums. I could either be in the club or not; I had to say I was a woman or not. My elders questioned me. My feminist communities questioned me. I am still questioned to this day. And I wonder if the women in MdM went through their own mourning of my body or my identity at some point. If it happened, I never heard about it, but it could've been in those very few years I wasn't called to participate. I really don't know...

Around this time, I remember that there was the Michigan Womyn's Music Festival in 2006 and I had been asked to take part in it. This was around the time that I was asking mostly to be referred to by male pronouns, though I was identifying as something (stud/boi) that would now be called nonbinary trans masc (also pre-top surgery and pre-testosterone). I took the gig because my dear friend and powerhouse Toshi Reagon invited me with the heads up that this was the time for me to come and expand the conversation around the transphobia that was happening at the Michigan Womyn's Music Festival. I got there and while there were really beautiful experiences I had, there were other moments that were hard, including other artist peers questioning my attendance. I went home fully anxious and sad, almost regretful that I was living more authentically as myself. And sadly, when I came back to L.A., the trans community shunned me for going to MichFest—no one asked me questions or even wondered why I would go or what I was doing there.

Because I performed at MichFest, another festival in the Pacific Northwest invited me to come and perform at their woman-centered event. When I told them that I was no longer identifying as a woman, but that I still passed as one and I still loved as one, and I would love to use my time on stage to share as a feminist, they rescinded their invitation saying that they would allow me to come and do a gender workshop, and that I could come as an attendee.

These exclusionary rules around my trans identity were isolating, and it felt as if there was no home, no place for my art, my feminism, my herstory as someone who was even up until less than 10 years ago, was perceived as a woman. I was being erased, kicked out and now I had no expansive community to lean into. I stayed touring while the world became more expansive and I am still looking for the silver lining in all this.

TOBACCO (2011)

1.

The last of any tobacco in my house has been smoked
Save for the cigarillo that was given to me by Ana before I even went to the D.R.
It sits on my altar as an offering, for me to remember her, remember preciousness

I sit outside with my thoughts and palm trees' silhouette
And remember, try to at least,
Everything I have in my soul is my claim
To getting better, to being not well
To dream bigger than my vices have pulled me to extremes of not caring

I care, is the truth.
I care that I live long and well for my loves
For the promise of new life, in the form of new horizons
In the form of children that are mine to teach.

I sit with Moraga's words,
of how she mourned her boy child's life even while he was alive . . . and still is.
I am grateful that I know Moraga well enough to testify to life.
His.

And I am sure that if I decided to have my own child, I will never be free of anxiety or
    fear.

I wonder if the joy I might have over my own child
will be trumped by my fear of death or calamities—
from the big to the silly.
From the car crashes to the table bumps,
to the queerphobia.
The constant kneading it does in my muscles.
If I will be happy with the new responsibility, this rite of passage
Or if I will remember why I decided against children.

I sit with Moraga's words,
of how she mourned her child's life even while he was alive . . . and still is.
I am grateful that I know her well enough to testify to life.
His.

As for mine, I am a him, too.
I sing for myself when something pulls me away from that cliff
and there are songs about me
I can only hear when I am off stage, literally right after.
I wonder and crave to know how many more will sing my hymns in this lifetime.
How many more will be witness, will testify to my change.
How many more will be able to fulfill my desire to be seen
To exist, in this body, during this era
Just as is.

I am curious about safety, how there is none for me to grasp a hold of.
I am reminded of spiritual texts that tell me to forget about the day to day,
focus on the me
to remember that to be okay with groundless-ness
is to be okay with me.
And that real freedom is unmatched by my own notions of freedom.

I beg to differ, and yet I still maneuver around this desire to be free of expectations

Only soon after do I recognize that I cannot
My life is not tragic, I am just not able—
I am a hymn in a him body that is read as only melody
As I strive to find rhythm in my step
To succeed in the next moments.

And I think of other hymns
Songs I sing of my thambi, of my soul bro, my sibling,
of my boys in many different cities.
I wonder if they crave safety as I do, or if they believe that they got it
When actually, they don't.

I think of efforts to personalize our lives
The one I met in 1998 who has turned to be a beacon of hope in the lives of so many of us who long to be sung
And I think of you, my boy, who hasn't met any of my other hymns
And how do you know what song to sing when you are struggling with the weight of everything.

We are female-assigned.
We carry the fear of getting raped because we are holding, still, as females do.
We push aside our needs in order to tend to other female bodies who are fems.
We try hard to be men, or manly, while we frustratingly,
but naturally
emote as female bodies do.
And we sit and think and ponder
As masculine,
As female bodies
As butches and bois who never grow up
because holding both is never revered as a form of adult
As men who are trying to create examples of new versions of men
who are trying to cut away to the core of this reality
As people who always need validation
In the encouraging words of our partners,
In the world's view on us being legal
Because we are trying to make sense of this world that seemingly doesn't want us,
Definitely doesn't hold space for us.

I wonder
Why we battle
And what the new masculinity is
That remembers that we feel
That we try not to
That we want to be strong enough to hold everyone else

But us.
And I wonder
What will become of our tribe
Where will we go to get the tools,
Who will provide us with rites of passages
To ensure that
It is alright to take up space
Sometimes
Because we are
Female bodies
Our reality must be honored
Instead of being erased.
Even when we are passing as men, our realities must be honored.
Isn't there a space that will also see us with all our secrets and glory?
After all, who is better equipped with strength
to hold/stand beside
men and women?
We crave to be honored for the space we keep.
Not the space we don't.

So goodbye to girls who say we are too manlike
And goodbye to women who say we are still women
And goodbye to men who claim that they can still have us as women
And goodbye to everyone who can't see us as whole
Who think we perform
Who don't know that we don't
Who understand gender to be 2.

And hello to the beautiful people
Who help create the ceremony to honor our gifts

Hello to the women who understand that we have something to say too,
Even when it seems like we don't.

Hello to those who love us regardless

Hello to those who respect their own complexities, who have compassion for
    their layered selves, who can therefore see us whole and without holes.
Hello to my people
Who understand
I am trying to push aside my own fears, thoughts, and inhibitions
I am trying to hold space for you too
For liberation, for freedom
It's tiring trying to be a man, when I feel things as a woman does
It's tiring to push aside me, because the men of your past took up so much space
It's tiring to just be, when people are asking me to decide what I want to be, still.

Hormones or not, just say

Hello to me
Sing my hymn
Loudly
With reverence for this Divine.

Sing, so I don't have to exhale smoke
Or ingest spirit
To feel the most Godly
In me
To feel God
Around me.
Sing for me, my hymn.

> My journey has brought me here. To a solid place of
> understanding that this soul may want a change from the
> understanding I have of it now, as it has done in the past.
>
> And where I land is a happy place. One where I can be revered as one would
> revere a woman, but I am trans. One where my herstories are honored,
> one where my hymns are being sung, where my genderqueerfuckitall
> is a beautiful mess that no one averts their eyes to. This place is the
> MdM collective that has grown with me, side-by-side, as I have been
> growing. And in being witnessed and seen as a sibling to this sisterhood,
> I have witnessed the power that this collective has cultivated.

In this day in age, it is a gift to be witnessed. To see someone is to honor them.

It only makes sense that those who have been herstorically silenced and had violence put upon their bodies would expand to bring in their trans sisters and siblings.

MdM Performance: I was called to host the MdM Live Art Show with Bamby Salcedo one year. This was a beautiful big deal that two trans-identified people were hosting. I applaud the collective for thinking of Bamby to host as she is Latinx and a warrior in the trans and immigrant communities.

Mujeres de Maiz was a space to be among other women of color who were passionate about what was happening in the world from a social justice and feminist perspective. I cannot think of my life without thinking about how lucky I was to have a family-like community in which I had a place to sit with other creative women.

NOTE

It took me forever to try to figure out what I was going to say for this anthology. In all seriousness, I wanted to write a piece that would show how much I revere and respect the womxn who have put their lives into Mujeres de Maiz, the organization itself, and the ongoing spiritually based movement work that the organization fosters. I also wanted to make sure, as someone who identifies as trans-masculine and queer, that I could do a service to the person I was and how I identified in the past, while also allowing for the beautiful person I was not allowed to be, to be honored in this retelling as well. *This is me, a trans masculine Tamil Sri Lankan American, male-pronoun using, womxn- and femme-loving, feminist-warrioring herstorical recollection filled with old poems and new understandings.*

12
Recollections

My Personal Journey with Mujeres de Maiz

SKRYB ANU

MUJERES DE Maiz has been and will always be a pivotal point in my life. On a personal level, I had just lost the life of my mother, so it was a time of mourning for me. There was something about feeling like the rug was snatched from underneath my feet, that gave me a numb I don't give a f*** attitude, that caused me to be ripe for an outward release. Speaking from my own perspective, I love how the Universe works because expression was healing for me. Just so happened, Mujeres de Maiz was birthing its existence on a premise I needed, a safe space where all women were welcome to express themselves. This was a venue that offered a level for women's voices that I had never before encountered, especially coming from an extremely conservative religious background. Yet, there I was, emotional baggage and all, ready to let go that fateful night, embarking on this new journey. Not only as a Black woman, but as a lesbian performing with an LGBTQ artivist group. This was the first time I would ever be so bold in public. Usually, I stayed behind the scenes, producing tracks, audio engineering, or writing lyrics for others. Even when it came to recording my own material, I hid behind the shield of a studio, enclosed in a recording booth. That pivotal moment with MdM opened a new chapter in my life.

I was in awe when I entered the womb of Mujeres de Maiz's creative space and saw all the women organizers, performers, and artists working together. I remember myself, D'Lo, and Sphear walking in and the excitement we shared. I kept pivoting my view to everything around me with a big grin on my face. It was like getting initiated into this secret underground movement of women. Something in me stood taller, being among those who would take the stage. Once we reached the top of the staircase and entered the main area, the amount of people that were there was daunting at first—but still—surprisingly, I wasn't afraid. I was anxious. The three of us being there together as the group Wadda G played a large part in my confidence because that was our premiere night. I stepped to the microphone feeling uninhibited, releasing my words, allowing the power of my voice to project across the room. After we finished performing, hearing the applause, whistling, and loud cheers coming from the audience, marked the beginning of the end of me biting my own tongue.

I was living in City Terrace on Buelah when I met D'Lo. My partner at the time, Sphear, had been out at an open mic spot. I decided to hang back at the house to listen to albums and work on music. When she returned, Sphear brought D'Lo with her. They met at the open mic. Sphear introduced me to D'Lo, and I found her particularly interesting because she was another dark sister, but with a culture tied to a different region of the world.[1] I had never met anyone personally from Sri Lanka before. Quite honestly, my limited knowledge of India had me only reference it in general terms. We all started hanging out, choosing and spinning records in my collection. The topic of creation came up in our circle discussion, so D'Lo asked if she could hear what I'd been working on, so I played some tracks. She started bobbing and freestyling to herself. Sphear jumped in, and it became a call-and-response lyrical dance, back and forth. I started improvising vocals in the background, they opened the floor. I started cross rhyming, and singing and we all kept circling back around. D'Lo called the next morning, inspired and just was ready to kick it off.

When we met that next day, she showed up with a flier for Mujeres de Maiz's event in Boyle Heights. She proposed that we form a group and prepare for it. A slight hesitation in me rose out of fear. But it didn't last. I was still feeling numb from a loss like novocaine. Fear was present but fleeting. Plus, the event felt right. Once we all came to an agreement that this was what we were going to do, we started brainstorming, tossing names out around the kitchen table on what our group name would be. Pieces of the name came together from each of us, and Wadda G (Women Aware, Deep, Dark, and Gay) was born—glaring, blatant, and what. . . . No apologies here. There wasn't a day that went by where we didn't rehearse or share music and staging ideas. We all had our notebooks out in our own little vibe spaces writing quietly. I kept my headphones on, producing tracks on my Emu Emax III sampling keyboard, way off into the dead of night, which was perfect for me anyway because I'm an owl influenced by the moonlight type anyway. Since I had a mic, stand, mixer, and speaker hookup, we would run through our full-on show several times in a row until it was flawless. No one of us could forget our lines and have to rely on a notebook. No reading was allowed, and we all had to come from memory. Also, there was the dramatic aspect of it. We weren't just reading poetry—there was a theatrical aspect added for emphasis. We added some props, like the most remembered machete by those who attended that performance, used to mimic a female beheading.

As I mentioned before, everything about my life was in flux at this time. So even living in City Terrace was a huge change for me. This was the first time I ever lived outside of my comfort zone, within a different demographic group, mainly Latinx. There was only one other Black family that lived on my block, and that's all I saw really represented in the city. Me and them. That was a stark difference coming from the predominantly Black community of Crenshaw, Leimert Park district.

The night of the show we met a couple of hours prior at my house on Buelah. We sat around the kitchen table and gave each other one last pep talk—this was it. I didn't know what to expect because this was me embarking on something beyond my personal experience. After that, we packed up and rolled out. . . . No turning back.

Notably, what grabbed my attention when we first rolled onto the block where the event took place was the police station we passed one block ahead of where we were going. I turn to the significance of that memory today, shaking my head, as being such a prominent memory etched in my mind as a person of African descent in this country, and how it automatically raised anxiety in me, for just being in and of itself, in such close proximity. The thought leaped in my mind, *Well this is interesting.* We as a people still had fresh wounds and, even more so, a soured relationship stemming from the Rodney King rebellion. Some time had passed, yes. But those groups of people who create public humiliation for law enforcement know that those bygones aren't just bygones on either end. And that was something I learned that a lot of the Chicana(o) peoples that I was among shared. We were all getting slammed on hoods, thrown handcuffed onto backseats. Silence wasn't an option. So, pulling up to the actual parking lot of the building where Mujeres de Maiz was hosting their event and seeing this vibrance of life with mujeres hanging out by their cars with doors open playing music respectfully out loud, conversing, laughing, sharing a cigarette, was an incredibly stark difference from the loom and gloom we just passed. That night was filled with a much-needed medicine, and for once in my mind women of color ruled, from a variety of backgrounds, it didn't even matter. Prior, I had mixed everything down on a DAT file, so I brought my portable player with us queued up for the sound man, ready to go. There was nothing major to carry; this was it. We walked up those outside stairs, entered the building, and got checked in. And the rest was her-story.

From that moment, Wadda G grew in popularity and expectancy as participating members. We even expanded to a fourth member, Kim, an African American vocalist whose vocals, presence, and performing energy were a perfect fit. We spent time creating new material at my house and at the bench of D'Lo's upright piano when she was still renting a place near the UCLA campus. Both her and Kim were students at the time. I also started producing tracks for Aurora, who was another poet we met as a result of Mujeres de Maiz. All was well and wonderful with our group until it wasn't, for personal reasons that I won't mention here. But I will say that the day Wadda G broke up was a deeply sad one indeed.

After we parted and went our separate ways, at the proceeding Mujeres de Maiz event, I reemerged on the stage with Sphear as the duo "Untitled." It too grew its admirers, with our sharp words, trip-hop beats, and visual syncs to sound with the use of videos. I would edit together a montage of clips to our tracks and burn it down to VHS. For our shows, we would set up a TV and VHS player on stage facing the audience as part of the scene. I would hold a remote to the player and hit play on cue when we began performing. Wadda G had already stepped outside the bounds of poetry with its incorporation of theater, and Untitled pushed even further. I was able to be experimental, utilizing both my audio engineering and postproduction skills.

With Untitled, I started getting introduced to other opportunities for community artivism. The pirated station Radio Clandestina was one of them. It was based in an abandoned prison located around Chinatown. Me and Sphear started doing a program called "BlakHole." We named it that due to its eclectic nature. We had audio skits that we had created that we would use as transitions between sets as our own audio commercial breaks. Our audio palette would sway listeners from Portishead, to The Isley Brothers, to Depeche Mode, while injecting our news segments that kept our audience up to date on topics such as what was happening with protests against the death penalty issued to Mumia Abu Jamal, fighting over the native lands of Chiapas, President Bush implementing the wiretapping program in everyday households, and more.

During that time in my life, I was a participating protestor on and off stage. One of the largest was the march against the criminal justice building, located in Downtown Los Angeles. It began with us performing at a pre-show before everyone assembled at the assigned meeting area to start the march. I felt so incredibly honored, because not only were we having the opportunity to participate in this mass gathering in opposition to Proposition 187 and the three strikes rule, but also, we were an opener for Burning Spear. Following that march, not long after, which was all taking place around the late nineties, we traveled to Tijuana to perform in protest to the border. After we finished, it was such an amazing moment for me to hear the beating native drums echo out, followed by the screeching, razor-sharp guitar sounds coming from Aztlan Underground, as they broke out into the song, "We Didn't Cross the Borders, the Borders Crossed Us!"

With Mujeres de Maiz, a kinship and sense of community was built that transcended the spaces where they were held. I have friendships to this very day, created from those moments. Even if we haven't seen each other in years, those bonds remain intact, strong, and unbroken. What we did had depth and meaning. Today, I carry that same spirit into how I approach my work as an augmented reality and virtual reality developer. My concerns always fall on the question, "How am I contributing to my culture and community?" Founding the Afro Innovator Exhibition is an outlet I've been nurturing to do this work. Changing the negative narrative that's constantly spewed out, with no reference to positive development or mention made of those great inventors who were people of color. Creating a space for talented minds to flourish and receive well-deserved recognition is my new journey.

In closing, it's beautiful to see what was started by the determination of a simple few, reaching so many, withstanding the tests of time. Mujeres de Maiz has blossomed and grown to be a legacy.

NOTE

1. D'Lo has given permission to be referred to as female with she/her pronouns in Skyrb's testimonio.

13
The Will of the Water

MARISOL LYDIA TORRES

I WAS BORN into the Valley of San Fernando, Califas, United States, encircled by the Verdugo mountains, Tataviam and Tongva grounds, and between ancient walkway-highways now known as the 5, 134, and the 170. I am a daughter—one of four girls—Mexican, Nicaraguan, part "valley girl," and all-Chicana. A granddaughter descended from Cuyuteca/Nahuatlaca and Matagalpa/Basque migrant farmworkers, restaurant cooks, revolutionary seamstresses, musicos, and poets. My father worked as a machinist my whole life and trained me in the art and vital importance of joke-telling. My dancer mother came to the United States as a teenager in the sixties, and for that reason, the musical dance mix that filled our home growing up included the Beatles, the Doors, the Rolling Stones, not to mention José José, *cumbia*, *merengue*, and the best dance music throughout the decades of the eighties through today.

Does she speak English? This is a question I heard from age three well into my thirties. As a child, I was extremely quiet. I was put into ESL in kindergarten because my teacher thought I didn't know how to speak English. Truthfully, I just didn't want to talk to her. *Habla español? Es muda, o que?* I pissed people off in two languages—offending them with my quiet functionality. I've battled extreme shyness my whole life; too afraid to speak up in moments when I felt like I could explode with everything I held in. I learned to rely on my facial expressions to communicate—my *muecas*—as my mother put it, and I realized I could make people laugh with my spontaneous facial "responses" to their intrusive questions. Drawing and painting are where I found comfort. Ever since I could remember, I gravitated toward the arts, my one voice. My father was also a musician, and my grandparents were storytellers and poets. I trained in piano for ten years. I began chorus at age eleven, and in high school I performed in a competitive show choir and hip-hop dance. My family couldn't believe it when they saw me on stage, I wasn't the same person. Once offstage, I'd retreat to my realm of quiet timidness. Sometimes the silence came naturally, other times, I thought it was what I needed to survive.

In college, I studied visual arts and Latin American studies. I eventually began to organize on campus. Proposition 187 had entered California politics. As a young college student, I couldn't believe such legislation could become law. I had experienced racism, overt xenophobia, and entitled hostility from my neighbors and community where I grew up. I still have vivid memories of being hollered at, "Go back to Mexico!," in elementary and junior high. I'll never forget the smug faces of neighbors and strangers young and old who threatened to call the cops and constantly tried to remind us "Mexicans" of "our place." I felt that this dangerous proposition would legalize these and other vicious acts of inhumanity. As a student organizer, I fought my instinctual shyness and focused on creating awareness about Props 187 and 184, immigration, and Indigenous rights, and many other issues. I helped raise funds and organize conferences, educational multimedia events, demonstrations, and other events in solidarity for schools and communities from the Mexican border and down south to Chiapas, Cuba, Central America, and throughout Latin America (Anahuac), as well as for communities here in the States. In 1996, a friend and fellow organizer was suddenly killed in a hit-and-run car accident. The months that followed his death were tremendously difficult. This young man, a good person, with sincere ideals, someone I organized alongside, was gone. His death hit me hard. In my mourning, I felt I lost my drive.

That summer, my cousins and I piled into my 1980 Malibu to an event where our cousin Danny Rosales performed teatro at Regeneración, the PRC (Popular Resource Center) in Highland Park. We didn't make it in time, but we ran into Rudy Ramirez—one of the key members of the PRC and Aztlan Underground—who told us there was another event at the Loft in Downtown. He tried to give us directions, but listen, we were from the Valley. We didn't know what the heck streets he was talking about. I did my best to follow him into this unknown LA territory. My loud *primas* screamed and laughed as we drove the windy curves of the antiquated 110 freeway. We made it to the show. Each room was packed with unfamiliar people, live bands, artwork, poets, and theatre. It was nothing like a dance club. No "fronts," no pickup lines, no competitive vibe—everyone was in a good mood and genuinely friendly. We made it to the space where my cousin performed with a Chicano/a theatre group called ChUSMA. My cousins and I cracked up at his hilarious antics amongst this conscious crowd. The student/organizer side of me was reawakened with the content of their skits, which were not only funny but carried a deeper meaning. We had a great time listening to live music and seeing artists share entertaining work that had politics, critique, and community perspectives mixed in. Calling it a night, we walked back to my car. I ran into one of the theatre members who asked if I wanted to audition for a play they were going to produce for a month at a Silver Lake theatre. I had never acted in a play. I don't know why, but I thought of my departed friend and things he would never be able to do. In my mind, I thought, "'F'-it, why not?" Try something new. It doesn't matter if I don't get chosen for the part. Just try something new. I looked back and simply said, *Okay*, then left with my cousins back home. It felt good to let go of a little bit of fear of the approaching unknown.

With all my anxiety back, I showed up at what I thought was an audition. The director had us do improvisation exercises together. It was strange but I gave it my best shot. At the end of the night, I asked someone, *So how many people are auditioning for this part?* The response was, "You're in." With this, I began my life as a teatrista. Rudimentary to say the least, but I always had a deep, inherited passion for comedy and gave all that I could for each performance. After the run, I was asked to officially join ChUSMA. We performed at local events, cultural centers, colleges, and produced new comedy and plays—eventually touring the country.

In early 1997, Claudia Mercado, whom I had met through events and venues we performed at, approached me about the possibility of collaborating with other female performers for a one-night performance on International Women's Day. It was a bit of an odd concept for me but there was something intriguing about the idea. It's not that female artists and performers weren't represented on stage in the L.A. Chicano/a community scene at the time; there was Martha of Quetzal, our theatre group had two women and three men, there were also solo poets, visual artists, and organizers, but there weren't moments when all these women would simultaneously occupy the stage. So, delving deeper into the unknown waters, I said yes.

We had our first meeting at the PRC. Funny, I thought the first time I found myself at the PRC with my lost primas would be my last. But there I was, outside of my comfort zone, once more. It was Claudia Mercado, myself, Cristina Gorocica, Liza Cohen Hita, and Celestina Castillo, the other woman from our theater group. We faced our chairs in a circle within the PRC's small radio studio and Claudia explained her idea. March 8th was coming up and she wanted to create a night where different women (us) could present a collaborative performance, right there at the PRC. On this first night we met, we brought out our personal journals and took turns reading. Listening to the other women read left me speechless. Even now, it's difficult to explain the feeling I had in that little studio. It was so moving. These women were brave, there was no fear, no shyness—they didn't hide anything in their poetry. When I performed theatre, I wasn't afraid to be loud, to be silly, or to move in ridiculous ways. But these poetic words that were shared that night were not masked in wacky movements or comedy or any strict dogma, it was just us. Sitting amongst this courage, I didn't even notice when deeply personal grief and trauma began emerging out of the pages of my journal and unloosened from vocal cords I always held tight. I was speaking them aloud for the first time but I felt like I was in a safe place. In a circle, we laughed and listened to one another. With support. With encouragement.

Four of us committed to putting on the performance. Liza, Claudia, myself, and Cristina. (What was I thinking? What did I get myself into?) I was nervous. We weaved our voices and experiences into one live art piece. Together, on the stage, our individual poems were brought to life for an audience. With these young, educated, and like-minded women on the stage with me, I felt that my story was important enough to acknowledge and share. In our collective piece, we spoke about relationships, trauma, abuse, activism, sexuality, labels, racism, love, earth, self, sexism, violence, and community. Our stories and styles were individually unique, but on this night, we found a shared language, a voice to speak our personal truths and communicate to the world. It felt like... strength. I was not afraid.

Afterward, we felt thrill and relief—it was over. It felt gratifying to follow through this act. I didn't know how the audience would respond and I was too occupied in making sure I had all my verses memorized to worry about much else, but the action was revealing itself to be more powerful than I anticipated. It was like another level to the activism I hadn't considered toward my own path of healing. And the striking thing was that people really responded well to us. We received a lot of positive feedback. People remarked how they connected to our experiences and words. This was an added bonus I didn't expect. I didn't think someone I didn't know could relate to my experience. The night ended well.

Unexpectedly, we were asked to perform at USC and then UCLA. We met to pull together our so-called one-time performance again, and Felicia 'Fe' Montes was invited to integrate her work into our piece. A beautiful connection between us was that we were all also organizers. Most of us were involved in organizing the 1997 Chicana/o Zapatista Encuentro in Chiapas. I remember us arriving back at the PRC after the USC performance to participate in a Big Frente Zapatista meeting. Still in complete face paint, semicostumed up, a couple of us still in hairsprayed high copetes and dangling props from our necks, we talked logistics with the rest of the collective. Surprised with more performance invites, we realized that maybe there is a need for a group like this because there wasn't enough representation of women on the stage—conscious women sharing the mic at the same time. It was at the Aztlan Cultural Arts Foundation (the old city jail) in Lincoln Heights, where we decided to name our group In Lak Ech (tu eres mi otro yo/you are my other me). We brought in Rachel Negrete Thorson, and our group was complete for a few years with six strong poets, writers, performers, painters, organizers, students, danzantes, and teatristas who would, over the years, also become teachers, mothers, doctorate and graduate degree holders, filmmakers, actors, muralists, musicians, producers, entrepreneurs, singers... and the list will hopefully keep growing. In 2004, we were blessed to meet and bring Marlene Beltran, a performing artist who added her beautiful singing voice and heart to our circle. A radiant energy that has re-joined our group since her time on stage with us in her infancy and childhood is Textli Gallegos; a multi-discinplinary artist and Cristina's oldest daughter. What began as a one-night performance became a group with a 25+ year history, pardon me, "her-story."

In those early days of In Lak Ech, a male Chicano friend, someone I considered a peer artist, called me on the phone and ranted, "I think what you're doing is wrong." *What?* What was he talking about? *Oh really? What are you saying?* "I don't think you women should be working against us [men]. It's wrong." He went on to fume that what we were doing was "anti-MAN" and was a complete disservice to the movement. I questioned him about this. *Why was it that women coming together had to be equated with being anti-male?* I pushed on. *Have you ever seen us perform?* I knew the answer. He had NEVER seen us on stage. But the mere idea of it was a complete threat. *Why don't you wait 'til you see us perform before you start making any judgments?* Of all people, I never expected to hear him say something like that. Sadly, he wasn't the only one who made similar assumptions about women. A male "elder" of the movement once remarked something of striking negative resemblance to us before a performance at East Los Angeles College, vowing that he "will never support what we do." But after he saw us perform that night, he changed his tone. He approached some of us to shake our hands in support. It was fascinating that both of these activists had such extreme opinions and fear about something they had never even seen. Women sharing together equaled something powerful indeed.

For me, these experiences affirmed the urgency to carry on. More space needed to be facilitated as forums for women. The concept of Mujeres de Maiz began to brew. Felicia and Claudia organized a callout for a self-published 'zine to premiere in a culminating event featuring women of color artists set for June 1997 at the PRC. The event was a transcendent night of all-female poetry, visual art, musical collaborations, and ended with a full performance by In Lak Ech. It was standing room only. After this night, more women began to participate in meetings to envision what this collective could be. We met at different houses and cultural centers and opened safe spaces for all to share their ideas equally. Some nights, the meetings simply became a therapeutic circle where the women would begin to share difficult situations. This further supported the need to keep the collective going and expand it for others to participate. The movement was important, but our holistic health was equally important.

Our first shows were filled with artists and performers at all levels of their disciplines. The collective was born out of collaboration, and so collaboration was encouraged among the artists who were invited to participate. Visual artists curated exhibits for each new live show. In the first year there was an incredible amount of experimentation with new art/performance produced by artists of different backgrounds, styles, and disciplines. Imagine the mezcla of poets, filmmakers, singers, musicians, visual artists, MCs, classically trained dancers, photographers, and flamenco dancers devising work together to be showcased amid community.

The atmosphere at the shows was always positive and invigorating. Giving the microphone to women of all ages was a powerful experience for the performer and the audience. People lined the street to get into the show and gave the artists extraordinary love and encouragement. It felt like community. L.A. has so much homegrown talent. We had many courageous performers and artists who held common tragic experiences that were articulated through song, poetry, paintings, and so forth. This was a very healing experience for so many of us. I was equally lifted by watching new diverse voices grace the stage with eloquent words, movement, and sounds that tended to their raw pain. The concept of In Lak Ech—*Tu eres mi otro yo* (*You are my other me*)—continued revealing itself to me in life-changing ways, deepening my experience immensely as an early performer/organizer. We were young, making "mistakes" to various eyes, but we grew up and matured upon these makeshift to professional stages together—sometimes with a mic, many times without a sound system for miles and miles—or was it dollars and dollars? We intended to continue building together even if it led to disagreement. This taught us essential lessons on the vital act of dialogue and the overwhelmingly transformative act of organizing in a circle (literally) for their potential impact on our multilayered communities.

The layers of reflection I encountered were magnified with the many elders Mujeres de Maiz were fortunate to nurture relationships with. Olivia Chumacero, writer, filmmaker, and elder of the Teatro Campesino, shared much with me about the sacred act of teatro through a multigenerational, ancient-based lens. I was a young teatrista without formal training. With generosity, no-nonsense elder candor, and stage direction, Olivia further verbalized, guided, and coalesced what I had sensed for years. Yes, this was my role. The space I occupied was not merely a physical space. It is shared, communal, and ACTIVE—not reactive. I recall her words and envision them as an animated painting: In a strong current of water, what will I be? Where will my feet be? Would I let myself bend to its will or stand feet planted diagonally upon earth like my mother taught me before I chose to begin walking through, moving, dancing, creating, living like my tias and abuelitas trained me through their life examples? This intersection of time onstage is experienced in a circle. And then as wondrous as it is, it must move on. You can't bottle the will of the water. These moments on the stage for us became impromptu ceremonies. Like a spark from a deep memory we related to. It was an ancestral call to arm the stage with our creativity. With In Lak Ech and MDM, we analyzed, practiced, and tripped over ways that decolonization might manifest in our poetry, our songs, our drums, and our lives.

My time with ChUSMA ended after almost twelve years, and I later co-founded Las Ramonas, an all-Chicana theatre comedy group. Due to the collaborative spirit of MDM, the relajo and satire of "Las Ramonas" was able to make its way onto the stage. Myself, Jo Anna Mixpe Ley, and Marlene Beltran first integrated our comedy, politica, music, and teatro at a Mujeres de Maiz live event together in 2007. We fused our teatrista "Zap-artista" organizer tactics to present larger-than-life actos with the motive of sparking dialogues and integrating the vital medicine of laughter within our movements through the lens of a Chicana with an X.

Through my participation with MDM, my paintbrush and my hands sculpted the words that I had never found before as a child—those accumulated words that had been wedged in the middle of my throat for most of my life. MDM made gallery space where it never existed before to hang our paintings, sculptures, photos, screen films, display our printed words and rhythmic stanzas. With these spaces I further developed the range of my color palette, the ease of my brush strokes along with the layers of my sculptures. Yes. I found a place where so many of my other selves could coexist: the teatrista, the poet, the painter, the sculptor, the comedian, the singer, the writer, performer, producer, artivista, as well as the amiga, the sister, the Chicana. I could say that in my childhood I never felt that college was for people like me. I truly thought it was something reserved for those in positions of privilege, money, or status. With exposure to so many women of color with higher degrees during those early years of MDM shows, I was inspired to return to graduate school and received my MFA in writing from the school of television, film, and theatre.

Early in my performance career, my artistry and activism became one. Via the collective process, the stage revealed itself to us as a temporal space to actualize our ideals. All we knew was our hunger and necessity to express ourselves and share it. The Zapatistas verbalized what we desired most—*a world where many worlds fit*. Performance was not solely a one-sided performative act to be observed or consumed for sole entertainment. It was a dual experience lived between the audience member and artivista. We were fighting for our survival together via this ceremony, via this impermanent experience, this intersection upon the earth where we found ourselves together within these very moments. We were moved to help lift women's voices out from the stations that were prescribed to us by the leftover colonial exploits that evolved and descended into neocolonial and neoliberal structures of our present.

Mujeres de Maiz has transformed itself and myself along the way. I'm proud to be part of its legacy. It never sought fame, only channels to build relationships, dialogues, and connect women together via our existing talents. We sought to amplify our indecipherable whispers and screams even further from out of our notebooks, classrooms, from our blocks, from the kitchen we thought we'd never leave, from those f'd up relationships we thought we needed to keep, the f'd up jobs we were forced to take, from the cycles we thought could never break. We sought methods to convert any space into a stage, calling us to empower the pens and spatulas and keyboards and recipes and tortillas and spray cans and cameras and all the etceteras already in our hands. To make music and films and murals and teatro and zines with those rhymes and jokes on the tip of the tongue and on the verge of a poem. To care for ourselves, the earth beneath our feet, and speak our collective truths.

Throughout the existence of MDM and In Lak Ech, I have felt the space to nurture and grow as a performer, writer, and visual artist. I'll always be grateful for the vision we were able to bring to life. I can look back at my old journals, early paintings, old flyers, photos, and see a woman who matured within a collective and on the stage in front of my community. I can say so much more, but it's about sharing the mic and space with my other sisters, right?

I look to the future with hope, and even in moments when I still struggle to find the words to speak, I'm accompanied with a song in my throat, with a paintbrush in hand, a pen, and a mic at my reach. With all my heart, thank you, mujeres.

PLATE 1
Linda Vallejo, "Flores de Aztlan Danza Cosmica"

PLATE 2
Margaret Alarcón, "Mujer de Maiz"

PLATE 3
Margaret Alarcón, "Hermana de Maiz"

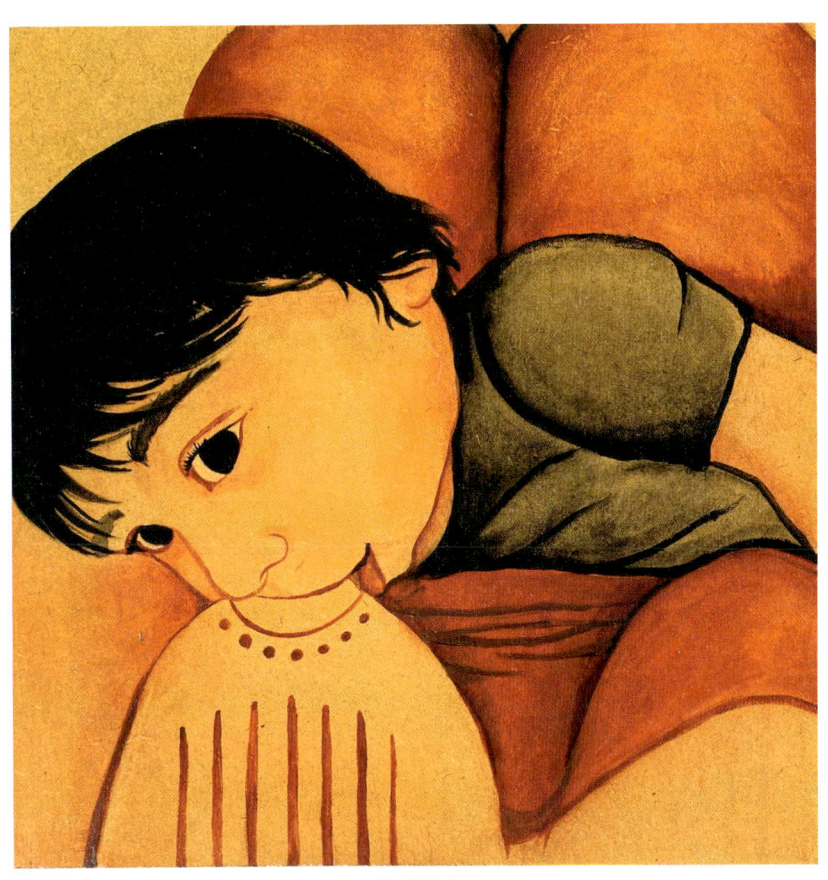

PLATE 4
Rachel Negrete Thorson, "Imix"

PLATE 5
Marisol Torres, "In Lak Ech: Flor y Canto"

PLATE 6
Gina Aparicio, "Cihualamachiliztli, Woman of Wisdom,"
Hawaiian red clay and iron oxide, 32×13×14 inches

PLATE 7
Linda Vallejo, "Madre Celestial"

PLATE 8
Felicia 'Fe' Montes, "Loteria Xicana"

PLATE 9

Lilia Ramirez, photograph by Carlos Callejo, "Xilonen: Angel of Los Angeles. Protest to Legalize Mural Ordinance at City Hall and Save Youth Art Programming"

PLATE III
Mariela de la Paz, "La Machi"

PLATE II
Pola Lopez, "Corn Mother"

PLATE 12
Pola Lopez, "Queen Fly Stone"

PLATE 13
Crystal Galindo, "29: Dolor"

PLATE 14
Crystal Galindo, "Coatlicue State"

PLATE 15
Celina Jacques, "Labor of Love"

PLATE 16
Christine Vega, "Walking the Red Road: Sisterhood Transformation,"
2012, color pencil on paper

PLATE 17
Felicia 'Fe' Montes, photograph by Roberto Q. Loza,
"Occupy LAcMAztlan performance art"

PLATE 18
Lilia Ramirez, "Coyo Comes Alive"

14
Contusions

FAITH SANTILLA

Contusions
mass confusion
worldwide disillusion
a fusion of a
star-spangled noose, abuse
and false news
nike shoes anchor blues
material consumption's so
delicious;
Hollywood-bound greyhound full of
young girls so ambitious
Born again prey, busy praying
as they are now ambitious
'cause as vicious as this world is that we live in
it's a given
that
we all try to stay hidden . . .

Behind our material submission
Behind our ambitions

Behind being christian, or any other religion.
Or through relentless deception receptions
Put on by societal inventions
Promising thee
success and freedom you once envisioned
But of these things
make an educated incision
And you'll see you're just slicing air
So make the decision to find
Liberation in something else,
Your mind,
Your words,
The front lines
'cause although we all seem fine
A spirit can be broken without breaking the skin or spine
Contusions
mass confusion
Worldwide disillusion.

The solution?
Mass inclusion.
Revolution.
Peace.

Mujeres de Maiz, Flor y Canto: Birth of La Diosa de Maiz, no. 1 (1997): n.p.

15
Cuscatlan

LIZETTE HERNANDEZ MOORE

Something in the gut hits me
when I say
El Salvador
That place of pretty silver sand
beaches
And dense foliage leaving one
not knowing
what's hiding now
Or what once hid
behind the green
The carnage
the suffering
the blood
Los llantos
Of people whose spirits now are
whole
O no?
Brown glistened skin from sun
sweat and heat
upon them
Fincas de cafetales

Tattooed foreheads
imprinting the pain of parents
lost
Unto the soil
forgotten it seems
But people like me
remember
And so when we say
El Salvador
it comes from a deep place
Inside my soul
like when I remember that young
sister
Esa compatriota
luchadora
hermana
en esa batalla
Laying on the dirt road
Revolutionary fatigue
pants down
Pussy blown up

so no evidence
stays behind
only gunpowder black
Eyes closed
pretty wavy hair
You almost forget
when u see in the picture
how lovely she once was
What family did she come from?
What town was she at?
What street was she found on?
Was she ever buried right?
Quien fueron sus madres?
El Salvador makes you wonder
How not right
humanity can be
to each other and how
things can go so astray?
With external help

Of course
Ya lo sabes todo
And by now we should all know
The root
Think hanging of Feliciano ama
But when will it all end?
Does that young girl have a
chance?
Bamboo holding red flag
People will rise
To liberate that land
Of CUSCATLAN

Los Angeles, Calif.
Mujeres de Maiz, Flor y Canto: Soldadera de Amor, no. 9 (2011): 26.

16
farm for meme

VIRGINIA GRISE

mash the kernels in a metate
5,000-year-old oaxacan blue corn
walk a circle of protection around the
    house
throw away barrels and barrels of
    broken glass
so we can grow
green amarth, yerba buena, chayote
eat the fruit
turn the root into tea
alache and chipilin
purple flowers
rich legumes
we didn't learn this in school

how to turn the guayaba leaf into
    medicine
what day to plant the yierba mora
how to mix the malabar gourd with
    honey

make palenquetas
know where the sun sets and rises
where the mountains are
in what direction is the ocean
xempasuitli/orange and yellow
marigolds welcome nuestros
    antepasados
our ancestors

first showed us
how to work the land with our hands
so that we could have something to
    call our own
14 acres of farmland
in the middle of South Central Los
    Angeles
after the riots
we have known more than violence

the first thing that grew was the cactus

one of the siete guerilleros
nopal is strong and independent
then the other plants grew too

in january, avocados, bananas, and cabbage grew.
in february, mushrooms, squash, and mangoes grew.
in march, artichokes and grapefruit grew.
in april, radishes, pineapple and spinach grew.

we planted
prayed for the farm
and it grew

Vanessa who we call V is an emcee. spins records and poetry. raisin three boys. four, three, and two on prayers and a whole lotta love. in between gigs, she stays at home with them and teaches them to read. Emmanuel, the middle child, can't decide whether or not he wants to be a ninja or a warrior, switchin his bandana from face to head, insisting that you cannot be both. he once told me how one day he was gonna build a farm and everyone could live on his land with their tents. V and the boys used to live on the South Central Farm in an encampment, tryin to save it from the police and bulldozers. Emmanuel told me he didn't like bulldozers but explained in his old man voice that when you pull something out the ground it grows back. don't worry. We're going to plant more things, he said.

even after the bulldozers came and
    tore our garden down
los nopales siguen creciendo
la caña/the sugar cane and the banana
    still grow . . .

San Antonio, Tex.
Mujeres de Maiz, Flor y Canto:
Somos Medicina, no. 6 (2008): 7.

17
Tortilla Warrior

CLAUDIA SERRATO

My Beautiful Aztlan
Brown, Purple, Yellow, Green
Gente de Maize
Fighting to Live Autonomously
Centuries of Struggle
Violated, Captured
Grown Unnaturally
Genetically Modified
¡Monsanto You Will Not Defeat Me!
For In the Pueblos Magicos
I Continue to Breathe
My Tierra, Mi Tonanztin
Living Vibrantly
First as a Teocentli, Xinachtli, a Seed
Grown in Milpas
Dried and Grounded
To Feed Nuestros Ecological Communities
Shaped into a Rounded Delicacy
Toasted on a Comal
A Blanket I Become

A Giver of Life, A Protector of Ancestral Cuisines
Nurturing Healthy Foodways
3,000 Years Strong
Creating Decolonized Free Zones
As the Xicana Indigena Body
Food is a Carrier of Knowledge
It is My Palabra
I Am Not Just a Tortilla
I Am A Warrior Queen
I Live and Fight for My People
I Am a Mother, a Mujer de Maize

Pomona, Calif.
Mujeres de Maiz, Flor y Canto: Soldadera de Amor, no. 9 (2011): 13.

18
Revolutionary Rants

MARIBEL MARTÍNEZ

I am tired a being your kind of revolutionary
Of being the self-appointed savior to those who have not tapped into the larger consciousness
Of sending out news updates to the ones
who don't bother reading it
Of always having the right words to your
bruised ego after your words and actions
have disrespected yourself
Of the late-night meetings listening to you speak of "our" issues forgetting that I
too have a voice in what's ours
It's exhausting; I'm done

My fist has been held too tight and too high for too long
That the muscles are beginning to atrophy
Waiting for you to lift a finger

And these arms

They were designed to be soft and comforting
Welcoming embrace
Yet, they have been flexed in ready alert
for a while
Muscle in distress

But these arms

These arms will one day hold babies
And these babies will need to know a

world filled with love and compassion;
not more angry faces

After all, the greatest tool for
   resistance is
love

I am tired of being your kind of
revolutionary
Of being the one in the office always
sounding the alarm
Tired of counting on angels of bread to
end poverty
Of tending to prison poppy fields and
cemetery parks
Of seeing rivers of tears overflowing for
years
My eyes that have been waterfalls are
now experiencing drought I force my
teeth to feel the breeze
Fake a smile

My fist has been held too tight and too
high for too long
And I'm not getting any younger

The joints are beginning to swell
My arthritis is starting to set in
Carpal tunnel vision
And there were so many songs I have
   yet
to play on my guitar
We grow sick and in need of healing
we turn to a government that is more
   broken
than us to cure our aliment
Pero los ancestros gave us gifts of

medicine in music and the arts.
They bequeath us ritual and ceremony
Board meetings and Robert's Rules
   are not
in our roots

My fist has been held too tight and too
high for too long
That I have started to go numb and
   tingly
Fallen asleep at the post

So blinded by the militancy:

in being anti-imperialist, in a
   consumer-driven
capitalistic economic apartheid,
globalized refugee overly sexualized
repressive society
That I forgot
the simplicity

Of a struggle not built on anti-
But on being visionary

Creativity

I,

you,

We are luminaries

This fist

This fist was supposed be a connection
Representing the strongest muscle of my

being (My heart)
A life force used to give meaning
And if we truly want to change the
    world
"Hate can't live here anymore"

My legs are tired of marching

I want laugh lines instead of stress lines
I want high fives not fingers like knives

I want understanding not overstating

I want forgiveness

I want hope and inspiration

Solutions that make our hearts happy

My fist has been held too tight and too
high for too long
Until now

Now I will leave it open,
    like the universe
and await the possibilities
Now I will unclench it and embrace
myself
Now I will let the air blow through it and
feel my connection with my mother
    Tierra
Now I will stretch out my hand

And invite you to walk this journey
    with
me.

East San José, Calif.
Mujeres de Maiz, Flor y Canto: Identity Blinging, no. 11 (2013): 23–24.

19

The Spiritual Activism of Mujeres de Maiz

Queering the Boundaries of Art and Action

KAREN MARY DAVALOS

THE CLASSROOM was packed. Every chair taken. With my child in hand, I maneuvered through the crowd and found a spot on the floor, placing the toddler in my lap. I adjusted our bodies for our comfort. It was one of the earliest performances of Mujeres de Maiz, and I recall that the room was filled with people, heat, and sound. Making the front of the classroom their stage, Mujeres de Maiz sat around a drum and beat in unison the tempo of their music. The evening event continued with ritual song, drumming, and trance-like movement. Although Mujeres de Maiz moved and swayed from their chairs, I refer to their bodily gestures as dance. Torsos refined and responded to sound and the movements of each other, heads marked rhythm, and feet maintained a beat; their improvised choreography called out to me and my elder child.

In the small space, the sounds of the drum and their amplified voices echoed in my ears and rocked in my chest cavity. The group of four performers actualized for the audience cum participants our shared earthly and cosmic rhythm, as our hearts pulsed their individual beats but with the same pattern of diastolic and systolic phases. Soon I felt the timbre of the drum in my body and focused my breath on the drum's rhythm. This mindfulness transported me from audience member to participant in the ritual song and dance, and I too began to sway like the Mujeres de Maiz on the stage.

My child, who had been enthralled by the music since it began, finally broke from my grip and bounced to the ground. They danced, as only a toddler can—moving between balance and imbalance, grace and stiffness, and with indifference to others. Watching my child, I immediately became aware again of the surroundings—a college classroom converted into a performance space as part of the 2001 Summer Institute of Mujeres Activas en Letras y Cambio Social at California State University, Northridge—and wondered about the power of Mujeres de Maiz to shift my consciousness with the sounds of their voices and the vibrations of their drum.[1] I was puzzled and amazed by their ability to move me—to transport me to interior awareness and to transform a site I knew well, the academic classroom and the site of my daily labor—into a sacred space.

Starting with this memory of the event embraces the affective experience and avoids marking the genre, a strategy I borrow from theatre and performance studies scholars and artists who interrogate the "static codes of reception" through their work and writing.[2] The strategy also aligns with the practices of Mujeres de Maiz (MdM): they defy conventional classification. As Reid Gilbert has observed about First Nations playwright, Marie Clements, MdM is an art collective that "undulates in and out of various genres and in and out of various responses to spectators, . . . [exposing] its own hybridity."[3] The group has worked in all media of the visual and performing arts for over twenty-five years in the Los Angeles metropolitan area. The members write poetry, perform spoken word, and sing and dance to their own musical compositions. They create photography, ceramics, prints, film, textiles, video, murals, drawings, sculpture, and paintings, and some works are collaboratively produced. Additionally, each media is taught to students of all ages, making education a central component of the collective's activities. Mujeres de Maiz also functions like a production company that annually publishes a zine, and regularly organizes art exhibitions and performances that combine all of the above. Not tied to disciplinary boundaries, specific media, or a set of activist tactics, Mujeres de Maiz queers categories in order to create social and personal change through art.

Further blending art and spirituality, MdM is also an advocacy organization that mobilizes communities for better health care and environmental sustainability and against sexual violence and police brutality.

For example, a workshop about herbal gardens is a platform for environmental justice, spiritual healing, and decolonial foodways. Because MdM is a collective without a brick-and-mortar facility, arts workshops and exhibitions, as well as other practices, literally form coalition. The collaborations are pragmatic and ethical, joining with allies committed to social justice. The emphasis on coalition-building allows the collective to expand and contract as necessary, although a core group of intergenerational members—Felicia 'Fe' Montes, Marisol L. Torres, Linda Vallejo, Margaret 'Quica' Alarcón, and Claudia Mercado—has been consistent since its earliest years.[4]

From its perspective, Mujeres de Maiz is an *artivist* organization. For over a decade, the collective has identified as "spiritual artivists" and "holistic artivists." This "hybrid neologism," which combines "art" and "activism" to express "an organic relationship between art and activism," may encompass the range of activities of the collective, but their activities also trouble political spectacle, specifically the emphasis on demonstrations for public mobilization.[5] Although MdM traces its influence to the Chicano and the Zapatista movements, their vision and praxis are more expansive than the political activism of these social justice campaigns. The public march or protest rally is not a strategy for MdM, although its members have participated in political demonstrations. The activities of MdM join societal and personal liberation.

While I respect the collective's self-identification, this essay is an exploration of how Mujeres de Maiz follows Gloria E. Anzaldúa's epistemology and ethics of "spiritual activism," as the collective "connects the inner life of the mind and spirit to the outer worlds of action."[6] This essay seeks a capacious account of Mujeres de Maiz and their activities and orientations, and therefore I place the collective within the historical and intellectual trajectory of queer, Indigenous, and Chicana feminist thought and arts practice. Mujeres de Maiz employs multidisciplinary and multimodal tactics to produce social and individual change. Such a broad and inclusive strategy emerges from an epistemology that shifts and expands the consciousness and stage for action. As spiritual activists, MdM values the interconnectedness of the planet, drawing ontological insight from the Maya moral philosophy of interconnection, In Lak'ech (tú eres mi otro yo / you are my other me). This principle produces a politics of individual and collective engagement as spiritual activists promote self-care and societal transformation. The Maya principle is foreign to Western thought; indeed, it queers western notions of self and other and being-in-the-world by complicating Western philosophy's constituting of the self as distinct from the other.

Anzaldúa articulates this Maya principle through spiritual activism, which expands the platforms for mobilization as well as deepens the tactics for producing systematic change.[7] It is not simply that the beings of the planet—the animals, plants, air, water, earth, and humanity—are metaphysically joined but that one is known or understood through one's neighbors and specifically through one's unfamiliar coresidents. Spiritual activists interrogate binary thought, identifying "us/them" constructions as unproductive, by locating veracity in the expression of incorporation: tú eres mi otro yo/you are my other me. When the self and the society are the site of engagement, the quest for justice depends on healing each aspect of life-force: women, people of color, colonizers, trees, bears, clouds, to name a few inhabitants who suffer from the pervasive and culturally imbricated logic of settler colonialism and its binary mode, we/they.

I hypothesize that Mujeres de Maiz builds on the bridging tactics, visual arts vocabulary, and spirituality of Las Mujeres Muralistas of the San Francisco Mission District and Las Flores de Aztlan of Los Angeles whose members included Analuisa Espinoza, Xochimilco Portillo, Irma Cui Cui Rangel (a very well-known Chicana vocalist), Norma Pedregon, Cecilia Castaneda, and Linda Vallejo, who would become a mentor to MdM.[8] Directly influenced by Vallejo, Mujeres de Maiz is also inspired to conceptualize *ceremonia* as an art form and art as a type of spiritual expression. Following their mentor's lead, MdM performs rituals within arts institutions, creates a ritual cycle for communities of color and women, and employs various interventionist tactics that can function as institutional critique. The essay concludes with an observation that Mujeres de Maiz has activated a new political platform for change, one that is deeply personal and yet collectively effective. It is the hybrid, complex, and diverse activities of Mujeres de Maiz that had led to its twenty-five years of generative differential consciousness and praxis.[9] It offers artists and advocates for social justice new strategies for mobilizing and healing.

SPIRITUAL ACTIVISM: INNER WORK / OUTER ACTION

Although Anzaldúa did not coin the term "spiritual activism," she amplified its meaning, particularly how it functions as an epistemology and ethic.[10] As oppositional knowledge, it challenges "official and conventional ways of looking at the world, ways set up by those benefiting from such constructions."[11] It is a metatheory of Anzaldúan thought, which as AnaLouise Keating observes requires examination "of at least ten interrelated Anzaldúan theories" if "a comprehensive analysis of Anzaldúa's spiritual activism" is desired.[12] For the purposes of this essay, I focus on the spiritual because it is essential to her oppositional theory and praxis of spiritual activism. Drawing on ancient wisdom, Anzaldúa posits that the spirit inhabits all creatures and it creates "a deep common ground and interwoven kinship among all things and people."[13] This ontology of interconnectedness and ineradicable relationships therefore informs action. The mobilization of one segment of the planet's residents—women of color, let's say—is partial and incomplete.[14]

Latina feminist theologian María Pilar Aquino made a similar observation when she called for "authentic liberation," the elimination of all suffering due to injustice and violence that is experienced at the personal and social levels.[15] In this way, Aquino acknowledges the matrix of oppression—the interwoven structures and ideologies such as racism, sexism, capitalism, homophobia, environmental devastation, and ableism—and holds accountable the privileged and the oppressed in the call to transform society from its forms of injury and inequality. No residents of the planet—human and nature—are left out of the coalition to create justice and health.

A similar politics of liberatory energies is proposed in the work of José Esteban Muñoz. According to Muñoz, the artistic realm is a site of potentiality, a space-time enunciation of queerness, the not-yet possibility of queer liberation. The aesthetic practices of poetry, performance, visual art, club scenes, and correspondence, argues Muñoz, generate a network of hopefulness, a conceptual making-do that anticipates future sanction.[16] Whereas Muñoz locates transformative power within thought that emerges from aesthetic practice, J. Dolan applauds the value of the spectator in transformation, pointing to the relationship between the performer and the audience as a generative space and time of social change.

To this inclusive, engaged ethic and strategy for social transformation, Anzaldúa adds self-care. The brutality of structural inequalities harms our most inner selves, and thus spiritual activism attends to the personal as well as the social body. Inner work takes many forms, including creative expression, the major activity of Mujeres de Maiz. As Clara Román-Odio argues about Chicana artists and authors, "art and writing become methods to explore this process of reformulation and a significant tool in the creation of oppositional agency."[17] Writing is a form of self-care as it serves as a springboard for critical engagement and consciousness. Anzaldúa views "writing as a form of activism" because it fundamentally engages the mind/body/spirit, and it is a way of "making alliances" because it opens lines of communication.[18] Thus Anzaldúan thought disrupts Cartesian dualities that separate mind from body and Western dichotomies that separate self from other. A holistic understanding of mind/body/spirit leads spiritual activists to nurture their entire being and to understand "inner work" as the first step in healing social ills.[19]

It is important to note that this inner work is not like the egocentric methods of self-help popular psychology or New Age spirituality in which the individual retains their autonomy. Inner work is not intended for "self glorification or other types of solipsistic individualism."[20] Inner work is rooted in the ethic of social justice. As Brenda Sendejo demonstrates in her analysis of Tejana politicians, helping others through political mobilization and spiritual change is the same type of work; it is "interrelated" social justice action.[21]

This orientation may be traced to the influence of Linda Vallejo. As an elder guide, Vallejo's life and work demonstrate a profound Indigenous epistemology that allows her to blend multiple sources of aesthetic inspiration and life experiences into a decolonial imaginary. For more than forty-five years, Vallejo has negotiated a practice that joins arts and spirituality, spirituality and political consciousness, and personal healing and community empowerment. Vallejo's integration of art and life crystallized in the late 1970s when she joined Flores de Aztlán.[22] Vallejo studied Maya and Azteca ritual dance forms with the troupe for over eight years and even after she stopped dancing and teaching, she continued her spiritual devotion. Since the 1980s, she has "poured water" and accepted leadership roles in the practice of North American sacred Indigenous ceremony, eventually bringing her two sons and mentoring other young people in the traditions of healing and homage.[23] She learned these leadership roles at "sweats run by Lakota, Navajo, Chicano, and California Indian tribes," and in turn shared her knowledge through these same ceremonies with the founders of MdM.[24]

Mujeres de Maiz connects political practice and spiritual activism, finding, as do Tejana politicians, that the self and one's ability to transform and employ a critical consciousness are connected to larger social structures.[25] For instance, the workshops that teach the art of herbal steam baths for female reproductive health attend also to the empowerment of women and the ceremony of healing the whole body. Likewise, descriptions for the monthly Full Moon Circle, or Coyolxauhqui Circle, have stated that the talking circle included "self-identified wombyn/womyn/women and grrrls/girls and Queer/Trans, Gender nonconforming individuals."[26] MdM invites participants to share traditional and contemporary Indigenous knowledge and participate in a healing ritual and *platicar*, a verb whose vernacular meaning connotes nonhierarchical, organic, and informal communication. Named for the moon goddess of Aztec cosmology, the circle of participants light candles and share small offerings that adorn the space where they gather. In the circle, *platica* joins the group, through which the listener deems the speaker an expert in *platicando*; professional credentials are not the source of value. Honored speakers are known for their keen ability to listen and anticipate the needs of their audiences.

Because the circle meets in public spaces, such as Hollenbeck Park or Coyolxauqhui Plaza, MdM activates a nonnormative presence, claiming social emplacement in a context of ongoing displacement. Both the park and the plaza are contested sites and document a history of struggle. For instance, against the wishes of Mexican-heritage residents, in 1960 urban planners built the Golden State Freeway across one perimeter of Hollenbeck Park, reducing its size and lake as well as the urban tranquility of the Boyle Heights community. Coyolxauqhui Plaza is a small monument with a public sculpture by David Moreno in City Terrace, a predominantly Mexican-heritage neighborhood of Los Angeles. Dedicated to the Mexica moon goddess, Coyolxauqhui, the plaza was created in 1976 during the Chicano movement, and it historicizes the community but also announces a feminine deity, an intervention against patriarchy. Emplacement—as both a physical and social location—offers a method of healing from injustice, isolation, erasure, or alienation, the strategies of violence established during colonial occupation.[27] In this way, the Coyolxauhqui Full Moon Circle is generative, remedying the historical and ongoing colonial and patriarchal displacements to which Indigenous, Mexican, African, and Chicana/o/x people are subject.[28] This maneuver activates the otherwise ignored, disparaged, and marginalized cultural knowledge for "self-identified wombyn/womyn/women and grrrls/girls and Queer/Trans, Gender non-conforming individuals." This complex list of participants and use of the virgule requires further discussion, and later I engage an analysis of the self-identities of MdM members and participants. At this juncture, I point to the decolonial tactic that operates through the monthly full moon gathering.

Similarly, workshops on vegan cooking contextualize this diet as a form of decolonial foodways, environmental sustainability, and healthy living. A plant-based cuisine is recognized for its lower cholesterol and higher fiber, which are known to reduce the risk of type-2 diabetes, obesity, high blood pressure, and heart disease—illnesses that disproportionately impact communities of color. Vegans also reject foodways that prioritize the human species of the ecosystem and select a plant-based diet because it requires fewer resources, especially water, than an animal-based diet. A plant-based diet may also refuse to treat animals as commodities, a stance that aligns with the philosophy of interconnectedness and sacredness of all beings. Keating's account of spiritual activism is applicable. MdM employs "specific actions designed to challenge individual and systemic racism, sexism, homophobia, and other forms of social injustice."[29] What is fascinating about MdM is the broad range of "specific actions"—workshops for self-defense, women's health, poetry readings, and organic gardening; presentations about nontraditional jobs in communities of color and Chican@ art from the 1960s to the present; and talking circles about sobriety, social justice, sexism, and culturally informed safer spaces.

Fundamental to these actions is the principle of In Lak'ech, which requires bridge-work, a phrase that indicates the cross-race, cross-gender, and other forms of alliance-across-difference that Anzaldúa and Cherríe Moraga acknowledged in their groundbreaking anthology, *This Bridge Called My Back*. Coalition is necessary for social transformation, and MdM has joined in solidarity with a variety of groups, including the Ovarian Psyco Bicycle Brigade, Womyn Image Makers, and People's Yoga, a studio in East Los Angeles, a predominantly Mexican-heritage neighborhood. Without a facility, MdM arts workshops, exhibitions, and productions are staged at community arts venues that echo their mission, and this strategy has produced collaborations at Self Help Graphics & Art, one of the oldest arts organizations to emerge from the Chicano Movement in Los Angeles, as well as institutions that emerged in the twenty-first century, Corazón del Pueblo, Tonalli Studio, and Legacy L.A. The nomadic mode of operation has its benefits and history, which I address in the following section. The consistent need to join in solidarity across difference guaranteed for several years the maintenance of the L.A. Womyn's Calendar, a clearinghouse produced by MdM that announced activities and events in the Los Angeles area that supported individual and community wellness in multiple forms. This calendar was the cyber bridge that facilitated face-to-face connections across social borders throughout the city.

ANTECEDENTS

Mujeres de Maiz embrace and expand the tactics developed during the Chicano movement, specifically among Chicana artists. Las Flores de Aztlan directly and indirectly nourished and inspired the spiritual activism of MdM (plate 1). The dance troupe, which operated from 1979 to 1984 under the direction of Josefina Gallardo, focused on Indigenous spirituality and inextricable relations, blending Native American and Mexican Indigenous as well as Catholic symbols, beliefs, and practices into its work. Las Flores de Aztlan performed *ceremonia* "based on Mesoamerican traditions and values 'while incorporating present day spiritual growth and reality'" and taught workshops about ancient cultures and arts of the Americas, traveling throughout the Southwest to cultural centers, schools, colleges, and public parks and building a network of Indigenous artists, scholars, and community cultural workers.[30] According to Linda Vallejo, Las Flores de Aztlan organically and yet defiantly would hold "ceremonies all over the place."[31] Notably, the troupe utilized the emergent feminist of color tactic of bridge-work and established coalitions throughout the Southwest, performing with the musical group Kukulkán and various Native American collectives. The collaborations of Las Flores de Aztlan challenge the view that Chicana/o indigeneity relied on an "Aztec-centric celebration of the Indigenous past of [Mexico]" while ignoring American Indians and contemporary Indigenous communities of Mexico.[32] Although the dance troupe clearly invoked Aztlan in their name, their sense of this "doubly colonized space" did not "end at the U.S.-Mexico border" as found in other Chicano cultural productions.[33] Their nomadic practice that acknowledges Indigenous presence and land by crediting elders and seeking their permission is a significant form also found among MdM.

Moving throughout California, the troupe produced new rituals that were part of a larger "Chicano calendar of ceremony" to "acknowledge the different directions and the continuation of the cycle of life."[34] The most significant ceremony was Fiesta de Maíz, an annual communal celebration of summer that joined spiritual communities from Los Angeles, San Diego, Sacramento, and the Bay Area. According to religious studies scholar Lara Medina, Las Flores de Aztlan, and two other groups created "the first Fiesta [which] was held in Los Angeles on June 5, 1979." "Esplendor Azteca, the danzante troupe of the now-deceased maestro Florencio Yescas of Tacuba, Mexico,"[35] along with Kukulkán and Calmécac (Nahuatl for "school of learning"), a group of Chicana/o health care professionals that focused on mental health through spirituality, collaborated with Flores de Aztlan to organize the inaugural event.[36] Artists from Self Help Graphics & Art also joined the first collaboration and those from the Royal Chicano Air Force (RCAF) of Sacramento later contributed to the Fiesta. MdM continues this "calendar of ceremony" with talking circles, celebrations to honor the seasons and four directions, and other events that form an annual series of rituals.

Mujeres de Maiz builds on the ethic and epistemology of Las Flores de Aztlan, which simultaneously conceptualized art as spiritual practice and spiritual practice as social engagement. Indeed, at the annual Fiesta de Maíz, Indigenous sensibilities infused celebration with a decolonial consciousness. Corn was presented as more than a food and agricultural resource; it structures Maya religion, and it allowed for sophisticated governance, urban development, art, trade, and migration across the Americas. It is foundational to Indigenous civilization and resilience.[37] With this insight, the organizers described the Fiesta de Maíz as a "ritual of resistance," which supports a new way of thinking about the major food source for Indigenous people of the *Américas*. It validated rather than belittled corn as a crop only fit for animals or eradicated through exploitation of the arable land.

The ritual also challenged "Western norms, which fail to provide young people with rites of passage acknowledging their importance for the future of the community."[38] Fiesta de Maíz centered Indigenous ways of being and knowing and negotiated this epistemology with contemporary Indigenous elders. The ceremony began with the construction of *altares* in homage to the four directions, a Native American practice based on the ontology of interconnectedness. It included a blessing by the elders of the community and the offering of spiritual advice or *consejos* and material gifts to the youth.[39] It concluded with the youth offering their own consejos to the community.[40] The holistic, inclusive, and relational annual ceremony supported the community's health, future, and empowerment. It is this type of interdisciplinary, intergenerational, and intercultural mode that informs the practice and ethics of MdM.

While Chicano nationalists favored neo-indigeneity and "selective[ly] appropriate[ed]" ancient civilizations, namely Mexica, Flores de Aztlan directly worked with contemporary Indigenous communities, an ethic also of MdM.[41] As such, their invocation of "Aztlan" did not reproduce Native American displacement in California but joined with them. Important conversations have yet to occur within Critical Latinx Indigeneities, which can learn from Flores de Aztlan, and its legacy within MdM, that challenges to Chicano indigeneity are generative of coalitions across contemporary Indigenous communities. Furthermore, these coalitions celebrate spatial and temporal concurrence and oscillation, rather than domination over space and time.[42] For Shifra M. Goldman, the art historian who established Chicana and Chicano art criticism as a serious endeavor, it was difficult to see the spatial and temporal oscillation, as she described Flores de Aztlan as "romantic" and "traditional."[43] Both terms were used as critique. Goldman overlooked the use of Maya dance forms as a significant divergence from the Chicano movement's emphasis on Aztec culture, in this case, Mexica danzante. Flores de Aztlan aimed for hemispheric solidarities but understood and refused to collapse differences across various Indigenous communities.

The use of ceremony, particularly within the venues hosting art exhibitions, also confounded critics who inherit the expectation of modernism as the break from tradition, particularly from religion. Chicana artists, such as Vallejo, who enacted *ceremonia* within an art exhibition to bless the space, and the Indigenous practitioners invited to lead these rituals, were expanding rather than contracting aesthetic fields. Exceeding the boundaries of visual arts, for example, Vallejo developed Madre Tierra Press, with coordination from Susan E. King, Women's Graphic Center studio director. This limited-edition offset, letterpress, and silkscreen fine art portfolio premiered at the Woman's Building in 1983. From June to December 1982, Vallejo was invited to develop the production and publication of a portfolio by twelve Chicana artists. She conceptualized a project that would pragmatically address the "economic pressure and lack of support for the arts, [and the fact that] the women artists of [her] community needed a professional publication of their works as well as collective support and networking."[44] The participants included artists Yreina Cervántez, Olivia Sanchez Brown, Cecilia Castañeda Quintero, Anita Rodriguez, Sylvia Zaragoza-Wong, and Linda Vallejo; photographer Judy Miranda; writers and filmmakers Juanita Cynthia Alaniz, Osa de la Riva, Juanita Naomi Quiñonez, and Mary Helen Ponce; dancer Josefina Gallardo; and feminist advocates Rosemary Quesada-Weiner, a leader of Comisión Femenil Mexicana Nacional, and Susan E. King.[45] Vallejo asked them to "respond to the concept of *Madre Tierra*, the 'Great Mother,' in her life. During a series of collective meetings and individual printing sessions, each woman was asked to express her beliefs to the group and finally to design and print a visual image or written work that would reflect her *Madre Tierra* experience."[46] It was an art practice that valued the process of art-making, community formation, and spirituality as much as the product. While an emphasis on women's experiences and especially motherhood had been discredited by Chicano movement politics, Vallejo and her contemporaries were registering a "decolonial motherhood" that challenged the narrow definition of politics and called out patriarchy for its injustices against women and families.[47]

Through *Madre Tierra Press* and Las Flores de Aztlan, Vallejo united spirituality, art, and self-reflection into a public ritual that could inspire observers to contemplate the interconnectedness of the cosmos. This practice that unites spirituality and creativity into a public gesture to celebrate the earth, women, and ancestors has informed MdM.[48] While witnesses in the 1980s may have placed Vallejo's practice within the genre of performance art, the emergent but important media of Los Angeles feminists, these rituals were intentionally not symbolic. According to the artist, she was communicating with and paying homage to the Divine. Her engagement of spirituality within the context of an arts organization transformed the site into sacred space. In short, *within the space of an arts organization*, Vallejo embodies a type of institutional critique not yet theorized by mainstream art historians who compartmentalize the arts and spirituality, especially since modernism became the de facto method of valuation.[49] Vallejo, her collaborators, and MdM use ritual to value womanhood, aesthetics, and Indigenous knowledge against heteronormative and racist propositions.

QUEERING NATIONALISM AND GENDER

Similarly, MdM empowers "mujeres" in their practice but expands notions of womanhood as well as racial and ethnic solidarity. Although a quick reading of the collective could assume it privileges cisgender women because of the English translation of "mujeres," its usage does not mimic conventional or heteropatriarchal meaning. Building on the mobilization strategies of Las Mujeres Muralistas, an arts collective of San Francisco, the group uses "mujeres" as a signifier across difference. In the 1970s, Las Mujeres Muralistas united a diverse group of Latinas who aimed to challenge gender norms and create new imagery for the Mission District, a neighborhood of Latinos in San Francisco. Founding members Patricia Rodriguez, a Tejana who migrated to California to study art; Graciela Carrillo, a Chicana from Los Angeles; Consuelo Mendez from Caracas, Venezuela; and Irene Perez, a Chicana "from a migrant farmworker family that had settled in East Oakland," were joined by other Latina artists, including Susana Cervantes, Ester Hernandez, Xochilt Nevel, Miriam Olivo, and Ruth Rodriguez.[50] Scholars, such as María Ochoa and Guisela Latorre, observe that the collective "created a space" in which their various identities and backgrounds were not "reduced to a polarized expression" based on cultural nationalism. Las Mujeres Muralistas was a platform "for [a] cooperative venture and mutual support."[51] This ability to find unity in difference was an emergent mode among women of color in the San Francisco–Oakland Bay Area, the region that gave rise to the collective behind the anthology *This Bridge Called My Back*. Within Las Mujeres Muralistas, their cultural and individual identities did not become a roadblock to solidarity but the groundwork for the realization that "these distinct groups often shared the same physical and cultural spheres and suffered under the same systems of oppression."[52] This responsive approach to collectivity was strengthened by a cross-ethnic and cross-race aesthetic sensibility as evidence in the mural *Latinoamérica* (1974), which visualizes a pan-Latino cultural setting, mirroring the demography of the Mission District. The mural created a new visual vocabulary in the neighborhood by referencing Bolivian, Peruvian, Guatemalan, Mexican, and Chicano landscapes, symbols, people, and spiritualities.

For MdM, the Spanish-language name speaks to some of the local residents of the Latin American diaspora. Written in Chicano Spanish (the word for corn appears without an accent), the name signals to the long-term Mexican-heritage residents of the region who invented their own living vernacular, *caló*. Artists and participants identify variously: Xicana indígena, Chicana, Salvadoreña, Latina, Native, and Guatemalteca—to name a few social signifiers. Additionally, MdM frequently reaches across racial and hemispheric identities to form coalition with other women and trans people of color, particularly among communities ignored due to the black/white binary and its undercurrent of white racial primacy. MdM has been attentive to violence against Middle Eastern women prior to mainstream media discussions of U.S.-sanctioned regimes of power in the Middle East, North Africa, and South Asia that displaced millions of women and families since the end of the twentieth century. One indication of this transnational coalition has been the inclusion of D'Lo, transgender Tamil-Sri Lankan-American actor, writer, and comedian, as the MC for multiple Live Art Shows that showcase "intercultural, interdisciplinary, and intergenerational" performers at the annual event to honor "International Women's Day, Women's Herstory Month, spring equinox and the Mexica new year."[53] MdM recognizes and celebrates the value of specific cultural heritages otherwise deemed insufficient, backward, or unnecessary by Western hegemony, and the collective rejects the ways in which global capitalism commodifies Indigenous and non-European cultures as exotic or foreign. Thus MdM acknowledges specific cultural, racial, and ethnic identities, *as well as* cross-racial solidarity, a strategy that emerges from the Maya principle, In Lak'ech. Their spiritual activism allows Mujeres to see themselves in the face of others, even as their own identities are clarified, transformed, and mystified.

DISIDENTIFICATION

As noted previously, MdM invites a range of participants, and its narratives echo José Muñoz's concept of disidentification. A common phrase in their online publications speak to the emergent, evolving, porous, and fluid view of their constituents: "self-identified wombyn/womyn/women and grrrls/girls and Queer/Trans, Gender non-conforming individuals." The first two terms (wombyn and womyn) disidentify the gendered identity that embeds masculinity within femininity (wo-MAN). The transgressive nomenclature is rooted in queer, intersex, and African American feminist activism, connecting MdM to a capacious history and community of feminists. It is both an identitarian maneuver and a counter-hegemonic act that opens and challenges narrow readings of identity politics. While some feminists worry about the privileging of biology, MdM expands its activities to include a broad range of "self-identified" individuals as clarified by the extensive use of the virgule: wombyn/womyn/women and grrrls/girls and Queer/Trans, and gender nonconforming individuals. Lived realities are not presumed or subsumed, and the backslash has the ideological function of "challeng[ing] exclusion and encompass[ing] multiple identities."[54] These narrative gestures are an invitation to participants to see and create themselves within and through MdM activities.

More significantly, it is their agency—the ability to self-identify—that becomes the fulcrum for solidarity. That is, self-identification is a mode against the heteropatriarchal violence that unnames, misnames, or obliterates the lives of "wombyn/womyn/women and grrrls/girls and Queer/Trans, Gender non-confirming" people. Rather than social harmony based on shared identity, MdM proposes collaboration based on self-determination.

While scholars and activists have taken a critical view of self-determination since the 1980s, often seeing it as an anachronism or a problematic mode of resistance, MdM values identity as an ethic and epistemology of spiritual activism. One's spiritual health depends upon self-care which includes self-naming. It might appear dated to some critics, but the ability to determine one's identity rather than accept popularly held misrepresentations of mujeres continue to engage a critical consciousness that can support social transformation. The linchpin for MdM is self-identification, a vital stage in the process of change: inner work/public acts, as Anzaldúa notes.

MOVIMIENTO

Enacting the legacy of Chicana feminist visual artists and Chicana feminist thought, MdM forges art, activism, and spirituality into a holistic practice that is mindful of metaphysical connections that urge us to care for ourselves, each other, and our world. The earliest programs of MdM, which I regularly attended, moved mind/body/spirit through song, dance, and invocation. As I note in the opening paragraph about one such experience, *movimiento* is central to the practice of Mujeres de Maiz, and I focus my closing remarks on the significance of movement.

While I acknowledge MdM identify as "spiritual artivists," I have explored their practice as "spiritual activism." These two categories are closely related, and I elected to focus on the phrase coined by Anzaldúa to illuminate collectivity and mind/body/spirit connections. I have also been mindful of how these two terms—spiritual artivists and spiritual activists—are a refusal to reduce their work to the Eurocentric discourse of "social practice," "public practice," and "socially engaged art." As Angelique Szymanek observes in a brief review of "socially engaged, activist, participatory, or new genre public art," these forms of "collaboration, community engagement, and participation as material, methodological, or conceptual artistic practice can be traced to pre- and post-colonial approaches to cultural production" in the Américas.[55] Szymanek follows W. Warner Wood, who observes the "'social practice' of Zapotec weaving" in which familial networks inform the weavers' work and the studios where the collective activity occurs. Similarly, I aim to challenge the myth that public practice is an avant-garde movement spearheaded by European and Euro-American artists of the late twentieth century or by "performative art-works that emphasize dematerialization."[56] Rather, I emphasize how participation is "a response to socio-political shifts" in power.[57] Spiritual activism is a strategy of resistance.

In closing, I turn my attention to the collective's *movimiento*—the communal, individual, somatic, and nomadic campaign for justice. I offer these final thoughts about the centrality of *movimiento*, or as Diana Taylor argues in her search for a term to encompass performance in the Americas, to "*Olin*, meaning movement in Náhuatl." Taylor notes, "*Olin* is the motor behind everything that happens in life, the repeated movement of the sun, stars, earth, and elements." She continues by explaining its meaning in the calendar and the name of a deity who "intervenes in social matters," observing that "the term simultaneously captures the broad, all-encompassing nature of performance as reiterative process and carrying through as well as its potential for historical specificity, transition, and individual cultural agency."[58] This emphasis on "historical specificity, transition, and individual cultural agency" is the collective's signature approach—mobilization of groups of people without denying their identities, engagement in public spaces across the city to center these identities and experiences, and the bustle of activities that inform each other—these approaches are essential to the collective's work, and particularly to the range of work, programs, performances, and projects as well as collaborations and coalitions for solidarity.

The framework of spiritual activism highlights attention to coalition building or bridging with others, and this tactic also requires movement and a strategy of mobility to avoid the limitations of any one ideology, identity, framework, or space. In her analysis of Chicana lesbian feminists' action during the Chicana/o movement, Edwina Barvosa observes that diverse subjectivity requires "cultivation of a geography of selves" or the ability to move and shift one's positions as one moves among a range of people.[59] "This new awareness [among Chicana lesbian feminists]," argues Barvosa, "fostered calls for 'solidarity,' rather than for the identity sameness of collective unity, as an organizing principle."[60] To achieve solidarity, one must shift, morph, and transition among the "geography of selves" that are available, imagined, and formed by the act of forging coalition. Movimiento is animated through relations that redistribute and expose the art historical evaluations and politics of audience engagement. These evaluations include assumed binaries of passive/active audiences in the arts and politics.

As such, *movimiento* and *olin* are the signature tactics for individual and collective experience within Mujeres de Maiz. The collective inspires individuals to shift and change their views of, responses to, and engagements with the world. MdM motivates one to leap to one's feet into action and supports a critical reorientation that moves against the grain of one's thinking. A bedrock for MdM is this inner work as it not only allows for a new approach to *movimiento* and *olin*, but it provides the foundation that allows Mujeres to embrace change. MdM does not settle, idle, or mimic the latest fad; to do so would risk the demise of the coalitions it builds or the destruction of the bridges it has crossed. MdM is constantly reinventing itself with new members, collaborations, or innovative strategies on social and technological platforms. As Chela Sandoval noted about U.S. Third World feminists of color, MdM practices differential consciousness, shifting as needed to modes of resistance that support broader coalitions. The strength of MdM is their willingness to continuously shift, to develop alternative modes of engagement and collaboration. The mantra of American culture and corporate management—change produces fear—does not resonate or find meaning within the collective, because transformation of self and society is both a goal and strategy. Movement is honored. Movement is sought. Movement is realized.

I propose that this investment in *movimiento* and *olin* is a lesson for radical, liberal, and Left social justice activists. The collective has much to offer in its attention to healing from domination, power-over in all forms. Mujeres de Maiz informs us that social justice platforms must be infused with spiritual work, and spiritual work is linked to social justice movements since attention to the self or caring for self allows for nurturing of the social body. The spiritual activism of MdM illustrates that the social body cannot be healed unless inner work is simultaneous and acknowledged as a vital tactic of justice.

NOTES

1. My memory is unclear, but my elder child and I first encountered Mujeres de Maiz at a Summer Institute of MALCS and later through two NACCS Annual Meetings in Chicago, Illinois, in 2002 and in Northridge, California, in 2003.

By the time they reached teenagerhood, they had experienced multiple performances, exhibitions, and ceremonies of MdM. But I might have been holding my son in 2001.

2. Ann Haugo, "Decolonizing Motherhood: Images of Mothering in First Nations Theatre," *Theatre History Studies* 35 (2016): 269; Jill Dolan, *Utopia in Performance: Finding Hope at the Theatre* (Ann Arbor: University of Michigan Press, 2005).

3. Reid Gilbert, "Marie Clement's *The Unnatural and Accidental Women*: Denaturalizing Genre," *Theatre Research in Canada* 42, no. 1–2 (2003): 125–46.

4. Amber Rose González and Michelle L. Lopez joined in 2011.

5. Chela Sandoval and Guisela Latorre, "Chicana/o Artivism: Judy Baca's Digital Work with Youth of Color," in *Learning Race and Ethnicity: Youth and Digital Media*, ed. Anna Everett, The John D. and Catherine T. MacArthur Foundation Series on Digital Media and Learning (Cambridge, MA: The MIT Press, 2008), 82. Although Sandoval and Latorre acknowledge that artists are "committed to transforming themselves and the world," they do not specify the relationship between the artivist and the world, a central component of my argument regarding Mujeres de Maiz and spiritual activism (83).

6. AnaLouise Keating, ed., *Interviews/Entrevistas: Gloria E. Anzaldúa* (New York: Routledge, 2000), 178.

7. Keating, *Interviews/Entrevistas*.

8. Linda Vallejo, interview with Karen Mary Davalos, August 20 and August 25, 2007, Los Angeles, California. CSRC Oral Histories Series, no. 2 (Los Angeles: UCLA Chicano Studies Research Center Press, 2013), 39; Lara Medina, "Los Espiritus Siguen Hablando: Chicana Spiritualities," in *Latina/o Healing Practices: Mestizo and Indigenous Perspectives*, Brian W. McNeill and Joseph M. Cervantes, eds. (New York: Routledge, 2008), 223–47.

9. Chela Sandoval, *Methodology of the Oppressed* (Minneapolis: University of Minnesota Press, 2000).

10. AnaLouise Keating, "Appendix 1: Glossary," in *The Gloria Anzaldúa Reader*, ed. AnaLouise Keating (Durham, N.C.: Duke University Press, 2009), 323.

11. Gloria E. Anzaldúa, "now let us shift . . . the path of conocimiento . . . inner work, public acts," in *This Bridge We Call Home: Radical Visions for Transformation*, eds. Gloria E. Anzaldúa and AnaLouise Keating (New York: Routledge, 2002), 542.

12. AnaLouise Keating, "Shifting Perspective: Spiritual Activism, Social Transformation, and the Politics of the Spirit," in *EntreMundos/AmongWorlds: New Perspectives on Gloria E. Anzaldúa*, ed. AnaLouise Keating (New York: Palgrave Macmillan, 2005), 243 and 253.

13. Anzaldúa, "now let us shift," 567–68.

14. While Sandoval and Latorre's notion of digital artivism acknowledges the necessity of "multidimensional meaning systems," which "provide access to a myriad of cultures, languages, and understandings," it does not depend upon

interconnectedness (83). However, the authors describe how young artists working at SPARC developed a "symbiotic connection" with the residents of Estrada Courts, the public housing site of their digital mural project (95). Spiritual activism seeks alliances across difference not only because one wishes to challenge oppression or "seek egalitarian alliances" (83). Spiritual activism conceptualizes that our very liberation depends upon global equity. Furthermore, spiritual activism is fundamentally a double project of both inner and outer work, an aspect not intrinsic but certainly observed in some forms of artivism. Chela Sandoval and Guisela Latorre, "Chicana/o Artivism: Judy Baca's Digital Work with Youth of Color," in *Learning Race and Ethnicity: Youth and Digital Media*, ed. Anna Everett, The John D. and Catherine T. MacArthur Foundation Series on Digital Media and Learning (Cambridge, Mass.: The MIT Press, 2008), 81–108.

15. María Pilar Aquino, "Latina Feminist Theology: Central Features," *A Reader in Latina Feminist Theology: Religion and Justice*, eds. María Pilar Aquino, Daisy L. Machado, and Jeanette Rodriguez (Austin: University of Texas Press, 2002), 139.
16. José Estaban Muñoz, *Disidentifications: Queers of Color and the Performance of Politics* (Minneapolis: University of Minnesota Press, 1999); José Estaban Muñoz, *Cruising Utopia: The Then and There of Queer Futurity* (New York: NYU Press, 2009).
17. Clara Román-Odio, *Sacred Iconographies in Chicana Cultural Production* (New York: Palgrave: Macmillan, 2013), 56.
18. Keating, *Interviews/Entrevistas*, 206 (first quotation) and 197 (second quotation).
19. Keating, "Shifting Perspective," 244.
20. Keating, "Shifting Perspective," 244.
21. As Brenda Sendejo clarifies in her analysis of Tejana leaders who employ spiritual activism as an ethic, inner work is a form of self-care that continuously looks outward. According to Sendejo, activists such as María Elena Martínez, the first woman to lead a political party in Texas, made "the shift from political activist to spiritual healer [and it was] not such a big leap" (61). Brenda Sendejo, "The Cultural Production of Spiritual Activisms: Gender, Social Justice, and the Remaking of Religion in the Borderlands," *Chicana/Latina Studies: The Journal of Mujeres Activas en Letras y Cambio Social* 12, no. 2 (2013): 58–109.
22. Sybil Venegas, "Walking the Road: The Art and Artistry of Linda Vallejo," in *Fierce Beauty: Linda Vallejo, a Forty-Year Retrospective* (Los Angeles: Plaza de la Raza and Cultural Center for the Arts and Education, 2010), 102. Exhibition catalog.
23. Linda Vallejo, interview with Karen Mary Davalos, 263.
24. Medina, "Los Espiritus," 231.
25. Sendejo, "The Cultural Production of Spiritual Activisms," 64.
26. *Mujeres de Maiz*, Programs. Web. Accessed August 12, 2015.
27. Unlike embodiment, emplacement is a spatial allegory, tactic, or imaginary that does not depend upon representations of the body. This work implies that emplace-

ment can extend the notion of social location because it is both physical and ideological. The central aspect of emplacement is agency. All people have a social location, but emplaced communities are empowered in their sites and discursive places of habitation. Karen Mary Davalos, "The Landscapes of Gilbert 'Magu' Sánchez Luján: Remapping and Reimagining the Hemisphere," in *Aztlán to Magulandia: The Journey of Chicano Artist Gilbert "Magu" Luján*, eds. Hal Glicksman and Constance Cortez (Munich: DelMonico Books-Prestel and Irvine: University Art Gallery, University of California, Irvine, 2017), 37–57. Exhibition catalog.

28. For more on the Coyolxauhqui Full Moon Circles, review chapter 5 by Nadia Zepeda in this collection.
29. Keating, "Shifting Perspective," 242.
30. Medina, "Los Espiritus," 230.
31. Linda Vallejo, interview with Karen Mary Davalos, 40.
32. Maylei Blackwell, Floridalma Boj Lopez, and Luis Urrieta, "Introduction: Critical Latinx Indigeneities," special issue, *Latino Studies* 15, no. 2 (2017): 131. Ella Maria Diaz documents additional collaborations among Chicana/o/x artists and Native Americans and Mexican Indigenous communities at Deganawidah-Quetzalcoatl University (D-Q University) and among the Royal Chicano Air Force. Ella Maria Diaz, *Flying under the Radar with the Royal Chicano Air Force: Mapping a Chicano/a Art History* (Austin: University of Texas Press, 2017).
33. María Josefina Saldaña-Portillo, "Losing It: Melancholic Incorporations in Aztlán," in *Indian Given: Racial Geographies across Mexico and the United States* (Durham, N.C.: Duke University Press, 2016), 197. I am not sure that Las Flores de Aztlan or MdM are melancholic in their invocations of indigeneity or engagement with Indigenous people. Thus I remind readers that Saldaña-Portillo's observations are about a novel and require mixed methods when applied to lived experience.
34. Linda Vallejo quoted in Medina, "Los Espiritus," 231.
35. Linda Vallejo quoted in Medina, "Los Espiritus," 196.
36. Medina, "Los Espíritus," 230.
37. Roxanne Dunbar-Ortiz, "Follow the Corn," *An Indigenous Peoples' History of the United States* (Boston: Beacon Press, 2014), 15–31.
38. Medina, "Los Espiritus," 238.
39. Medina, "Los Espiritus," 238.
40. Medina, "Los Espiritus," 239.
41. Lourdes Alberto, "Topographies of Indigenism: Mexico, Decolonial Indigenism, and the Chicana Transnational Subject in Ana Castillo's *Mixquiahuala Letters*," in *Comparative Indigeneities of the América: Toward a Hemispheric Approach*, eds. M. Bianet Castellanos, Lourdes Gutiérrez Nájera, and Arturo J. Aldama (Tucson: University of Arizona Press, 2012), 40.
42. Maylei Blackwell, F. Boj Lopez, and Luis Urrieta, "Introduction: Critical Latinx Indigencities," *Latino Studies* 15, no. 2 (2017): 126–37; María Josefina Saldaña-Portillo, "Critical Latinx Indigeneities: A Paradigm Shift," *Latino Studies* 15, no. 2 (2017): 138–55.

43. Shifra M. Goldman, "Madre Tierra: una idea, una exposicíon, una publicacion," *La Opinion*, January 1983, 9.
44. *Linda Vallejo*, About, Publications, Critical Reviews, and Interviews, Tierra Madre Press, 1982, Web. Accessed March 17, 2022.
45. Shifra M. Goldman, "Madre Tierra: una idea, una exposicíon, una publicacion," *La Opinion*, January 1983, 8–9.
46. *Linda Vallejo*, About, Publications, Critical Reviews, and Interviews, Tierra Madre Press, 1982, Web. Accessed March 17, 2022.
47. Ann Haugo, "Decolonizing Motherhood: Images of Mothering in First Nations Theatre," *Theatre History Studies* 35 (2016): 269–84.
48. Madre Tierra Press and archival documentation about the project were included in the exhibition, *Doin' It in Public: Art and Feminism at the Woman's Building*, which opened at the Ben Maltz Gallery in October 2011 as part of the Getty Foundation initiative in Southern California, Pacific Standard Time: Art in L.A. 1945–1980; Vallejo again led a ritual blessing at the reception. Her consistent practice as a feminist in the context of male privileging and her specific engagement with California references offers important pedagogical lessons for MdM.
49. Laura E. Pérez, *Chicana Art: The Politics of Spiritual and Aesthetic Altarities* (Durham, N.C.: Duke University Press, 2007).
50. Terezita Romo, "A Collective History: Las Mujeres Muralistas," in *Art, Women, California 1950–2000: Parallels and Intersections*, eds. Diana Burgess Fuller and Daniela Salvioni (Berkeley: University of California Press, 2002), 179; Sybil Venegas, "The Artist and Their Work: The Role of the Chicana Artist," *Chismearte* 1, no. 4 (Fall/Winter 1977): 3–4.
51. María Ochoa, *Creative Collectives: Chicana Painters Working in Community* (Albuquerque: University of New Mexico Press, 2003), 37.
52. Guisela Latorre, *Walls of Empowerment: Chicana/o Indigenist Murals of California* (Austin: University of Texas Press, 2008), 27.
53. *Mujeres de Maiz*, Program Overview, Live Art Show, Web. Accessed March 17, 2022.
54. Karen Mary Davalos and Alicia Partnoy, "Translating the Backlash," *Chicana/Latina Studies* 4, no. 1 (2004): 6.
55. Angelique Szymanek, "Elina Chauvet: Decolonizing Disappearance," *Latin American and Latinx Visual Culture* 4, no. (2022): 64.
56. E. Carmen Ramos, "Printing and Collecting the Revolution: The Rise and Impact of Chicano Graphics, 1965 to Now," *¡Printing the Revolution! The Rise and Impact of Chicano Graphics, 1965–Now* (Princeton and Oxford: Princeton University Press in association with the Smithsonian American Art Museum, 2020), 28. Exhibition catalog.
57. Szumanek, "Elina Chauvet," 64.
58. Diana Taylor, *The Archive and the Repertoire: Performing Cultural Memory in the Americas* (Durham, N.C.: Duke University Press, 2003), 14–15.

59. Edwina Barvosa, "Mestiza Consciousness in Relation to Sustained Political Solidarity: A Chicana Feminist Interpretation of the Farmworker Movement," *Aztlán: A Journal of Chicano Studies* 36, no. 2 (Fall 2011): 127.
60. Barvosa, "Mestiza Consciousness," 129.

BIBLIOGRAPHY

Alberto, Lourdes. "Topographies of Indigenism: Mexico, Decolonial Indigenism, and the Chicana Transnational Subject in Ana Castillo's *Mixquiahuala Letters*." In *Comparative Indigeneities of the América: Toward a Hemispheric Approach*, edited by M. Bianet Castellanos, Lourdes Gutiérrez Nájera, and Arturo J. Aldama, 38–52. Tucson: University of Arizona Press, 2012.

Anzaldúa, Gloria E. "now let us shift . . . the path of conocimiento . . . inner work, public acts." In *This Bridge We Call Home: Radical Visions for Transformation*, edited by Gloria E. Anzaldúa and AnaLouise Keating, 540–78. New York: Routledge, 2002.

Aquino, María Pilar. "Latina Feminist Theology: Central Features." In *A Reader in Latina Feminist Theology: Religion and Justice*, edited by María Pilar Aquino, Daisy L. Machado, and Jeanette Rodriguez, 133–60. Austin: University of Texas Press, 2002.

Barvosa, Edwina. "Mestiza Consciousness in Relation to Sustained Political Solidarity: A Chicana Feminist Interpretation of the Farmworker Movement." *Aztlán: A Journal of Chicano Studies* 36, no. 2 (Fall 2011): 121–54.

Blackwell, Maylei, F. Boj Lopez, and L. Urrieta. "Introduction: Critical Latinx Indigeneities." *Latino Studies* 15, no. 2 (2017): 126–37.

Davalos, Karen Mary. "The Landscapes of Gilbert 'Magu' Sánchez Luján: Remapping and Reimagining the Hemisphere." In *Aztlán to Magulandia: The Journey of Chicano Artist Gilbert "Magu" Luján*, edited by Constance Cortez and Hal Glicksman, 37–57. Munich: DelMonico Books—Prestel and Irvine: University Art Gallery, University of California, Irvine, 2017. Exhibition catalog.

Davalos, Karen Mary, and Alicia Partnoy. "Translating the Backlash." *Chicana/Latina Studies* 4, no. 1 (2004): 6–18.

Diaz, Ella Maria. *Flying under the Radar with the Royal Chicano Air Force: Mapping a Chicano/a Art History*. Austin: University of Texas Press, 2017.

Dolan, Jill. *Utopia in Performance: Finding Hope at the Theatre*. Ann Arbor: University of Michigan Press, 2005.

Dunbar-Ortiz, Roxanne. "Follow the Corn." In *An Indigenous Peoples' History of the United States*, 15–31. Boston: Beacon Press, 2014.

Gilbert, Reid. "Marie Clement's *The Unnatural and Accidental Women*: Denaturalizing Genre." *Theatre Research in Canada* 42, no. 1–2 (2003): 125–46.

Goldman, Shifra M. "Madre Tierra: una idea, una exposicíon, una publicacion." *La Opinión* (Los Angeles), January 1983, 8–9.

Haugo, Ann. "Decolonizing Motherhood: Images of Mothering in First Nations Theatre." *Theatre History Studies* 35 (2016): 269–84.

Keating, AnaLouise. "Appendix 1: Glossary." In *The Gloria Anzaldúa Reader*, edited by AnaLouise Keating, 319–24. Durham, N.C.: Duke University Press, 2009.

———. "Shifting Perspective: Spiritual Activism, Social Transformation, and the Politics of the Spirit." In *EntreMundos/AmongWorlds: New Perspectives on Gloria E. Anzaldúa*, edited by AnaLouise Keating, 241–54. New York: Palgrave Macmillan, 2005.

Keating, AnaLouise, ed. *Interviews/Entrevistas: Gloria E. Anzaldúa*. New York: Routledge, 2000.

Latorre, Guisela. *Walls of Empowerment: Chicana/o Indigenist Murals of California*. Austin: University of Texas Press, 2008.

Medina, Lara. "Los Espiritus Siguen Hablando: Chicana Spiritualities." In *Latina/o Healing Practices: Mestizo and Indigenous Perspectives*, edited by Brian W. McNeill and Joseph M. Cervantes, 223–247. New York: Routledge, 2008.

Mujeres de Maiz, Web. Accessed August 12, 2015, and September 17, 2015; Program Overview, Live Art Show, Web. Accessed March 17, 2022.

Muñoz, José Esteban. *Cruising Utopia: The Then and There of Queer Futurity*. New York: NYU Press, 2009.

———. *Disidentifications: Queers of Color and the Performance of Politics*. Minneapolis: University of Minnesota Press, 1999.

Ochoa, María. *Creative Collectives: Chicana Painters Working in Community*. Albuquerque: University of New Mexico Press, 2003.

Ramos, E. Carmen. "Printing and Collecting the Revolution: The Rise and Impact of Chicano Graphics, 1965 to Now." In *¡Printing the Revolution! The Rise and Impact of Chicano Graphics, 1965–Now*, edited by E. Carmen Ramos, 23–70. Princeton and Oxford: Princeton University Press, in association with the Smithsonian American Art Museum, 2020. Exhibition catalog.

Román-Odio, Clara. *Sacred Iconographies in Chicana Cultural Production*. New York: Palgrave Macmillan, 2013.

Romo, Terezita. "A Collective History: Las Mujeres Muralistas." In *Art, Women, California 1950–2000: Parallels and Intersections*, edited by Diana Burgess Fuller and Daniela Salvioni, 177–87. Berkeley: University of California Press, 2002.

Saldaña-Portillo, María Josefina. "Critical Latinx Indigeneities: A Paradigm Shift." *Latino Studies* 15, no. 2 (2017): 138–55.

———. "Losing It: Melancholic Incorporations in Aztlán." In *Indian Given: Racial Geographies across Mexico and the United States*, 195–232. Durham, N.C.: Duke University Press, 2016.

Sandoval, Chela. *Methodology of the Oppressed*. Minneapolis: University of Minnesota Press, 2000.

Sandoval, Chela, and Guisela Latorre, "Chicana/o Artivism: Judy Baca's Digital Work with Youth of Color." In *Learning Race and Ethnicity: Youth and Digital Media*, edited by Anna Everett, 81–108. The John D. and Catherine T. MacArthur Foundation Series on Digital Media and Learning. Cambridge, Mass.: MIT Press, 2008.

Sendejo, Brenda. "The Cultural Production of Spiritual Activisms: Gender, Social Justice, and the Remaking of Religion in the Borderlands." *Chicana/Latina Studies: The Journal of Mujeres Activas en Letras y Cambio Social* 12, no. 2 (2013): 59–109.

Szymanek, Angelique. "Elina Chauvet: Decolonizing Disappearance." *Latin American and Latinx Visual Culture* 4, no. 2 (2022): 58–74.

Taylor, Diana. *The Archive and the Repertoire: Performing Cultural Memory in the Americas.* Durham, N.C.: Duke University Press, 2003.

Linda Vallejo, About. Publications, Critical Reviews, and Interviews, "Tierra Madre Press, 1982," Web. Accessed March 17, 2022.

Linda Vallejo, interview with Karen Mary Davalos, August 20 and August 25, 2007, Los Angeles, California. CSRC Oral Histories Series, no. 2. Los Angeles: UCLA Chicano Studies Research Center Press, 2013. Web.

Vallejo, Linda. "Artist's Statement." In *Fleshing the Spirit*, edited by Elisa Facio and Irene Lara, 263. Tucson: University of Arizona Press, 2014.

Venegas, Sybil. "The Artist and Their Work: The Role of the Chicana Artist." *Chismearte* 1, no. 4 (Fall/Winter 1977): 3–4.

———. "Walking the Road: The Art and Artistry of Linda Vallejo." In *Fierce Beauty: Linda Vallejo, a Forty-Year Retrospective*, 101–3. Los Angeles: Plaza de la Raza and Cultural Center for the Arts and Education. Exhibition catalog.

ROUND III

LA CULTURA CURA

Artivist Aesthetics

20
Art Is Ceremony

GINA APARICIO

As a young adult, I dedicated my spirit and energia to community activism. I have been an activist in the city of Los Angeles for more than thirty years. While on this path, I discovered how art could be used as a political tool and for personal transformation. The subject matter of my work is influenced by my spirituality, political activism, and cultural-historical background. I see my work as a political act. As an artivist (activist/artist) I use art as a political tool for social justice, to raise human consciousness, and to heal our communities from the trauma caused by colonization and continued violence waged against our communities.

After the passage of NAFTA in 1994, the Indigenous communities of Chiapas and greater southern Mexico took up arms in defense of their existence and ways of life. I was inspired by the Zapatistas to organize for the self-determination of our communities. They led by example on how we can organize to control our own destinies as a people—whether this be creating spaces such as Mujeres de Maiz, or working with the community in the fight to keep the South Central Farm, an important space for the community. It provided a safe space for children, organic foods in a food desert, and medicinal herbs for a vulnerable segment of our community.

I first became engaged with Mujeres de Maiz (MdM) in 1997 at their first Live Art Show at the Popular Resource Center (PRC). I was so inspired by the spirit food these mujeres were sharing. Their voices reflected my experience and the shared experience of the women around me. Although I had worked with several Chicano organizations and held leadership roles within some of them, I had never felt as empowered as I did leaving that event. Those women touched the very core of my espiritu and left a mark that is forever with me. For that, I am most grateful.

My journey with this group of chingonas began in 1998. I received a call from my student activist friend Margaret 'Quica' Alarcón to work on the upcoming zine. I jumped at the chance. Margaret, Felicia 'Fe' Montes, Claudia Mercado, and I worked for several days and nights, piecing together that third zine with little sleep. We sat around a table in Margaret's living room sifting through books and magazines, searching for material. Once in a while, we were lucky enough to all squeeze onto the futon in the living room for a quick power nap before continuing the work. We have come a long way from toiling for hours working on those first zines. Fast-forward over twenty years, and the network created by MdM has brought together a community of mujeres whose original works of art now grace the zine pages. It is a beautiful sight to see all the submissions before us.

I have played many roles within MdM both as a "core member" (decision-making body of the group) and as an individual artist. For the first fifteen years, the core consisted of four mujeres: Felicia, Claudia, Margaret, and myself. Most of the work I did for MdM consisted of helping Margaret with the editing and layout of the zine, photographing the Live Art Shows, and curating the art exhibits. I have been gifted the opportunity to document the medicina offered by all the artists who have contributed to the spirit of MdM throughout the years. Through the taking of the photographs, I have witnessed many magical moments. One that stands out occurred during a collaboration between Susana Baca, Martha Gonzalez (from the band Quetzal), and La Santa Cecilia. I will never forget the moment when La Marisoul's (La Santa Cecilia) voice brought Susana Baca to tears as she sang the lyrics to Susana's song "Maria Lando." It raised the hair on my arms and pierced my spirit. This is but one of many, many, moments that will forever be part of my MdM experience. Photographing and attempting to capture the spirit of all the women of MdM has been a transformative experience. I receive a small piece of each of them with each performance; In Lak Ech (you are my other me).

Taking on these roles within the group has given me the opportunity to engage with the artists' works on an intimate level. Sifting through the submissions of poetry, reading them over and over again while simultaneously looking at the visual art, unearthed our interconnectedness within this cosmic web. The work was a reaffirmation of the road I was on. The women's work "gave me permiso" to create the work I wanted to create despite the resistance from the mainstream art world.

We decided to document our herstory for ourselves. We were creating a safe space for women artists regardless of age, sexuality, ethnicity, or formal training to share of themselves for ourselves, creating sacred space whenever this happened. I think this was especially important for me as a queer Xicana. The collaborations with queer Xicana performance groups Tongues and Butchlalis de Panochtitlan and having transgender MCs D'Lo and Bamby Salcedo helped to wedge a space for the queers of our community. The work on stage and in print has served to question and redefine the social history of our experiences. It created a space where it was safe for my own coming out. I now have a community to belong to.

Women of color artists' work historically and in the present is still pushed to the margins. This is why I feel that the art exhibits curated by Mujeres de Maiz are extremely important. As the former curator for MdM, I felt a sense of urgency to fill this void. Women's art was hung in unconventional venues such as coffee shops, hallways, and basements of community spaces like Casa del Mexicano for an audience that normally would not go to museums or galleries. It is my belief that art is theory and philosophy and instigates discourse. These exhibits have served to bring people together to experience and talk about art.

Mujeres de Maiz has opened up the space for us to tell our stories, to share herstory, to heal our wounds, and to give hope. Mujeres de Maiz has been part of my journey in reconnecting with my spiritual self. The work by all the women throughout the years reminds us what it means to be human. It is my hope that the cultural production of Mujeres de Maiz will create a shift in human consciousness. Like all of creation, the work of these women is imbued with spirit and in constant change. Through this work, we are spiritually connected. Art Is Ceremony.

Humbly,
Gina Aparicio

21
Queer Xicana Indígena Cultural Production

Remembering Through Oral and Visual Storytelling

SUSY ZEPEDA

VISUAL CULTURE is a form of storytelling. Usually storytelling is conceptualized in the form of oral tradition as it is passed on from generation to generation; here I meditate on the possibility of learning or remembering history, ancestry, medicine, language, and other forms of ancient knowledge through visual culture. In particular, I present visual representations that have been intentionally created by queer Latina and Xicana Indígena artists to address colonial forms of epistemic violence or missing memory. Queer Latinas and Xicana Indígenas enact forms of remembering through their art to regain cultural and ancestral memory and story. Building with Indígena women of color artists who were influenced by and connected to Los Angeles–based Mujeres de Maiz since their inception, my analyses take form to focus on visual art as a space of ceremony and healing, where forgotten histories are rewritten from rooted, non-heteronormative matriarchal perspectives. The consciousness of Xicana, Latina, and Indígena women of color formations of collectives who are remembering through ceremony is a generative site of knowledge. The direct participation of many of the featured artists here—including Gina Aparicio, Claudia Mercado, and Dalila Paola Mendez—in the creative circles and visionary events of MdM, as well as the deep friendships, connection, and collaborations with key members of

Mujeres de Maiz, including Margaret 'Quica' Alarcón, Felicia 'Fe' Montes, and Lilia 'Liliflor' Ramirez, illustrates the interconnected community of artists and social justice activists and critical thinkers that frame the remembering and visual storytelling in this essay.

Remembering through storytelling is particularly important in discussions of Xicanx and Latinx communities who have, to differing degrees, been displaced, "de-tribalized," and "de-Indianized" (Gonzales 2012). Colonization was a source of harmful fragmentation for most peoples in Mesoamerica and continues in the present day through colonial legacies of forgetting or misremembering. Cherríe Moraga (2007) suggests that it is important for Xicanas and Xicanos to "re-member" the histories that have been erased due to colonization in order to recover the connections among ancient cultures, stories, art, architectures, languages, spiritualities, and diverse and distinct sexualities. Diana Taylor (2003) sheds light on this debate by speaking of "the colonizing project" and directly addresses the intentional destructiveness of ancestral cultures and memory. Taylor argues, "Part of the colonizing project throughout the Americas consisted in discrediting autochthonous ways of preserving and communicating historical understanding. As a result, the very existence/presence of these populations has come under question. Aztec and Mayan codices, or painted books, were destroyed as idolatrous, bad objects. But the colonizers also tried to destroy embodied memory systems, by stamping them out and discrediting them" (34).

I argue through the work of the featured artists that what continues to exist despite this violence is the sacred knowledge that lives within the people—a resistance spirit, *la palabra* or word, cultural memory, which many times can manifest through visual imaginings and representations, such as sculptures.[1]

Marita Sturken (1997) suggests "that memory is a narrative rather than a replica of an experience that can be retrieved or relived" (7). Memories are not exact evidence of something; instead, the narratives tell collective rememberings or imaginings. She continues, "All memories are 'created' in tandem with forgetting.... Forgetting is a necessary component in the construction of memory. Yet the forgetting of the past in a culture is often highly organized and strategic" (7). Sturken (1997) offers a vital piece of knowledge in this formulation that is needed for remembering, since the forgetting is not random. There are significant reasons for the forgetting, including historical and sexual traumas. As Andrea Smith (2005) argues in her text *Conquest*, sexual violence was a central component of colonization. The effects of colonial legacies are still being felt in epidemic forms in various communities today through incest and other forms of harm, such as domestic violence. There is a need for intentional remembering for the purpose of transformation or healing. I am suggesting that remembering, becoming aware of or clarifying a memory, can assist in the process of healing historical and/or sexual traumas.[2]

The question becomes: How do generations remember particularly when records and memories have been destroyed or mutilated due to forced dislocation? Or as transnational feminist scholar M. Jacqui Alexander (2005) asks, "How, why and under what conditions do a people remember? Do spiritual practices atrophy? Or do they move underground, assuming a different form? What is the threat that certain memory poses?" (293–94). Her theorizations of memory and the sacred prove to be extremely useful for this project. She asks: "How does one know the stories and histories of one's people? Where does one learn them?" Later stating, "We had forgotten that we had forgotten. Missing memory. . . . How will I come to know the stories and histories of *my* people?" (262–63, emphasis original). This is where visual representations can assist to reroot practices and memories that have been displaced over generations. Macarena Gómez-Barris (2009) says of visual art, it "has the capacity to speak to, contest, elaborate upon, and produce collective experiences that escape the domain of 'politics as usual.' . . . Visual art carves out new modes of representation that escape the binary logic of history and memory whose reductionist outcome expresses itself as erasure of the experience of violence" (78–89). The very experience of remembering creates meaning through a particular context (time and space), while bringing life to a specific topic, genealogy, or legacy.

A queer Xicana Indígena methodology of remembering generates a productive tension between colonial and noncolonial frameworks that signify the entangled complexities of historical narratives and memories. While the term queer on its own is often understood as a Western hegemonic term that erases women of color or queers of color, the writing of the phrase "queer Xicana Indígena" signals a disruption or queering of colonial legacies that impose norms of gender, race, sexuality, class, ceremony, and spirituality—actively creating space for decolonized alterities

(Muñoz 1999). Similarly, the use of the "X" in the term Xicana signals a conscious politicized identity that insists on intentionally remembering Indigenous cultures, language, roots, and hidden histories of Mesoamerica (i.e., the concept of Ometeotl; dual energies of male and female) that can be likened to the Native American concept of Two-Spirit (Driskill 2016). Gina Aparicio's work shows the possibilities of remembering through a queer Xicana Indígena methodology.

GINA APARICIO'S CLAY STRUCTURES AS VISUAL STORYTELLING: DISRUPTING BORDERS OF GENDER AND NATION

Sculptor Gina Aparicio, who regards Celia Herrera Rodríguez, Rocky Rodriguez, and other Indígena and Native American women as her mentors, was the featured artist on the cover of the Mujeres de Maiz 2009 annual zine, and an invited artist to the Thirteenth Women of Color Film and Video Festival entitled *Regenerations* on the UC Santa Cruz campus.[3] Aparicio, a self-identified queer Xicana Indígena artist with Apache and Mayan K'iche' lineages, who was born and raised in Los Angeles, exhibited multiple clay sculptures that evoked a deep remembering of tragedy and healing for Indigenous communities of Mesoamerica. Evident in her clay representations are her intense studies of ancient hieroglyphs, close examination of contested Mexican and Latin American histories, as well as her engagement in Xicana/x politics and spiritual practices.

Aparicio's clay sculptures, although created in the modern day, are reminiscent of ancient art forms that simultaneously disrupt and renarrate heteropatriarchal stories by centering mujer or genderqueer generational memory and knowledge. The creation of her art is a ceremony, beginning with her queer feminist Indígena vision guiding the molding of the clay. Aparicio mixes red earth color clay with water as she begins to intentionally create a full female-bodied figure that has Indigenous features and is adorned with ceremonial elements associated with life and death—in a sense creating an earth-centered story in harmony with the four elements (water, earth, air, and fire) and based on her imagination of and connection with ancestors. Aparicio uses a kiln (fire) to solidify the clay sculpture before she paints her creation, to further bring her piece to life. This contemporary appearing sculpture incorporates multiple modern colors (as opposed to other singular-toned sculptures by Aparicio) to show her insistence that *diosas* continue to exist in the current moment (i.e., walk the urban streets of Los Angeles).

Aparicio's art is a form of oral tradition and visual storytelling in the sense that she creates a revised narrative that is rooted in gender balance and a remembering that Indigenous women led and continue to lead and practice ceremony today (Boone and Mignolo 1994). According to Taylor (2003), "Cultural memory is, among other things, a practice, an act of imagination and interconnection" (82). Cultural memory requires a deep focus and belief in something more than what is immediately visible in historical narratives or representations. As Taylor argues, "Sometimes memory is difficult to evoke, yet it's highly efficient; it's always operating in conjunction with other memories" (82). For Aparicio, constructing memory through her clay structures is a disruption to male-centered Indigenous narratives, such as Chicano cultural nationalism and Chicano assertions of Aztlán, that disremember the significant role of female or queer counterparts. Aparicio's artwork appeared in the Mujeres de Maiz zine in 2006, and has continued to be part of the archive of this long-time-running self-identified women of color zine that made intentional space for critical lens, and the building of matriarchal feminist knowledges.

In this sculpture, Aparicio is also remembering the process of rerooting, or creating an Indigenous-centered ceremonial space for Xicanxs and Latinxs who are in diaspora. Patrisia Gonzales (2012) argues, "Indigenous Mexican practices in Mexico and the United States are examples of how communal peoples maintain ancestral practices without a defined communal base" (235). Further suggesting, "Indigenous/traditional medicine creates a relationship with nature, the place-cosmos. Through activating Indigenous values of respect, responsibility, and renewal, disconnected original peoples can restore their teachings and cultures. They can change the effects of domination" (235). Through Aparicio's careful and intentional art piece she creates a space that allows for connection and ultimately healing from colonial legacies.

Aparicio's sculpture, titled "In the Spirit of the Ancestors" (figure 21.1a), features a 4-foot, 9-inch Indígena mujer, a sort of replica of Aparicio herself, sitting in prayer. Made of clay, she resembles the red earth

FIGURE 21.1 Gina Aparicio, 2005. "In the Spirit of the Ancestors," Clay. Gina Aparicio.

and wears moon-shaped earrings to show her connection to the stars and cosmos.[4] She is holding both of her arms and hands out to the heavens with her head in a similar incline, signaling a humble connection to the ancestors above and below. A heart-centered necklace lines her yellow-green top, while her belt holds a calavera (skull) at her core, sitting cross-legged and rooted in blue jeans and matching green shoes. According to Aparicio, the skull signifies cycles of life and rebirth experienced many times during a lifetime, directly challenging linear notions of life and death, while the heart of the necklace is representative of the way one connects with spirit, through the corazón.[5] Her left hand has a swirl or spiral etched in her palm, a symbol that rethinks time, space, and story, representing nonwestern circular ways of imagining those concepts. Her black hair is pulled back in a braid, signaling an urban diosa en ceremonia, prayer.

In the *Regenerations* Art Exhibit display (figure 21.1b), she sits with burgundy maize (corn) in her right hand on top of a layer of red-colored rocks, with ceremonial elements around her, including sage, feathers, a rattle, a lit candle, and a ceramic mug with water—strongly resembling an altar for sacred teachings and cleansing ceremony (Halfmoon 2006). The practice of ceremony is a method of survival that provides growth of spiritual consciousness for Indigenous people who have been "detribalized" (Gonzales 2012). Cleansing ceremonies are grounded traditional ways to do healing work when someone experiences a form of trauma—that is, susto (fear), vergüenza (shame), and tristesa (sadness) (Román 2012). Using artistic representation and visual culture as a means to pass on stories and sacred teachings are significant for evoking memory and forgotten histories since practices such as cleansing ceremonies (limpias) are not easily represented through the written word. Aparicio's work encourages remembering of sacred healing tools that can be used on an everyday basis to connect with spirit, thus not requiring a connection to an outside institution (i.e., church).

Aparicio's exhibition setup further illuminates her process of ceremony and vision in constructing this piece. Aparicio said about this sculpture:

> A lot of times people see Indigenous cultures as something that is dead, as something that no longer exists . . . it is very much alive, and it's alive

in us and we have a responsibility to keep those things alive for the future generations, so it's an attempt to document our history, to document the lineage that has been passed down and to leave that for future generations. So she's bringing in a lot of these metaphors, but very contemporary, she is like a goddess, but she has on jeans and shoes for instance . . . She is not the traditional, what you are used to seeing, maybe an unclothed goddess. (Halfmoon 2006)

Aparicio's intention for this sculpture was that it would bring together "things that have been passed on from generation to generation, over hundreds and hundreds of years, through our mythology, through our stories, through our oral traditions, and through our spirituality and spiritual practices" (Halfmoon 2006). Her efforts to create this piece of visual culture are a direct response to colonization and legacies of forgetting ancestral connections. I witnessed the possibility of passing the sacred knowledge represented by this art piece when a young woman of color from Los Angeles, who traveled with Aparicio and other mujeres from Los Angeles, explained to a two-year-old the sacred elements that surrounded the sculpture. This young woman's knowledge reflected a deep wisdom by enunciating the story and uses of the ceremonial elements; she explained the process of burning sage, sounding a rattle, and lighting a candle as a form of prayer.[6] She explained how anyone could use these tools, giving the young one permission. As a participant observer, this moment made clear to me the possibility of passing generational knowledge through cultural production. It also demonstrates how the formation of an art exhibit in women of color, Chicana, Latina, and Indígena space allowed for subaltern and sacred knowledge to be remembered in a respectful and interactive way.

DECOLONIZATION OF AZTLÁN

The decolonization of Aztlán is a complicated task, however, as Chicana feminists have successfully theorized critiques of heteropatriarchy, exclusivity, and male dominance; this has led to a reconceptualization of Chicano cultural nationalism. Strengths of this framework and movement are critiques of imperialism, racist structures, and the search for

Indigenous roots. Aparicio's work is an example of honoring the land through ceremony, without continuing the colonial legacy of territorial regulation through borders, a practice the concept of Aztlán ironically purports. Through the decolonization of Aztlán, there is a possibility to reconstruct a relationship with the land that is not based on ownership or re-colonized borders. Through a queer Xicana Indígena methodology there is intentional respect and solidarity building with Indigenous peoples who are connected to the land. Property is a white supremacist notion rooted in colonization that requires adherence to the "pillar of genocide" as theorized by Andrea Smith (2006), and is based on the elimination or disappearance of Native American peoples. Similarly, Morgensen (2011a) argues, "White supremacy and settler colonialism are interdependent and must be theorized together" (109).

Aztlán, like Chicano nationalism, has been severely contested and disrupted by Chicana and Latina feminists (Ramírez 2002; Fregoso and Chabram 2006; Blackwell 2011). The mythical homeland of Aztlán was based on a notion of territory that positioned the ancestors of Chicanos as the original peoples of the U.S. Southwest, disregarding other Indigenous peoples and histories. The settler colonial logic of Aztlán was central to the formation of Chicano cultural nationalism. It emerged as a result of the 1848 Treaty of Guadalupe Hidalgo and Mexican "loss of land," which ended the war between the U.S. and Mexico. The treaty legalized the "transfer" of land from Mexico to the United States, including California, Texas, Arizona, Colorado, New Mexico, and Nevada, among other territories. In addition to land that was taken by force and subsequent reconstructing of political nation-state borders, racial hierarchies were established through the divisive language of the Treaty of 1848.

A critical Xicana Indígena methodology asks, What does focusing on the "loss of land," due to the Treaty of Guadalupe Hidalgo in 1848, obscure in terms of ancestry in Central Mexico and a shared history with Native peoples? The mythical formation of Aztlán was an important strategic formation for Chicanos who had been forcibly displaced during the conquest and the construction of nation, and thus denied access to Indigenous historical narratives, languages, and cultures. Still, the ownership claim to the land known as the U.S. Southwest must be uprooted within Chicano/a consciousness.[7] Employing Indigenous decolonization as a methodology facilitates the disrupting of the settler colonial logic emphasized by Chicanos who claim Aztlán as a literal territory without the acknowledgment of other tribes and peoples. Further, I argue that the focus on the legacies of the U.S.-Mexico war is limited because it overlooks the Spanish conquest in central Mexico as a significant moment of colonization for Chicanos. Critically revisiting the history of Mesoamerica, particularly from a feminist perspective, makes Indigenous and genderqueer ancestry become increasingly central to forgotten stories of the "Mexican-American." As Blackwell (2011) argues, Aztlán made women "invisible through the construction of nationalist patrimony that universalizes masculine subjects through the category of 'Chicano,' encoding a gendered mode of remembrance" (95).

Aparicio's vision and creation of "In the Spirit of the Ancestors" shows the layers of sacred knowledge that are informed by a spirit of resistance to the annihilation of Indigenous cultures. Central to Aparicio's narrative is a concern for future generations to know non-heteronormative Indigenous cultures, histories, and spiritual practices that have been disappeared, or read as nonexistent in modern-day society. Her effort to produce this representation allows the viewer to integrate contemporary forms of an urban Xicana who is walking a spiritually connected road, ancestry in the present day. This is of particular significance because, according to Gonzales (2012), "the ceremonial discourse and rites were precisely the spaces of Mesoamerican knowledge that the Spanish sought to annihilate" (71). It is to the conquest of Indigenous people by the Spanish that I move to through continued analysis of Aparicio's clay structures that assist in remembering forgotten histories.

CUICA MAQUIXTIA, NAHUATL LANGUAGE, AND FORMATION OF MEXICAN NATIONALISM

Aparicio displayed another clay sculpture at the *Regenerations* art exhibit. It features "a woman crucified on the cross," who is "impregnated and her womb is the earth,"[8] a representation that is reminiscent of an outcast who challenges dominant structures (figure 21.2). According to Aparicio, her name in Nahuatl is Cuica Maquixtia, "which translates into she who sings to be free, she's blind folded" (Halfmoon 2006); she is unclothed, and she wears a long braid. Her hands and feet are literally crucified, nailed, and tied on the large cross behind her. In this extraordinary political sculpture, Aparicio expresses her critique of "issues from institutionalized religion to patriarchy," formations of dominance that were central to the conquest of Indigenous people in Mesoamerica (Halfmoon 2006). This sculpture visually represents the colonization by the Spanish Crown in the early 1500s and the resulting disruption of Indigenous spiritual practices and ways of life through their forced disconnection with the land. It is significant that Aparicio created this artwork to remember the trauma experienced by the ancestors of "detribalized" and "de-Indianized" Xicana/x and Latina/x. Cuica Maquixtia opens a path for healing.

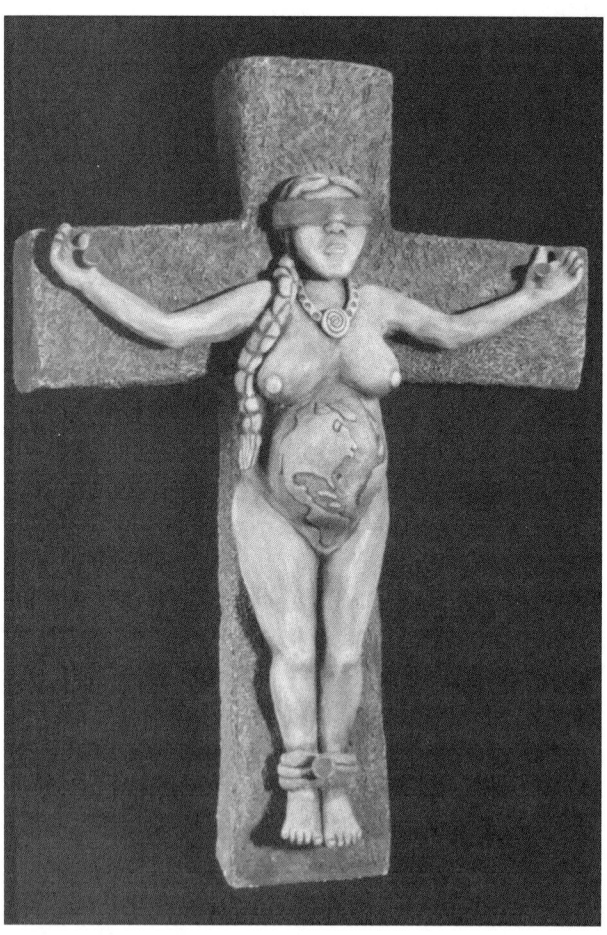

FIGURE 21.2 Gina Aparicio, 2004. "Cuica Maquixtia" (She who sings to be free, in Nahuatl.) 27"×19"×7", clay. Gina Aparicio.

Māori scholar Linda Tuhiwai Smith (1999) identifies "Remembering" as one of "Twenty-Five Indigenous Projects." Smith (1999) writes, "The remembering of a people relates not so much to an idealized remembering of a golden past but more specifically to the remembering of a painful past and, importantly, people's responses to that pain" (146). In this case, Aparicio creates a stunning piece of art as a response to layers of complicated histories that caused multiple forms of destruction through forced dislocation, sexual violations, and intentional erasures of spiritual practices. Smith (1999) continues, "Both healing and transformation become crucial strategies in any approach which asks a community to remember what they may have decided to unconsciously or consciously forget" (146). Through a queer Xicana Indígena tracing of colonial historical occurrences it is possible to bring sanación or healing to the ancestors of displaced peoples, by remembering the dominant forces of conquest.

Aparicio, with this layered and complex piece, critiques the imposition of Christian ideology and a white-centered racial hierarchy, while centering a female-gendered body that holds the earth in her womb.[9] Fittingly, Alexander (2005) suggests, "If healing work is a call to remember and remembering is embodied then we want to situate the body centrally in this healing complex" (316). Aparicio's sculpture accomplishes this by centering a naked body of a full-figured Indigenous mujer that is rarely seen or honored in dominant forms of religion. According to Guillermo Bonfil Batalla (1996), the process of forced Christianization can be conceptualized as the de-Indianization of a population.[10] Aparicio's piece is a resistance to the de-Indianization that resulted from colonization: "De-Indianization is a historical process through which populations that originally possessed a particular and distinctive identity, based upon their own culture, are forced to renounce that identity, with all the consequent changes in their social organization and culture. De-Indianization is not the result of biological mixture, but of the pressure of ethnocide that ultimately blocks the historical continuity of a people as a culturally differentiated group" (Batalla 1996, 17).

During colonial times, in what became New Spain or colonial Mexico, the mixed-blood mestizo had higher authority than the Indigenous (pure blood), simply because mestizos possessed Spanish blood. Historian María Elena Martínez (2008) names this "limpieza de sangre," which translates to "purity of blood."[11] Martínez argues, "Spanish notions of purity and impurity of blood were fictions, ideological constructs based on religious and genealogical understandings of difference that despite their invented nature were no less effective at shaping social practices, categories of identity, and self-perceptions" (61).

Within this fictive spectrum of "purity and impurity" blood characterization, Indigenous people were deemed to have "stained ancestry." One of the biggest fears the Spanish Crown held was that converted people, even those who accepted baptism, would not let go of their ancestral beliefs. As a result of this fear based on fiction, Martínez (2008) described, "Indigenous people were . . . policed and punished" for religious "transgression" (101). This historical context is operative in narrating the purpose of Aparicio's remembering while creating Cuica Maquixtia.

COMPLEXITIES OF NAHUATL LANGUAGE AND "INDIAN" IDENTITY

Aparicio's earth-toned provocative sculpture has a Nahuatl name. This is also a significant form of remembering since Nahuatl was a dominant Indigenous language that is often associated with the Aztec, since the Aztec were the ruling power during the Conquest in the early 1500s.[12] Batalla (1996) makes a striking argument about the language of Nahuatl, in relation to domination and conquest; he says, "Nahuatl was the preferred tongue, and its teaching was proposed as a general method of facilitating preaching in all of New Spain. To a large extent the 'Nahuatlization' that can be observed in many parts of the country resulted more from missionary action than from Aztec expansion. . . . The ability to communicate was converted into a means of control and domination" (87).

Nahuatl was used widely in New Spain and among Indigenous people in the Americas until 1821, the year that Mexico became a nation (Forbes 1973), although the widespread use of the Nahuatl language was not necessarily by choice. To reduce the effort in learning multiple Indigenous languages, the Spanish rulers mandated the use of Nahuatl by all the tribes as the language of communication.

This example shows us the complexity and cooptation of the language. Aparicio purposefully names this piece in Nahuatl to remember and reroot the language in its Indigenous context through a strategy of decolonization. Aparicio says of the significance of using Nahuatl, it is "one of the Indigenous languages from the central valley of Mexico, and so in an attempt to try to preserve those Indigenous languages . . . so many have been lost. Not lost, but . . . very violently taken away . . . so it is an attempt to preserve that and to reintroduce that into the community . . . in Los Angeles" (Halfmoon 2006).

It is a layered and complicated history that surrounds the Indigenous language of Nahuatl. Its reclamation despite the misuse by colonial forces is significant, as is the tracing, honoring, and learning of other Indigenous languages that have been disappeared or are currently marginal to the Spanish language (a colonial language). Language holds knowledge, history, and culture.[13]

Aparicio, who is Apache through her matrilineal side and Guatemalan (Mayan K'iche') through her patrilineal side, has several other clay figures that are named in the Nahuatl language, actively remembering and centering an Indigenous worldview. The exposure of this language to her (mostly urban and "detribalized") audiences provides a consciousness of Indigenous concepts not available if Chicana/x and Latina/x are only engaging with the Spanish and English languages. Aparicio's artwork links an analysis of colonization to the ever-receding access and fragmented or forgotten knowledge concerning Indigenous languages, cultures, and spiritual practices that was connected with the formation of the Mexican nation.

A central project in the establishment of the Mexican nation, similar to earlier forms of colonization, was to de-Indianize the people so that Indigenous and ancestral roots were not the center of identity formations or understandings of self. Instead, a mixed-blood or mestizo race took form that was legitimated because of its malleability within the imperial world; most importantly for the purposes of colonial strategy, it eliminated the "Indian." As Indigenous scholar Renya Ramirez (2002) argues, "The dominant discourse says that Indian identity must remain silent and hidden," "in both Mexico and the United States, the Indian is supposed to disappear" (6). Ramirez further argues that "if a criterion utilized in the United States to determine Indian identity were employed in Mexico, almost ninety percent of Mexican population has enough Indian blood to be considered Indigenous, if Mexicans knew their tribal ancestry. These figures demonstrate how the Mexican Nationalist narrative [of] mestizaje has decreased the power of the numerically strong Indian population in Mexico" (4).

This knowledge of ancestry is particularly significant in that, as Ramirez notes, "if mestizos in Mexico decided to identify as Indians, it could transform the political and ethnic composition in Mexico dramatically" (4). Ramirez offers an important argument for interrogating the categorization of mestizo, which as a form of identity can homogenize, and consequently can impede the work of tracing one's ancestral lineage.[14] Similarly, Batalla (1996) critiques the way the Aztecs are centralized in narratives of Indigenous people in Mesoamerica. He suggests that their hypervisibility obscures other Indigenous tribes and, as a result, Indigenous people in Mesoamerica tend to be subsumed, homogenized, or assimilated into the categories of a constructed nation, such as Azteca-Mexica, Mexicana/o, or Mexican American. There is an argument here to reclaim Indigenous roots, subjectivity, and methodologies, while doing the work to excavate one's familial history for tribal affiliations that go beyond the popularized or dominant narratives that Chicanos and Chicanas, or Latinas or Latinos tend to claim. I now turn to a discussion of Womyn Image Makers, a filmmaking collective who joined forces to support each other on their journeys to tell their stories and remember.

WOMYN IMAGE MAKERS: COMMUNAL AND COLLABORATIVE DISRUPTIONS OF HIERARCHIES

Womyn Images Makers (WIM) came together in May 2000 (Mercado 2001). This collaborative of queer Indígena Xicanas and a Centroamericana who have roots in El Salvador, Guatemala, Mexico, the San Francisco Bay Area, and East Los Angeles collaborated and coconspired together for over ten years. They individually or collectively belong to other LA-based collectives such as Mujeres de Maiz, In Lak Ech, and EpiCentro. The four members who made up this nonhierarchal Indígena centered filmmaker collective were Maritza Alvarez, Aurora Guerrero, Dalila Paola Mendez, and Claudia Mercado. According to Mercado (2001), "These urban Xicana, Indígena, Mestiza filmmakers and visual artists . . . share a passion for representing our stories: sensual morena narratives, obsidian experimental digital collages, slice of life adventures and herstorical ancestral portraits" (29).

They build on a Xicana Indígena subject formation that is transnational and diasporic, in the sense that it defies the boundaries of nation-state demarcations. Aurora explains, "Latinos who identify as Xicanas are starting a resistance to mainstream culture and colonialism and have a spiritual base that is rooted in their indigenous ancestry."[15] In their films, there is a visible constant connection with Indigenous practices—spirituality, prayer, and ceremony are central elements of their storytelling. Queer Xicana filmmaker Aurora Guerrero recalls the emergences of her spiritual practices that influence her visual storytelling:

> For me, my identity as a mujer Indígena really surfaced when I started to learn about my history and that was [during] my freshman year in college, so coming into my identity as a Chicana meant wanting to learn more about my own history. [I started] reading about other people who weren't ashamed of acknowledging their Indigenous ancestry, I felt a very profound need to connect to that, it felt very organic.... I felt an immense pull to come back to my spiritual self and so I started to connect to Indigenous practices, mostly through Native North American sweats, Lakota sweats and then Diné tipee ceremonies, and I had done a few Mexican Indigenous sweat lodges. I really started to connect my spirituality, between 18 and 24, my Indígena side, and then I started connecting beyond that to Santería which brings a lot different spiritual practices together, from the Indigenous, to the Catholic, to the African and that is what feels like home to me because its representative of all my ancestry.[16]

Aurora's story demonstrates the non-linear complexity of her spiritual journey, as well as her influence and connection with multiple forms of spirituality, including the influence of Native North American practices.

The four mujeres who make up Womyn Image Makers (WIM) joined forces and created a sacred space, mirroring Mujeres de Maiz, to build collective trust for storytelling through film, "with the intentions of opening up dialogue and documenting their art and methodologies of collaboration and visual art production" (Alvarez and Zepeda 2006, 128). Their filmmaking was groundbreaking, as queer Indigenous-identified mujeres who collectively burned sage and copal, participated in ceremony, and mentored a youth circle. Their intentional collaboration defied Hollywood's individualistic film industry strategies, as well as Hollywood's whiteness and heteronormativity. WIM also defied dominant structures through critiques of colonization, imperialism, retelling histories of violence, and addressing the complexities of war and police brutality. As independent filmmakers, WIM managed to not only put the stories of Indigenous-identified queer women of color on the big screen, but intentionally worked to create a space for women of color and people of color to be a part of the filmmaking crew—as a result, opening doors for aspiring artists to develop their creative talents and receive guidance in the process of film production.

Womyn Image Makers methodologies for creating art and storytelling are reflective of a larger collective vision that can be encapsulated in what Mendez named the philosophy or legacy of Indigenismo, which she also referred to as "people of the land." Mendez, who handles the production design in the collective, suggests that "*indigenismo* or people of the land" is "reflective of our working-class backgrounds, and how we realize that we have to work together as a whole and that each of us has our strengths and we can build upon that.... [T]he way that we are doing it is through visual communication, a visual language" (Alvarez and Zepeda 2006, 130). It is insightful to see how the philosophy of Indigenismo is conceptualized by Mendez and then applied as a practice within this filmmaker collective. Their form of collaborating is a manifestation of ceremony, again similar to MdM. Womyn Image Makers created a circle of creativity with one another that honors everyone's work, talents, and vision. Guerrero, remarks, "we are really creating something very new. We don't really have anyone, at least within filmmaking, to model ourselves after, so we are creating a new space" (Alvarez and Zepeda 2006, 129).[17] With these reflections both Mendez and Guerrero show not only the significance of their work for future generations, but also how their critiques of hierarchy and individualism are central to their methodology and ceremony of filmmaking and community building.

PURA LENGUA: PRACTICING DECOLONIZED FILMMAKING

As previously mentioned, the four collaborators have roots in various regions of Latin America, hold different familial histories of migration to the United States, and have traveled to different parts of the world. It was their particular life histories and experiences that inspired their collective critical perspective of nation-state politics and their desire to constantly make visible the violences and injustices inflicted on poor, working-class, queer, and Indigenous communities.[18] It is an awareness of colonial legacies and fierce critique of neoliberal politics that seeps through the central themes of WIM's intense short film *Pura Lengua* (All Tongue). This eleven-minute short film is based on real events that were scripted by Maritza Alvarez, the director of photography. Alvarez, notes that WIM is often referred to as a "gang" because of the way they present themselves collectively. She received funding and access to equipment through a Los Angeles–based film school to produce Womyn Image Makers' award-winning film *Pura Lengua* (Alvarez and Zepeda 2006).

This groundbreaking short film, shot with a backdrop of the L.A. punk scene, features an urban queer Xicana's story of healing from heteronormative and state violences. According to Mendez, it was a "one-week shot" with "long hours" that was filmed while the cast and crew were also working full-time or part-time jobs aside from the making of the film.[19] Their efforts to produce this film reflect the vital impulse of grassroots collective creativity mirrored in women of color methodologies.

The storyline of the film *Pura Lengua* features the tragic and healing narrative of an urban Xicana's experience and struggle with queer love and heteronormative state violence. The connections between the different layers of state and colonial violence are shown through the main protagonist, Reina Armas (played by Karla Legaspy), an urban Xicana from Los Angeles, whose heart is broken by her woman lover and whose body is beaten by the police, reflecting the layers of violence in her urban environment.

The film begins with a community poetry reading where Reina turns to an Indigenous women's drumming collective and asks for a "beat." Reina's poetic storytelling ensues with the shake of a rattle and Reina remembering the call she made from a California jail, proclaiming, "They fucked me up," referring to the police beating she received. Betrayed by her queer lover, who decided that her son "needed a father," the film flashes to Reina sharing story and drink at Placita Olvera with friends to relieve her heartbreak. Reina finds a turquoise necklace on display that resembled a necklace she was wearing, one that Reina's ex-lover had honored her with and won't accept back when they broke up; her ex-lover insisted she keep it since her grandmother, whom the necklace originally belonged to, "would have liked for you to have it."

The contradictions of the necklace resembling the store display angered Reina. Especially when the white-appearing store owner from Delaware asked Reina accusingly if she will be "buying anything." Reina reacts by saying "I guess you would call this a free market." All collides in the next scene as the disgruntled owner calls the police to notify them of Reina's supposed criminality. When the police arrive, they accusingly ask her, "Why are you running?" This moment critically makes visible the way neoliberal policies (i.e., NAFTA and state police) function as structures of domination. This is further enacted when Reina responds to the interrogation of where she got her necklace: "From my girlfriend you pinche puerco." The cop replies, "So you like pussy, huh?" Confirming that her story is plausible, yet due to her resistance as a brown queer Indigenous womyn, she is in violation of the law and will suffer the consequences. The film ends with Reina speaking her truth in a circle of mostly women, "armed by her ancestors," a force that cannot be taken away.

This short film identifies heteronormativity as a form of relational and state violence where patriarchy and racism meet as systemic culprits that have been internalized and legitimized in multiple spaces. Reina is fully aware of these contradictions, and WIM's filmmaking supports the main character's growing awareness of the injustices she is experiencing. It also shows the implications of colonial history and cross-border neoliberal policies in the urban environment of Los Angeles. Simultaneously, the film collaborative's intentionality in representing Reina's healing through poetry, drumming, and storytelling offers the viewers and the protagonist a way to deal with the layers of violence in her complex urban landscape.

What is perhaps most impressive about this film collaborative is their dedication to breaking with the hierarchies of filmmaking and working as a collective to tell their personal stories, what Mendez called "stories from spirit," narratives that have a meaning and purpose.[20] In addition to their methodology of working in a communal collective, Aurora, who described the making of *Pura Lengua* as "a combination of guerrilla filmmaking skills with dashes of formal training," said, "We have lots of respect for each other as artists, which makes it easier for us to trust each other when it comes to making those spontaneous creative decisions. We're also similar communicators. We're both good listeners and extremely patient."[21] A collective dream WIM held, before they parted ways, was to start a Xicana/x and Latina/x community media center with a theater and gallery space, a place where community members could learn storytelling and filmmaking skills to write and create representations of their own narratives.

CONCLUSION

This essay traced how queer Xicana Indígenas, Latinas, and Indigenous women of color consciousness and collectivity create art and space to do the work of remembering and healing. The work of the cultural producers primarily happening in the LA area is threaded with the vision and praxis of Mujeres de Maiz in various ways, including in the Live Art Shows and other forms of collaboration. I have shown how the featured cultural producers in this essay participate in various forms of ceremony and actively work to evoke ancestral memories in shared spaces and through practices of creative ritual. Both their visual productions and process of creating are forms of ceremony. These artists provide a space of healing for communities who have been disconnected from their ancestry. They intentionally work toward decolonizing Indigenous lineages, and regaining knowledges and cultural memory through intentional critique of heteropatriarchal state and nationalist politics.

Through their own narratives and visual representations these queer Xicana Indígenas are doing the collective work of remembering and decolonizing knowledge with the purpose of regaining cultural memory. The artistic production of these cultural artists and visionaries, as well as their methods of collaborating to create sacred knowledge, contributes to queer Xicana Indígena and Latina discourses of remembering. The decolonized subjectivities these artists create for themselves are a direct result of their respective self-reflection and self-naming, as well as a testament to their tracing of Indigenous ancestry.

Within the subjectivity of Xicana Indígena presented here there is a desire to connect with the land, despite the disconnection that has occurred due to violence. Xicanas are actively doing the work to acknowledge settler colonial legacies and the displacement of Native

American peoples. There is an intention to build solidarity, dialogue, and spaces of healing despite the missteps of early formations of Chicano nationalism.

Memory, the way one remembers; forgetting, what is left out or forgotten due to traumas; and historical narratives of ancestry have also been central themes in this chapter. The work of remembering makes it possible to piece together expressions, perspective, and theories through mediums of alternative (creative) methodologies. These representations can engage the complexities of difference and the interconnections of local and global relations of power. The remembering I focus on occurs through various forms of cultural production, including media-film, music, poetry, sculpture, or a fusion of these. The process of remembering entails enacting ceremony to recall ancient memories, stories, and practices whose existence has been previously threatened by forms of colonization (i.e., de-Indianization and detribalization). Remembering is about healing. The purpose of remembering is to enable the telling of a story or the retelling of forgotten or misremembered history, and the creation of subaltern historical narratives that open space for transformation. The "remembering" I conceptualize here facilitates a "rerooting" in the present moment through a revised perspective on the importance of restoring the connections among history, culture, language, land, and spirituality.[22]

NOTES

Reprint with minor edits of Susy Zepeda, "Queer Xicana Indígena Cultural Production: Remembering Through Oral and Visual Storytelling," *Decolonization: Indigeneity, Education & Society* 3, no. 1 (2014): 119–41.

1. The emphasis on images and performance echoes the insightful formulation that Taylor (2003) draws in her critique of writing that was introduced by the Conquest, that is, "The writing = memory/knowledge equation is central to Western epistemology" (24). Taylor argues, "Although the Aztecs, Mayas, and Incas practiced writing before the Conquest—either in pictogram form, hieroglyphs, or knotting systems—it never replaced the performed utterance. Writing, though highly valued, was primarily a prompt to performance, a mnemonic aid" (17).
2. This logic follows that of post-traumatic stress, when one becomes aware of what caused the trauma that knowledge facilitates the path of overcoming the memory.

3. The Research Cluster for the Study of Women of Color in Collaboration and Conflict film festival organizers coordinated with the Nineteenth Annual MALCS (Mujeres Activas en Letras y Cambio Social) Summer Institute, titled: *Transfronteras: Generations and Geographies. Activistas en la lucha!* (August 2–5, 2006) to host an artist exhibit where Aparicio and others were featured. University of California, Santa Cruz.
4. Aparicio Interview, 2013.
5. Aparicio Interview, 2013.
6. It is significant to note that the burning, lighting, or offering of sage is primarily a Northern Native American practice that has been adopted by Xicanas/os and Latina/os. In Mexico and other places in Latin America, it is copal that is burned, lit, and offered during ceremony. The Catholic Church makes use of frankincense during occasional services, showing how a colonial institutional force co-opted ceremonial elements of the people.
7. Both Saldaña-Portillo (2003) and Contreras (2008) make similar arguments.
8. Halfmoon (2006). This image appears on page 64 of Hidalgo de la Riva (2006) special issue, *Chicana Spectators and Mediamakers*.
9. As argued by Martínez (2004), particularly in her arguments of la "limpieza de sangre."
10. Bonfil Batalla (1996) details, "The colonial enterprise engaged in destroying Mesoamerican civilization and stopped only where self-interest intervened. When necessary, whole peoples were destroyed. On the other hand, where the labor force of the Indians was required, they were kept socially and culturally segregated" (62).
11. Martínez (2008) argues further, in the Americas, "the colonial discourse of purity of blood was . . . initially propelled by the Christianization project and by Spanish distrust of the religious loyalties of Jewish converts—by religious utopias and anticonverso sentiment" (129).
12. Bonfil Batalla (1996) claims, "Mexico City is the place with the largest number of speakers of indigenous languages in all the Americas" (52).
13. For an important discussion on Chicanos/as and variations and uses of the Spanish language, review Anzaldúa (2007), "Chapter 5: How to Tame a Wild Tongue," in *Borderlands/La Frontera: The New Mestiza*.
14. Chicana writer Ana Castillo does this form of ancestral tracing in her 1995 text, *My Father was a Toltec*.
15. *Pure Filmmaking: "Pura Lengua,"* CreativePlanetNetwork.com, http://www.creativeplanetnetwork.com/digital-cinematography/news/pure-filmmaking-"pura-lengua"/6716, accessed December 2, 2013.
16. Guerrero Interview with author, 2013.
17. Mercado, script supervisor of *Pura Lengua*, further observes, "There are other Xicanas and Latinas that have been making films and Latinos that have been making films, but they have been following the conventional protocol of the system, following the hierarchy of filmmaking . . . and there was no collective or

collaborative collective of *mujeres* [that could help us]. We had to go to each other to help feed our dream and make it possible" (Alvarez and Zepeda 2006, 130).

18. WIM's second short film, *Viernes Girl*, directed by Aurora Guerrero and funded by HBO has a marked scene when one of the leads, a queer Salvadoreña who lives in Pico Union, "flips-off" a poster representation of the civil war in El Salvador. Although this film is humorous in nature, the collectives' critiques of repressive nation-state politics make the final cut.

19. Mendez Interview with author, 2010.

20. Mendez Interview, 2010.

21. *Pure Filmmaking: "Pura Lengua,"* CreativePlanetNetwork.com, http://www.creativeplanetnetwork.com/digital-cinematography/news/pure-filmmaking-"pura-lengua"/6716, accessed December 2, 2013.

22. Central to this remembering are critical forms of mapping race, gender, sexuality, and class in all its complexities and structures—an analytic that is akin to what Lugones (2008) calls "the modern/colonial gender system," which she partly characterizes as a form of "intersectionality" that has been theoretically formulated by women of color feminists. Lugones (2008) illuminates, "Intersectionality reveals what is not seen when categories such as gender and race are conceptualized as separate from each other" (4).

REFERENCES

Alexander, M. Jacqui. 2005. *Pedagogies of Crossing: Meditations on Feminism, Sexual Politics, Memory, and the Sacred*. Durham, N.C.: Duke University Press.

Allen, Paula Gunn. 1989. "Lesbians in American Indian Cultures." *Hidden From History: Reclaiming the Gay and Lesbian Past*, edited by M. B. Duberman, M. Vicinus, and G. Chauncey Jr., 106–16. New York: New American Library.

Alvarez, Sandra, and Susy Zepeda. 2006. "Womyn Image Makers: A Colectiva of Queer Indígena Visionaries." In *Chicana Spectators and Mediamakers: Imagining Trans-Cultural Diversity*, edited by Osa Hidalgo de la Riva. Special issue, *Spectator: USC Journal of Film and Television Criticism* 26, no. 1 (Spring): 127–34.

Anaya, Rudolfo. 1989. "Aztlán: A Homeland Without Boundaries." In *Aztlán: Essays on the Chicano Homeland*, edited by Rudolfo A. Anaya and Francisco Lomeli. Albuquerque: University of New Mexico Press.

Anzaldúa, Gloria. 2007. *Borderlands/La Frontera: The New Mestiza*, 3rd ed. San Francisco: Aunt Lute Books.

———. 1998. "To(o) Queer the Writer—*Loca, Escritora y Chicana*." In *Living Chicana Theory*, edited by Carla Trujillo, 263–76. Berkeley, Calif.: Third Woman Press.

Bacchetta, Paola. 2007. "Introduction to Third Edition: Circulations: Thinking with Gloria Anzaldúa in Paris." In *Borderlands/La Frontera: The New Mestiza*, 3rd ed. San Francisco: Aunt Lute Books.

Blackhawk, Ned. 2006. *Violence of the Land: Indians and Empires in the Early American West*. Cambridge, Mass.: Harvard University Press.

Blackwell, Maylei. 2011. *Chicana Power! Contested Histories of Feminism in the Chicano Movement*. Austin: University of Texas Press.

Bonfil Batalla, Guillermo. 1996. *México Profundo: Reclaiming a Civilization*. Translated by Philip A. Dennis. Austin: University of Texas Press.

Boone, Elizabeth Hill, and Mignolo, Walter, eds. 1994. *Writing Without Words: Alternative Literacies in Mesoamerica & the Andes*. Durham, N.C.: Duke University Press.

Boyd, Nan Alamilla. 2008. "Who Is the Subject? Queer Theory Meets Oral History." *Journal of the History of Sexuality* 17, no. 2: 177–89.

Brown, Lester B., ed. 1997. *Two Spirit People: American Indian Lesbian Women and Gay Men*. Binghamton, N.Y.: Haworth.

Carrasco, David. 2008. "Imagining a Place for Aztlán: Chicanismo and the Aztecs in Art and Resistance." In *The Aztec World*, edited by Elizabeth M. Brumfield and Gary M. Feinman, 225–40. New York: Abrams.

Castillo, Ana. 1995. *My Father Was a Toltec and Selected Poems 1973–1988*. New York: Norton.

Contreras, Sheila. M. 2008. *Blood Lines: Myth, Indigenism, and Chicana/o Literature*. Austin: University of Texas Press.

De la Mora, Sergio. 2006. *Cinemachismo: Masculinities and Sexuality in Mexican Film*. Austin: University of Texas Press.

Denetdale, Jennifer Nez. 2007. *Reclaiming Diné History: The Legacies of Navajo Chief Manuelito and Juanita*. Tucson: University of Arizona Press.

Driskill, Qwo-Li. 2016. *Asegi Stories: Cherokee Queer and Two-Spirit Memory*. Tucson: University of Arizona Press.

Driskill, Qwo-Li, Daniel Health Justice, Deborah Miranda, and Lisa Tatonetti, eds. 2011. *Sovereign Erotics: A Collection of Two-Spirit Literature*. Tucson: University of Arizona Press.

Estrada, Gabriel S. 2007. "An Aztec Two-Spirit Cosmology: Re-sounding Nahuatl Masculinities, Elders, Femininities, and Youth." In *Gender on the Borderlands: The Frontier Reader*, edited by Antonia Casteñeda with Susan H. Armitage, Patricia Hart, and Karen Weathernon, 10–14. Lincoln: University of Nebraska Press.

Forbes, Jack D. 1973. *Aztecas del Norte: The Chicanos of Aztlán*. Greenwich, CT: Fawcett.

Foucault, Michel. 1980. *Power/Knowledge: Selected Interviews and Other Writings, 1972–1977*, edited by Colin Gordon. New York: Pantheon Books.

Fregoso, Rosa Linda. 2003. *meXicana Encounters: The Making of Social Identities of the Borderlands*. Berkeley: University of California Press.

Fregoso, Rosa Linda, and Angie Chabram. 2006. "Chicana/o Cultural Representations: Reframing Alternative Critical Discourses." In *The Chicana/o Cultural Studies Reader*, edited by Angie Chabram, 26–32. New York: Routledge.

Gluck, Sherna, in collaboration with Maylei Blackwell, Sharon Cotrell, and Karen S. Harper. 1998. "Whose Feminism, Whose History? Reflections on Excavating the History of (the) U.S. Women's Movement(s)." In *Community Activism and Femi-*

nist Politics: Organizing Across Race, Class, and Gender, edited by Nancy Naples, 31–56. New York: Routledge.

Goeman, Mishuana. 2013. *Mark My Words: Native Women Mapping Our Nations.* Minneapolis: University of Minnesota Press.

Gómez-Barris, Macarena. 2009. *Where Memory Dwells: Culture and State Violence in Chile.* Berkeley: University of California Press.

Gonzales, Patrisia. 2012. *Red Medicine: Traditional Indigenous Rites of Birthing and Healing.* Tucson: University of Arizona Press.

Griswold del Castillo, Richard. 1990. *The Treaty of Guadalupe Hidalgo: A Legacy of Conflict.* Norman: University of Oklahoma Press.

Guerrero, Aurora. 2013. Keynote: LGBTQIA Western Regional College Conference, University of California, Santa Cruz, February 24, 2013.

Guerrero, Aurora, and Claudia Mercado. 2010. "Screening and Discussion of Films: *Lagrimas de Café*, *Pura Lengua*, and *Viernes Girl.*" American Studies 157: Sexual Identities and Communities Course, University of California, Santa Cruz, Fall 2010.

Halfmoon, Mark with Gina Aparicio, Monica Enriquez, Aurora Guerrero, and Dalila Paola Mendez. 2006. "Voices." Interview. 13th Annual Women of Color Film Festival. Santa Cruz Community Television, Santa Cruz, Calif. August 3, 2006.

Hanh, Thich Nhat. 1992. *Touching Peace: Practicing the Art of Mindful Living.* Arnold Kotler, Ed. Drawings by Mayumi Oda. Berkeley, Calif.: Parallex Press.

Herman, Judith. 1997. *Trauma and Recovery: The Aftermath of Violence from Domestic Abuse to Political Terror.* New York: Basic Books.

Kaiser, S. 2005. *Postmemories of Terror: A New Generation Copes with the Legacy of the "Dirty War."* New York: Palgrave Macmillan.

Latina Feminist Group. 2001. "Introduction: *Papelitos Guardados*: Theorizing *Latinidades* through *Testimonios*." In *Telling to Live: Latina Feminist Testimonies*, edited by The Latina Feminist Group, 1–24. Durham, N.C.: Duke University Press.

Leyva, Yolanda Chavez. 1998. "Listening to the Silences in Latina/Chicana Lesbian History." In *Living Chicana Theory*, edited by Carla Trujillo, 429–34. Berkeley, Calif.: Third Woman Press.

Lugones, María. 2008. "The Coloniality of Gender." *Worlds and Knowledges Otherwise* 2 (Spring): 1–17.

Martínez, María Elena. 2008. *Genealogical Fictions: Limpieza de Sangre, Religion, and Gender in Colonial Mexico.* Stanford, Calif.: Stanford University Press.

Mercado, Claudia. 2001. "Womyn Image Makers: Las Nuevas Doñas?" *Tongues Magazine* 1: 29–30.

Moraga, Cherríe. 1993. "Queer Aztlán: The Re-formation of Chicano Tribe." In *The Last Generation: Prose and Poetry*, 145–74. Boston: South End Press.

———. 2001. *The Hungry Woman.* Albuquerque: West End Press.

———. 2011. *A Xicana Codex of Changing Consciousness, Writing 2000–2010.* Drawings by Celia Herrera Rodríguez. Durham, N.C.: Duke University Press.

Moraga, Cherríe, and Celia Herrera Rodríguez. 2007. "Mission Statement." La RED Xicana Indígena.

Moraga, Cherríe, Celia Herrera Rodríguez, David Carrasco, and Dr. Loco. Book Reading and Panel: *A Xicana Codex of Changing Consciousness, Writing 2000–2010*. Stanford University, January 17, 2012.

Morgensen, Scott. 2011a. *Spaces Between Us: Queer Settler Colonialism and Indigenous Decolonization*. Minneapolis: University of Minnesota Press.

Morgensen, S. 2011b. "Unsettling Queer Politics: What Can Non-Natives Learn from Two-Spirit Organizing." In *Queer Indigenous Studies: Critical Interventions in Theory, Politics, and Literature*, edited by Qwo-Li Driskill, Chris Finley, Brian Joseph Gilley, and Scott Morgensen, 132–52. Tucson: University of Arizona Press.

Muñoz, José Esteban. 1999. *Disidentifications: Queers of Color and the Performance of Politics*. Minneapolis: University of Minnesota Press.

Pérez, Emma. 1999. *The Decolonial Imaginary: Writing Chicanas into History*. Bloomington: Indiana University Press.

———. 2003. "Queering the Borderlands: The Challenges of Excavating the Invisible and Unheard." *Frontiers* 24, no 2/3: 122–31.

Ramírez, Catherine S. 2002. "Alternative Cartographies: *Third Woman* and the Respatialization of the Borderlands." *Midwestern Miscellany* 30: 47–62.

Ramirez, Reyna. 2002. "Julia Sanchez's Story: An Indigenous Woman Between Nations." *Frontiers: A Journal of Women's Studies* 23, no 2: 65–83.

Román, Estela. 2012. *Nuestra Medicina: De Los Remedios Para el Aire y Los Remedios Para el Alma*. Bloomington, Ind.: Palibrio.

Saldaña-Portillo, María Josefina. 2003. "Toward an American 'American Studies': Postrevolutionary Reflections on Malcolm X and the New Aztlán." In *The Revolutionary Imagination in the Americas and the Age of Development*, edited by M. Saldaña-Portillo, 259–90. Durham, N.C.: Duke University Press.

Smith, Andrea. 2005. *Conquest: Sexual Violence and American Indian Genocide*. Cambridge: South End Press.

———. 2006. "Heteropatriarchy and the Three Pillars of White Supremacy: Rethinking Women of Color Organizing." In *Color of Violence, The INCITE! Anthology*, edited by INCITE! Women of Color Against Violence, 66–73. Cambridge: South End Press.

———. 2010. "Queer Theory and Native Studies: The Heteronormativity of Settler Colonialism." *GLQ: A Journal of Lesbian and Gay Studies* 16, no. 1/2: 41–68.

Smith, Linda Tuhiwai. 1999. *Decolonizing Methodologies: Research and Indigenous Peoples*. New York: Zed Books.

Soto, Sandra K. 2010. *Reading Chican@ Like a Queer: The De-Mastery of Desire*. Austin: University of Texas Press.

Sturken, Marita 1997. *Tangled Memories: The Vietnam War, The AIDS Epidemic, and the Politics of Remembering*. Berkeley: University of California Press.

Taylor, Diana. 2003. *The Archive and The Repertoire: Performing Cultural Memory in the Americas*. Durham, N.C.: Duke University Press.

Wilson, Angela Waziyatawin. 2005. *Remember This! Dakota Decolonization and the Eli Taylor Narratives*. Lincoln: University of Nebraska Press.

22

Bringing Art to the People

Decolonizing Art Spaces and Exhibitions

MICHELLE L. LOPEZ

THE ANNUAL art exhibition of Mujeres de Maiz (MdM) takes place during the spring season.

In the early years, the exhibition was part of their Live Art Show, but eventually, it became a separate event of its own. Rather than being held in a traditional gallery, the exhibitions would take place in nontraditional spaces: local community centers on the eastside of Los Angeles such as Casa del Mexicano, Corazón del Pueblo, and Self Help Graphics & Art, breaking down elitist notions in art presentation. If a community center was not available, MdM would have the exhibition in local coffee shops, hallways, and basements—any place that had a wall they could use. They sought local community members as their audience, not the usual gallery or museumgoers. Sometimes their exhibition would be up for a month, sometimes one day depending on what the space would permit.

Art creation by artists associated with MdM transcends art for viewing pleasure and contemplation—it sometimes calls for spontaneous participation. At one of the Live Art Show events, for example, a collaborative and spontaneous onsite mural was created by Yreina Cervántez, Blossom, Noni Olibisi, Petal, Summer, Timoi, Marisol Lydia Torres, and Rachel Negrete Thorson. Each artist was able to create in the moment as their spirit moved them. MdM also pushes art creation beyond the wall and gallery space through the use of public performance. They believe that in order to truly bring art to the people, you must go to and be where people are. This means going out to perform in the street, in marches, at parks, on sidewalks, and in barbershops; anywhere there is a potential for an audience. This essay will explore the importance of the content and symbolism in some of the artworks that have been presented at MdM exhibitions and the ways the collective decolonizes art and exhibition spaces by bringing art to the people in their communities.

MUJERES DE MAIZ AND THE GODDESS COYOLXAUHQUI

One remedy has involved looking to the stories created by our ancestors. A popular image used by the artists of Mujeres de Maiz is the Mexica[1] goddess Coyolxauhqui who has been embraced by contemporary Chicanas. Since the Chicano Movement of the 1970s and the discovery of the Coyolxauhqui stone in 1978, Chicanas have been drawn to the image. Artists have been using her likeness in art, jewelry, and clothing ever since. The interest in Coyolxauhqui sprouted out of the Chicano Movement when people of Mexican descent living in the United States began to embrace, identify, and claim their Indigenous roots.

The Coyolxauhqui stone was found in February of 1978 during the excavation of the Templo Mayor in Mexico City, when electrical workers made an interesting discovery. They had unearthed a carved pinkish stone that was more than ten feet wide, featuring a depiction of the Mexica moon goddess Coyolxauhqui in the moment after she had been dismembered by her half-brother Huitzilopochtli.[2] Archeologists found fragments of offerings and colonial rubble on the stone leading them to believe she had been buried where she was originally placed—at the base of the great pyramid in what was once the capital of the Mexica empire, Tenochtitlan.[3] The stone of Coyolxauhqui was placed at the base of the temple in order to symbolize the reenactment of Huitzilopochtli killing his sister, and throwing her dismembered body down Mount Coatepec.[4]

The goddess Coyolxauhqui comes from the postclassic period of Mesoamerica and there are several variations of her myth. The most popular version is that she was the half-sister of Huitzilopochtli and "she symbolically represents the Mexica's first victorious conquest, for in both, Coyolxauhqui challenged Huitzilopochtli, only to be defeated."[5] Coatlicue, the mother of Coyolxauhqui and Huitzilopochtli, became pregnant one day while sweeping. A mysterious ball of feathers appeared, made its way into her skirt, and impregnated her. Because of the mysterious circumstances of her pregnancy, Coatlicue's children became enraged and sought to kill her. Coyolxauhqui, the only daughter of Coatlicue, led her four hundred brothers, called the Centzon Huitznahua, in an attack upon their mother.[6] Coatlicue was able to communicate with her unborn child Huitzilopochtli while he was in her womb. She relayed to him the tragic situation that was happening with her other children, but Huitzilopochtli assured his mother that he would take care of her. On the day Coyolxauhqui and her forces were about to strike and kill Coatlicue, Huitzilopochtli was born fully grown, wearing full war regalia, ready to fight. He immediately killed his sister by decapitating her, and then he proceeded to chop off her limbs and threw them down the side of Mount Coatepec. He then turned to kill many of his brothers. The ones who escaped became the stars in the night sky.

To fully understand the impact of Coyolxauhqui on the contemporary Chicana psyche, it is important to also look closer at the Coatlicue myth to gain a better understanding of how Coyolxauhqui relates to her mother. Coatlicue or Snake Skirt is Mother Earth in most legends. In some myths, parts of her body formed South America. She also goes by other names and titles including Ilamatecuhtli, which means Old Goddess; Itzpapalotl, meaning Flint Butterfly; and Tonantzin, meaning Our Mother.[7] Some believe that she was a shapeshifter with her favorite form being a woman with talons, wearing a skirt of snakes. In this form, she is adorned with a necklace made of the skulls, hands, and hearts from her sacrificed victims.[8]

There is little written about Coatlicue's relationship with her only daughter Coyolxauhqui. From what has been written, one can gather that Huitzilopochtli was the favored child of his mother. In her essay "Dismemberment and Reintegration: Aztec Themes in Contemporary Mexican Practice," Patricia Michán described Coatlicue as "an archetypal image of the Great Mother with her polarities. As positive, she suggests religious order and respectful cleanliness. She sweeps the temple steps. As a negative figure, she is terrifying, depicted with snakes and skulls on her head and skirt. She is a devouring mother who would hold her children in submission."[9] One could say this mirrors the relationship a single mother might have with her children. The mother is the giver of life, the one who keeps the house together, but she must also be the disciplinarian. To a child, this could be terrifying. Michán continues, "Coyolxauhqui is sitting under a tree crying about the absence and abandonment of her mother Coatlicue that with the pregnancy of her son to be born would accentuate."[10] Favoring sons over daughters is common in many cultures. However, this tradition remains prevalent within Latino cultures in the United States, which is illuminated by the myth of Coatlicue and her relationship to her children. Like Coatlicue's reverence for Huitzilopotchli, males are often favored within the Latino family unit. Patriarchal dynamics are common, and these dynamics have been a topic of debate and discussion in Chicana feminist discourse for years. Unfortunately, patriarchy continues to be embedded into religion and the social constructions we are surrounded by.

Some of the artists of Mujeres de Maiz have been drawn to the Coyolxauhqui image because they are able to see themselves reflected in her. Coyolxauhqui was torn apart, dismembered, and abandoned psychologically by her mother in favor of her new son. Many Chicanas have felt as though they have also been torn apart by the world, physically and psychologically ripped to pieces. They are constantly being pulled in different directions by home, work, family, friends, and marriage, metaphorically cut into pieces and dismembered, with each piece taking care of something or someone. Michán described the identity for women of Mexican descent as "the product of the interweaving of two cultures in Mexico, the pre-Hispanic and the Spanish, both of which have been imprinted on the collective psyche, influencing the role of women in their relationships and in society at large. The relationship between Coyolxauhqui and Coatlicue illustrates an archetypal configuration behind women's entrapment with their mothers, who along with their religiosity, women have no sense of worth or empowerment. The over-responsibility and tendency toward self-sacrifice has become the imprinted pattern of emotional intoxication and masochistic purgation."[11]

Despite these struggles, Chicanas manage to pull themselves together. In this day and age, we are seeing more and more Chicanas getting advanced degrees, sometimes multiple degrees, holding high positions, and healing the community, because they are piecing themselves back together. Coyolxauhqui serves as a reminder that out of tragedy something beautiful can be born, which has led to increased use of her image by Chicanas in general and by Mujeres de Maiz in fashion, ritual, and art in particular.

For some, the goddess Coyolxauhqui is associated with the moon and women because the cycles of the moon resemble a woman's monthly menstrual cycle. In some legends, she is understood as the moon because the sun Huitzilopochtli vanquished her. As the sun rises the moon is extinguished every day. MdM honors Coyoloxauhqui's connection to the moon in their monthly "Coyolxauhqui Full Moon Circle" ceremonies that have been organized and held since 2010.[12] In these talking circles, women gather under the full moon to share their stories, providing a forum for women to express concerns and situations they may be experiencing in their lives, in a safe space. It is an opportunity for women to come together, support each other, and assist in the healing process. Felicia 'Fe' Montes expressed her own personal feelings toward the moon goddess, saying, "Coyolxauhqui womynifests [sic] in many ways for me. She is the moon goddess, the broken sister/sistar, the hurt women, the healing women, the strong warrior, and the leader of many (her 400 brothers/sisters the stars). Many Xicanas including me relate to her because our own experiences of pain and violence, but also the resiliency to heal and transform from it."[13] The support system of the talking circles not only brings women together that identify with their Indigenous roots and ancestors, but it also provides them a platform to heal. González observes, "The circle is organized around Indigenous teachings of respect, healing, interconnectedness, and the notion that women are sacred carriers of knowledge and culture."[14]

Chicana writer Gloria Anzaldúa extends our understanding of Coyolxauhqui by likening the goddess to the writing process. She eloquently described written drafts as Coyolxauhqui, stating:

> The Coyolxauhqui you put together is a grotesque figure with arms sticking out of her back, her skull hanging between her legs. She has eye sockets for knees. You pull your hair and snarl at the screen. You will have to take the text apart bone by bone; go through psychic dismemberment once more; fly apart, implode, splinter once more. This stage of writing feels violent y

siempre te desmadra (and always messes you up). This stage reminds you of helping your mother desgranar (peel) corn, scattering the hard kernels and then waiting for them to sprout. The second time you re-member the bones, Coyolxauhqui emerges less malformed. The text begins to take comely shape, begins to discover its own grace, its own organic force.[15]

Anzaldúa describes how one puts Coyolxauhqui back together through the editing process, rewriting until your paper is complete, making Coyolxauhqui whole again. The talking circles for many are a step on the journey to becoming whole again.

Artists from Mujeres de Maiz have utilized various methods and mediums to depict Coyolxauhqui, from literal representations mirroring

FIGURE 22.1 Rosalinda Ruiz, *Ascension*, oil on canvas. Photograph provided by Mujeres de Maiz.

the traditional Coyolxauhqui stone to more contemporary interpretive themes. A painting completed by Rosalinda Ruiz titled *Ascension* is an example of a more traditional representation (figure 22.1). In this image, Coyolxauhqui is ascending to her place as the moon, joining her brothers the Centzon Huitznahua in the sky. There are also nontraditional images such as Lilia Reynoso's *Coyolxauhqui: Pachamama Lucharemos Contigo*, which combines Coyolxauhqui with the myth of Mother Earth (figure 22.2). Coyolxauhqui is joined together with the goddess Pachamama from Inca mythology. The combination of Indigenous thought represents the different combinations of Chicana ancestral heritage, serving as a reminder that not all Chicanas share Aztec heritage. The text on her shirt translates to "we will struggle with you." This statement within the image is another reflection of the struggles that Chicanas face daily but it also points to the struggles faced by Mother Earth.

Coyolxauhqui being put back together represents mujeres pulling themselves together as women and as warriors, ready to face the battle of daily life. Lilia "Liliflor" Ramirez depicted Coyolxauhqui as a warrior in her piece titled *Coyo Comes Alive* (plate 18). In this image, Coyolxauhqui is painted in warrior regalia. She is not wearing the traditional Mexica garb that was worn by warriors in the ancient empire, but a contemporary feminine style of war gear. Coyolxauhqui has readied herself for battle and looks as though she is ready to make her move to fight patriarchy and colonial systems of oppression. There is a hummingbird within the image that most likely represents her brother Huitzilopochli. The Nahuatl word for hummingbird is huitzilin, which comes from his name. Hummingbirds are also believed to be warriors that died and have been reincarnated.

Crystal Galindo's piece *Coatlicue State: Josie Channels the Goddess* speaks directly to themes of decolonization and empowerment of women (plate 14). Crystal's work is known to celebrate multidimensional Chicana identity. She frequently uses bright colors and women with diverse body types as models. The woman at the center of this painting is Coatlicue and she is a queen showing off her necklace made of human hearts and hands. At its center is a black widow, indicating her fearlessness of death. She appears confident and powerful through her body language as she gazes directly at the viewer. The expression on her face seems to be saying, "Be confident, be powerful, and love who you are." Taken together,

FIGURE 22.2 Lilia Reynoso, *Coyolxauhqui: Pachamama Lucharemos Contigo*, paint, collage. Photograph provided by Mujeres de Maiz.

the artwork discussed thus far displays the goddess Coyolxauhqui in a variety of ways that intrigue viewers.

The image of Coyolxauhqui has been used by Chicana artists for quite some time. Yreina Cervántez, whose influence and guidance have been instrumental to MdM over the years, created a lithograph triptych in 1995 titled *Nepantla* that incorporates Coyolxauhqui, which Laura Pérez described in this way:

[It] works to destabilize racist and sexist histories of representation. She reinscribes alternative and healing visions of reality. The first panel introduces nepaltilism as an ongoing struggle between two cultural legacies, as revealed in their different ways of seeing: that of an ostensibly universal, European scientific perspective that measures difference against the standard of European man, and that of American Indian worldviews, represented by several objects symbolic of the spiritual and social ideal of harmonious balance between all beings, including the Nahua glyph *ollin*,[16] signifying continuous change and balanced differences.[17]

Within the first panel there is imagery from *The Annals of San Francisco* that depicts what was determined to be "civilized and employed Indians." There are also images of protestors of Pete Wilson's Proposition 187, the California initiative meant to deny education to undocumented immigrants. In 1984 when Proposition 187 was passed by 60 percent of California voters, there was a lot of hostility and false information spread about Mexican migrants that impacted Latinx-appearing individuals in California regardless of their citizenship status. In the aftermath of the Trump administration, we have seen how this hostility is still prevalent in the United States.

The second panel *Mi Nepantla* contains several self-portraits of Cervántez depicting herself as Coyolxauhqui. In one, she has her eyes closed and bells on her cheeks. Another self-portrait is of her as a child along with a *Nagual*,[18] suggesting that she feels pulled apart as a Chicana in the United States. Pérez suggests, "The artist's visual identification with Coyolxauhqui speaks of her own fragmentation as a Chicana artist, through a continuum of gendered and racialized cultural losses that the lithographs document."[19] The final panel *Beyond Nepantla* contains a circle with a spiral of Quetzalcóatl, the feathered serpent. The spiral is so prominent in the image that it immediately draws the attention of the viewer. Pérez suggests, "Quetzalcóatl represents both wisdom and the arts, and the unity of the spiritual and the material."[20] The triptych depicts art's ability to heal the artist and possibly the viewer. Not only is it loaded with Indigenous cultural references and symbolism, but it also appears almost unfinished, which challenges the Eurocentric notion of beauty and what is considered fine art.

Coyolxauhqui has come to represent identity, struggle, and spirituality in Chicana art and has a meaningful effect on the collective psyche of Mujeres de Maiz. In fact, Yreina is a mentor to several MdM members and has assisted them in growing as artists. Although Coyolxauhqui comes from Aztec culture, the contemporary interpretations of her have developed into something new. The image of Coyolxauhqui is used by MdM artists to not only connect to their ancestors, but to also make sense of their own lives within the patriarchal social structures we currently live in. They also use her representation as a way to find strength and heal. Coyolxauhqui reminds us that women must persevere through the struggles of life. If they get knocked down, they have the ability and tools to pull themselves together, not only to pick up the pieces, but to put the pieces back together again, creating something even stronger than before.

SPIRITUALITY AS ART FORM

Works exhibited and published by Mujeres de Maiz are multilayered and combine themes of spirituality, rites of passage, cultural art-making practices, motherhood, fertility, love, loss, social justice, and identity, which I discuss in this section. According to Lucy Lippard, "Art with spiritual depth and social meaning is homeless in this society, trapped in an art world dedicated to very different goals."[21] Mujeres de Maiz gives spiritual art a home. Many mainstream galleries and museums turn away artwork with spiritual components, whereas MdM views embracing spirituality not only as a form of self-expression, but also as a way of determining one's own identity.

Combining Indigenous and western spiritualties can be seen in the artwork created by MdM artists. Liliflor combines Catholicism and Indigenous spirituality in her mural *Mujer Bendita*, which prominently features the Mexica goddess Coyolxauhqui next to the Virgin Mary, who is portrayed with Indigenous features. Next to Coyolxauhqui is a hummingbird, which likely represents her brother Huitzilopochtli. The two main figures in the mural represent and embrace the complex duality of Mexican culture, the combination of Spanish and Indigenous cultures.

This is significant because it not only reflects the reality many Chicanas live with of balancing Catholicism with Indigenous traditions, but it illustrates the Virgin Mary as Our Lady of Guadalupe. The Virgin of Guadalupe who appeared to the Indigenous man Juan Diego on Mount Tepeyac holds a special place in Mexico and many Mexican American families.

For Mujeres de Maiz, spirituality and rites of passage are connected. This is evident in Gabriela Zapata's *Malinalxochitl, Mi Primera Luna* (my first moon), which investigates the creative energy of women. The first moon marks an important rite of passage in the life of many women. The womb and the menstrual cycle are the focal point, but it also speaks to fertility and a major life change. For centuries many cultures have looked to the first moon (period) to indicate when a girl transitions into womanhood and can bear children. Some women create life within their bodies, but they also hold a creative energy that enables them to create art and life indicated by the radiating symbol on the womb. The symbol is important because it not only represents the moon and the uterus; it is the same symbol used in ancient Mexica artwork to represent Chicomoztoc where the seven Aztec tribes originally departed from.[22] Another piece that combines spirituality and a rite of passage is Sarah Espinoza's *Warrior* (figure 22.3). Not only does this watercolor and ink piece investigate pregnancy and childbirth; it looks to ancient spiritual beliefs. In the ancient Aztec mindset women that died during childbirth were seen as warriors.[23] This image situates the pregnant woman as Coatlicue, indicated by Huitzilopochtli's image on her bare belly. She is far along in her pregnancy cradling her belly in one hand while holding a dead hummingbird in the other. The image of Huitzilopochtli's sister Coyolxauhqui can be seen within the moon. The painting evokes feelings of fear as the mother is nearing the battle of childbirth and then motherhood. Coatlicue, a mother whose son went straight into battle upon his birth, must have also been afraid just as many mothers are.

Finally, Gina Aparicio's *Ipan Nepantla Teotlaitlania Cachi Maztlcayotl* also combines art with spiritual practice (figure 22.4). The interactive mixed-media installation offered the viewer a multisensorial experience combining sight, sound, and smell. The art piece took place in a small room with a dirt-covered floor. Upon entering the room, the viewer hears the sound of a women's drumming circle playing subtly and the nostrils are filled with the smell of fresh earth. There were four *Naguals*

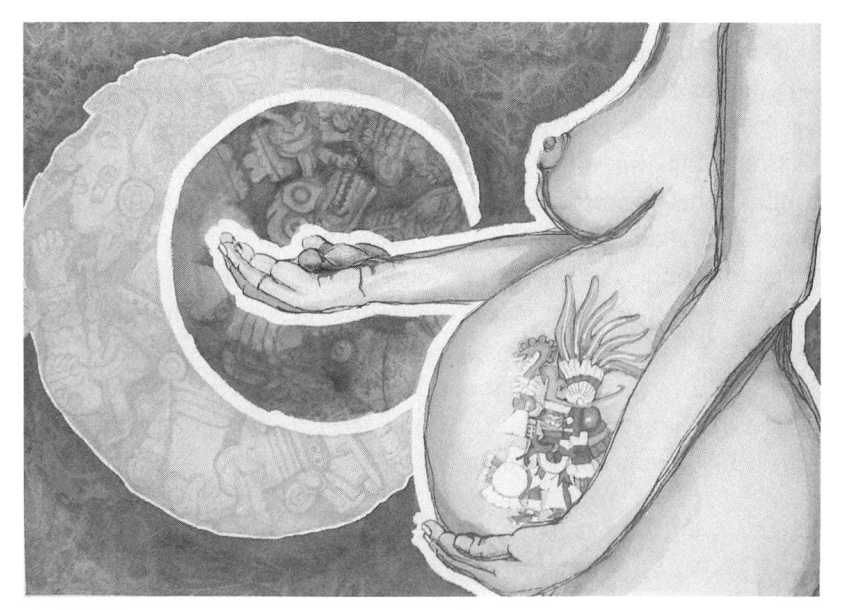

FIGURE 22.3 Sarah Espinoza, *Warrior*, watercolor and ink. Photograph provided by Mujeres de Maiz.

FIGURE 22.4 Gina Aparicio, *Ipan Nepantla Teotlaitlania Cachi Maztlcayotl*, mixed media. Photograph provided by Mujeres de Maiz.

in the room, each standing over seven feet tall arranged in ceremony with one another. The moon, represented by the goddess Coyolxauhqui, was placed prominently in the center of the room. Gina describes them as "caught between worlds, praying for a better future."[24] The heads and hands of the *Naguals* are made of fired clay, each weighing over one hundred pounds. All four hold instruments in their hands to play music, which is an important part of Indigenous prayer practices.

Taken together, these pieces created by the artists who work with Mujeres de Maiz convey their spirituality freely through their artwork. This is a stark contrast to traditional Eurocentric ideas toward spirituality in art. The fine art world appears to only accept contemporary themes of spirituality if it is a critique of organized religion.

MOTHER | EARTH

The combination and overlapping themes and subject matter in the artwork of Mujeres de Maiz is complex. The artwork and mediums vary between the artists, just like the subject matter. In this section I center artists whose work expresses the theme of motherhood in various forms, across time and place.

Sheila Rodriguez's piece *Madre de la Vida* (Mother of the Life) incorporates *papel picado* (Mexican paper cutting), fertility, and heartache into her painting (figure 22.5). The focal point is a woman's exposed heart that has been stabbed with knitting needles, suggesting the loss of motherhood or the loss of a mother. Her face is covered by hanging papel picado, but we can see that her eyes are closed. The image conveys heartache and pain while holding tightly to her culture signified by her *rebozo* (Mexican shawl).

Honoring Mother Earth is a theme prevalent in the artwork of Mujeres de Maiz epitomized in *Madre Celestial* by Linda Vallejo, a veteran Chicana artist and longtime MdM advisor, mentor, participant, and supporter (plate 7).[25] This painting is part of a series titled *The Los Cielos Series* that Linda describes as integrating her "understanding and experience, recollections, and healing through nature. This series often depicts the female form superimposed on a brilliant sky to discuss a metamorphic relationship with nature and as a symbol of nature's creative force. I

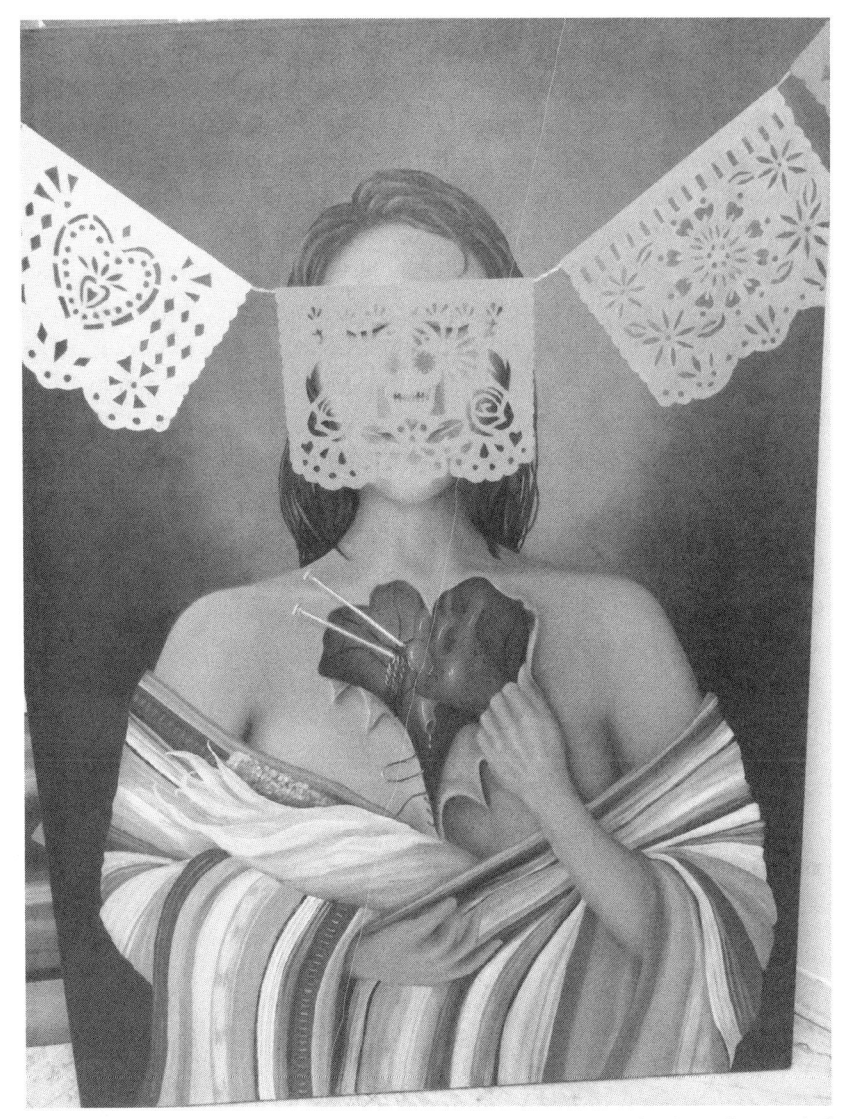

FIGURE 22.5 Sheila Rodriguez, *Madre de la Vida*, oil on canvas. Photograph provided by Mujeres de Maiz.

meticulously rendered and proportioned each figure as a reflection of a balanced and harmonious countenance."[26] Healing through nature honors Mother Earth and recognizes the creative energy of the earth and women in the universe. Margaret 'Quica' Alarcón's *Hermana de Maiz* also speaks to honoring the earth and understanding women as creators and givers of knowledge (plate 3). The woman at the center of the image is growing out of an ear of corn much like the Mujeres de Maiz logo. She appears to be handing an object to the viewer—the Nahua symbol for voice. She is giving voice, the ability to speak and understand within the universe. Behind her is the moon with the image of Coyolxauhqui in it. The woman and moon exist within the universe embraced by the power of creation. The woman must use her ability to honor herself and those around her. Alarcón also created the piece *Mujer de Maiz* to honor the earth and recognize her as the giver and taker of life (plate 2). Large colorful ears of corn sprout from the earth while a woman's body returns to it, and we can see her skeleton becoming part of the surrounding landscape. Margaret is honoring Indigenous cultural traditions and spiritual thought with this work. It is as if she is making the statement, "We come from the land and we shall return to it."

While much of Margaret's work embraces spirituality, it also explores identity through experimental art practices. Her piece *Ojo de Maiz* combines printmaking with papel picado (figure 22.6). Within this piece are

FIGURE 22.6 Margaret 'Quica' Alarcón, *Ojo de Maiz, Intaglio*, aquatint with chine colle. Photograph provided by Mujeres de Maiz.

four separate intaglio prints, each executed with great precision. We can see the human heart in one, which represents life and love. The image with the human figure has corn growing through it. This honors not only corn as the giver of life but also as a unifier of tribes and peoples. The print with the foot is adorned with ayayayotes, a type of instrument made from the seedpods of the Ayayayote tree, also known as *chachayotes* and *coyoles*. They are most commonly used in Danza.[27] When the dancers move a rattling noise is made. Alarcón's cultural connection recognizes Indigenous forms of prayer. In the fourth and final image, hands are holding a symbol that represents the moon and uterus, recognizing the power of creation that is within women, similar to that of *Malinalxochitl, Mi Primera Luna*. The symbols and practices within this piece are part of Margaret's identity as an Indigenous Xicana with Otomí, Taíno, and Spanish ancestry. Mother Earth is a prevalent theme in the work of many of the artists who work with MdM because she encapsulates so much of what it is to be a woman—the power of creation, motherhood, and feminine knowledge and power.

ARTIVISM IN ACTION

ARTivism combines art with activism, essentially turning art into a verb. When art is put into action, it can be used as a tool to raise social awareness and consciousness and to educate and create change. MdM has a long history of using art as a tool for change. Many of the Mujeres use art to support community, ecological, and labor causes. In *Another City Is Possible: Mujeres de Maiz, Radical Indigenous Mestizaje and Activist Scholarship*, Amber Rose González describes them as a critical component of artivism in Los Angeles, stating: "Mujeres de Maiz is a cornerstone of the artivist movement in Los Angeles. The collective creates spiritually and politically charged cultural production to construct and assert an urban Indigenous mestiza identity and consciousness grounded in transnational feminist of color histories, politics and aesthetics to open up meanings in such a way that any audience member can subscribe to their form of liberatory consciousness and being and to create reparative narratives that challenge dominant cultural representations and that critique social injustices."[28]

Action is a critical component of ARTivism; it allows for important work to be done, which requires both collective and individual action. Mujeres de Maiz participates in political action events such as the May Day, Women's, and Black Lives Matter marches in Los Angeles. They also do work to support community centers and organizations such as Proyecto Jardin, a community garden located in Boyle Heights near White Memorial Hospital. Gloria Anzaldúa spoke about the importance of action in feminist spaces: "Speaking and communicating lay the groundwork, but there is a point beyond too much talk that abstracts the experience. What is needed is a symbolic behavior performance made concrete by involving body and emotions with political theories and strategies, rituals that will connect the conscious with the unconscious. Through ritual we can make some deep-level changes. Ritual consecrates the alliance. Breaking bread together, and other group activities that physically and psychically represent the ideas, goals and attitudes promote a quickening, thickening between us."[29]

FIGURE 22.7 Felicia 'Fe' Montes, *The Politricked Public Art Cart*, mixed media installation, wood, video monitor, and silkscreen press, 2011. Photograph provided by Mujeres de Maiz.

MdM is able to connect the physical and psychological through their actions in community. Not only participating in political action and volunteering in community spaces, but also by creating talking circles and hands-on workshops that allow for expression and the exchange of ideas.

ARTivism allows for art to be interactive and move through communities. *The Politricked Public Art Cart* created by Felicia 'Fe' Montes is an example (figure 22.7). The piece resembles a cart used by Los Angeles area street vendors who are typically migrants from Mexico or other Latin American countries. They use carts to vend food items on the street

FIGURE 22.8 Felicia 'Fe' Montes, *Botanica del Barrio*, mixed media installation. Photograph provided by Mujeres de Maiz.

such as ice cream, *elote* (corn), chips, cotton candy, and hot dogs. This cart resembles the elote cart, but it is equipped with a silkscreen, TV monitor, and PA system. The cart allows for the public to interact with it and create artwork of their own with the silkscreen press attached. Felicia describes the cart as "a small political art hub and mobile unit for the sharing of political platforms through image, video, performance, poetry, and protest. It is also a place for dialogue with informational brochures, flyers, and know your rights information."[30] Felicia designed a second cart titled *Botanica del Barrio* that brings herbal remedies to the community (figure 22.8). When the cart is in motion Felicia will stop and make homemade mixed herbal teas for the community free of charge. The cart provides a platform to inform the public about health, wellness, and non-Western medicines. Montes said, "It is different because it is of, by, and for the people rooted in their daily realities of family, work, and issues of racism, sexism, and classism and their attempts to end these issues and fight for justice."[31] Mujeres de Maiz does not simply address issues of injustice; they provide solutions. Art in action is a remedy, not a declaration.

HONORING THROUGH ALTARS

Another exemplification of ARTivism in action is the creation of altars that deliver both a cultural message and social commentary. Mujeres de Maiz has created traditional three-dimensional and nontraditional altars to honor ancestors and culture across Los Angeles. Yreina Cervántez's mural *La Ofrenda* under the First Street Bridge in Los Angeles is an inspiration to the collective. This altar is unique because it is presented in a two-dimensional form and it honors an individual who is alive, paying homage to Dolores Huerta, the co-founder of the United Farm Workers union. Guisela Latorre, in her book *Walls of Empowerment: Chicana/o Indigenist Murals of California*, says the following about the work:

> Latinas have fought for a more important role within the private sphere of the home and the family, as well as for the right to work or earn an education. . . . Cervántez's images of *La Ofrenda* suggests she intended to establish a strong foothold for Latinas in both spaces. The iconography of

the mural includes elements commonly seen in both spheres. The viewer can readily link the candles, the calla lilies and the craft elements to private domains, for many home altars include these objects. The word "ofrenda" (offering) suggests that the artist intended the entire mural to be a gigantic altar dedicated to Dolores Huerta.... The very inclusion of Huerta's figure and her obvious links to both the UFW and the civil rights movement implies that the lessons to be learned from *La Ofrenda* also belong to the public domain.[32]

The resiliency and persistence of women is a strong theme within Cervántez's mural and the focus on Dolores Huerta was a new concept when the piece was originally created. Much like Chicanas, this mural constantly struggles for survival due to its location under the bridge at Toluca and Second Street in downtown Los Angeles, a prime target for graffiti.

The artists who participate with Mujeres de Maiz use cultural symbols and Indigenous references within their altars in an effort to not only decolonize and challenge Eurocentric aesthetics and ideals of beauty, but also to heal from the generational trauma of colonization. They recognize art is a tool for healing that can be used to educate. The artists have

FIGURE 22.9 Mujeres de Maiz, *Mesa de las Madres*, installation, mixed media, 2014. Photograph, Felicia 'Fe' Montes.

collectively constructed altar installations such as *Mesa de las Madres*, originally part of a Day of the Dead altar exhibition in Downtown Los Angeles's Grand Park in 2014 and has since been exhibited in several other locations upon request (figure 22.9). The inspiration behind the work was my great-grandmother's kitchen table. The heart of any family home is most often this location as so much happens around the table other than eating food. Events and holidays take place there, birthdays, anniversaries, heartache, long conversations with family and friends, just to name a few. In my own family experience, I can recall as Mexicans living in a Euroamerican world, the place we felt most comfortable was our kitchen table. It was our homeland since we had no other. Even though assimilation has attempted to take language and culture from Chicanxs, it could never take away our food. Along with food items typically seen in a Mexican kitchen such as beans and chili peppers, herbal remedies such as gordolobo tea, honey, and rosemary were included in the installation. My father's ashes, along with photos of family members who died, were placed in the pots and bowls on top of the table to acknowledge they are still with us.

The installation also represents the three levels of the universe: the underworld, the terrestrial world, and the astral world. The four directions are represented with corn, beans, and seeds. In the underworld there are photographs of women who have died and whom the collective greatly admire such as Gloria Anzaldúa, Frida Kahlo, and Rosa Parks, to name a few. The terrestrial world contains the food items on the tabletop and the astral world is above all. When incense or sage is burned on the table, it goes up into the astral world. This installation challenges and attempts to decolonize traditional art not only with representations of Chicanx culture, but by including spiritual and healing elements.

We Are the Land was another interactive installation completed by the collective, which actually began to grow in several ways. This piece contained three large maps for viewers to interact with. The collective provided small tags and invited viewers to write where they came from on the tag and then pin it to the map. As tags were added to the maps, the installation grew. This action was intended to convey the notion that we are all connected. Viewers could see how close they really are to one another by seeing that distance is not so great. Dirt was placed at the base of the artwork to represent the earth. The women combined live plants along with artificial constructions of corn at the base. Seeds of corn were left in the dirt, and within a couple of weeks a seed had sprouted. The actions of the living artwork reaffirmed the collective's belief that the notion of planting seeds of liberation/culture/love/etc. can create change in the world.

Another example of spirituality as art form is the altar installation *Mujer Maiz*, created by Lilia Ramirez, that featured a dress made of cornhusks as the centerpiece. Corn is significant to many Indigenous cultures across the continent of America. In some traditions, it represents the cycle of life, in others knowledge. Some ancient Mayan peoples bound their heads to resemble the shape of corn, reflecting their deep connection to it. To the Mexica, the corn goddess Chicomecoatl is associated with fertility and nourishment. Lilia has worn the functional dress for several of her performance pieces around the Los Angeles area and has created other companion works while wearing the dress, such as *Xilonen: Angel of Los Angeles* (plate 9). In the altar environment cornhusks, live plants, and flowers surrounded the dress. Within *Xilonen: Angel of Los Angeles*, the artist added wings to the dress and carried a staff with an ear of corn on the end. She proclaimed herself to be the guardian and patroness of Los Angeles. In the dress, Lilia is Xilonen or Chicomecoatl bringing nourishment in the form of art to us. Both the installation and digital photograph speak to the sacredness of corn and honor the ancestors, while also recognizing women as creators and holders of divine energy.

The artists associated with Mujeres de Maiz honor and practice altar-making in a variety of ways from traditional home altars to innovative interactive mixed-media altars. Through the years they have pushed the boundaries of altar-making just as their predecessors did, like artist Amalia Mesa-Baines and master altar maker Ofelia Esparza. Both women inspire MdM with their craft, content, and fearlessness in their art practices.

The subject matter and themes expressed by MdM artists defy the traditional Eurocentric standards of universalism, beauty, and what has traditionally been considered fine art. The artworks discussed in this chapter embrace a multifaceted Chicana identity, and spiritually and just like the Chicanas themselves, they are complex and fierce. For years traditional art spaces, art schools, and galleries told these artists that their work was "craft" or "folk" art and they were encouraged to veer away from using cultural symbols. Despite this, they stayed true to their art and have persevered for more than two and a half decades. Mujeres de Maiz continues to create and push the boundaries of the art world, and their contributions to the Los Angeles Artscape continue.

NOTES

1. One of the seven Aztec tribes. Known to be the largest and most dominant.
2. Leonardo Lopez Luján and Judy Levin, *Tenochtitlan* (New York: Oxford University Press, 2006), 28.
3. The great pyramid of Tenochtitlan was dedicated to Huitzilopochtli the god of the Sun and War, and Tlaloc the god of rain. However, Huitzilopochtli was the patron god to the Mexica people.
4. Eduardo Matos Moctezuma, "Archaeology and Symbolism in Aztec Mexico: The Templo Mayor of Tenochtitlan," *Journal of the American Academy of Religion*, December 1985, 798.
5. Fray Bernardino de Sahagún, *The Florentine Codex: A General History of Things in New Spain, Book 3*, trans. Arthur J. O. Anderson and Charles E. Dibble (Santa Fe, Salt Lake City: School of American Research, University of Utah Press, 1952), 1–4.
6. Fray Bernardino de Sahagún, *The Florentine Codex*, 1–4.
7. Manuel Aguilar Moreno, "Aztec Art and Culture," Lecture. California State University, Los Angeles, Calif., February, 2016.
8. Manuel Aguilar-Moreno, *Handbook to Life in the Aztec World* (Oxford: Oxford University Press, 2006), 190.
9. Patricia Michán, "Dismemberment and Reintegration: Aztec Themes in Contemporary Mexican Practice," *Journal of Analytical Psychology* 45, no. 2 (2000): 310.
10. Michán, "Dismemberment and Reintegration," 307–329, 310.
11. Michán, "Dismemberment and Reintegration," 313.
12. For more on this ceremony, review chapter 5 by Nadia Zepeda in round 1.
13. Felicia 'Fe' Montes, email message to author, February 22, 2016.
14. Amber Rose González, "Another City Is Possible: Mujeres de Maiz, Radical Indigenous Mestizaje and Activist Scholarship." PhD dissertation (University of California, Santa Barbara, 2015), 80.
15. Gloria Anzaldúa, "Chapter 22: Putting Coyolxauhqui Together: A Creative Process," *Counterpoints* 90 (1999): 251–52.
16. The Aztec symbol for movement.
17. Laura E. Pérez, *Chicana Art: The Politics of Spiritual and Aesthetic Altarities* (Durham: Duke University Press, 2007), 41.
18. A human that has the power to transform.
19. Pérez, *Chicana Art*, 44.

20. Pérez, *Chicana Art*, 44.
21. Lucy Lippard, *Mixed Blessings: New Art in a Multicultural America* (New York: Pantheon Books, 1990), 11.
22. Chimalpahin Quauhtlehuanitzin, Domingo Francisco de San Antón Muñon, *Codex Chimalpahin, Volume 1: Society and Politics in Mexico Tenochtitlan, Tlatelolco, Texcoco, Culhuacan, and Other Nahua Altepetl in Central Mexico*, ed. Arthur J. O. Anderson and Susan Schroeder (Norman: University of Oklahoma Press, 1997), 69.
23. Aguilar-Moreno, *Handbook*, 163.
24. Gina Aparicio, text message to the author, May 27, 2016.
25. In 2015 *The Culture Trip* named Linda one of "L.A.'s 8 Most Influential Chicana and Chicano Artists." Michael Reyes, "L.A.'s 8 Most Influential Chicana and Chicano Artists," TheCultureTrip.com, updated December 2015, http://theculturetrip.com/north-america/usa/california/articles/l-a-s-8-most-influential-chicana-and-chicano artists/?utm_source=emails&utm_medium=featured&utm_campaign=250215losangelesart.
26. Linda Vallejo, "Los Cielos," *LindaVallejo.com*, accessed May 1, 2016, http://www.lindavallejo.com/artworks/paintings/los-cielos/page/2/.
27. Contemporary Aztec dance.
28. González, *Another City Is Possible*, 51.
29. "Bridge, Drawbridge, Sandbar or Island: Lesbians-of-Color *Haciendas Alianzas*," in *Bridges of Power: Women's Multicultural Alliances*, ed. Lisa Albrecht and Rose M. Brewer (Philadelphia: New Society, 1990), 154.
30. Felicia 'Fe' Montes, "Politricked Public Art Cart," *Feliciamontes.com*, accessed April 23, 2016, https://feliciamontes.wordpress.com.
31. Montes, "Politricked Public Art Cart," 52.
32. Latorre, *Walls of Empowerment*, 196–97.

23
Mythology of Flesh and Turquoise Serpents

DIANA PANDO

Mujeres offering flesh to nuestra gente
ofrenda of stardust, bone, and blood
our antepasados ciegos, sordos, mudos

El cuerpo va resumbando
Ombligo Womb Warrior

hermanas bust ass
in cubicle ten hours a day
and clean office buildings
to put food on table

Offerings of flesh observed
but we look the other way
cuz it's easier
          on the eye

"This is the body and blood of Christ"
Wait; no it's the body and blood
of maquiladoras making money for
men refusing to mourn
Mujeres de Júarez

Flowery offerings of flesh
strewn in desert
while female poets in Afghanistan
killed for penning poems

Out of my mother's barriga
I came forth, all blood,
copper retablos and bic pens
Chronicler of spectacles of flesh
forming and foaming at the mouth
Drenched in agua de romero
Entrega de ofrenda sin moneda

Turquoise fire serpent
Slithers in sharp opal teeth
Looking to devour
entrails of sueños left over on man-
    made altars

and realizing it's not the Universe
    demanding tribute
its our own hunger
our own ritual of flesh

secret cannibal in us revealed
we devour each other and ourselves
hold obsidian dagger high and plunge
it deep
and when it's over
all we can do is toss beautiful carnage
    from urban temple steps
and hope you don't become
                the next

                offering of
                flesh.

Mujeres de Maiz, Flor y Canto:
Ofrendas of the Flesh, no. 12 (2014): 3.

24

We Are

MARISOL CRISOSTOMO-ROMO

We were told we were made of
   cornhusk and
red earth.

Growing from a reality of tobacco
   leaves and
rich copal smoke,
We were the ones who drowned in
   pools of
our own blood,
Choking on forbidden tongues
We were the ones flung into mass
   graves,
Bodies
Upon bodies
Became ghosts
Upon ghosts
Roaming the Black Hills, Sand Creek,
   Acteal,
Plymouth Rock

We were the ones whose prayers were
stronger than any gunpowder
Or foreign church
Prayers stronger than the moment
   after the
gloomy rapes of Indian women whose
Small children are forced to watch as
Don Cabeza de Puto
Forces his greed into her cornsilk
   center
Leaving her with a sadness that lasts
   for
more than 500 years.

We were the ones who swam in
   corpses of
our dead
And walked on the limbs and heads
   of our
brothers in the Mexica Valley

While settlers chose to abuse our
    sacred alcohol and continued
To
Aimlessly
Rape.

As I prepare snuff can lids for my
    prayer
dress
I pray for the grandmothers whose
    medicine
was exterminated
And I pray
We were the ones chopped into
    bite-size
pieces with machetes in Cayetano and
    fed to
Dogs
Trained to disembowel
Us
Vomiting from the smell of where they
    burnt

our brains and scalps

As I prepare snuff can lids for my
    prayer
dress, I pray
And ask to forget
The nursing babies ripped from their
    mothers
breasts and thrown in the air for
Target practice
We are those mothers and
My god,
We are those babies,
Nursing on memory.

Mujeres de Maiz, Flor y Canto: Cantando al Amanecer, no. 5 (2007): 41.

25
My Body

A Sight of Violence

MARIANA AQ'AB'AL MOSCOSO

When I was a little girl, I asked my mother:
"Por qué no tengo pelo rubio y ojos azules?"
My mother gently responded: "Pero mírame a mí, mija . . ."
I did not understand.
Why was I not like the pretty girls?
I wanted long straight blonde hair
a normal name like Jessica or Jennifer
I wanted to be smart
but everything about me was a betrayal to my desires
because I wanted to be White.
White America had convinced me: You do not belong.

However, what I didn't know was
that this was an act of violence placed upon my body.
A violence that extended beyond my historical specificity,
it started more than five hundred years ago
it is intwined in my genes
I carry with me the violence unleashed upon my ancestors.
My body, a site of violence.
My Brown skin is more than a pigment, it speaks without words!

In White America, my skin gives permission against my will
for people to make assumptions
question my intelligence
sexualize my body
or view it in disgust.

Do not be fooled
I am not a victim and neither are you
My Brown sisters, your body does (not) define you.
Dedicate yourself
Decolonize. Organize. Love Yourself.
Be a Feminist.
Because no little Brown girl should ever want to be White.

Mujeres de Maiz, Flor y Canto: Ofrendas of the Flesh, no. 12 (2014): 21.

26
Mi Quierdo 24th and Mission

MAYA CHINCHILLA

Mi querido 24th and mission
Conjunto on a Tuesday night
Mostly men gathered around to listen
to the upright bass
Acoustic guitar
drum
and of course—
the accordion
Harmonizing
reminding stocky brown-skinned men
   of home

They will be home soon they think,
no need to do anything permanent here

And the bar on the corner always a
pop song, ballad, cumbia
salsita BLARING
The music sometimes draws me near
but the Men spilling out to the street ...
   ssst sst
mamacita

Reminds me that no mujer decente
   would be in there
Some reason I know to walk away,
hurried hips
not swaying
even though I've never considered
   myself especially decente
and Even though my father says
I sometimes talk like one of those
   women in
those bars
And we automatically know what one
   of those
women are.

Poor women aren't allowed liberation
Or maybe they find freedom in tight
   jeans and
A stretchy v-neck that shows every
   bump every
movement
Dripping ornaments dangle teasing
gold hoops lasso your eyes

You will see me!
Ay! He says, why do you women wear
    a dark bra under a white shirt
Only Nacas do that!

She sighs uncomfortable in skin she
    thought
she was comfortable in
She thought it looked fine,
hurls back: that the bra is pink and is
    close enough to her skin!
as she changes to a darker shirt

They say don't walk alone at night
    because
something
might happen to you
And if it does, well then you shouldn't
    have
been alone

Blame the victim reflex,
so you don't have to take any
    responsibility
What if you don't have someone to
    walk with?
Lock yourself inside until someone
    comes for you?
Until the world changes?

And he says yeah the world is a
    dangerous place for women
but how are we supposed to change
    things?
It will always just be dangerous for
    women to
be alone.

Some men will always rape some
    women.

I can't believe he says this, but then
    that is what
we are talking about,
right?
Fear, the ultimate power over a woman.

Rape
Confidence busted
trust gone disgusted
picked up from a black top smack down
substandard practices
negative in the place of a positive
accusatory sin and no redemption in
    sight.
It's dangerous to be a woman; even
    first world.
That is why I am connected to my
    hermanas on
the border.
I know what it is to fear to have body
    of mujer
Be careful I hear they are killing
    women over
there
My 1st world status means nothing?

Body parts, cut nipples,
legs disconnected from hips

Her brown eyes, her smile never seen
her laugh not heard anew
The last her mother saw of her was
    bone.
She didn't get to say goodbye.

Bone. No flesh to be ogled wounded.
What she most wants to hug her
　daughter again.

THE BORDER
this line that is not a bridge, not a line,
　it's a
ditch a hole an open wound,
like the Berlin wall the great wall of
　China,
apartheid wall, imaginary walls
not just one wall
but several, cement, iron gate, barbed
　wire
men with guns protecting who again?
Whose interests?
Eerie walls of silence

So we March, mourn,
we don't forget,
write letters, make speeches
hold discussions
Looking up from fear
and hopelessness
raising awareness
daring to be powerful

The Missing turned up raped &
　mutilated,
ni una mas
Ineptitude bungling of local
　authorities,

ni una mas
Blame the victim reflex
she must have run off with a boyfriend
maybe your precious daughter leads a
　double life.

Ni una mas

Young, pretty, long brown hair, poor,
　brown skin.
Ni una mas

Mexico lindo y querido has some dirty
　secrets
Yes la madre de las tierras is helping
　hide our
naughty dirty laundry
Out in the desert, only half hidden,
so you know what happens to women
　who step
out of line,
out of the house
NAFTA'S neglected, unprotected,
　migration
survival,
maquila women earning 4 dollars a day
working on electronics, working on
　clothes she
could never afford.

Explosion of exploitation!
Is only the half of it
Representing the condition
of women across the planet

Symptoms of a deeper problem.
Tener cuerpo de mujer es ser
amenazado de muerte
Her only crime was being a woman
Crimes against all our humanity

Pero sabes Que?
No Estan Solas. No Estan Solas. No
 Estan Solas!
WE ARE NOT ALONE

Mujeres de Maiz, Flor y Canto:
 Toltecayotl, no. 4 (2006): 45–46.

27
Femzines, Artivism, and Altar Aesthetics

Third Wave Feminism Chicana Style

NORELL MARTÍNEZ

IN THIS essay, I examine the grassroots publication project of the East LA Chicana collective Mujeres de Maiz (MdM). Since 1997 MdM has released an annual underground, self-published zine called *Flor y Canto*. This submission-based publication consists of poetry and visual art by women of color from across the nation. Fifteen volumes have been released since the organization's founding (figure 27.1). An annual art exhibit and performance event hosted by MdM in the barrios of East LA inaugurates the publication. The zine showcases the work of emerging and established female artists to advocate for and promote creative acts by women of color.[1] Considering that this demographic is gravely underrepresented in the art and literary world and that women of color face disproportionate economic and social inequality, MdM's work makes a significant contribution to the world of alternative media by publishing their work. This is especially important because, as some critics suggest, the zine scene has been dominated by white, middle-class youth, and zine history from the Anglo American viewpoint has erased people of color from the zine trajectory (Zoble 3).

My aim is to examine Chicanas' contributions to the world of feminist zines, or femzines, as they are called in the zine world. I am particularly interested in the ways that Chicanas enact their version of third wave feminist activism through their zine. Often associated with third

FIGURE 27.1 A total of fourteen issues of *Flor y Canto* were published between 1997 and 2016. Twelve of them are pictured here. Photo by Margaret 'Quica' Alarcón. Courtesy Michelle L. Lopez, 2018.

wave feminism, femzines are credited for being the vehicle of expression for third wave feminist thought. While the third wave expanded the topic of feminism to include women of diverse backgrounds and diverse identities, the contributions of Chicana zinesters are understudied. Although MdM's zine project reflects a typical third wave feminist trend of zine production, *Flor y Canto* diverges from the traditional zine-making approach in that MdM draws on a Chicana feminist epistemology inspired by Indigenous worldviews to denounce the gender status quo. Furthermore, they adopt a politicized spirituality influenced by Mesoamerican conceptions of art and poetry, one that expands understanding of creative expressions as transformative and healing that defies Western notions of art. MdM employs this notion in their femzine to make a larger critique of patriarchy, gender inequality, racism, sexism, and homophobia.[2] Thus I argue that their third wave activism is similarly a form of artivism because they view art and poetry as a form of healing from the trauma of violence experienced by marginalized women.[3]

When examining MdM's zines, I ask how Chicanas address violence and how it represents various aesthetic methods to make visible and speak against these issues. According to Piepmeier, gender violence is a prominent theme in femzines overall. For this reason, I choose to examine *Flor y Canto*'s volume 12, "Ofrendas of the Flesh," to consider the ways in which Chicanas use poetry and visual art to speak out against and heal from gender violence. MdM asked contributors to address the various ways women's "flesh" is taken or abused, or the ways in which women reclaim and take back their "flesh." The pieces in this volume respond to the pleasure and pain of women and convey how their bodies have been objectified, commodified, and misread, but also how women have taken agency and control and reclaim their bodies, create new meaning, and resist these forms of violence.

I claim that the pieces in this volume employ Laura E. Pérez's concept of aesthetic altarities, or altarities for short, a framework she uses to explore Chicana visual art that is infused with spiritual idioms. According to Pérez, altarities refer to art as offerings on an altar "where the material and the still disembodied are invoked" (*Chicana Art* 6). I will utilize this framework in this study as a lens to examine both the poetry and the visual art in "Ofrendas." Pérez explains that traditionally, altars have been spaces where one "invokes, mediates, and offers homage to the unseen but felt presence in our lives, whether these be deities, ancestors, or the memories of our personal, familial, and collective pasts" (7). However, she argues that for Chicana artists, the altar is a gendered aesthetic form that is used to acknowledge, make visible, and pay respect to that which is "disembodied," or visually, socially, and culturally invisible. In other words, creating art with an altar-like function can serve to invoke all those women who have gone unacknowledged, or whose pain has been ignored, or whose bodies have been abused, and thus this art-altar can be seen as a political act. Hence, a femzine that uses the altar as a framework allows Chicanas to speak out against misogyny, homophobia, and patriarchy, and likewise, validates women's diverse experiences and views them as worthy of being honored instead of deeming them disposable.

In what follows, I examine the world of femzines and third wave feminism. I then consider how contemporary Chicana feminists like MdM take an artivist approach in their third wave politics and employ their own cultural knowledge, histories, and politicized spiritual understandings using a Mesoamerican cosmology to make a feminist critique. Next, I shift my discussion to the texts and do an analytical reading of several poems and images in "Ofrendas" as altarities to illustrate Chicanas' deployment of artivism to speak against patriarchy and gender violence and ultimately heal from this trauma.

FEMZINES AND THIRD WAVE FEMINISM: A CHICANA ARTIVIST APPROACH

Third wave feminism was born in the 1990s when a generation of women witnessed a backlash against the initiatives won by the Women's Movement. Negative representations of feminist women on television, for example, alongside high-profile cases of rape that would often go unpunished revealed to young women that the work of second wave feminists was not yet done. Femzines, catalyzed by women in the punk scene in the 1990s, are often credited for being the vehicle of expression for the third wave generation. Young women who called themselves Riot Grrrls echoed what many women felt at the time: they were "tired of being written out—out of history, out of the 'scene', out of our bodies" (qtd. in Nguyen 176).[4] MdM's *Flor y Canto* zine comes out of this tradition to self-publish as a form of protest against this lack of visibility.

Chicanas like the MdM members, who came of age in the barrios of East LA in the 1990s when third wave feminism emerged, faced unique challenges that would politicize and shape their feminist ideas. In the 1990s the effects of global capitalism were being felt universally. The restructuring of world economies brought more urban decay, deindustrialization, low wages, and cuts to social programs and public education to communities of color in poor neighborhoods. The economic devastation led to gang violence, the crack epidemic, and high crime rates in LA inner cities. Police violence was also a focal point of that period, as the Rodney King beating by police in South Central LA indicated. Simultaneously, the large influx of Latina/os into LA fueled a xenophobic, anti-immigrant movement in the State of California that continues today. As is commonly the case, economic and social insecurity make women more vulnerable to exploitation and violence.

Aside from this, in 1994 the world would also see Zapatistas from the highlands of Chiapas take up arms against the Mexican government in protest of the North American Free Trade Agreement. Like the rebels in

Chiapas, urban youth of color in LA also felt persecuted by the State and relegated to second-class citizenship. They too experienced low-intensity warfare and police violence and were living the effects of neoliberalism in their barrios. This inspired Chicana/o youth to organize political and artistic movements grounded in the Zapatista vision: "un mundo donde quepan muchos mundos" (EZLN). MdM members looked to the Zapatistas, and especially the Zapatista women, who played critical leadership roles in the uprising, for inspiration to resolve gender disparities in their community. Three years after the Zapatista uprising, MdM launched their collective and published the first volume of their femzine, *Flor y Canto*. Their name, Mujeres de Maiz, is a reference to the Mayan Zapatista women whose people have since ancient times considered maize to be sacred food, highlighting women's vital role in the cultivation and preparation of the plant as well as in the struggle for liberation and access to land to continue their way of life, often invisiblized labor.[5]

While Zapatista women provided a new model of feminism for the women of MdM, the work of feminist writers of the second wave also had a strong impact on them. Chicana feminists who draw on Mesoamerican cosmologies to challenge gender inequality in their work were especially influential. In the introduction to each volume, MdM proclaims that the collective began "among the writings of empowering mentors" and credits the "penetrating power of Xicanisma" as having a profound impact on their generation of women. Coined by Ana Castillo, "Xicanisma" refers to a Chicana feminism particular to the experiences of Chicanas in the United States, a lens to examine the societal, political, and economic issues that they face. By using the "X," Castillo incorporates the Nahuatl language of the Mexica to pay homage to the Indigenous roots of Chicanas.[6] Xicanista writers such as Castillo, along with Cherríe Moraga and Gloria Anzaldúa among others, reclaim their Indigenous origins as a political act and as a step toward regaining cultural integrity.[7] Their theory engaged with Indigenous epistemologies that call for an end to racist and sexist oppression, to honor the feminine and female, and to recover what was lost due to colonialism.

Like their Xicana predecessors, MdM deploys a pre-Columbian vision of the world to challenge gender inequality and give voice and representation to urban women of color. The themes in *Flor y Canto*, the poetry and art within its pages, are an amalgamation of work that alludes to the Indigenous past while addressing the urban realities of the present. This framework is implemented to subvert racist stereotypes of women of color while questioning the social and economic issues women experience. There is certainly a wide diversity of voices and not all pieces conform to Xicana indígena ideology, yet a pre-Columbian imaginary is strongly present in each volume. Paintings of female goddesses, clay sculptures that employ an Indigenous aesthetic, and Nahuatl words sprinkled throughout the pages underscore the power of the feminine. Poems with titles like "Coyolxauhqui Rising" by Diana Pando invoke the Aztec moon deity and call on young women to rise like the moon, to tear down walls and be the "Next generation of Dolores Huerta, Soldaderas, Sor Juana y Gloria Anzaldúas" ("Rites," 39). Demeaning ideas of Mexican/Chicana women as weak and unintelligent are defied by naming brilliant and impressive female figures, mirroring Anzaldua's method of reviving female deities driven underground by the male-dominated Aztecs, to critique patriarchal societies that undermine women's power.

Perhaps the strongest intervention MdM makes when invoking a Mesoamerican epistemology is the way in which they view the role of the artist and art-making. For MdM art is a tool for "social change and transformation, connecting issues from local to global, personal to political," and is grounded in the Nahua concept of "teaching and healing by offering flower and song" ("Cantando").[8] The meaning of *xochitl in cuicatl*, or flower and song, refers to artistic expression, which was transmitted by the *tlamatini*—knowers of things—mainly through poetry. For the Nahua, the *tlamatinime* were trained specialists, the caretakers and interpreters of the codices, masters of the word, who transmitted the history of the people orally through poetry and "promoted communication with the divine through the arts rather than through warfare" (Medina). They engaged in teaching, healing, and mediating the well-being and spiritual growth of the beholder through *xochitl in cuicatl*, which translates literally to "flower and song" but means "poetry and truth," based on the idea that artistic expressions in the forms of words, songs, and paintings connect us to the divine. Miguel León-Portilla explains that for the Nahua "the only possible way to speak truthful words on earth was through the path of poetry and art" (314 qtd. in Pérez, *Chicana Art*).[9] When the artist "truly expressed his or her heart in flower and song the inner self was deified or filled with divine energy" (Carrasco 81). To perceive art through this lens, Pérez states, is to value the power of art as socially transformative, politically meaningful, and healing (*Chicana Art* 25).

The act of describing their zines as "modern day codices," and the women within the pages as "scribes," is politically meaningful and elevates women of color artists to *tlamatini*—modern-day healers and teachers. To honor a woman of color with this title, even if only on a symbolic level, is to sanction her as "knower of things" and "speaker of truth," a significant gesture in a racist, patriarchal, and hierarchical society. By providing a space for women whom society has silenced and marginalized to "speak their truths," the zine becomes a vehicle for such "truths" to be told—truths that are painful, that remind us that "poor women aren't allowed liberation," and truths that are hopeful, that remind women of their collective power, that "WE ARE NOT ALONE," as Maya Chinchilla proclaims in her poem ("13 Baktun" 15).[10] It is these narratives that do not get heard on nightly news shows, unseen and indiscernible in mainstream platforms.

MdM's artivism is realized by placing disproportionately impacted women in the elevated position of artist. In showcasing their poetry, art, and performances—through a zine or an art show—they give women the opportunity to be valued and respected by the public in a world that consistently devalues them, particularly in traditional art and literary spaces. Challenging the notion that art is reserved for the elite, MdM publishes and exhibits work by women who are not formally trained, whom the world would not consider "real" artists, women who are "recipient[s] of much negativity, but . . . producer[s] of much creativity," as MdM describes them, and deserve to have their work seen and their words read ("Cantando"). MdM disrupts the bourgeois notion that "artist" is a title determined by standards like formal training or obtaining mastery. They challenge this exclusivity by elevating all women to the position of "artist," deploying an artivist framework grounded in an ancient notion that art connects us to the divine.

Some critics question the effectiveness of artivist strategies to create material change in a capitalist society. Anthropologist Manuel Delgado argues that artivism "does not cultivate an ideological struggle nor does it create an organic base for transformation" (77). Delgado questions whether it is or is not revolution or at least an effective contribution to a real overcoming of the capitalist system (*Artivismo* 78). Indeed, the political strategies of artivists are not very well articulated or organized into a unified historic bloc, nor can one point to their theoretical underpinnings. Yet, when Chicana artists appropriate Nahua concepts of art and art-making, they challenge European notions of art as merely expressions of an individual's inventiveness and are instead reimagining art as socially transformative and healing. I agree that individual forms of healing will not dismantle an oppressive system like capitalism and there is no substitute for direct-action activism and mass mobilization on a collective level. Nonetheless, for many women of color, healing can be politically significant; healing can mean the act of liberating oneself from patriarchal and colonized constructions of sexuality, or unlearning dominant conceptions of race and gender hierarchies, or undoing the psychological damage of the legacies of colonialism, racism, and sexism passed down across generations.

For MdM, healing is connected to a spirituality grounded in Indigenous cosmologies that helps us imagine a socially just world. In *Flor y Canto*, the culturally hybrid spiritual aesthetics infused with visions of social justice and gender equality are not unique to MdM. Many Chicana artists combine spirituality and politics in their art and include hybrid forms of spirituality grounded in Indigenous beliefs because, as Pérez explains, these are often "inseparable from questions of social justice, with respect to class, gender, sexuality, culture and 'race'" (*Chicana Art* 20). *Flor y Canto* exemplifies these aesthetic traditions, particularly in their altar-like approach.

AESTHETIC ALTARITIES

According to Pérez, Chicana artists have used the altar as an art form for the past three decades. Most utilize it to make social commentary on culturally relevant matters in the Chicana/o community. While the altar does not function the same way in all art installations, altar-inspired art is oftentimes used to convey a gender-conscious, politicized spirituality that speaks to social issues, such as patriarchy in Mexican culture, or to validate the experiences of Mexican women, as is the case in the work of Chicana artist Amalia Mesa-Bains. Pérez explains the multiple ways Chicanas use the altar in their art: "Altar-installation and altar-inspired art inescapably references the altar's timeless and cross-cultural spiritual function, whether to sacralize the profane; to interrogate the spiritual claims and political effects of dominant religious beliefs; to figure the imbrication of the artistic, the spiritual, and the political; or . . . to articulate presently meaningful, hybrid forms of spirituality and spiritually conscious art making" (*Chicana Art* 92).

In this section I will focus on the overlap of the artistic, the spiritual, and the political in MdM's femzine. I discuss three ways I see altarities as described by Pérez: the altar as a site of invocation of the "unseen"; the altar as a site of ofrenda, or offering; and the altar as a site of sacrifice or death. This aesthetic approach is more palpable in the introduction of each volume, but is especially present in volume 12, "Ofrendas of the Flesh." Engaging with altarities to speak about these issues reveals a Chicana artistic, political, and spiritual aesthetic that diverges from other third wave femzine creators.

While many third wave femzinesters address gender violence by sharing personal stories or by offering guidance on how to respond to violence, here Chicanas write poetry that conveys their understanding of violence as a systemic issue that affects communities of color and women in particular on the local and global levels. Although several poems describe personal experiences with violence, the use of altarities creates a more nuanced understanding of that experience, one that draws on the spiritual and political as a form of healing. In the following sections, I define the three functions of the altar that I use as framework to analyze the poetry and art in "Ofrendas" and explain how the altar is evident in MdM's zine project in general.

ALTAR AS A SITE OF INVOCATION AND MEMORY

Chicanas adopted the altar to bring visibility to the "invisible." Altars, Pérez affirms, are sites of recuperation, recovery, or memory of those who are not "seen," or are "dead" in the eyes of many, those who are "not fully within social discourse," the ethnic "minority," the Latina/o, the sexually "queer" (*Chicana Art* 125). Pérez adds that altars are also sites of invocation of "that which is disembodied for reason of its *alterity* with respect to dominant cultural norms" (144). Pérez uses the Latin word for "the other," or the alter, to complicate the function of the altar as a site where Chicana artists invoke "the other," but also as an art form of "the Other" in the eyes of the dominant culture, which deems Chicanas as socially and culturally outside the norm.

By dedicating *Flor y Canto* to the community of women of the past, present, and future generations, MdM's publication project functions as a site of invocation and memory. "This *amoxtli*,"[11] they write, "is an offering to those before us and those to come. A seed in our struggle to remain human" ("Somos"). In paying homage to the generations of the past and future, MdM draws from the Dakota Sioux belief of the Seven Generations: the idea that actions represent learning from the previous three generations and the understanding that existing actions will influence the lives of three subsequent generations (Wildcat 121). As Wildcat affirms, "we are simultaneously shaped by history and are shapers of future history" (122). *Flor y Canto* documents their shaping of Chicana "herstory," while acknowledging that Xicana feminist activists shape their work. The altar is thus manifested in the simultaneous act of offering and paying homage to the past, present, and future generations, a promise of continuing to make this artistic ofrenda to their community by drawing on the legacy of resistance of the previous generations.

ALTAR AS A SITE OF OFFERING

The altar can also serve as a site of offering or ofrenda. To give an ofrenda is to pay homage to someone or something; it is the act of surrendering or sacrificing on one's own terms, in hopes that it will manifest into hopeful and better futures. For Pérez, when Chicanas invoke the altar in their art, it functions as an "offering on the altar," offering the fruit of artistic labor with the aspiration that it will be transformative and healing to the community (*Chicana Art* 6). In many spiritual traditions, altars are believed to be sites of "mediation between the material and the spiritual" worlds (124). Thus certain items are placed on the altar as an offering to the spirits during healing ceremonies or other special occasions. When Chicanas draw on the concept of offering in their altar-inspired art, they pay homage and respect to that which is not seen: the invisible, unheard, and unrecognized in their art. While the altar as a site of memory and the altar as site of ofrenda overlap—in fact, one cannot exist without the other, as is the case in the tradition of Day of the Dead, where the altar *is* the offering—for the purpose of this essay, they are discussed as distinct entities.

For MdM, the work they do to publish and distribute the zine is an offering to the community. In producing an amoxtli that is abounding with "poetry and truth" by women of color, MdM creates a "sacred object," which they place on the community "altar." They do this with the hope that the "flower and song" on the pages will be healing and empowering for other women. By "chronicling ourselves for ourselves," they write, "we inspire the minds and spirits of the younger generation to keep the dream alive" ("Somos").

ALTAR AS A SITE OF SACRIFICE OR DEATH

Chicanas have used the darker aspect of the altar in their art to represent a site of death, destruction, or sacrifice. The altar as "sacrificial slab," as Pérez calls it, signifies violence and annihilation, or that which has been sacrificed against one's will (*Chicana Art* 114). To be sacrificed often suggests the act of one being "crucified" for the common good, as was the case in many ancient religious practices. Here, however, artists subvert the idea of the "common good" and are instead speaking against the powers and systems that sacrifice people for the "common good" of the privileged few. In other words, when Chicanas invoke the altar as sacrificial slab, they depict those who have fallen victims of capitalism, patriarchy, sexism, and other types of violence. Each volume of *Flor y Canto* is centered on a theme that connects to larger social issues. The poetry and art in the zine make commentaries on the social, political, environmental, and economic oppression that people in communities of color face and how this inevitably affects women.

OFRENDAS OF THE FLESH: MEMORY, OFFERINGS, AND SACRIFICIAL SLAB

The volume "Ofrendas of the Flesh" takes an explicit altar-like approach on multiple levels. As the title indicates, the booklet concerns offerings;

more specifically, it asks women to consider how they offer their "flesh" or bodies in a world where women's bodies are abused and violated physically and institutionally. The theme of this volume echoes what Chicana feminist theorist Cherríe Moraga calls "a theory in the flesh," where women's "flesh and blood" experiences, their physical realities and struggles, their sexuality, skin color, and where they grew up come together to "create a politic born out of necessity" (23). Although artists interpret the theme in a number of ways, the submissions in the volume ultimately speak the raw knowledge women bring from their lived experiences. Some express that they reclaim their bodies by making offerings on their own terms: "Women's flesh is ours to offer," declare the editors, "it is ours to act, reclaim, take back, hide, and voice as we wish" ("Ofrendas"). Women "offer" what they consider sacred, whether that comes in the form of offering their flesh to the ink of a tattoo or offering their flesh to a sexual partner of their own liking. In this sense, women articulate their agency over their own bodies and their lives in the form of ofrenda. To offer herself in any way she wishes counters the misconception that women's bodies are readily available or that women have no control over their own bodies, especially important for women of color whose bodies have historically been violated.

However, the reader also finds that women interpret the theme by drawing on the altar as sacrificial slab. In the "Forward," Diea May makes a connection between the 1997 incident in Italy—when the Italian Supreme Court declared a man free because the woman he raped was wearing jeans—and the ways in which women's bodies have been and continue to be abused and assaulted without consequence today. The international movement known as Denim Day was born as a result of this incident, "a yearly reminder that women's flesh is abused and taken advantage of physically and institutionally" (May 2). The altar thus becomes a site of violence that women invoke to speak out against these abuses. Conversely, the altar as a site of memory and invocation of the alter, or "the other," is also suggested here, as women use their art to bring visibility to the often invisible, unheard, and untold stories of those who have fallen victim to the hegemonic powers that perpetuate gender violence. For instance, women draw on the Day of the Dead altar and the Aztec sacrificial altar to tell their stories or make critiques against the violation of their body.

Zuleica Zepeda, Justice for My Daddy. Digital Photography. 2013.

This photo was taken at the Statewide Mass March Against Police Brutality in Anaheim, Califas. Justice for Jose de la Trinidad! Shot [7 times] & killed by LA Sheriff's Deputies November 10, 2012.

FIGURE 27.2 "Justice for My Daddy." Zuleica Zepeda.

However, before presenting the poetry and art, MdM opens the zine by addressing racial and state violence against men of color. "Ofrendas" opens with a dedication, "to all the families who mourn because of the police state." In a poem titled "Too Many," Diea May speaks against police violence against men. She writes, "Heart clenches / brutality badged / soul shudders / personally / gun purloins people . . . wombyn nation mourns our people / we question / and we anger / and we continue" (ii). She not only describes an intimate scene of police brutality but alludes to the women who are left behind to pick up the pieces. They "mourn," she says, but they also "continue" to convey strength and perseverance in the face of adversity. She concludes the poem by stating, "May all the young men whose lives are taken by badged persons rest in power. . . . Blessings to the families that continue to mourn while many forget" (ii). On the opposite page sits a black and white photograph of a little girl holding a protest sign that reads "Justice for My Daddy" by Zuleica Zepeda (figure 27.2). In the middle of the sign, there is a picture of two young girls hugging a young man who squats down to embrace them, all three smiling at the camera.

It may seem out of place to honor the lives of men in the opening of a zine that focuses on women. Yet May invokes the altar as sacrificial slab here to educate readers about the larger structures of violence against communities of color. By placing this poem and photograph at the opening of the zine, readers are aware that police violence in communities of color is not separate from violent acts against women of color. To combat one, the other must also be combated; as Black Lives Matter activists remind us, "laws, policies, and the culture that underpin gender inequalities are reinforced by America's racial divide" (Asoka and Chatelain). By pointing to the way men's flesh is sacrificed by the police state, this piece also functions as a pedagogical tool to educate an audience of mostly women that violence is not merely behavioral but also structural.

Another form of structural violence that the poets in "Ofrendas" address is the exploitation of women. In Diana Pando's poem "Mythology of Flesh and Turquoise Serpents," she explicitly uses the altar as the sacrificial stone by placing it in the context of an Aztec human sacrifice to speak to the ways in which women's bodies are abused and exploited because of capitalist greed.[12] Pando uses the vivid imagery of a sacrificial ceremony—obsidian daggers, turquoise fire serpents, entrails, and carnage—as a way to compare this seemingly barbarous act to that of greedy capitalists who exploit women in the most inhumane ways. She writes, "Hermanas bust ass in cubicle ten hours a day and clean office buildings to put food on table. Offerings of flesh observed but we look the other way cuz it's easier on the eye" (3). She sets what we do not want to see before us in an altarlike fashion; even if we are not the exploiters, we are complicit if we refuse to see the Other. Implying that the victim is a mother by making a reference to putting food on the table adds to Pando's critique, as it is well known that women tend to be the most vulnerable to exploitation in the workforce. The worker is thus making a sacrifice for her family while simultaneously sacrificing herself to her employer.

Pando moves on from women workers to the femicides in Ciudad Juárez. She writes, "This is the body of Christ. Wait, no it's the body and blood of maquiladoras making money for men refusing to mourn Mujeres de Juárez. Flowery offering of flesh strewn in desert" (3). By specifically stating that maquiladoras make money for men, she points to a larger issue rooted in a system of patriarchy that deems women's bodies more exploitable and their lives less valuable, precisely because they are women. As Rosa Linda Fregoso states, "One way to politicize violence against women . . . is by highlighting the role of the patriarchal state in creating the conditions of possibility for the proliferation of gender violence" (133). Pando recreates this site of sacrificial violence to challenge perceptions of barbarity, considering the ways in which capitalist society sacrifices victims every single day.

Pando concludes the poem by describing the end of the sacrificial ceremony, alluding to mythical figures and leftover entrails: "Turquoise fire serpent / Slithers in sharp opal teeth / Looking to devour / entrails of sueños [dreams] left over on man made altars / and realizing it's not the Universe demanding tribute / it's our own hunger." Turquoise fire serpent is what the Aztecs called the Lord of Fire, Xiuhtecuhtli, who among other things was the patron god of the Aztec emperors and of the merchant class, the *pochteca*. It is he who devours the entrails of dreams "left over on man made alters [sic]" pointing to the Aztec's own elitist and imperialist culture, as human sacrifice was more tied to military strategies than spirituality. Thus, by pointing to the "man made altars" and "our own hunger," she is suggesting that violence is not inherent in the spiritual beliefs of the Aztecs but much more connected to human avarice. In utilizing the trope of human sacrifice to discuss the exploitation of women's bodies, Pando asks readers to take another look at capitalist society. In making parallels between the Aztecs and "our own hunger," she does not romanticize Aztec culture but rather illustrates Fregoso's assertion that violence is endemic to the State, "produced by an authoritarian government that has cultivated forms of violence . . . and even death" (132). Thus Pando's poem makes use of the sacrificial altar to make a larger critique of violence against women, pointing to the altar as a site of violence imposed on women that is linked to patriarchy, capitalism, and the State.

Like Pando, Fe Montes also provides a critique of gender violence but this time through a digital silkscreen image that points to the Americas as a site of sacrifice. Montes's image is a black-and-white photo collage of Latina faces cut out and clustered together. Their eyes and black hair stand out, while their faces look colorless. Each woman looks straight into the camera as if acknowledging the viewer's gaze. An image of murder or death is conveyed, as a slight random splattering of blood over the faces of the women is present, although subtle. A large map of the Americas, orange in color, sits above the collage with the words "America's Next Top Murder" in black (figure 27.3). The words head the North American section of the map and Christian crosses are dispersed throughout the north, central, and southern sections of the Americas, indicating that women have died in these locations.

Montes's image points to a global, interlocking capitalist system that functions, first and foremost, to make profit at all costs for its ruling classes, as they are complicit in the murders and exploitation of women. Although Mexico's high-profile femicides have drawn the most attention, Montes suggests that we should not limit the geographical sites of violence to one region; women's lives are devalued across the Americas. Countries like Guatemala, El Salvador, and Colombia have high numbers of female murders, yet reports suggest that rate of femicides in in the United States is staggering (Russell and Harmes). When Montes displays the words "America's Next Top Murder" across North America, she suggests that gender violence is not limited to "Third World" countries. She makes developed countries like the U.S. complicit in the femicides, as U.S. economic imperialist strategies such as free trade agreements rarely

Felicia 'Fe' Montes, America's Next Top Murder. Silkscreen. 2011.

FIGURE 27.3 "America's Next Top Murder." Felicia 'Fe' Montes, 2011.

benefit the poorest communities; women have suffered the most from these policies.

In placing the religious iconography of the cross throughout both continents, North and South America, a common item in domestic altars, Montes creates an altar-like aesthetic of memory, invocation, and coexistence with the spirits of the dead. Paying homage to these women counters the mostly apathetic reaction of officials who have done little to deal with this serious problem. Clustering the faces of these women, who are clearly Latina, into one unifying image, Montes is at risk of homogenizing the individual experience and story of each woman. However, these images also indicate what many have observed: that it is the dark-skinned, poor women who are most vulnerable to violence. Thus to pay reverence to them is also to make their social invisibility visible. As Pérez asserts, altars cultivate memory and "that in itself is political and that in turn can generate wider social and political effects" (*Chicana Art* 124). Montes's image attests to this phenomenon.

While some may revere or pay homage to the unacknowledged and unseen women in their altar-like art, some pay homage to themselves. In doing so, the altar functions as a site of healing. In "An Offering to the Silence," Mary Alvarado raises the question of sexual violence as she grapples with the deeply personal experience of rape, a particularly secretive issue not often discussed in public. Many femzine creators have used their zine as a platform to openly address their experiences of rape and incest. Piepmeier explains that discussing these personal issues in public through zines helps with the healing process (165). Similarly, Alvarado makes her story public, indicating that healing has begun to take place. Here she uses the Day of the Dead altar as a site to pay homage to the dead, but to Alvarado, the dead is a child, a young victim of rape. Using the second-person point of view throughout the poem indicates that she speaks to someone else, to the "dead" person she is invoking. To Alvarado, the "dead" is that little girl who learned to hate her body, repressed her sexual desires and curiosity, and stopped being who she was after she was violated.

The tradition of the Day of the Dead, a holiday celebrated throughout Latin America, is rooted in the belief that on November 2nd those who have departed will visit earth to celebrate with the living. The living prepares for the visit of the deceased by paying homage to them in the form of ofrendas, which include altars filled with flowers, food, and other treats. Alvarado gives her ofrenda to "la niña que se perdió" (the girl who was lost) when she was raped (11). She writes, "Mi cuerpo, el cuerpo mío. Una vela, una ofrenda a ese cuerpo virgen, that virgin body" (11). Alvarado lights a candle to pay tribute to the virgin body that died at the age of eight. Although virginity is usually attributed with purity, here Alvarado reappropriates spirituality from patriarchal institutions like the Catholic Church that equate virginity with a woman's worth. By placing her virginity on the altar as something that is dead, not because she allowed it to be, but because it was forcefully taken from her, she points back to a patriarchal culture that perpetuates forms of violence on female bodies while at the same time policing them.

Alvarado also pays homage on her altar to the person she used to be. She writes, "El 2 de noviembre comes and an offering is made to that dead person you let him make of you when he raped you at 8" (12). On her altar she places "an offering a esa vagina que te tardaste en aceptar, and you . . . castigated its sexuality and found aversion, repugnance, and grew antipathy, and animosity, and made it your nemesis" (11). As the Day of the Dead ritual is centered on a coexistence with the dead, here Alvarado makes peace by coexisting with her traumatic past, which also includes a past of self-loathing, both of her body and of her sexuality. Yet she invokes that part of her that is "dead" and gives it new life, and thus the process becomes a form of rebirth. When November 2 comes, she says, "I no longer give him, the one who rapes, the power to kill me; Instead, I celebrate to please, love, and feed my body daily! I give life to that pandemic disease called SILENCE on November 2" (12). The altar provides a space for healing but also has a cyclical function that illustrates the Mesoamerican notion of life and death itself; that life and death are inextricably intertwined is partially why the Day of the Dead is celebrated. Thus Alvarado's poem echoes this cycle in her own healing process, first presenting the little girl who "died" as a result of being violated, then presenting the "new" woman who is alive and happy, and finally connecting back to that little girl, that part of herself, who dwells in the realm of the dead. Silence turns into voice in the process, as silence is what sexual predators thrive on and what partially perpetuates the abuse of young children. Here Alvarado "gives life" to silence by transforming it on her altar.

Alvarado, Pando, Montes, and May's visual and literary art illustrates how Chicanas coalesce art, politics, and Chicana Indigenous spirituality to speak out against gender violence. In doing so, these women demonstrate a unique approach to third wave activism—one that is informed by their own cultural memory and traditions.

CONCLUSION

In creating an ofrenda-like zine, MdM assists in the healing process for both the women who are published and the community at large. MdM writes, "This work is a prayer for the healing of our selves, our communities, and our Mother Earth" ("13 Baktun"). While healing can take place in different forms, for women of color—who are often the least recognized for their creative talents—artistic expression allows more freedom to step out of prescribed roles and be artists, even if in just one volume of *Flor y Canto*. As Anzaldúa asserts, "language, fine arts and literature do not belong to women of color and culture and the social system enslave our hands in clerical, factory, field or secretarial work to service it" ("Haciendo," xxiv). Yet these voices deserve to be heard, published, and displayed.

Furthermore, when an aesthetic form like altarities is applied to honor a person or a people by remembering them, by making them visible and by coexisting with them, it makes a political statement; it conveys that they are worth remembering in a world that deems them not valuable. To make an ofrenda is to honor a person or community. Yet altarities also allow one to be aware of and point to the forces that sacrifice or kill and exploit members of the community. In other words, they allow one to name the enemy. Archuleta explains in her discussion of the power behind naming the enemy through writing for Native women: "Although Indigenous women face numerous enemies from the past into the present, we realize that healing and empowerment cannot take place until we identify the many sources of our oppression" (92). In "Ofrendas," Chicanas use altarities as an aesthetic language to name the enemy, so that healing, survival, and resistance can take place.[13]

MdM's *Flor y Canto* invites us into an intimate space where one can see how women of color grapple with violence. Articulating it through a medium like poetry and art signifies awareness, which is the first step in the process of healing and creating change. As Anzaldúa reminds us, "Awareness of our situation must come before inner changes, which in turn come before changes in society" (*Borderlands* 109). This idea links back to the question of third wave feminist activism. Although MdM are part of this feminist generation and engage with similar meanings of activism as their feminist counterparts, Chicanas like MdM draw from their own epistemologies, both spiritual and cultural, to enact their activism. In MdM's case, artivism is rooted in making other women art creators, and through that process elevates them as healers and wise women, like the tlamatini.

While zines do not offer an official platform for women of color to voice their concerns, their presence in these small publications is significant nonetheless. I say "small" because these little, grassroots, underground, self-published booklets are not high profile; they get easily lost in the world of official publishing. Nevertheless, Barbara Christian reminds critics of the ramifications of their work, of their choices of what to critique: "Literary criticism," she states, "is promotion as well as understanding, a response to the writer to whom there is often no response.... I know, from literary history, that writing disappears unless there is a response to it" (62). To look at these underground publications that gleam with the "poetry and truth" of women is to promote their work and ensure that it continues circulating and living in our imaginations. By making them the subject of analysis, critics put these artists on *altares* and keep their memory alive; it is how we coexist with them in our work.

NOTES

Reprinted with permission from Norell Martínez, "Femzines, Artivism, and Altar Aesthetics: Third Wave Feminism Chicana Style," *Chiricú Journal: Latina/o Literatures, Arts, and Cultures* 2, no. 2 (Spring 2018): pp. 45–67.

1. The Chicana members of MdM are editors and producers of *Flor y Canto*. Though a Chicana-led project, the poetry and art on the pages are not limited to a Chicana demographic. Hence I do not use the terms "Chicanas" and "women of color" interchangeably but rather deploy them to specify the difference between the producers and the contributors to the zine. I use the term "women of color" to refer to women who belong to racial and ethnic groups that have been legally and socially subordinated in the United States, which include Latina, Black, Asian American, and Native American women. I choose to use the term not to erase the individual concerns of each group or with the intention to cling to categories or labels that maintain restrictive forms of identity politics, but to unify across color lines in the struggle against sexism, racism, homophobia, and class oppression.
2. Throughout this essay, I use the singular form when referring to MdM as a single entity or group, and the plural form when referring to them as a collection of individual women.
3. A couple of definitions are useful here. Duncombe and Lambert argue that *artivism* is not "art about politics," meaning that using "social injustice and political struggle as a mere subject matter" will not do. *Artivism*, they say, is art "that intends to change the very way we see, act and make sense of our world—including what we understand to be politics itself." Although Anzaldúa does not use the term *artivism*, her understanding of women of color's "creative acts" is relevant, especially when considering the work of MdM. She declares that for women of color, "writing, painting, performing, and filming are acts of deliberate and des-

perate determination to subvert the status quo. Creative acts," she says, "are forms of political activism employing definite aesthetic strategies for resisting dominant cultural norms and are not merely aesthetic exercises" ("Haciendo," xxiv).

4. The "rrr" in front of "girl" represents an angry growl.
5. The name "Women of Maize" alludes to the cultural importance of maize in Mesoamerica as essential to the survival and livelihood of the people. It also makes visible the role Indigenous women have played throughout history in agricultural traditions and resistance struggles, work that has often been overlooked. Miguel Angel Asturias's classic novel *Hombres de maíz* (1949), for instance, about an Indigenous community whose land is under threat by outside interests, centers on male Indigenous leaders. The title references the creation story of the Maya K'iche' people, the *Popol Vuh*, a tale about the first people who were created from maize. The hero twins in the tale, Hunahpú and Xbalanqué, are often depicted as male. However, there is debate among scholars questioning whether Xbalanqué is actually female. If this is true, it is another example of the ways in which Indigenous women have been erased.
6. I will use the term "Xicana" when referring to Chicana feminists who embrace a Xicana indígena politics in their work.
7. I acknowledge that there are problems and contradictions with the use of Indigenous worldviews, including the essentializing and romanticization of a pre-Columbian past. It is beyond the scope of this essay to analyze these issues. Review the work of Sheila Marie Contreras for a thorough critique.
8. The term "Nahua" is used to discuss the group of Mesoamerican peoples that spoke the Nahuatl language. The Nahua people include the Toltecs and Mexica.
9. For a detailed study on the traditions and philosophy of the Nahua people, review Miguel León-Portilla. He explains that the Toltecs were highly regarded for their artistry, religious practices, and philosophical ideas.
10. Find the full poem in chapter 26.
11. "Book" in Nahuatl.
12. Find the full poem in chapter 23.
13. Review "Know Your Enemy: The Sham of Filipino Independence" in chapter 3 for a poetic analysis of this topic.

BIBLIOGRAPHY

Alvarado, Mary. "An Offering to the Silence." In *Flor y Canto*, "Ofrendas of the Flesh," Vol. 12. Los Angeles, 2014.

Anzaldúa, Gloria. *Borderlands: La Frontera*. San Francisco: Aunt Lute, 1999.

———. "Haciendo Caras, Una Entrada." In *Making Face, Making Soul*, edited by Gloria Anzaldúa, xv–xxviii. San Francisco: Aunt Lute, 1990.

Archuleta, Elizabeth. "I Give You Back: Indigenous Women Writing to Survive." *Studies in American Indian Literature* 18, no. 4 (2006): 88–114. http://www.jstor.org/stable/20737352.

Asoka, Kaavya, and Marcia Chatelain. "Women and Black Lives Matter: An Interview with Marcia Chatelain." *Dissent*, Summer 2015. Accessed February 22, 2016. htttp://www.dissentmagazine.org/article/women-black-lives-matter-interview-marcia-chatelain.

Asturias, Miguel Angel. *Hombres de maíz*. Buenos Aires: Losada, 1949.

Carrasco, David. *Religions of Mesoamerica*. San Francisco: Harper & Row, 1990.

Castillo, Ana. *Massacre of the Dreamers: Essays on Xicanisma*. New York: Plume, 1994.

Chincilla, Maya. "Mi Querido 24th and Mission." In *Flor y Canto*, "13 Baktun," vol. 8. Los Angeles, 2003.

Christian, Barbara. "The Race for Theory." *Cultural Critique*, no. 6 (1987): 51–63. https://doi.org/10.2307/1354255.

Contreras, Sheila Marie. *Bloodlines: Myth, Indigenism, and Chicana/o Literature*. Austin: University of Texas Press, 2008.

Delgado, Manuel. "Artivismo y pospolítica. Sobre la estetización de las luchas sociales en contextos urbanos," *QuAderns-e: Institut Catalá d'Antropología* 2, no. 18 (2013): 68–80. https://raco.cat/index.php/QuadernseICA/article/view/274290/362359.

Duncombe, Stephen, and Steve Lambert. "An Open Letter to Critics Writing about Political Art," Center for Artistic Activism, October 20, 2012, accessed September 9, 2015, http://artisticactivism.org/2012/10/an-open-letter-to-critics-writing-about-political-art/.

EZLN, "Cuarta declaración de la selva Lacondona, 1996," *Enlace Zapatista*. Accessed March 14, 2018. http://enlacezapatista.ezln.org.mx.

Flor y Canto. "13 Baktun." Vol. 8, 2003.

———. "Cantando Al Amanacer" Vol. 5. Los Angeles, 2007.

———. "Ofrendas of the Flesh." Vol. 12. Los Angeles, 2014.

———. "One: Body, Mind Spirit." Vol. 14. Los Angeles, 2016.

———. "Rites of Passage." Vol. 10. Los Angeles, 2012.

———. "Somos Medicina." Vol. 6. Los Angeles, 2008.

Fregoso, Rosa Linda. "The Complexities of Feminicide on the Border." In *Color of Violence: The INCITE! Anthology*, edited by INCITE! Women of Color Against Violence, 130–34, Cambridge: South End Press, 2006.

Hackman, Rose. "Femicides in the US: The Silent Epidemic Few Dare to Name." *The Guardian*, September 26, 2021. https://www.theguardian.com/us-news/2021/sep/26/femicide-us-silent-epidemic.

León-Portilla, Miguel. *Los antiguos mexicanos a traves de sus crónicas y cantares*. Mexico: Fondo de Cultura Económica, 2005.

May, Diea. Forward to "Ofrendas of the Flesh," *Flor y Canto*. Vol. 12, Los Angeles, 2014.

Medina, Lara. Forward to "Somos Medicina," *Flor y Canto*. Vol. 6, Los Angeles, 2008.

Moraga, Cherríe. "Theory in the Flesh." In *This Bridge Called My Back*, edited by Gloria Anzaldúa and Cherríe Moraga, 23–29. New York: Kitchen Table Press, 1981.

Nguyen, Mimi. "Riot Grrrl, Race and Revival." *Women and Performance: A Journal of Feminist Theory* 22, no. 2–3 (2012): 173–96.

Pando, Diana. "Mythology of Flesh and Turquoise Serpents." In *Flor y Canto*, "Ofrendas of the Flesh." Vol. 12. Los Angeles, 2014.

Pérez, Laura E. *Chicana Art: The Politics of Spiritual and Aesthetic Altarities*. Durham, N.C.: Duke University Press, 2007.

Piepmeier, Alison. *Girl Zines: Making Media, Doing Feminism*. New York: New York University Press, 2009.

Popol Vuh: The Sacred Book of the Maya. Translated by Allen J. Christenson. Norman: University of Oklahoma Press, 2007.

Wildcat, Daniel R. *Red Alert! Saving the Planet with Indigenous Knowledge*. Golden, Colo.: Fulcrum Books, 2009.

Zoble, Elke. "Cultural Production, Transnational Networking, and Critical Reflection in Feminist Zines." *Signs: Journal of Women in Culture & Society* 25, no. 1 (2009): 1–12. https://doi.org/10.1086/599256.

28

Teatro Heals

JO ANNA MIXPE LEY

CLOSE YOUR eyes and imagine seeing smiles blossom on people's rostros and observing the moments of epiphany that emanate off people's faces when the sisters take the stage. That is what happens when you attend a Mujeres de Maiz event. That's why it's hard to believe what some people, even those within the Chicana/o movement, envisioned when they thought about Mujeres de Maiz in the late 1990s. From the various comments, I thought I would be walking into a space where women had bras and sage in their hands, howling underneath the full-blood eclipsed moon while bringing down the walls of the system as they invited us to feast upon the hearts of misogynistic imperialistic men.

Yet, when I saw my first show in 1998 at the CSO, I entered a sea of beautifully diverse people of color, whom I did not have to necessarily worry about explaining myself to. To see sisters I attended college with at that time on stage, such as Martha Gonzalez, Felicia 'Fe' Montes, Sarah Rosencrantz, and D'Lo spit words of loving fire, Marisol Lydia Torres in her performance skit paraded the world's largest chancla I had seen in my life, followed by poems and songs by In Lak Ech—there was no doubt I was in the right place. In my college years, I emphasized the activist in the "student activist" label. I prioritized attending meetings, organizing rallies against the elimination of affirmative action, and so much more over my academics. As one of the last generations of affirmative action cohorts, ensuring access to college was a priority, which also left no space for my own creation of art.

Yet, in one hour, these sisters of Mujeres de Maiz and the space and the community they created redefined the role of the arts in my life as a community organizer by exemplifying how, in fact, it was not only a possibility but that the arts are necessary to reach a larger audience in ways that most traditional community organizing fall short of doing. So, I began to write narratives, mostly poetry again, with clear intention, and to share my writing at political manifestations and community events. The first shift into using art as a tool for social change was when I collaborated with my friend at UCLA, Desire Flores, who is a phenomenal dancer. She created a movement dance routine to one of my poems about farmworkers in America and we had the honor to perform this for Dolores Huerta. The way the movements and words simultaneously communicated her family's farm-working experience allowed me to break my own preconceived boundaries that I could not integrate my writing that I have created since I was eight years old into my political organizing. This performance motivated me to apply to a one-week writing seminar with Cherríe Moraga. The experience with all the writers and Cherríe Moraga herself was so life-changing that it is the reason why I now have my MFA and continue to write. A cycle of positive, transformative blessings abounds.

As the years passed, the Mujeres de Maiz events and yearly International Women's Day event was something I never missed. It became my safe space. I have been an educator for over fifteen years, and it is a place I still refer my students to attend because the knowledge gained from the performances, dialogues, and interactions with those present is not found in books. To witness and be a part of it all is such an amazing practice of community healing.

In time, I became fortunate enough to contribute to their yearly zine, allowing space for my voice to be heard.[1] I began to volunteer at the events, and I formed a sisterhood with many of these fierce mujeres. These bonds were strengthened because the compassion behind their art goes beyond the stage. Our roads and circles intersect and meld together many times in the educational setting, in ceremonial settings, community spaces/centers, and on the streets on the daily. In 2003 I traveled to Chiapas with some of the sisters. I organized binational efforts with them, I happily and nervously participated in their events as an MC, I taught, marched alongside, shared prayers with, and became sisters with them. These intersections enriched our art, and I saw the ever-lasting impact it was having, and I felt so blessed to be a part of it.

These sisters had their Chicana badassery together!

And then it occurred. One day, at one of the MDM events, Felicia 'Fe' Montes, Marisol Lydia Torres, Marlene Beltran, and I were hanging out. As we were talking about the next Mujeres de Maiz show, Fe suggested, "You three do theater. You should write a skit and perform it at the next show, we need Xicana theater." We pondered, looked at each other, and were like, "Yeeaaah." We've done theater together a few times and continue to do it on our own sooooo BOOM—Teatro M to the 3rd (get it: Marlene, Marisol, Mixpe) was formed, which later became "Las Ramonas." We renamed ourselves after Comandanta Ramona and the influence she had on our lives. Myself and Marlene of Las Ramonas were in Chiapas during Comandanta Ramona's passing. We were humbled to stay in the space where her velorio was held when we went to the Caracol of Oventic to have a cultural exchange between people of color and the Zapatistas. Flowers were still present in the room; we felt her presence envelop us as we slept on the dirt in preparation for our exchanges the next day.

With so much going on in our Chicana/o/POC community, we knew satire was the way to go. Laughter is a way to delve into things that oftentimes make us uncomfortable. It opens roads to dialogue. More than anything, we wanted the performance to act as a mirror of our community. The first performance we wrote, blocked, did costumes, sound effects, acted in, and produced was called "Mujeres Contra La Rabia del Machismo" (MCLRDM). MCLRDM was created as an infomercial format because unfortunately we all have had a toxic Chicano in our lives who is really a machista in disguise. Through our satirical performance, we offered women a clinic where a simple operation could "remove the machista out of him, so he can then become a gender and culturally sensitive compañero" in the movement.

I can't begin to express how liberating, comforting, and what an absolutely maniacally balanced and fun experience it is to create with Marlene and Marisol. It was instantaneously effortless. We brainstormed together, spent time writing the script together, and created a space where we knew our ideas mattered. We rehearsed in our small apartment spaces, late hours at schools, community spaces, wherever was available. I would reveal more details of our secret process, but if I did so, I might have my Ramona card revoked, and this Ramona don't play that.

Without any real expectations of how people were going to take our very satirical piece, we were excited to debut "Mujeres Contra La Rabia del Machismo" at a Mujeres de Maiz show in 2007, and people loved it. They laughed at our characters, our punch lines, our contorted body movements, and face gestures. It fueled us with so much energy to fully commit to our characters as we performed. At that moment, we knew it would not be a one-time thing. We shared our performance at various universities throughout the United States, at "Take Back the Night," "Dia de los Muertos," "Farce of July," antibanning ethnic studies events in Arizona, and mucho, mucho mas.

Through it all, we created various multimedia performances, our full-on "That's What She Said" show, our "Chihuahua in a Box," and "Freestyle Conspiracy" music videos, "Afterschool Freestyle Special," skits galore, and one that is still waiting to exhale. Las Ramonas is one of the best things that has happened in my life.

Mujeres de Maiz has created a space for communion and reunion. It is a place for dialogue, reflection, growth, laughter, tears, and creation. It has supported and challenged my role as a teacher, organizer, and artist in and for the community. And the best part is that many of these mujeres are my sisters por vida. They are the ones I turn to for anything. We have overcome so many struggles, losses, organized many events and actions, and, as the Zapatistas have taught us, celebrated many victories. It has been a part of my self-autonomy, my journey for growth, my journey for change, my and our journey for self-love.

NOTE

1. Review "Poema Para Abuela: Escúchame" in chapter 29.

29

Poema Para Abuela

Escúchame

JO ANNA MIXPE LEY

Camila went to her Quince
in a vestido de fine filagrina
Croched from Abuelita's strands
of white cabello.

Underneath seven layers of vestidos,
Abuelita hid the third creación
from her viejo,
wrapped up the first two around
her body—
retreating into wind spilling
with pozole from Rosita's stand.
All four pansitas groaned
as she escaped Las Brisas
Tijuana
to Boyle Heights
where cleaning solution X
ate through seven
layers of filagrina.

Pero mírame Abuela,
siete años of purging scalded mis
    tripas.
A plato de pozole is
a shot of cleaning solution X.
Que pena, mi cuerpo,
good for only libros
reading, eating, writing them.

Escúchame Abuela,
I know you don't rest,
I smelled you as I washed my hands
    and mouth in el baño,
I heard you as prima Camila
    performed el Baltz,
I see you jumping off this page.

Las nubes—
they are crotched from Abuelita's
    strands of white cabellos.

***

I wish I could tell you Abuelita,
cara a cara,
how you woke me anoche.
You came through in waves
Past the cup living
      underneath my bed
      blocking entryway for spirits
straight onto my chest.

I became you
      as you became me
an image lost in reflection—
I saw you,
occupying my seat
in the kitchen table,
stuffing napkins underneath
your leg, thinking
      no one was looking.
The moon broke in
the kitchen, illuminating a blue corn
   growing from your hair.
I walked up to you
tore off the husk,
and took a bite,
      intractable hairs clinging
      to the cracks in my teeth.

Abuelita, I fell asleep
on the kitchen table, again.

When I woke up,

a San Marcos cobija held me tightly.
A trail of baba
ran down imprints
creased into my cheek
from the cracks on the table.
Machupichu's grains de arroz reflected
off la laguna de baba
on the table.

Discomfort gnawed,
Alerting my seven senses
of the part
that was going to smell
acrid.

Cloistered napkins sought refuge
hiding within trenches underneath
my leg,
full of food
chewed
but never intended to be eaten.

Mujeres de Maiz, Flor y Canto:
Ofrendas of the Flesh, no. 12 (2014):
      5–6.

30
Una Muñeca

XITLALIC GUIJOSA-OSUNA

No hay que darle
no mas una muñeca
a una niña
Para que aprenda ser mama y esposa.

Dale un libro
Para que aprenda
A escribir poemas,
Ensallos, o nuestra historia

Dale un lapiz
Para que escriba
Todos los sueños
Que ella guarda en su Corazon.

Dale un pincel para que
Pinte el mundo
Que ella desea crear
A lo mejor es un mundo major

Dale apoyo en lo que
Ella quiera hacer
Para que lo haga
Con ganas e inspiracion.

Dale la posibilidad
De ser independiente
Para que tenga

El valor de volar lejos.

Dale la oportunidad
De que te diga
Lo que ella quiere
Hacer con su vida

Dale el espacio para sus
Equivocaciones y que
Ella misma aprenda
De los errors que ha cometido.

Dale el derrecho de
Escojer como ser
Una MUJER y como
VIVIR!

Inspired by the Swapmeet
Maywood, Calif.
*Mujeres de Maiz, Flor y Canto:
Somos Medicina,* no. 6 (2008): 45.

ROUND IV

MDM EPISTEMOLOGIES AND PEDAGOGIES

31
In the Spirit of the Voluta

CRISTINA GOROCICA

I HAD ONLY read a poem aloud once. It was at the Troy Café in Downtown Los Angeles in the mid-nineties where, by chance, I volunteered that night to read my poem. *Pavimiento* was about a young girl looking for adventure on a cold night at the bus stop on Cypress Avenue. Little did I know that the Troy Café reading would leave me wanting more, wanting to write more and to be able to share my writings with others. I kept writing poetry and prose related to my life as a shy, sheltered, Catholic Chicana from *NELAS*, Northeast Los Angeles. Most of my writings after the Troy Café reading would be about me trying to find a place in our big city of Los Angeles, searching for rattles and drums, searching for *comadres* who looked like me with black hair and brown almond eyes, speaking Spanglish and saying *dichos* our parents would yell at us across the living room, and searching for *compañeros* who would respect me as a conscious *mujer*. My *voluta*, the symbol for speech found in the Mayan codices, flowed. My *voluta* existed. My *voluta* came to life that night.

I remember sitting in the PRC, the Public Resource Center, in Highland Park in the fall of 1996. A few of us women started hanging out there and decided to meet up on a warm Wednesday evening and share poems and personal stories. We found out that we all were writers who had been keeping our poems and stories in notebooks and journals, and on receipts, napkins, and random sheets of paper. I remember how nervous I was. I didn't know these brown women very well but our hearts and revolutionary minds were in sync. I was tightly holding onto my Frida Kahlo journal where I had just written a new poem, "Sister in the Movement with an Attitude." There were six of us at the PRC that day: Felicia 'Fe' Montes, Marisol Lydia Torres, Claudia Mercado, Rachel Negrete Thorson, Liza Cohen Hita, and myself. We sat in a circle on a pink couch and black plastic chairs in the recording studio/radio station at the PRC. We each took turns sharing our poems out loud, a little hesitant, and self-conscious.

I remember reading "Sister in the Movement with an Attitude" and hoping that no one would take it personally and ask me to leave. The piece was about women judging women, being fake, backstabbing, and drama that women can create out of spite, jealousy, and trauma. I was calling out women without naming anyone specific, even though I could have. I let the wind take it.

I remember enjoying their pieces as they enjoyed mine. There was a silence that we shared that created spirals through the air, the *volutas*. We smiled, laughed, cried, and smirked at each other. We opened a door that had been kept shut for years. These stories and poems had been hiding in the shadows and pages of our pillows, our binders, our shelves at home. No one knew I wrote poems, wrote prose. It wasn't something my family talked about or encouraged. It wasn't something my closest friends and I shared. For me, they were my secrets and true feelings. Most of us had never shared out our poems and little did we know that these words would empower other young Chicana women. I hadn't really heard of women with strong minds sharing poems. This was the beginning of something, the beginning of *volutas*, flowing through the air, women filled *volutas*, creating wind, energy, filled with ancestral memory.

The next time we met up was the following week after Claudia's radio show at the PRC where she would play local music from Chicano artists and address issues related to the community. We met in the small room and once again sat in a circle to share our stories and poems. The silent *voluta* symbol was hovering above us, invisible but we could feel its presence. The power of sharing our gentle hearts and minds out loud in a safe space was incredibly inspiring. We could feel we had something special between all of us. We felt the world needed to hear our voice, a woman's voice that would not be interrupted or discredited. Weekend after weekend, we attended events at the PRC, and the majority of the events featured male bands or male artists. We wanted the stage and a chance to share our artistic creations.

After that gathering, the six women who had only sat together and shared the spiral *voluta* a few times decided to organize an event at the PRC to share our *palabras*, our true stories as young Chicanas, our desire to be heard, and hopefully inspire others. We had a desire to share our survival stories. We were and are survivors of our ancestral struggles. Our poems reflected our parents, grandparents, and their community-based teachings and struggles. Our poems had and have ancestral memories that we can only credit our ancestors for. Our songs of prayer and gratitude were gifted from those memories that we at times can only relate to those who came before us. We transmit their energy through our *poesia, danzas, y cantos*, our prayer, and our spirituality. We needed a space created by and for women that would honor our words and thoughts. We had created the first Mujeres de Maiz event and our own women's poetry group, In Lak Ech, which is a Mayan phrase that means *tu eres mi otro yo*, or you are my other me. Choosing *In Lak Ech* was a decision that came out of *platica* and debate. It was our responsibility to choose this name. We chose this term because we felt connected to it as conscious, first-generation, Indigenous Chicana women who share similarities and differences and have a strong connection to our identity. In Lak Ech was born out of inspiration and hunger for expression.

IN LAK ECH

Tayecana . . . Viento, Agua, Tierra, Fuego

I remember waking up from a dream early in the morning. When I woke, I started singing the *"Tayecana"* song. *"Viento, agua, tierra, fuego"* flowed like a *voluta*. *"Vente a mi lado, come to my side . . ."* I picked up my hand drum and started singing these words. I rushed to write them down on a napkin next to my bed. An *energia* took over and embraced my voice, my mind, and my will. The drum was a heartbeat and my voice cracked nervously as I sang along. *"Vente a mi lado, Come to our brother sisters, that are in Aztlán . . ."*

This *canto* has been shared at our performances, ceremonies we attended, and later throughout the continent. I credit the gift of these lyrics to the ancestors. The women who make up In Lak Ech—Felicia, Rachel, Liza, Marisol, Claudia, Marlene, and myself—have always recognized that what we do as a women's *flor y canto* group has been a blessing and responsibility. We were put together to create and resonate ourselves through poetry and song that reflect our ancestors' strength and love.

When the "Love Song" came to me, it was from a feeling that words could not express. Only ancestral chorus and Indigenous *weyas* in melodic patterns could exemplify the love I have for family, In Lak Ech, and the community. The "Love Song" is a song to sing to share and express unconditional love towards someone, something, or anything. That's part of the reflection of *In Lak Ech*—when we hold up the sacred mirror to ourselves, what we see reflecting back is another *mujer* that is just like me, just like you, just like any one of us. *In Lak Ech* reminds me that I am not alone, that we women are not alone.

GENERATIONS OF MDM

I was blessed with the pregnancy of my first daughter a few years after the MdM movement was initiated. I was excited to be able to have love and light within me as we created, sang, and organized in our communities. My pregnancy felt important and significant within the momentum and a voice we created as conscious Chicana women. Tayecana Gallegos, my daughter, is a little spirit who lived and thrived in me as I wrote and brought the *"Tayecana"* song to life. She walks with the four directions, the heartbeat inside, the fire in her blood. She is the passion and love behind *"Tayecana."* Ixchel Gallegos, my second daughter, is a little spirit that lived and thrived in me as I wrote the "Love Song." She is a bundle of love that was knotted too tight and waiting to be unraveled. The passion and upbeat momentum of the "Love Song" is a demonstration of the love I felt for Ixchel in my womb. Ixchel is the "Coyolxauhqui Song." She is Ixchel, *La mujer Maya de la luna, tu eres mujer, la imagen de ella, fuerte mujer*. I bled for her . . . *Sangramos*. I gave life to her . . . *Damos Vida*, I breastfed her, *damos leche y amor*. Her spirit is with me always . . . *Tu espíritu está conmigo, soy fuerte mujer*.

These two young women are an integral part of all my creations with In Lak Ech and Mujeres de Maiz. They were in the womb while I read poetry, wrote and sang songs, and supported my sisters in their poems, songs, and art. They were crawling, breastfeeding, and growing around the drum, the mic, the *voluta*, our expressions. Their presence served as an inspiration, a drive, a subtle force that fostered the desire for expression of a Chicana mujer. I needed to set an example, pave the way for them, and open doors. I needed to write our story, Herstory, and my two girls would live it to its entirety through In Lak Ech and MdM. My purpose was and is to show them that there is no other way but this way: her way, the way of the *voluta*, the Chicana way, the "*Todos Somos*" way—where they wouldn't ever question their identity and their place as a woman. I didn't want them to have to wait to sit in a Chicana Studies class to discuss issues of remaining quiet, docile, and accepting things the way things are—from male dominance to church-inflicted guilt to hypocrisy and double standards in our homes, families, and machismo mindsets. I wanted them to see through issues and solve them as they came our way. MdM was and is the place of higher learning, the place of education, the place of inspiration, and open doors. My daughters have those doors open as do many young women in our community. Some are not ready to walk through the doors but at least they know there is a door. MdM is their vessel.

32

Conocimientos from the Mujeres de Maíz Oral Herstory Project

GABRIELA MARTINEZ, PEDRO MARTINEZ, MEGAN PENNINGS, AND DIONNE ESPINOZA

"Creating work together we could change ourselves and we could change the world, really."
—FELICIA 'FE' MONTES, MUJERES DE MAÍZ CO-FOUNDER AND EXECUTIVE DIRECTOR

WITH THIS statement, community-based artivist and educator Fe encapsulates a central principle guiding the work of Mujeres de Maiz.[1] According to this principle, collective work ("creating work together") not only impacts the individual within the collective, it also resonates outward as a model of social change. As translated into praxis by Mujeres de Maiz, this principle explains how a grassroots community effort of Chicana/Latina women of color artivists has sustained itself for more than twenty years. Since it is rare for a collective to continue functioning over such a long time it is especially important to document individual herstories of MdM participants as part of a collective herstory that makes visible their labor, artistry, and "sacred" space-making as Chicana/Latina/women of color artivists.[2]

With this in mind, and through a collaborative process with Mujeres de Maiz, in 2014–15, a faculty member along with graduate and undergraduate students at Cal State L.A. gathered oral herstories of seven MdM collective members in anticipation of the collective's twenty-year anniversary (1997–2017).[3] The oral herstories aimed to document the lives of these artivists by asking questions such as how they came to consciousness as artists, their formative influences, and their choice of artistic medium. From their individual stories, we moved to the collective by asking how they became involved in Mujeres de Maiz and their ideas about the project, vision, and inspiration of MdM. The seven narrators represent co-founders who came together in the mid-nineties to birth the collective as well as more recent participants. Each of the participants saw Mujeres de Maiz as providing a space for their voice and art. Each had a unique story about their relation to the collective as they shared their narratives of family, education, community, spirituality, and activism both as individuals and as members of a collective.

What we came to call the Mujeres de Maiz Oral Herstory Project evolved from a course of fifteen students to an independent study in which a research team of three students and a faculty member met over eight months to continue the work. In addition to conducting two additional interviews as a team, we read articles on decolonial and Chicana feminist methodology and discussed the goals of research. We also listened carefully and took notes on the oral herstories. As a culminating task, and inspired by our reading and discussion, the student researchers wrote personal *testimonios* that examined their paths to higher education and the meanings and importance of Chicana feminism and community-engaged research. Although we were not sure how our research would be shared beyond conference panels where the oral herstory project was presented, when we were invited to contribute to this anthology, we were excited to be part of a retrospective honoring the pathbreaking work of Mujeres de Maiz and to have an opportunity to share the transformative knowledges that emerged for us from doing this work.

This chapter frames our research and the outcomes as rooted in *conocimientos*. Although we did not explore this concept during our meetings, in retrospect Anzaldúa's concept of *conocimiento*, which has many resonances and invites further exploration and application, describes the layers of knowledge, learning, and understanding that emerged from the oral herstories and from our process of conducting them.[4] As an overall framework, Anzaldúa's description of *conocimiento* as a "mode of connecting" seems especially relevant and meaningful for this work: "Conocimiento es otro mode de conectar across colors and other differences to allies also trying to negotiate racial contradictions, survive the stresses and traumas of daily life, and develop a spiritual-imaginal-political vision together. Conocimiento shares a sense of affinity with all things and advocates mobilizing, organizing, sharing information, knowledge, insights, and resources with other groups."[5]

For us, Anzaldúa's reference to how *conocimiento* "advocates mobilizing, organizing, sharing information, knowledge, insights, and resources with other groups" names the transfer that occurred between MdM's oral herstory narrators and our team as we conducted and listened to the oral herstories. Furthermore, Anzaldúa scholar AnaLouise Keating highlights the activist component of *conocimiento*: "Anzaldúa's theory of *conocimiento* offers a holistic activist-inflected epistemology designed to effect change on multiple levels."[6] Our essay explores the multiple levels of *conocimiento* embedded in the research process and highlights the knowledge that can emerge at the intersection of community engagement, academic research, and social justice. In other words, we frame the Mujeres de Maiz Oral Herstory project not only as research on activists, but also as activist research and as spiritually transformative research.

There are three components or flashpoints of transformative research experiences and learning that we present in this essay: (1) It matters who is doing the research and their own investments and life experience that they bring to the project. The student testimonios showed how their family and educational experiences are intertwined to yield resilience within the challenges of academia well as a deeper investment in community-based research that pushes against dominant ideas of the "academic." (2) A crucial aspect of oral history is the labor of listening. The work of listening solidifies learning and, through the labor involved, carries the knowledge as a kind of "bridge" between the narrator and listener, especially when there is an affective or feeling component that accompanies it. (3) The knowledges shared by the narrators of MdM in their oral herstories—what might be identified as "themes" in traditional social science interpretation and analysis—are best presented, given the context and value of the knowledge shared, as *conocimientos* that build upon, and contribute to, the legacies of women of color and Xicana Indigenous feminist praxis in local and global movements for social justice.

This essay represents a weave of individual and collective voices by including the narratives of the student researchers and the oral herstories of Mujeres de Maiz artivistas. The voices of the individual student researchers appear when quoting from their *testimonios* about the project and acknowledging their insights and analysis.[7] The faculty director of the project served as the editor, facilitator, and organizer of the essay, guided by input from the student researchers. In this way, the essay seeks to make transparent hierarchies of knowledge and power and to unsettle these hierarchies by putting student and community stories at the forefront. It also weaves the individual and the collective voice throughout, ultimately creating a collective *testimonio*, representing a different way of sharing research.

TESTIMONIOS OF STUDENT RESEARCHERS

Over eight months in 2015, our research team—Pedro, Megan, Gabriela, and Dionne—met regularly to conduct two additional interviews with MdM collective members, and then to process all seven of the interviews that had been conducted. Our meetings could be characterized as closer to a study group than a traditional class or independent study. We sat in a circle, whether we were in Dionne's office or in a conference room. Faculty and students both identified readings for discussion. Since our approach and goals had been different from the detached approach of traditional research due to our own investment in and connection to the issues that MdM embraces and centers, we selected essays that challenged traditional social science frameworks and that required us to reflect on our own relationship to this work.[8]

The most influential readings were those published in the field of education and centering Chicana feminist and decolonial methodology.[9] Building on the groundbreaking formulation of Chicana Feminist Epistemology by Dolores Delgado Bernal, a central premise of these essays is that it matters who does the research because a researcher's life experience and cultural intuition inform their interpretive work. "The Xicana Sacred Space" spoke to the possibility of having a dialogue that invited our whole selves to the conversation in academic space. These articles not only presented or related to a central or common set of ideas, they also allowed for multiple researcher voices and testimonies. We saw this scholarship as most appropriate to understanding the work of a collective of women of color and to how we would present that work in print to reflect our own group dynamics.

At one point, Dionne asked the student researchers to write short reflections on their experience of interviewing MdM as a "warm-up" to writing about methodology. What emerged was that each of the student researchers came to the project with their own stories of observing and/or experiencing marginalization based on race, class, and gender on the path to higher education. As a result, they came to the university with a deep sense of community and family of origin as a foundation that motivated their commitment to continuing their educational paths. Each person wrote about their struggles to access and to connect with higher education in their individual written *testimonios*. These struggles were inextricably tied to the meanings of doing research and to the way that participation in a research project with MdM empowered them and helped to bridge the academy with their community.

For Megan, a graduate student in Chicano(a)/Latino(a) studies who was also earning a post-baccalaureate certificate in women's, gender, and sexuality studies, the path had not been an easy one. She relates her roots in her community and her early experiences with education:

> I grew up in Baldwin Park, a small town within the San Gabriel Valley. Since I lived there most of my life and attended the same schools as my parents, I always called Baldwin Park home. . . . I struggled for years around my educational process due to my learning disability, and because of this the idea of higher education was never a part of my vocabulary: I always felt that I wasn't smart enough to go to college. . . . I spent the last year of high school focusing more on working and not so much on filling out a college application.

> The lack of support from my high school counselor, who encouraged me to graduate from adult school and get a job, and the fact that few of my friends were planning to go to the university, left me without a sense of purpose to go to college. My mindset quickly changed once I became a mom: I was no longer just responsible for myself. Now I was responsible for another person who depended on me. After months at a trade school, I shifted to a community college where I could get a degree that would lead me to a good-paying career. I then realized, *Why stop there, why not pursue a BA degree?* After I transferred to Cal State L.A., I started to find my identity not just as a single mother, but also as an individual and that is when I really started to understand the importance of education.

Gabriela, an undergraduate majoring in sociology with a minor in creative writing, similarly rooted herself in her community. She had observed the caregiving labor of the immigrant women of color in her community, labor that is often invisibilized, devalued, or taken for granted:

> As an adolescent growing up in El Sereno, a neighborhood on the Eastside of Los Angeles, I paid close attention to the lives of the *mujeres* in my neighborhood. But it was during my teen years that I began to learn more about my community. After a spinal cord injury accident which left me paralyzed from the neck down, I was mostly at home and had the majority of my day available to speak to my mom and to the women in the neighborhood who would come over to help us. My rehabilitation became the art of expressing myself with my mom and these *mujeres*. Their daily stories—shared among each other and with me—illustrated agony and inequality in their homes. When I went to college, I didn't know immediately what I would focus my studies on, however I knew that I wanted to help these *mujeres* to find a safe space where they could speak to other *mujeres*. I always carried their voices with me everywhere I went on the Cal State LA campus.

Finally, Pedro, an undergraduate, wrote about how he sought spaces that would align with his goal of bridging the community and the academy as a student activist:

> Entering the college environment as a freshman, I recall having three goals in my mind: "1. Get Involved! 2. Graduate with a B.A. in Political Science, and 3. Begin to change the world." Following the course of my college goals (especially numbers 1 and 3), I became involved with El Movimiento Estudiantil Chicano/a de Aztlán (MEChA) and The Queer Connection (TQC) during my second quarter. My politicization in the student movement on campus influenced me to select the major in Chicano/a Studies and a minor in Women's, Gender, and Sexuality Studies.
>
> As a "Queer Chicano," I wanted not only to integrate my intersecting identities in my studies and campus activism, but also to engage these intersections as a lived praxis as I ventured off campus. Stationing myself in the nearby community of Boyle Heights, I began to visit the community spaces and to meet the people who sustained these spaces. It was within

this community of fellow organizers and public intellectuals that I began to navigate my place within the world and academia.

For Pedro, the oral herstory project with a women of color-based collective also called for him to explore the question of gender privilege: "As a self-identified male, I questioned whether it was appropriate for me to begin speaking for/about or witnessing stories of women's oppression, resistance, and womanhood." After spending some time reflecting on his position he concluded, "I came to see the importance of bearing witness to *mujeres poderosas* retelling their stories for the generations of Xicanas to come."

Once at the university, for all of us (graduate student, undergraduate student, and professor), studying Chicana feminist herstory and learning about theories and perspectives such as the work of Gloria Anzaldúa and Cherríe Moraga influenced and nourished us as scholars and activists. Gabriela wrote, "When I discovered the Chicana Feminism class on campus I felt as if I had found a home on my college campus.... Chicana Feminist studies allowed me to understand where I came from." Pedro had also been influenced by a course in Chicana Feminism as he "became intrigued with questions of indigeneity, decolonization, and ways of countering colonial epistemology." Each of us found our voice and space in higher education and, especially, in ethnic studies and women's, gender, and sexuality studies courses, both sites in the academy that center marginalized perspectives and lives.

Additionally, the idea of learning from the artivists of Mujeres de Maiz through oral herstory motivated Gabriela, Pedro, and Megan to be part of this project. Megan had learned about MdM in her community college so when she started as an undergraduate at Cal State L.A., and then a graduate student, she was drawn to opportunities to work with MdM as a volunteer, and eventually as an intern.[10] Gabriela saw her studies in Chicana feminism as the starting point for which the opportunity to learn more about Mujeres de Maiz was a next step: "When I heard about the 'Chicana Narratives and Community Engagement' class, it included my passions and promised to bring together helping the community and Chicana Feminism." Finally, Pedro was drawn to MdM's artivism and to the prospect of challenging dominant research paradigms by participating in the oral herstory project.

THE LABOR OF LISTENING: EMOTIONS, KNOWLEDGE TRANSFER, AND HEALING

The director/professor coordinating the course and project (Dionne) saw in this project an opportunity to implement a pedagogy of praxis, one in which her role was that of a guide, mentor, coach, facilitator, and/or trainer who sought to empower a new generation of student researchers in oral herstory methods and methodology that could be applied to social change and activism. In adopting a more collective approach, she looked to Mujeres de Maiz and their fiercely collective process and to MdM cofounder Felicia 'Fe' Montes's suggestion of thinking about the interview in terms of storytelling.[11] She also consulted the work of Chicana feminist scholar María Cotera who had founded the Chicana por mi Raza online archive. Cotera had involved her students in gathering archival materials and invited them to be "critical witnesses" of the interviews she conducted with major figures in Chicana feminism.[12]

For the Mujeres de Maiz Oral Herstory project, each oral herstory involved teams of three students to conduct the oral herstory. Each team member had a specific role in the process: They might have been documenting the session by taking photographs, writing notes on the interview, or recording a backup copy on digital audio. Each group worked collaboratively to research the narrator and then to develop any additional narrator-specific questions. A team member selected by the group would serve as the primary interviewer who posed questions to the narrators. During the interview, Dionne participated as another witness and as a consultant who offered support to the students, videographer, and narrator as we all sat together for the interview. Additionally, through a partnership with the department of television, film, and media studies, each interview was filmed by a videographer (among them three undergraduate students and a former graduate student).

Regardless of specific "assigned" tasks, each team member had the job of listening, which involved our full presence and attention. The labor of listening throughout the oral herstory proved essential to *conocimiento*. In fact, the examples here show that the traditional language of "interviewer" in oral history fails to encompass the work involved for those posing the questions. "Interviewer" suggests an almost detached person in the journalistic sense and leaves out the circular nature of questions and the responses that bridge knowledge back to the interviewer from the narrator. In our project, the idea of an interviewer-listener more accurately reflects the *labor* and *activity* of listening as well as the collaborative nature of a narrator and the listener/interviewer in the dynamic of the oral herstory process. For the interviewer-listener, this is a very active process. Pedro unpacked the dynamics of interviewing and listening as labor when he mentioned "stress" to describe some of his feelings during his interview with Marisol Lydia Torres: "The stress of both actively listening and navigating the interview to ensure that we asked the questions we were seeking to have answered was overwhelming, to say the least." He noted that not only must the interviewer-listener bear witness, but they are also responsible for "facilitating the flow of knowledge."

The process of listening brought forth an array of emotions, expressed at different times by interviewers, team members, and narrators. Researcher Pedro emphasized the "labor" of listening and the link to emotions in the process of decolonization as these emerged in an interview with MdM collective member Marisol Lydia Torres. At one point, she recounted her participation in the Encuentro Intercontinental por la Humanidad y Contra el Neoliberalismo (1997). As she was describing her experience, Pedro stated that he "was particularly struck when she quotes Comandanta Ramona and the ethos/transformative pedagogy that was manifested through a simple question, 'Where is your heart today?'" He continued, "I remember while conducting this interview being amazed and even at a point being brought to tears (during the Comandanta Ramona account) from the testimony that Marisol had shared with us. The Zapatistas had served as a major catalyst and focal point for my organizing, so as I was hearing a first-person account of the wisdom of Ramona, I could barely control the reaction I had. This profound moment revealed the power that storytelling can have on our communities." Because Marisol's account of Ramona registers on an emotional level for Pedro, it activates a transfer of knowledge or *conocimiento* at a deep level of understanding.

Another example of the emotions that accompanied knowledge transfer around storytelling is shared by Gabriela. In this case, the narrator's emotions evoked in the interviewer-listener responses of both pain and joy through recognition of similar experiences. Gabriela was drawn to Iris De Anda's *corazon de pocha* when she described her *pocha* experience as a second-generation daughter of Latina/o immigrants and as someone raised in El Sereno, like her: "Throughout my interview with Iris there were specific moments when I wanted to cry with her, to laugh with her but I maintained a straight face while my heart was cradled by her words of wisdom. In the beginning of our interview, she spoke like my lifetime next-door neighbor." Gabriela remembered the effect of one of Iris's *pocha* stories in particular: "When the interview arrived at the climax in which she told me about the incident with her mom in the first grade, where she didn't want her mom to be the lady that spoke Spanish, her eyes began to water and her voice grew deep. I wanted to grieve out loud with her, I wanted to say, 'I did something like that to my mom too when I was in elementary school, you're not alone.' But I let my heart cry with hers silently while the camera recorded every breath she took."[13] Gabriela articulated a feeling she held within that she was able to name and express as a result of how this moment enabled "griev(ing)" to work through a moment of pain within a space of healing.

Another example of healing that was supported through the interviewing-listening praxis of conducting an oral herstory is reported by researcher Megan, who interviewed Amber Rose González. Weeks prior to the interview, Megan's mother had passed away from kidney disease, so she had taken some time away from the team meetings to mourn. After two weeks, she returned to conduct an interview with Amber Rose González because she felt that doing the interview supported her own healing process. As she listened to Amber's story, Megan began to reframe her own family herstory:

> As [Amber] talked about her family and understanding the lines between academics and the collective, I knew and understood where she was coming from. Dr. González talked about how school was never really important, but that she had always had a love for books. I knew just what she was talking about: School was never for me, but I shared the same love for books, which reminded me of how my mother showed me books at a young age and would share the stories of all the books she would read to me and my sister.

For Megan, returning and doing the work, while difficult, gave her a space to remember her mother: "It was the interview with Amber Rose

González that helped me to realize that my mother was and will always be a major impact in my education because of her teaching me that books were important and the stories in those books can have a deep connection to ourselves." Megan also noted the moment in the interview when Amber became emotional as she discussed the healing of the ancestors as essential to decolonization. This, too, spoke to Megan as she went through her own process of mourning her mother and healing her ancestors.

Listening also sparks the possibility of an internal change for the interviewer-listener by centering an epistemology rooted in collaboration and community. Pedro theorized about the deep work of listening in oral herstory as mobilizing social change through "communal affect": "Could Oral Herstory present itself further as an essential tool for decolonization and (re)kindling subaltern affect that is buried under colonialism by forcing the viewer to share with the narrator these communal emotions that permeate and take existence through our lived experience as people of color?" Pedro's concept of "communal affect" crystallizes the notion of *conocimento* as crucial to decolonization. As Pedro reflected on the two interviews he had participated in, one as a witness (Iris De Anda) and the other as the interviewer/listener (Marisol Lydia Torres), he declared, "The act of storytelling and sharing creates new opportunities for (re)bridging the lost, forgotten, and unknown parts of ourselves." Gabriela also observed the idea of *conocimiento* as a knowledge transfer in her interview with Iris De Anda: "Iris and I not only shared our *corazones de Pocha*, but we created a Chicana collective atmosphere with my other research partners in the interview room." She also framed the atmosphere as "creating a sacred space for collectivity" as guided by the healing words of *conocimiento* shared by the narrator.

MUJERES DE MAÍZ CONOCIMIENTO(S) AND XICANA INDIGENOUS FEMINIST PRAXIS

In addition to reflecting on how the interviewing-listening process served as a space of deep learning and understanding, we discussed the concepts that motivated MdM's artivism and feminism as rooted in the legacy of women of color feminist and Indigenous feminist thought and praxis.

In our conversation about the central *conocimientos* we heard and felt deeply, we identified Zapatismo (Megan), the values of sharing and interdependence (Gabriela), ideas about decolonization (Pedro), and concepts of Indigenous feminism (Dionne) across several narratives. These knowledges resonate as central to the foundation of MdM as a collective along with other areas that we had asked about (spirituality, collectivity, and indigeneity). We each were assigned to write short reflections about these ideas as they appeared in the oral herstories. It was after our initial writing that Dionne introduced Gloria Anzaldúa's concept of *conocimiento*. We understood *conocimiento* literally as a knowing or teaching that was communicated across several of the MdM oral herstories. For us *conocimiento* was a more culturally accurate and appropriate language for interpreting MdM's work than "themes" or "findings," as used in traditional social science or interview-based research.[14] Since there was more than one *conocimiento*, we reference the central philosophies and teachings as *conocimientos*, in the plural.

For example, Zapatismo had been often written and spoken about as a profound influence in Chicana/o social movements in Los Angeles and, specifically, as influential for founding members of Mujeres de Maiz, several of whom traveled to Chiapas for historic *encuentros* between allies and activists around the globe and the Zapatistas including, among our narrators, Marisol Lydia Torres and Felicia 'Fe' Montes. Two specific tenets of Zapatismo praxis were voiced in the interviews: "Todos Somos" and "A World Where Many Worlds Fit."[15] Megan identified how these ideas were brought up by three of the MdM narrators: "Within the interviews Felicia 'Fe' Montes, Marisol Lydia Torres, and Iris De Anda referenced how they have been inspired by the movement of the Zapatistas and how their work and the work of the MDM collective focus on the concept of 'Todos Somos'(We All Are)." Megan defined "Todos Somos" as a way "to bring a consciousness to the idea that 'we are all' ARTivist in various forms and ways." Drawing on Fe's interview, Megan further sees how Mujeres de Maiz implements "Todos Somos" as a concept that also extends to new generations: "By using their ARTivism MdM is able to inspire others especially the younger generation that they too can do the same in their own forms of ARTivism."

Todos Somos is a radically inclusive concept, as is another Zapatista philosophy voiced by Fe and Marisol, "A World Where Many Worlds

Fit." Marisol translates this philosophy as a form of radical inclusion when asked about her hopes for Mujeres de Maiz. In her thoughtful response, she summed up: "I love the philosophy of the Zapatistas, 'a world where many worlds fit.' Like, that to me is my—what I have taken on my whole life, 'a world where many worlds fit,' how can I continue to share that concept and extend that concept into daily life for others to feel they can just grow and be and complete themselves without any inhibitions, without judgement, without worry . . . how can we lift each other?"[16] In Torres's terms, that world must empower others to live out their potential.

In thinking about the way Mujeres de Maiz upheld their fierce collectivity, we saw sharing and interdependence weaving throughout the narratives. Gabriela observed: "The women we interviewed from Mujeres de Maiz illustrated a powerful collective ethic that bonded together eighteen years of sacred sharing and interdependence." Gabriela applied the idea of "The Xicana Sacred Space" to the work of Mujeres de Maiz.[17] She identified quotes by Fe, Liliflor, and Iris that described MdM's "sacred space." Fe described how MdM was "giving a space" through living, singing, creating, and sharing:

> We are living In Lak Ech and Mujeres de Maiz. We are still singing in ceremonies, learning songs, some still creating songs and sharing poetry. Our daughters now are dancing or doing danza, it's just a different type of manifestation of In Lak Ech. And Mujeres de Maiz has continually created those spaces for women of color artivists through the zine and through the events we were able to give a space, a stage for performers, a page for writers, and a wall for visual artists who have never exhibited and giving them that possibility.

Liliflor presented the full moon circle gatherings as a space of sharing, "In the full moon circles . . . we honor grandmother moon as women and give offerings of gratitude and we play music and songs . . . and we share our experiences, and we help each other, and we network and it's a day to gather our forces as feminine energy."[18]

Finally, Iris gave examples of the kind of space created by Mujeres de Maiz:

They have created a safe space for all of us to be able to share our art. When I say all of us, I mean the mujeres, but I know that we have male allies that help us make Mujeres de Maiz what it is. So, they allow that safe space, they allow us to take up space in this world where a lot of the media . . . [show] a lot happening for the male, but Mujeres de Maiz came along and opened up a doorway where it's like, "We're going to put on a show and it's just going to be women, we're going to highlight women, we're going to open the road and pave the way for women to share their art" whether it was poetry, music, film, or painting there's no boundary, we're not in a box, we can do everything and be everything and when you're doing it with your sisters it's very transformative.[19]

According to Gabriela, "For the mujeres of Mujeres de Maiz sharing means creating a safe and sacred space for women of color where they can connect with the experiences of other women. Ultimately, this is what the essence of the path of their collectivity illuminates."

The third *conocimiento* we explored, decolonization, had been part of our interview questions as we asked narrators to describe what it meant to them, and how they implemented it, whether individually or collectively. According to Pedro, "Waziyatawin [Angela Wilson] and Michael Yellow Bird describe decolonization *as a process*." Pedro cites their definition: "As a process, decolonization means engaging in the activities of creating, restoring, and birthing. It means creating and consciously using various strategies to liberate oneself, adapt to or survive oppressive conditions; it means restoring cultural practices, thinking, beliefs, and values that were taken away or abandoned but are still relevant and necessary to survival; and it means the birthing of new ideas, thinking, technologies, and lifestyles that contribute to the advancement and empowerment of Indigenous Peoples."[20]

There were a number of practices shared by MdM narrators that connected to this definition, one that emphasizes an ongoing and daily commitment at many levels. Pedro cited several quotes from the interviews with Liliflor and Fe. Liliflor offered these thoughts on decolonization as a process: "Decolonizing myself from the food I eat every day, that's decolonizing. Growing my own garden is decolonization," "Decolonizing our conditioning. . . . Our humanity has been conditioned," and "Decolonizing ourselves from that patriarchal conditioning that was instilled in us as children." Felicia 'Fe' Montes presented her understanding of decolonization: "Deconnect, or unconnect or take away from some of the different ways of being and lifestyles and interactions, that came with colonization . . . going forward in a way that's healthy for us in body/mind spirit. . . . An act of not only survival and resistance but affirmation for my culture and my people." As Amber expressed in an emotional moment of her interview decolonization is also about "healing our ancestors who suffered through these things." For MdM narrators, decolonization goes beyond survival (although survival is key) but also to building, affirming, thriving, healing, and finding a way forward.

As we have documented here, the philosophies and praxis of Mujeres de Maiz ignited connections and powerful validation at individual-personal levels, communal-collective levels, and beyond. By sharing our stories as researchers alongside the teachings of Mujeres de Maiz, we want to demonstrate how new spaces of *conocimiento* are created that have the power to continue to radiate and transform through activism, art-making, education, and pedagogy. As Pedro wrote, "It has been a life-changing and radically informing experience to be a part of the MdM Oral Herstory research team." He acknowledged the gathering of energies that made the work possible: "What allowed me to enter this space and actively engage in this project was the supportive environment provided by Dr. Espinoza, the fellow students (graduate and undergraduate), the camera production team, and the boundless collaboration of Mujeres de Maiz." Megan reflected, "The MdM Oral Herstory Project helped to show me that we can reframe research and help communities tell their own stories in their own voices, as well as show the impact of collectives, especially those that focus on womyn of color." She especially connected the importance of storytelling as integral to generational survival: "This process was even more clear to me now that my mother's story is gone and now it's up to me to uncover her story for my daughters to have. I wanted to bring that to the women of MdM and bring out their stories of struggles, healing, and community activism."

In fall 2015, as the group prepared to give a presentation about the work at a social justice conference, we talked about having a "giveaway" at the end of our presentation.[21] Gabriela offered to bring flower pens that her mother had made, a beautiful gesture that also brought her mother's creativity into our presentation. Gabriela suggested attaching an inspirational quote to the pens and brought us several quotes by Gloria Anzaldúa. We chose the often-cited and essential quote, "May we do work that matters. Vale la Pena."[22] For us, the Mujeres de Maiz Oral Herstory Project exemplified "work that matters," and while we had spent many hours of our time on campus, in preparation, and in the interviews, we felt the work had tremendous value. And we were thankful to the narrators for their open-hearted willingness to be part of it.

Collective research impacted our selves as researchers, students, and faculty. In other words, by learning about the formation, history, and praxis of Mujeres de Maiz as artivists in a collective and reflecting on our own positionalities through the practice of listening and learning about their core beliefs and principles, we grew to realize the many levels of transformation possible through collective work by students and faculty in higher education. For us, this transformation was made possible because the narrators of the oral herstories shared their experiences as members of a community-based grassroots collective. Through reading, discussion, listening, analysis, and reflective writing, we came to a deeper place of self-knowledge and rootedness that we feel demonstrates the transformative potential of community engagement work for student researchers.

NOTES

The project was supported by an Instructionally Related Activities Grant; the Television Film and Video Student Production Unit; Community Engagement Undergraduate and Graduate Research and Internship Grants from the Center for Engagement, Service, and the Public Good (awarded to Gabriela Martinez, Pedro Martinez, and Megan Pennings); and the Faculty Fellows program of the Center for the Study of Genders and Sexualities (awarded to Dionne Espinoza) at Cal State L.A. We wish to acknowledge the WGSS 484 Chicana Narratives and Community History course participants who completed five of the interviews in Winter 2015 and to thank the many faculty colleagues and staff members who helped with the logistics of equipment and location.

The Mujeres de Maiz Oral Herstory Project Team would also like to thank Martha R. Gonzales, Amber Rose González, and Felicia 'Fe' Montes for their feedback on an early draft of this essay. We send a corazon-filled *mil gracias* to Mujeres de Maiz for their collaboration and inspiration, which has been profound and without which this project would not have been possible. This project was reviewed by the Institutional Review Board at Cal State L.A.

1. Felicia 'Fe' Montes, interview, conducted by Denysse Nuñez with team members Megan Pennings and Bamby Salcedo, supervised by Dionne Espinoza, Cal State L.A. Campus, February 25, 2015, videotaped by Ysabel Gonzalez.
2. Throughout the essay, the term "oral herstory" appears in order to emphasize and mark "women" or "womyn" as the generators of the narrative. In doing so we follow MdM's own practice of challenging masculinist language. MdM also changes language as needed to ensure inclusion, especially in reference to trans*, queer, and gender nonconforming people who participate in MdM's collective or in their events as artivists, emcees, and performers.
3. The Mujeres de Maiz Oral Herstory Project developed out of conversations between two members of the collective, Felicia 'Fe' Montes and Michelle L. Lopez, and Dionne Espinoza, a faculty member at Cal State L.A. The oral herstories were gathered over two quarter terms in 2015. During the first course, offered in Winter 2015, "Chicana Narratives and Community History," a group of fifteen student researchers prepared for and interviewed five collective members in teams of three to four people. In addition to conducting the interviews, students volunteered at the collective's annual International Women's Day Event. In Spring 2015, three students from the original class of fifteen enrolled in an independent study to continue the project. The four of us interviewed an additional two collective members.

    The list of narrators came directly from Mujeres de Maiz themselves and represented the diversity of their members, past and present. Although we were not able to interview all of those on the list for reasons of time, we interviewed four long-term members—Felicia 'Fe' Montes, Lilia 'Liliflor' Ramirez, Margaret 'Quica' Alarcón, and Marisol Lydia Torres—and three of the more recent members—Amber Rose González, Iris De Anda, and Michelle L. Lopez. In addition to the previously cited interview with Felicia 'Fe' Montes, we list here the other six interviews conducted in Winter and Spring 2015: Iris De Anda, interview by Gabriela Martinez, with team members Pedro Martinez, Samantha Sandoval, supervised by Dionne Espinoza, Cal State L.A. Campus, February 17, 2015, videotaped by Lucas Benitez; Marisol Lydia Torres, interview, conducted by Pedro Martinez with team members Megan Pennings and Gabriela Martinez, supervised by Dionne Espinoza, Cal State L.A. Campus, May 30, 2015, videotaped by Marla Ulloa; Lilia 'Liliflor' Ramirez, interviewed by Lizvette Flores, with team members Josefina Williams and Brenda Prieto, supervised by Dionne Espinoza, Cal State L.A. Campus, February 19, 2015, videotaped by Dillon Kinkead; Michelle L. Lopez, interviewed by Tony Braccamonte, with team member Sandra Parra, supervised by Dionne Espinoza, Cal State L.A. Campus, February 19, 2015, videotaped by Ysabel Gonzalez; Margaret 'Quica' Alarcón, interviewed by Christina Mancera, with team members Lainie Escovedo and Beatriz Arreola, supervised by Dionne Espinoza, Cal State L.A. Campus, February 13, 2015, videotaped by Ysabel Gonzalez; and Amber Rose González, interviewed by Megan Pennings, with team members Pedro Martinez and Gabriela Martinez, supervised by Dionne Espinoza, Cal State L.A. Campus, May 17, 2015, videotaped by Marla Ulloa. Our hope is that, with the consent of Mujeres de Maiz, the oral herstories will be made available at Cal State L.A. in the future.

4. Scholars have been theorizing and applying *conocimiento* as a part of Anzaldúa's body of theories such as borderlands and *mestiza* consciousness in fields such as education, psychology, and art history for at least fifteen years. Review, for example, a recent essay in educational research by Tanya J. Gaxiola Serrano, Mónica González Ybarra, and Dolores Delgado Bernal, "'Defend Yourself with Words, with the Knowledge That You've Gained': An Exploration of *Conocimiento* Among Latina undergraduates in Ethnic Studies," *Journal of Latinos and Education*, doi.or/10.1080/15348431.2017.1388238, accessed January 25, 2018; in the field of psychology, Aida Hurtado, "Gloria Anzaldúa's Seven Stages of Conocimiento in Redefining Latino Masculinity: José's Story," *Masculinidades y cambio social* 4, no. 3 (2105): 44–84; and in studies of art and activism, Edward McCaughan, "Notes on Mexican Art, Social Movements, and Gloria Anzaldúa's 'Conocimiento,'" in *Social Justice* 33, no. 2, (2006): 153–64, to name only three. Dionne first heard the term *conocimiento* from Belinda García, Executive Director and Co-founder of Sisters of Color United for Education in Denver, Colorado, when she discussed the how the concept was central to her art and healing workshops.

5. Gloria E. Anzaldúa, "now let us shift . . . the path of conocimiento . . . inner work, public acts," in *This Bridge We Call Home: Radical Visions for Transformation*, eds. Gloria E. Anzaldúa and AnaLouise Keating (New York and London, Routledge, 2002), 571.

6. AnaLouise Keating, "Introduction: Shifting Worlds, Una Entrada," in *EntreMundos/Among Worlds: New Perspectives on Gloria Anzaldúa*, edited by AnaLouise Keating (New York: Palgrave Macmillan, 2005), 8. Review also Keating's essay in that volume, "Shifting Perspectives: Spiritual Activism, Social Transformation, and the Politics of Spirit," 241–54.

7. It is important to state that while the essay has been primarily edited by Dionne, who coordinated and served as the facilitator, guide, and femtor of the project, the essay represents a collective voice based on our group research experience. Members of our research team are referenced by name in relation to their individual contributions. In addition to their testimonios, Dionne and the student researchers brainstormed the *conocimientos* and then each person wrote short papers from excerpts of the interviews. We then discussed these ideas in a team meeting. As we explain later, the format for this essay is rooted in readings

in Chicana feminist epistemology and methodology that emphasize collectivity and that balance the individual and collective voice. Additionally, Dionne was inspired in her editing of the essay by the model of Susan Cayleff, Melissann Herron, Chelsea Cormier, Sarah Wheeler, and Alicia Chávez-Arteaga, whose essay presents a way to write up a community oral herstory project that involves faculty, graduate student researchers, and research participants. "Oral History and 'Girls' Voices': The Young Women's Studies Club as a Site of Empowerment," *Journal of International Women's Studies* 12, no. 3 (2011): 22–44. Accessed through Virtual Commons.

8. One of these essays was Gaile S. Cannella and Kathryn Manuelito's "Feminisms from Unthought Locations: Indigenous World Views, Marginalized Feminisms, and Revisioning and Anticolonial Social Science," *Handbook of Critical and Indigenous Methodologies*, eds. Norman K. Denzin, Yvonna S. Lincoln, and Linda Tuhiwai Smith (New York: Sage, 2008), 45–59.

9. Dolores Calderón, Dolores Delgado Bernal, Lindsay Pérez Huber, Maria C. Malagón, and Veronica Nelly Vélez, "Chicana Feminist Epistemology Revisited: Cultivated Ideas a Generation Later," *Harvard Educational Review* 82, no. 4 (Winter 2012): 513–39; Lourdes Diaz Soto, Claudia G. Cervantes-Soon, Elizabeth Villarreal, and Emmet E. Campos, "The Xicana Sacred Space: A Communal Circle of Compromiso for Education Researchers," *Harvard Educational Review* 75, no. 4 (Winter 2009): 755–75.

10. Megan Pennings completed her M.A. thesis in Mexican American studies in summer 2017, titled, "Restoring the Mind, Body, and Spirit: Mujeres de Maiz and Social Media as a Tool of Spiritual Activism and Education for Communities." Since this work, she has become a member of the Mujeres de Maiz collective and is involved in their programming. An adaptation of her thesis is included in this anthology.

11. This occurred over lunch and coffee conversations over several months beginning in Spring 2014 and continuing in Fall 2014 with Fe and Michelle. During the fall, we developed agreements about the project and how to approach it. Fe and Michelle attended the final session of the course in Winter 2015 where student teams presented excerpts of their work. We maintained communication throughout Spring 2015 and through the retrospective exhibition at LA Plaza de Cultura y Artes in Spring 2017. Excerpts of the oral herstories were edited as a short video about the collective and included in the exhibit.

12. María Cotera generously discussed her model and approach with Dionne as she planned for the class. Review Cotera's brilliant essay about her work and student participation, "'Invisibility is an Unnatural Disaster': Feminist Archival Praxis After the Digital Turn," *South Atlantic Quarterly* 114, no. 4 (2015): 781–801.

13. Gabriela is referring here to Iris De Anda's poem "To Be a Pocha or Not to Be" from her collection *Codeswitch: Fires from Mi Corazon, Los Writers Under-*

ground Press (2015), 82. The specific phrase in the poem that is referenced is as follows:

> ashamed of spanish in the 1st grade
> i'm sorry mami I never meant to hurt you
> ashamed of english in abuelas embrace
> I know you never meant to hurt me . . .

14. Anzaldúa, "now let us shift," 571.
15. *Todos Somos* in Spanish is translated as "We All Are." In English, "A World Where Many Worlds Fit," is translated as *Un Mundo donde Quepan Muchos Mundos* in Spanish. The phrases appear here as they were spoken by the narrators.
16. Marisol Lydia Torres, interview.
17. Diaz Soto, Cervantes-Soon, Villareal, and Campos.
18. Lilia 'Liliflor' Ramirez, interview.
19. Iris De Anda, interview.
20. Wazityatawin and Michael Yellow Bird, "Decolonizing Our Minds and Actions," *Unsettling America: Decolonization in Theory & Practice*, https://unsettlingamerica.wordpress.com/2013/05/08/decolonizing-our-minds-and-actions/, accessed January 29, 2018.
21. This presentation was for the Fullerton College Social Justice Summit, November 20, 2015, hosted by the Ethnic Studies Department. The researchers also presented in the Center for the Study of Genders and Sexualities Faculty Fellows Presentation at Cal State L.A. as "Bridging Conocimientos: The Mujeres de Maiz Oral HerStory Project," April 4, 2017. Members of MdM attended the presentation at Cal State L.A.
22. The quote in context can be found in *The Gloria Anzaldúa Reader*, ed. AnaLouise Keating (Durham, N.C.: Duke University Press, 2009), 314. It appears at the end of Anzaldúa's short essay, "Let Us Be the Healing of the Wound," written in 2000.

33

Becoming an Activist-Scholar-Organizer with Mujeres de Maiz

AMBER ROSE GONZÁLEZ

THIS CHAPTER chronicles revealing moments and experiences in my graduate research where I sought to document the creative, political, and spiritual practices of Mujeres de Maiz (MdM) from 2011 to 2014. Written from the perspective of an insider-outsider Indigenous Xicana feminist researcher and student activist, I hope to provide a useful account of the joys, struggles, and opportunities that can come with community-engaged ethnographic research that students and activist-scholars can look to as they embark on their own projects. It took me nearly a decade to revisit this essay, providing a necessary critical distance to be able to reflect on a time that was emotionally, intellectually, and spiritually taxing. I can now view my graduate school experience and my written work with appreciation and compassion, something I was not able to do at the time. In "Becoming An Activist-Scholar-Organizer with Mujeres de Maiz," I strive to honor my younger author's voice—inexperienced, self-conscious, and determined—and blend it with my current voice and perspectives that have the advantage of hindsight.[1]

Weaving together personal narrative and ethnographic field notes, this story opens with my approach to gaining entry into the MdM circle, facilitated by Felicia 'Fe' Montes, emphasizing the importance of building collaborative relationships. The beginning of my journey was a critical period of personal and professional growth as I sought to make sense of my role as a young feminist scholar working in and for a community that I care about deeply. As I began to reflect on and write about my research methodology, the following inquiries became central: How can researchers develop respectful and reciprocal relationships with community research partners? What does accountability look like in Indigenous feminist research? What mechanisms will I use to evaluate myself (my thoughts, words, and actions)? How can I ensure my research is useful to the community? How can I integrate my research into my teaching? Asking these questions early on and throughout the project allowed me to metawitness myself and my research experiences, which became integral to my growth as an activist-scholar-organizer.[2]

Next, I discuss the difficulties that resulted from the interplay between my roles and identities as a graduate student researcher, MdM organizer, first-generation college student, and Indigenous Xicana, and my attempts to bridge these in an academic context. I document my struggle to escape nocuous settler social science methods and to align with anticolonial, feminist, Indigenous, and activist approaches to ethnography. I think through everyday embodied research activities with Gloria Anzaldúa's path of conocimiento, leading me to newfound understandings of my identities and my work. The chapter concludes with a summary of what an activist research praxis means to me and offers a blueprint for those who, like me, are compelled to disobey normative research conventions by combining their academic and activist goals while being accountable to their community and to themselves.

VENTURING OUT, ENTERING THE COMMUNITY

The following provides a snapshot of the first year of my dissertation research, culled from my research notebook, which consists of formal dated entries as well as incomplete ideas scribbled on the back of napkins, flyers, and Post-it notes. I begin with a brief timeline that captures important moments that I spent investing in building a relationship with MdM.

> 2010, March. *I finally decided on a dissertation topic! The MdM collective. But what exactly will I write about? Explore their website and Facebook page to learn about the history of the group and to find out who I should contact to ask permission to take on this project.*

2010, April 7–10. *Attended the National Association of Chicana and Chicano Studies (NACCS) Conference in Seattle, Washington, to meet with MdM members Felicia 'Fe' Montes and Martha Gonzalez and attend their panel "Mujeres de Maiz: L.A. Artivism Live."*

2010, June 19. *Attended the "Celebrating Words Festival, Written, Performed, Sung" at Los Angeles Mission College in Sylmar to follow up with Felicia.*

2010, December 9. *Organized an Indigenous Xicana fashion show and cultural fair in Santa Barbara that featured MdM designers and local artisan vendors.*

2011, January to March. *Organized the 2011 MdM Live Art Show.*

2011, March 6. *The 14th Annual MdM Live Art Show "Soldadera de Amor" (Soldier of Love) at the Casa Grande Ballroom in Boyle Heights.*

2011, March 30–April 2. *Participated in a roundtable presentation "Chicana Cultural Activism and Spaces of Belonging" with MdM members at NACCS in Pasadena, California.*

⌘

After attending the 2009 and 2010 Live Art Shows as an audience member and deciding to write my dissertation about MdM, I thought that a good place to begin my research would be to explore the MdM website and Facebook page. I discovered that Felicia 'Fe' Montes is a co-founder and the director of the group and that she was scheduled to present at the National Association of Chicana and Chicano Studies (NACCS) conference on April 7–10, 2010, in Seattle, Washington. I decided to attend the conference so that I could attend the panel "Mujeres de Maiz: L.A. Artivism Live" organized by Felicia and Martha Gonzalez, lead singer and percussionist of the Grammy Award–winning band Quetzal, long-time performer and organizer with MdM, and at the time, a PhD student at the University of Washington. The panel was a combination of spoken word, musical concert, academic presentation, and interactive dialogue with the audience.

After the session, I approached Felicia to thank her for sharing her work and to introduce myself. After a few minutes of small talk, I took a deep breath, swallowed my nervousness, cleared my throat, and said, "I'd really love to write about Mujeres de Maiz and I'd like to know what's the best way for me to ask for permission from the group?" As someone who has worked with and belonged to different Indigenous and women of color organizations and student groups, I was familiar with protocols around seeking inclusion in a new community. I was sure to ask for permission and not automatically assume that I could take on this project. I also knew that being granted permission would likely take time and require me to "show up in a good way"—that is, to demonstrate through my actions that I was coming to MdM with good intentions and willing to put in work—that I too had something to offer. I also knew that there was a possibility that I would not be given permission, which would mean that I would have to change my research topic. Felicia and I spoke for a few more minutes before going our separate ways. She seemed intrigued with my offer, told me that she would talk to the other core members, and asked me to keep her updated on any developments from my end.

A few months later, on a sweltering hot day in June 2010, I attended the fifth annual "Celebrating Words Festival, Written, Performed, Sung" at Los Angeles Mission College in Sylmar hosted by Tía Chucha's Centro Cultural and Bookstore, where Felicia was scheduled to perform.[3] I hadn't reached out to her since NACCS because I preferred to establish relationships in person and this event was the perfect opportunity to update her about my project. I arrived in time to see Tía Chucha's resident danzante group Danza Temachtia Quetzalcoatl offer the opening ceremony, giving thanks to the Creator, and blessing the space and attendees. Afterward, I walked around the outdoor grassy area in the one hundred-plus-degree heat where the vendors were set up. As I perused the artisan booths I ran into a few classmates from undergrad. We sought relief in the shade and chatted for a while. I noticed Felicia's booth and made my way over. She was selling clothing, jewelry, handbags, and other handcrafted items from Urban Xic.[4] I browsed the merchandise while she assisted a customer. I selected a few items to purchase and handed them to Felicia, we hugged and kissed on the cheek, and talked about how school was going.

Since we last spoke I had developed more concrete ideas about the MdM project. I shared with her that I would like to interview organizers and audience members and that I was interested in gathering ephemera to create an MdM archive at a university or city library. I asked if that would be something the collective would be interested in. Felicia said MdM wanted to create an archive for some time and that she would put me in contact with their documentarian and other members who could help. She also said the core members were excited about my project. After meeting with Felicia at NACCS and at the festival, I felt it was appropriate to continue connecting online while I completed my dissertation proposal. We kept in touch through email and Facebook over the next few months.

BUILDING RECIPROCAL RELATIONSHIPS

Fast forward to the fall when I designed and taught the class "Indigenous Women Resisting Representation" for the feminist studies department at the University of California, Santa Barbara. Before the term began, I met with my comrade Gloria Sanchez-Arreola to discuss ways we could collaborate to create a service-learning project for my course. Gloria was in charge of cultural programming at Casa de La Raza, a nonprofit community center on the Eastside of Santa Barbara. She also curated live performances and art exhibits at Del Pueblo Café, her family's Mexican restaurant in nearby Goleta. We decided to organize an Indigenous women's fashion show and marketplace that would function as my student's final project and as a fundraiser for Casa de la Raza youth programs. Gloria and I invited Felicia to be the featured clothing designer and Lisa Rocha, a longtime member of MdM, to be the featured jewelry designer. The fashion show served multiple purposes. My students learned how to organize a fundraising event, it provided a space for them to connect feminist theory to praxis, and it allowed me to build my relationship with Felicia and MdM by bringing them to my community in Santa Barbara. "The Good Red Road: Cultura Conscious FEshion" took place Thursday, December 9, 2010, at Casa de La Raza, with an audience of approximately one hundred students and community members.[5] A few weeks later Gloria, Felicia, and I submitted a proposal to present on our fashion show collaboration at the 2011 NACCS conference "Sites of Education for Social Justice." We intended to share our experiences working together in our different capacities as educators and artivists from Southern California. Gloria ended up not being able to participate, so Felicia and I invited visual artist and MdM member Lilia Ramirez to participate in her place.

We began the panel with introductions and Felicia asked the ten or so audience members to introduce themselves as well, which helped create a more intimate space. Before Felicia began her formal presentation, she lit a medicine bundle and placed it in a seashell. She lifted the shell toward her forehead, lowered it in front of her heart, moved it across her chest from shoulder to shoulder, and said a prayer. This ceremonial opening is common in all MdM organizing meetings, presentations, and performances. By bringing in sacred medicines and giving thanks to the ancestors and to the Creator, the conference room was transformed and the people in it were made aware of our sacred connection. Felicia proceeded to share a detailed history of MdM, recounting the first Live Art Show in 1997 and the cultural, educational, and political projects MdM has worked on since then. She deferred to me in some instances, asking for my input and to support the points that she made. I did the same with her during my presentation titled "Collaborative Research Relationships and Art-Based Activist Curriculum" using the fashion show as a case study. It was important that our roundtable be interactive between presenters and also with the audience. Felicia, Lilia, and I shared our experiences of collaboration and community building and we attempted to also develop a sense of community at the conference, however rudimentary or fleeting, by demonstrating the ways we interact in organizing meetings. The examples described in this section provide a glimpse into the ways I developed reciprocal relationships with Felicia and other MdM members early on. I continued to deepen my involvement with MdM in spring 2011 as an organizer of the fourteenth annual Live Art Show and as a participant-observer to gather dissertation data, which I recount in the following section.

FINDING COMMUNITY AS A MUJER DE MAIZ

On Monday, January 3, 2011, I drove from Santa Barbara to the Boyle Heights community center Corazón del Pueblo to attend my first Live Art Show planning meeting. As soon as I exited the freeway and turned onto First Street, I was overwhelmed by strong feelings of nostalgia. I passed familiar landmarks like Mariachi Plaza and the smells coming from the taquerias on what seemed like every corner welcomed me home. I drove by the meeting at 6:45 p.m. and noticed that no one was inside. Not wanting to be the first person to arrive, I stopped for tea at Primera Taza Coffee Shop before heading to the meeting. As I entered Corazón del Pueblo, I was immediately struck by the vibrant art exhibit featuring creative interpretations of La Virgen de Guadalupe. Three paintings captured my attention in particular. La Virgen with a luchador mask, the Virgen as Coatlicue, and finally as a homegirl with an East L.A. aesthetic. I sat down on a chair facing the center of the room notating my observations in my notebook, smiling and saying hello to folks as they began to arrive one by one. Most of them smiled back, some seemed shy and remained quiet as we waited for the meeting to start, and others conversed among themselves. I would come to learn that seven out of the ten women were also new to the circle, which is probably why most of us waited for a more formal cue to interact.[6]

Felicia arrived just past 7:00 p.m., greeted everyone individually, and asked us to take a seat in the circle of chairs. She sat down, burned some medicine, introduced herself, and shared an opening prayer. Felicia passed the bundle to the woman on her left and asked that we introduce ourselves and share a few words. When it was my turn to speak I introduced myself, gave thanks for being a part of the circle, announced that I was a graduate student in Chicana and Chicano studies writing my dissertation about Mujeres de Maiz, and said, "With everyone's permission, I'd like to take notes and pictures during the meetings." I looked around the circle for approval and was happy to see all the women shaking their heads in agreement. A mujer named Lorena was sitting on my left. She whispered to me that she graduated from UCSB and said, "I think your project is great." Her verbal validation and the energy that filled the room made me feel at ease. I was also beginning to feel more comfortable because the space felt culturally and spiritually familiar. A mix of Mexican Catholic and Indigenous iconography and practices were present throughout the evening.[7] The meeting ended around 10:00 p.m., and as I was packing up my things, Felicia told me that the core members were very excited that I was going to document MdM's history and experiences, which reaffirmed my sense of belonging in the space. I was glad to get the approval of the other core members who weren't present at the meeting. Many of them worked full-time jobs in addition to being artists, caretakers, and graduate students who work on MdM projects behind the scenes, so I had not had the opportunity to meet them yet. On the drive back to Santa Barbara, I had a renewed sense of excitement about my project, about being a graduate student, and the forthcoming academic year.

As the weeks passed, my confidence grew and I began volunteering for various tasks and offering my opinion more often during discussions. Many organizers attended the weekly meetings sporadically because they had other obligations. I had the privilege of having funding to travel back and forth to Los Angeles and an open schedule dedicated to conducting research. I attended nearly every meeting and, consequently, I was able to connect with many of the women. There were usually anywhere between five to ten women at the meetings, and those who were new, like me, also seemed to grow more comfortable over time. The meetings themselves were healing for me and sometimes functioned as group therapy. We always gave thanks or said a prayer, shared stories, offered advice, encouraged one another, and we all seemed to care deeply about our city, our cultures, and future generations. After a few meetings, I began using "we" and "our" when talking about MdM in the meetings, including myself as a part of the group.

As time passed, I felt as though I should take on a more participatory role to show that I was fully committed to the collective and not just some dubious researcher who would leave after I got the data I needed. It wasn't that anyone told me that I should do more, but my upbringing and my student activist background taught me how to comport myself in a new group setting, particularly the expectation of earning one's place through active participation—or what we would call "putting in work." And although I was growing comfortable at the organizing meetings, I faced an inner struggle integrating my role as a researcher. This struggle surfaced in my feminist methods seminar, which I consider next.

INTIMACY, AFFECTIVE TIES, AND BRIDGING ACADEMIC-COMMUNITY RELATIONSHIPS

While on campus, I struggled to fully articulate my experiences as an MdM organizer and my commitment to the group. My use of "we" and "our" became "them" and "their." In academic settings in general and in my feminist methods seminar in particular, I felt as though I had to be objective and use academic jargon despite my apprehensions about terminology, such as fieldwork, informant, and research subjects. Those words could not capture the spirit of my experiences. Talking about my personal and communal intellectual-spiritual-emotional journey as research illustrated by technical academic parlance made me feel as though I was participating in some exploitative project and being honest about my work would risk being seen as not rigorous at best and illegitimate at worst by my professor and peers.

These feelings became especially salient for me after reading Opaskwayak Cree scholar Shawn Wilson's *Research is Ceremony: Indigenous Research Methods*.[8] I turned to this text, and others like it hoping to learn how other Indigenous and decolonial scholars grappled with concerns similar to my own.[9] Wilson explains, "The purpose of any ceremony is to build stronger relationships or bridge the distance between aspects of our cosmos and ourselves. The research that we do as Indigenous people is a ceremony that allows us a raised level of consciousness and insights into our world."[10] As soon as I read this passage, I thought, "At last! I have a way to explain what I, or rather, what we (MdM) are doing in terms that I can understand!" I planned to write about the work of MdM as spiritual artivism, but with Wilson's perspective, I understood that *my research* is also ceremonial. In Wilson's view, research methodology defined through an Indigenous paradigm is essentially the building of relationships, which I was certainly already invested in. However, Wilson questions his ability to illustrate research as ceremony in his writing and in situations with non-Native audiences who tend to value individualism and typically view time as linear, history as fact, and ceremony as metaphor. At the MdM meetings I was able to slowly make connections and build relationships with the women, but similar to Wilson, there was a disconnect for me in the seminar and in my writing.

FREE WRITE JANUARY 5, 2011

Feminist Methods Seminar Week #1 In-Class Writing Prompt: "What question concerning the social world would you like to investigate if you were guaranteed not to fail?" *This is an extremely hard question for me to address—one that I'm not sure how to approach. What do I care most about in the world? I interpret "what question" as "what socio-political issue" or "problem" would*

I most like to solve? At the very least I think I understand the question as, "If answered, what question would most benefit my community or the communities that I care about?" And what does it mean to fail at answering a question about the social world? Shouldn't "failure" just lead to more useful questions? I find myself trying to pick apart the prompt rather than attempting to answer it directly. I keep rereading what I wrote hoping it will give me clues as to how I want to respond; maybe the words will come if I just keep writing. But nothing yet. Maybe it's because this question is depressing. It makes me think about all of the unanswered questions I have about my research. Or maybe it's because I feel the impossibility of any immediate solutions to social problems. There are only partial answers, minor shifts, and disruptions. How does this prompt help me think about my own research? Can I fail?

POST-FREE-WRITE THOUGHTS, JANUARY 6, 2011

Maybe a more relevant question for me is what is activist scholarship? Is it only defined as working in/with/for grassroots social justice movements? Is activist scholarship limited to research or can it include teaching? Can teaching be considered a mode of activism (e.g., shifting consciousness, mentorship, building relationships/beloved communities, etc.)? Can't I just be involved in social justice work that is not about/for my research? What about short-term involvement with organizations? What's the difference between volunteerism and activism? Is volunteering less important? How is activism defined and (de)valued in academia? Being a student organizer has always been necessary for me. Why should this change now that I'm in graduate school?

These journal entries are the first documented critical reflections that mark the beginning of an introspective journey brought on by a writing prompt that would be compounded by future writing exercises, discussions, and fieldwork activities. At the time I didn't understand why I was having such a difficult time. Hindsight and self-exploration would provide me with some clarity. First, I felt constrained because I believed I needed to perform my intelligence, which meant I needed to appear rigorous, detached, and well-spoken. I felt compelled to use academic jargon in order to be viewed as a legitimate scholar. I had many negative experiences throughout my education that drove this posturing impulse.

On multiple occasions in graduate school, my ideas, values, and character were criticized and my intelligence was questioned, sometimes blatantly and maliciously by faculty whom I had once admired. Being a first-generation college student, I didn't know how to defend myself or push back in that setting, so I often remained silent. I struggled with the concept of ethnography, participant observation specifically, because it stems from cultural anthropology and has been, and to some degree still is, a method used by scholars to conduct unethical research in marginalized communities. I was aware that scholars of ethnic, feminist, and Indigenous studies have decolonized and reconfigured a number of qualitative methods, participant observation included, but the language used to describe these processes still left a bad taste in my mouth. I also felt resentful because immersion and observation are part of intuitive processes for me since my family raised me with these cultural approaches to learning. Nonetheless, I still needed to understand the vocabulary and techniques required by my PhD program.

Most importantly, I was conflicted because I didn't feel comfortable discussing my emotional investment and affective ties to MdM with my peers, despite the fact that we read and discussed articles on the topic of intimacy in research including "Into the Dark Heart of Ethnography: The Lived Ethics and Inequality of Intimate Field Relationships" by feminist sociologist Katherine Irwin.[11] In this introspective article, Irwin examines personal experiences of "marginality, conflicting loyalty pulls, professional and personal angst, moments of intense pleasure and joy as well as devastating bouts of self-doubt and failure."[12] I didn't want to appear vulnerable in the seminar by admitting that I too had those feelings articulated by Irwin. I had difficulty bridging the perceived divisions between MdM and my academic community; in this instance, it was the feminist methods seminar. On numerous occasions my discomfort resulted in me censoring myself, often shutting down completely, assuming that if I discussed the intimate ties that I felt, I would be labeled as overly emotional. First Nations education scholar Margaret Kovach notes how Indigenous scholars often feel apprehensive in bringing cultural knowledges into Western research spaces that have only recently begun to accept "other" or "diverse" epistemologies and approaches to research.

I developed friendships and connections with many of the MdM organizers in different ways. I attended ceremony with some and shared meals in their homes. I have presented with them at conferences; invited them to perform and give guest lectures in my classes; exchanged advice about graduate school, family, health, spirituality, and food ways; and we had many informal conversations that took place "off the record." Feminist sociologist Ann Oakley insists that meaningful feminist research depends on empathy and reciprocity, pointing out how researchers rarely comment on the social or personal characteristics of the interviewer, the affective rapport between the researcher and the interviewees, and how interactions can develop into "more broadly-based social relationships," including friendships.[13] Similarly, Chicana researchers Maxine Baca Zinn and Patricia Zavella consider the advantages and challenges of being a Chicana "insider-outsider" researcher arguing this position can facilitate access to Chicanx communities, lead to understanding subtleties in language and actions, insights through critical self-reflection, and higher levels of sensitivity, mutual trust, and respect.[14] Zinn and Zavella suggest that the insider-outsider status can also create ethical dilemmas for the Chicana researcher because she often feels a high level of accountability and responsibility in conducting fieldwork and analyzing the data. For me, the difficulty did not result from the affective ties themselves, but because I felt overwhelmed by a high level of accountability and responsibility to represent MdM and my own experiences in an academic setting.

ACTIVIST SCHOLARSHIP AND THE PATH OF CONOCIMIENTO

My identities as MdM organizer and researcher constantly shifted depending on the context. I struggled to maintain confidence as I negotiated between what I perceived to be the incongruous values and practices of these respective roles. As a graduate student specializing in Chicana feminisms, it was ironic that I hadn't considered my research journey was part of what Gloria Anzaldúa calls the path of conocimiento, which is a deeply self-reflexive process consisting of seven interconnected stages a voyager undertakes that can ultimately lead them to unearth a critical self-awareness and a deep inner-knowing, creating space for meaningful outward social action. I was unable to understand my experiences in this way until after I emerged from the process drastically transformed. In this section, I define conocimiento and explore my journey with attention to especially difficult and revelatory moments that led to shifts in perception about myself and my work.

Building on her foundational concept mestiza consciousness, Gloria Anzalúa extends this epistemological theory as conocimiento in her later works.[15] Conocimiento represents a process of questioning old doctrines and dominant ways of thinking and the search for intuitive, spiritual, and transformative forms of knowledge and modes of being. Describing the journey that is conocimiento, Anzaldúa explains: "Breaking out of your mental and emotional prison and deepening the range of perception enables you to link inner reflection and vision—the mental, emotional, instinctive, imaginal, spiritual, and subtle bodily awareness—with social, political action and lived experiences to generate subversive knowledges. These conocimientos challenge official and conventional ways of looking at the world, ways set up by those benefiting from such constructions."[16]

The path of conocimiento entails ongoing processes of death and rebirth—parts of you die on the journey, parts that no longer serve you or humanity, and you are reborn anew again and again. There are seven stages or stations on the path of conocimiento representing the seven sacred directions: south, west, north, east, below, above, and center/heart. Grounded in a Mesoamerican cosmovision, Anzaldúa connects the seven stages to other embodied-spiritual practices such as the seven chakras and the seven planes of reality.[17] The stages do not happen in any particular order or for a specified period of time. Here I provide a summary of the seven stages, followed by a discussion of my experiences within them.

1. "El arrebato . . . rupture, fragmentation . . . an ending, a beginning." In this stage, your world is turned upside down and what you thought you knew to be reality begins to fracture. You are faced with "opposing accounts, perspectives, or belief systems" that challenge your frames of reference, your comfort, your complacency. "The urgency to know what you're experiencing awakens la facultad, the ability to shift attention and see through the surface of things and situations." Attempting to recover from the rupture, you are propelled from the so-called safe place you once called home into nepantla.[18]

2. "Nepantla . . . torn between ways." Nepantla occurs most often. It is a transitional space of critical reflection and transformation that emerges between each of the other stages.
3. "The Coatlicue state . . . desconocimiento and the cost of knowing." I spent a great deal of time in the Coatlicue state confronting feelings of confusion, anger, guilt, and despair that result from historical traumas and resistance to self-knowledge. The Coatlicue state is a period of incubation where one vacillates between desconocimientos, ignorance or denial of knowledge, and the urge to examine oneself, teetering on the edge of awareness. This inner confrontation occurs often and "every increment of consciousness, every step forward is a *travesía*, a crossing."[19] Every crossing is part of a larger creative process that can result in large-scale cultural shifts. The Coatlicue state is necessary to sort through pain and confusion in order to make the soul, develop the psyche, expand consciousness, and come into being. In a 1994 interview with Debbie Blake and Carmen Abrego, Anzaldúa illustrates the link between the Coatlicue state and nepantla by explaining:

> When you come out of the Coatlicue state you come out of nepantla, this birthing stage where you feel like you're reconfiguring your identity and you don't know where you are. You used to be this person but now maybe you're different in some way. You're changing worlds and cultures and maybe classes, sexual preferences. So you go through this birthing of nepantla. When you're in the midst of the Coatlicue state—the cave, the dark—you're hibernating or hiding, you're gestating and giving birth to yourself. You're in a womb state. When you come out of the womb state you pass through the birth canal, the passageway I call nepantla.[20]

Anzaldúa describes nepantla as "the overlapping space between different perceptions and belief systems,"[21] and she associates it with "states of mind that question old ideas and beliefs, acquire new perspectives, change worldviews, and shift from one world to another."[22] In this stage, you have agency to tap into la facultad, or what Patricia Hill Collins calls the skills of the outsider within, which also comes from living on the margins.[23]

4. "The call ... el compromiso ... the crossing and conversion." In this stage, you are called to transform your condition. In an attempt to change your situation and in reaching for the future, you move beyond your bodily limits—also known as "yoga of the body." You cross the threshold of awareness and surrender aspects of your old self.
5. "Putting Coyolxauhqui together ... new personal and collective 'stories.'" Anzaldúa uses the mytho-historical figure Coyolxauhqui to illustrate this stage because she exemplifies "the wish to repair and heal, as well as rewrite the stories of loss and recovery, exile and homecoming, disinheritance and recuperation, stories that lead out of passivity and into agency, out of devalued into valued lives."[24] Here, you rewrite your autohistoria, which is a self-reflective personal life story and collective history in the service of social transformation.
6. "The blow-up ... a clash of realities." It's a struggle to enact your new vision in the world and you clash with those who hold onto their *desconocimientos*.
7. "Shifting realities ... acting out the vision or spiritual activism." You become a *nepantlera*—a negotiator, bridge-builder, mediator, truth seeker, and truth speaker—who facilitates connections and alliances.

Anzaldúa explains, "Together the seven stages open the senses, increasing the breadth and depth of consciousness, causing internal shifts and external changes. All seven are present within each stage, and they occur concurrently, chronologically or not."[25] Reconstruction takes place in all stages and no change is permanent on the path of conocimiento.

I incubated in the Coatlicue state for extended periods as I painfully worked to integrate my identities as an activist-scholar and community organizer, exemplified by my participation in the Live Art Show. I was conflicted with how to be involved as an audience member and organizer because I could not fuse these roles with what I thought I should be doing as a researcher. Next, I reflect on my original plans to participate in the 2011 Live Art Show, "Soldadera de Amor," followed by an account of what actually took place and my emergence from the Coatlicue state.

In order to respectfully take part in the MdM Live Art Show, I carefully considered various aspects and specific tasks in my role as a participant-observer. I considered the following logistical questions in anticipation of the show: What is my role as a participant observer? What are my guiding questions going into the space? What aspects of the show will I document—my own experiences and interactions, interactions between audience members, MdM organizers, performances? What technologies will I rely on to document the show and what are the pros and cons of using each technology? What are the pros and cons of bringing undergraduate student volunteers and how can I ensure they are prepared and understand their roles and responsibilities to me and to MdM?

During the time I was making plans to attend the Live Art Show, I was also an advisor-mentor to Mujeres Unidas por Justicia, Educación y Revolución (MUJER), a Chicana/Latina feminist undergraduate student organization at UCSB. During the 2010–11 academic year I mentored two members who accompanied me to an MdM planning meeting where we discussed the need for volunteers at the Live Art Show. The following week, I asked one of my mentees to recruit additional members, so there was a need for me to determine their roles and responsibilities. I led a mandatory volunteer meeting a few days before the show in order to ensure they were prepared. I created an agenda that included an event schedule, volunteer stations with a description of duties and expectations, and a list of what to bring, including comfortable shoes and spending money. After reviewing each agenda item in detail, we collectively decided to arrive in L.A. a few hours before the show to eat breakfast together, which I provided in appreciation for their labor, to meet the MdM organizers, assist with setup, and familiarize ourselves with the venue.

I carefully evaluated the tasks that the student volunteers and I would be responsible for. I considered taking pictures with a digital camera, recording with a video camera, writing notes in a journal, dictating my observations into a digital voice recorder, or doing it all in some combination. I decided to take pictures with my personal digital camera, shop in the marketplace, eat food, talk with friends, roam around on my own, and enjoy the show as I had in the past. I also planned to use a digital voice recorder to dictate things that I wanted to make sure I remembered, which seemed less distracting and less time-consuming than journaling. Writing notes in a journal was also impractical for me because it would detract my attention from being present in the moment to participate as an audience member. I decided to create a digital audio entry before and after the show and throughout when I felt compelled, stepping outside or into the green room when it was too loud. I also planned to document the show with a digital video camera, setting up one stationary camera to record the performances on stage and a secondary mobile video camera to record interviews with vendors, audience members, performers, and MdM members. In order for me to be present as an audience member and organizer, I decided to have two student volunteers run the video cameras who would be provided with basic training and technical instruction.

I made numerous decisions as a participant-observer and deliberated on my responsibilities as a researcher working with eight student volunteers. I felt a great deal of stress because the Live Art Show only happens once a year and I believed it to be my primary data source. Days prior to the show I had a major realization that came in a flash during a moment of panic—a rupture that thrust me into nepantla and through el compromiso. I recognized that my experiences also matter, that I'm a member of this community, and that my participation as an audience member and organizer is just as important as my role as researcher. I began to stitch Coyolxauhqui together by remembering that I chose participant-observation because it closely resembles the "learn by doing" approach that I was raised with. My family taught me to be a participant-observer, to listen to my intuition, to be respectful, and to build meaningful relationships my entire life. Despite this awareness, my newfound certainty "blew up" the moment I arrived at the venue as I struggled to enact my new vision in the world.

My detailed plan fell apart due to my compulsion to take a hands-on role and participate as an organizer. Anxiety surged through my body as I imagined missing some piece of critical data, even though I knew it was impossible to observe every detail. Chicana anthropologist Olga Nájera-Ramírez notes similar apprehensions in documenting a festival in Jalisco, Mexico, writing that it is, "Impossible to report all points of views discovered in the field. This problem becomes further complicated when dealing with festivals because of its multidimensional/multivocal aspect."[26] No literature review could have prepared me for the uneasiness that arose in that moment. As the morning went on, I relaxed a bit and tried to stop overthinking what I should do next. The doors were not yet open to the public, so I went with my instinct to participate as an organizer. As time went on, I realized that I could in fact bridge my roles as participant and observer. I was moving through nepantla and beginning to shift my reality. I trusted the student volunteers could handle the tasks I had assigned to them. This included setting up chairs in the main stage area, placing a paper questionnaire on each chair for the audience to complete, using a tally counter at the entrance to track admissions, assisting vendors with setting up their booths, collecting the questionnaire as the audience exited after the show, and other miscellaneous tasks such as restocking the bathroom and acting as ushers throughout the event.

As the show got underway, I browsed the marketplace, took pictures, purchased jewelry and food, caught up with old friends that I ran into, and floated in and out of the performance area. I decided to take charge of the video cameras rather than have the students be responsible for this important component of my research. I set up the stationary camera to record the performers on the stage upstairs and asked that one volunteer change the tapes as needed during the times I was not there to do so myself. I ran the mobile camera and interviewed performers in the green room and vendors in the marketplace. A few of the MdM organizers, myself included, stayed at the venue until 11:00 p.m. to clean up and make sure all loose ends were tied up. By the end of the night, I felt compelled to put Coyolxauhqui together and write about my experiences as a community organizer, audience member, and activist-scholar in my research journal. The following week I began to piece myself and this story together. In the final section of this chapter, I offer a sketch of engaged community work and activist-scholarship as an offering to Coatlicue and Coyolxauhqui and to other activist-scholars seeking autohistorias that might help them think through their own research methods.

A BLUEPRINT FOR ACTIVIST-SCHOLARSHIP AND COMMUNITY ORGANIZING

A form of spiritual inquiry, conocimiento is reached via creative acts—writing, art-making, dancing, healing, teaching, meditation, and spiritual activism—both mental and somatic (the body, too, is a form as well as site of creativity). Through creative engagements, you embed

> *your experiences in a larger frame of reference, connecting your personal struggles with those other beings on the planet, with the struggles of the Earth itself. To understand the greater reality that lies behind your personal perceptions, you view these struggles as spiritual undertakings.*
> —GLORIA ANZALDÚA, "NOW LET US SHIFT," 542

This written product would not have been possible unless I opened all my senses, metawitnessed my mind-body-emotion matrix, and came home to myself.[27] It's critical to note that while I was on the path of conocimiento, I engaged in numerous liberatory-spiritual-creative-embodied practices that facilitated my journey. I took Afro-Brazilian dance classes, practiced yoga, worked with a nutritionist/Lac./TCM (licensed acupuncturist, Traditional Chinese Medicine) practitioner, and attended ceremony. I intentionally ate more ancestral foods and local produce and cut back on processed foods, I spent time with myself at the beach, and I went on hikes. I also studied Theatre of the Oppressed and Spoken Wor(l)d Art Performance as Activism (SWAPA) with Chela Sandoval. My own Indigenous Xicana/feminist of color research praxis called me to simultaneously engage in somatic work, creative expression, and retribalization/reconnection while engaging in a community research project. These practices helped me realize that I was struggling to use feminist, Indigenous, and anticolonial research methods because I was approaching them intellectually. I also needed to use my intuition, spirit, body, and emotions to know on a visceral level and to purge colonial ways of knowing, learning, and being. These practices helped me develop my facultad and understand that I was on the path of conocimiento.

I first entered the MdM community as an organizer and researcher over a decade ago. I now understand my research agenda was a localized part of a global Indigenous project of validation, survival, social justice, self-determination, and decolonization by Indigenous Xicana researchers working in and for our own communities. To honor my journey, I conclude by providing my seven personal tenets of activist-scholarship, crafted in the hopes of providing guidance for others interested in liberatory community-engaged research.

1. Reflexivity: Closely examine my positionality and how that shapes the research. Consider issues of power, intimacy, and emotional investment in the project;
2. Collaboration: Define research goals and intentions with the research community before beginning the project. Work with key community members from research design through publication and beyond when possible;
3. Build Relationships: Ask for permission, be respectful, caring, and work to equalize power with students, academic colleagues, community research partners, and myself. Also build my relationship to knowledge and the writing process. Revisit "The Path of Red and Black Ink" as needed;[28]
4. Transparency: Document outcomes, challenges, and opportunities. Represent these clearly and candidly in the writing and presentations;
5. Accessibility: Decide how to communicate findings to both an academic and a popular audience, guided by the question: *Could my mom read this?* Consider using culturally relevant storytelling structures/styles and accessible language. Present in academic settings and community venues, in personal and virtually;
6. Accountability: To the research community: check in, show up, put in work, and be honest. Check in with others often to determine what they need and create opportunities for feedback on my process, behaviors, and actions. Accountability to myself: check in with myself often. Address my physical, mental, emotional, and spiritual needs. Set realistic goals, be flexible, be honest, listen to my intuition, don't be afraid to take risks or ask for help. Remember that there is no such thing as failure only opportunities to learn;
7. Recall this quote by Gloria as needed: "By redeeming your most painful experiences you transform them into something valuable, algo para compartir or share with others so they too may be empowered."[29]

NOTES

This chapter is a revised version of my dissertation methods chapter. Amber Rose González, "'Autobioethnography': How I Became an Activist-Scholar-Organizer" in "Another City Is Possible: Mujeres de Maiz, Radical Indigenous Mestizaje and Activist Scholarship" (PhD diss., University of California, Santa Barbara, 2014), 17–50.

Thanks and gratitude to my colega Lucha Arévalo for providing thoughtful feedback on an earlier draft of this essay and to my dissertation chair, mentor, and life-long maestra, Chela Sandoval, for your guidance, support, and love. This essay is dedicated to the memory of Horacio N. Roque-Ramírez, who helped me develop a love for research methods and who continues to teach me to write from the corazón.

1. There is a dearth of published work on ethnographic methods from the perspective of the graduate student who is in the thick of negotiating unfamiliar terrain, which can be particularly foreign for first-generation college students. As I worked on the literature review for my methods chapter, I unsuccessfully sought out publications from novice researchers who chronicled their struggles, which in part, motivated the publication of this chapter. An excellent exception is Carolina Alonso Bejerano, Lucia López Juárez, Mirian A. Mijangos García, and Daniel Goldstein, *Decolonizing Ethnography: Undocumented Immigrants and New Directions in Social Science* (Durham, N.C.: Duke University Press, 2019).

2. Decolonial theorist and liberation philosopher Chela Sandoval names the act of witnessing one's own consciousness, one's own mind-body-emotion matrix, as metawitnessing.

3. Tía Chucha's was founded in 2001 as a creative and educational bookstore, art, performance, and cultural space to serve the community in the Northeast San Fernando Valley. In partnership with the Los Angeles Department of Cultural Affairs, they presented a one-day, free family event to celebrate and promote literacy and the arts. The festival featured local artisan and food vendors, live musical, theatrical, and spoken word performances, children's activities, a book fair, author readings, community resources, and family literacy workshops.

4. *Urban Xic*, now El MERCADO y Mas, is an online cooperative marketplace that Felicia created for Los Angeles–based socially conscious artivists, musicians, and fashion designers who connect with Xicanx-Indígena worldviews—that is, the spiritual-politics that call for respect, peace, and dignity for all Indigenous peoples, to sell their merchandise. El MERCADO is the official shop of Mujeres de Maiz. https://elmercadoymas.com/.

5. For an account of this and other Indigenous fashion shows, review Chela Sandoval, Amber Rose González, and Felicia 'Fe' Montes, "Urban Xican/x--Indigenous Fashion Show ARTivism: Experimental Perform-Antics in Three Actos," in *meXicana Fashions: Self-Adornment, Identity Constructions and Political Self-Presentations*, eds. Aída Hurtado and Norma Cantú (Austin: University of Texas Press, 2020), 283–316.

6. The organizers of the Live Art Show vary from year to year with a few consistent members returning. New people are invited by returning organizers or by core MdM members. This open practice allows organizers to participate when they are able, perhaps for one season or a single event, without any pressure to contribute more or to return the next season. All contributions are valued equally. The openness of MdM's organizing framework is key to the group's longevity.

7. I was raised Catholic by my father and with pan-Indigenous religious traditions by my mother who reconnected with her Apache culture and spirituality when

I was a pre-teen. Some familiar practices that I experienced at the organizing meeting include a circle structure, opening and closing prayers, burning medicine, giving thanks, Guadalupe-Coatlicue art, and more. Chicana scholars have named the blending of these practices spiritual mestizaje, Indianizing Catholicism, and nepantla spirituality. Gloria Anzaldúa, "Border Arte: Nepantla, El Lugar de La Frontera," in *The Gloria Anzaldúa Reader*, ed. AnaLouise Keating (Durham, N.C.: Duke University Press, 2009), 176–86; Theresa Delgadillo, *Spiritual Mestizaje: Religion, Gender, Race, and Nation in Contemporary Chicana Narrative* (Durham, N.C.: Duke University Press, 2011); Yolanda Broyles-González, *Re-Emerging Native Women of the Americas: Native Chicana Latina Women's Studies* (Dubuque, Iowa: Kendall/Hunt Publishing, 2001); Elisa Facio and Irene Lara, eds., *Fleshing the Spirit: Spirituality and Activism in Chicana, Latina, and Indigenous Women's Lives* (Tucson: University of Arizona Press, 2014); Lara Medina, "Los Espíritus Siguen Hablando: Chicana Spiritualities," in *Latina/o Healing Practices: Mestizo and Indigenous Perspectives*, eds. Brian W. McNeill and Joseph M. Cervantes (New York: Taylor & Francis, 2008), 223–48; Cherríe Moraga, *A Xicana Codex of Changing Consciousness: Writings, 2000–2010* (Durham, N.C.: Duke University Press, 2011).

8. Shawn Wilson, *Research Is Ceremony: Indigenous Research Methods* (Nova Scotia: Fernwood, 2008).

9. Other texts that shaped my understanding include Irene I. Blea, *Researching Chicano Communities: Social-Historical, Physical, Psychological, and Spiritual Space* (Westport, Conn.: Praeger, 1995); Leslie Brown and Susan Strega, eds., *Research as Resistance: Critical, Indigenous, and Anti-Oppressive Approaches* (Toronto: Canadian Scholars Press/Women's Press, 2005); Margaret Kovach, *Indigenous Methodologies: Characteristics, Conversations, and Contexts* (Toronto: University of Toronto Press, 2009); Charles Menzies, "Reflections on Research with, For, and Among Indigenous Peoples," *Canadian Journal of Native Education* 25, no. 1 (2001): 19–36; Olga Nájera-Ramírez, "Of Fieldwork, Folklore, and Festival: Personal Encounters," *Journal of American Folklore* 112, no. 444 (1999): 183–99; Sarah Pink, *Doing Sensory Ethnography* (Thousand Oaks, Calif.: Sage Publications, 2009); Linda Tuhiwai Smith, *Decolonizing Methodologies: Research and Indigenous Peoples* (London: Zed Books, 1999).

10. Wilson, *Research Is Ceremony*, 11.

11. Katherine Irwin, "Into the Dark Heart of Ethnography: The Lived Ethics and Inequality of Intimate Field Relationships," *Qualitative Sociology* 29, no. 2 (June 2006): 155–75.

12. Irwin, "Into the Dark Heart of Ethnography," 160.

13. Ann Oakley, "Interviewing Women: A Contradiction in Terms," in *Doing Feminist Research*, ed. Helen Roberts (London: Routledge, 1981), 31.

14. Maxine Baca Zinn, "Field Research in Minority Communities: Ethical, Methodological and Political Observations by an Insider," *Social Problems* 27, no. 2 (1979): 209–19; Patricia Zavella, "Feminist Insider Dilemmas: Constructing

Ethnic Identity with Chicana Informants," in *Feminist Anthropology: A Reader*, ed. Ellen Lewin (Malden, Mass.: Blackwell, 2006), 186–202.
15. Gloria Anzaldúa, "now let us shift . . . the path of conocimiento . . . inner work, public acts," in *This Bridge We Call Home: Radical Visions for Transformation*, eds. Gloria E. Anzaldúa and AnaLouise Keating (New York: Routledge, 2002), 540–79; Gloria Anzaldúa, "Preface: (Un)natural Bridges, (Un)safe Spaces," in *This Bridge We Call Home: Radical Visions for Transformation*, eds. Gloria E. Anzaldúa and AnaLouise Keating (: Routledge, 2002), 1–5; Gloria Anzaldúa, "Let Us Be the Healing of the Wound: The Coyolxauhqui Imperative—La Sombra y El Sueño," in *The Gloria Anzaldúa Reader*, ed. AnaLouise Keating (Durham, N.C.: Duke University Press, 2009), 303–14.
16. Anzaldúa, "now let us shift," 542.
17. Anzaldúa, "now let us shift," 545.
18. Anzaldúa, "now let us shift," 546–47.
19. Anzaldúa, *Borderlands/La Frontera, The New Mestiza*, 3rd ed. (San Francisco: Aunt Lute Books, 2007), 70.
20. Gloria Anzaldúa, "Doing Gigs: Speaking, Writing, and Change: An Interview with Debbie Blake and Carmen Abrego (1994)," in *Interviews/Entrevistas*, ed. AnaLouise Keating (London: Routledge, 2000), 225–26.
21. Anzaldúa, "now let us shift," 541.
22. Anzaldúa, "(Un)natural bridges, (Un)safe Spaces," 1.
23. Patricia Hill Collins, "Learning from the Outsider Within: The Sociological Significance of Black Feminist Thought," in *Beyond Methodology: Feminist Scholarship as Lived Research*, eds. Mary Margaret Fonow and Judith A. Cook (Bloomington: Indiana University Press, 1991), 35–59.
24. Anzaldúa, "now let us shift," 558–63.
25. Anzaldúa, "now let us shift," 545.
26. Nájera-Ramírez, "Of Fieldwork, Folklore, and Festival," 186.
27. I was introduced to the mind-body-emotion matrix by Chela Sandoval in her course "The Shaman-Nahual/Active-Witness Ceremony Through Story-Wor(l)d-Art Performance As Activism," or SWAPA, at the University of California, Santa Barbara.
28. Gloria Anzaldúa, "The Path of Red and Black Ink," in *Borderlands, La Frontera—La Nueva Mestiza*, 3rd ed. (San Francisco: Aunt Lute, 2007), 87–98.
29. Anzaldúa, "now let us shift," 540.

34

Restoring the Mind, Body, and Spirit

Mujeres de Maiz and Social Media as a Tool of Spiritual Artivism and Education

MEGAN PENNINGS

I WAS FIRST introduced to MdM as an undergraduate student at California State University, Los Angeles, where I was starting to find my cultural identity. I was starting to understand why my family distanced themselves from our culture, why I was not allowed to learn Spanish, why my community saw me as just "another white girl," and why I battled with my identity as a mixed-race mujer. I enrolled in my first course in "Chicana Feminism" with Dr. Dionne Espinoza, where I was introduced to the ideology and praxis of Chicana feminism. Although I had heard of the term "Chicana," it was not until this course that I fully understood how Chicana feminism had become this powerful identity-based movement for many women of color. It was in this course that I formed my own identity as an Irish-Chicana. I felt a sense of belonging and learned that I was not alone as others also struggled to come to terms with their identities.

One impactful experience during this course was a presentation by Felicia 'Fe' Montes who showed a video performance of her spoken word poetry "Overcompensating Xicana Complex." Her words brought up this new power and raw emotion within me. I felt a sense of deep learning and connection with a sisterhood collective that I long sought after to help me understand more of my cultural identity. I felt inspired to understand more about Felicia's work as an artivist and to learn more about Mujeres de Maiz (MdM) as a collective and what they have done for their communities—from creating spaces to interact with art and poetry to promoting personal and ancestral healing. Upon completion of the Chicana Feminism course, I felt motivated to start my journey to reconnect my mind, body, and spirit.[1] Over the course of the next three years, I would go on to be mentored by Chicana feminists, take courses that included MdM content, and attend many MdM events as a volunteer and later as an organizer and intern.[2] However, it was not until I was a graduate student and I took another course with Dr. Dionne Espinoza that asked students to interview core members of MdM, that I truly began my journey with MdM.[3]

This chapter is an adaptation of my graduate thesis project where I researched MdM's social media practices and analyzed their Instagram posts from 2016 to 2017 to understand how they use social media platforms as an educational tool for spiritual artivism.[4] Here, I examine how MdM engages in spiritual artivism to engage communities of WOC and QWOC by bringing awareness to their followers on social media.[5] The following sections focus on how MdM's Instagram has benefited their followers in their process of healing and/or reconnecting to the mind, body, and spirit. The first section, "Through the Lens of Digital Spiritual Artivism," will define the concept "spiritual artivism" and examine how MdM deploys this womxn of color feminist praxis on social media. I then move on to discuss the impact of "Reposting to Reconnect the Mind, Body, Spirit" by analyzing memes to illustrate how MdM uses the reposting feature to further engage in digital spiritual artivism. The next section will focus on how social media has emerged among "A New Generation of Digital Artivists and Feminists Followers." And, finally, I conclude with a discussion of my research process and personal interactions with MdM's social media.

My first experience with managing MdM social media was during the Live Art Show in 2015. Since then, I have been involved with multiple aspects of their social media including posting on Instagram during their many events, posting information on artists, performers, and vendors during the Live Art Show, and with the new features of Instagram and Facebook, I have been in charge of "Going Live" during events with artists, performers, vendors, and audience members about their experiences during the events. Through these interactions, I was able to get a sense of how important the MdM digital space had become for many of their followers; for example, being able to use a digital format to bring the events live to followers who are not able to attend, or to introduce artists, performers, and vendors to new audiences by "tagging" their social media, or by reposting from other accounts as a way to support, but also to create a digital community around the ideology of MdM.[6]

As I was starting my journey with MdM in 2015, I was also on a new path of reconnecting and healing my mind, body, and spirit. It was during this time that I had lost my mother and was looking for guidance. I felt lost and disconnected to myself spiritually. I have learned that our deepest connection is to our mother, and I felt like my connection was gone. I didn't understand how life was supposed to keep going on. I would post memes and quotes about loss on my personal Instagram as I struggled with depression and experienced all five stages of grief all at once. Physically I was here, but mentally and spiritually I was lost. During this time, MdM's Instagram posts would help me get through my days. The motivational words and images helped me reconnect my mind, body, spirit—it was the images that displayed strength, reality, knowledge, and spiritual connection that reminded me of my path and the importance of community, even on the digital level. It was also within MdM's social media that I found I was not alone, and many others dealt with the same pain and struggles I did. I was beginning to see the power of social media as a form of healing and a space for individuals to connect as a community. The interactions among followers through comments illustrate how MdM posts have allowed individuals to find some form of coping mechanisms—whether it be based on the images, words, or comments—these interactions have helped their followers manage painful or difficult emotions in the moment.

As I analyzed MdM's Instagram feed, I started to understand how they have adapted social media as an educational and outreach support platform, especially for individuals who have been impacted by their mental health. Through my research, I learned that MdM posts have educated their followers, myself included, on various social issues, on understanding the self, and the connection we have to our ancestors. These empowering posts are teaching tools that help followers understand the impact of oppression within our communities. I began to understand that the mind, body, and spirit have a purpose, and through MdM social media this becomes a form of a daily affirmation, for not just myself but others, which helps followers connect and understand the impact of healing through a digital platform in the form of spiritual artivism.

THROUGH THE LENS OF DIGITAL SPIRITUAL ARTIVISM

> @MujeresdeMaiz "The Instagram account for an empowering community space in Los Angeles also works to empower those of us not in the area through their connection to the earth, each other, their work and the world."[7]
> —MODERN TEJANA

Interaction on social media has become a daily routine for many individuals, with a generation that is all about becoming "Instafamous."[8] Many base their daily activity on the interactions among followers. While many people also use social media to connect to family, peers, and network, other accounts focus on community activism and use social media as a tool to resist marginalization. For MdM, social media has become a platform for digital expression, artivism, education, and healing. Based on my personal observations, I've noticed the idea of social media as a form of education has become a new concept in the last five years. Social media images have the potential to connect communities to information that is not widely available within mainstream media and has become an alternative news outlet that allows people to see firsthand accounts of what is happening at the moment. For artists, the role of social media impacts their content and actions. Bart Cammaert explains, "The internal role refers to the decision making while external roles relate to mobilisation, recruitment, and the creation of alternative or independent channels of communication that contribute to a vibrant public sphere."[9] As an activists/artivists internal role, their decisions of what content will be shared are based on the ideology of that organization or individual. The external role covers the platform that is used to communicate their ideology, such as live stream, video, or photo posts that connect communities and share content among their followers. By creating digital communication and documentation, followers are allowed access to information on an unlimited basis through the touch of an application on a smartphone, tablet, or computer.

In the epigraph at the beginning of this section, Modern Tejana, an online blog that focuses on culture, style, food, and fun for contemporary Latinas in Texas, founder Melissa Rodriguez points out how Mujeres de Maiz's Instagram has become a major outlet to promote empowerment, positivity, awareness, and pride in a digital community by allowing space for followers from various communities to heal and learn through live streams, videos, and photos. As a grassroots, Xicana-led, feminist of color organization, MdM's Instagram posts keep true to their mission statement, which is: "Mujeres de Maiz (womxn of the corn) provides holistic wellness through education, programming, exhibitions, and publishing in order to empower women and girls through the creation of community."[10] MdM first started using social media in 2012, and during this time they only used Facebook and Instagram. MdM's Facebook was used for inviting followers to events, where Instagram became the space to post images or repost images, with content that focused on their work in the community including documentation of their yearly Live Art Shows. Over time, MdM began using additional platforms such as YouTube, X (Twitter), and Twitch, and their online presence has become much more active because of the COVID-19 global pandemic.

By using social media to advance their mission, MdM has opened an ideology around spiritual healing by creating a loving and sustainable digital world to build space for marginalized communities to transform their consciousness—this is spiritual artivism in the digital realm. Gloria E. Anzaldúa coined the term spiritual activism, encapsulated in the following quote: "With awe and wonder you look around, recognizing the preciousness of the earth, the sanctity of every human being on the planet, the ultimate unity and interdependence of all beings-somos todos un país. Love swells in your chest and shoots out of your heart chakra, linking you to everyone/everything. . . . You share a category of identity wider than any social position or racial label. This conocimiento motivates you to work actively to see that no harm comes to people, animals, ocean–to take up spiritual activism and the work of healing."[11]

By engaging in spiritual activism on social media, MdM opens a space for conversations around healing and reconnecting the mind, body, and spirit using an artivist framework. Through my research, I found MdM posts and reposts of many images that could be interpreted as a form of spiritual artivism. From protests in the streets to art on the walls, these images reflect the ways MdM uses digital art toward educating and healing communities. In what follows, I analyze four representative examples of MdM posts from 2016 to 2017.

Figure 34.1 is a drawing of an Indigenous woman, split down the middle, with two sides depicted. On the left side, her dark hair is braided, and she is wearing a T-shirt that partially reads "No Dakota Access Pipeline." A can of pepper spray held by a white hand is being discharged straight to her face, and as a result, her eye is tearing up. On the other side, she is in

FIGURE 34.1 They love us and hate us. Mujeres de Maiz Instagram. Illustration by Tyler Amato.

Indigenous dress, her hair is light and styled with a tribal headband and feathers, she is wearing dreamcatcher earrings, and someone is holding a cell phone camera up to her to take a photo. The cell phone displays wording as if the person was ready to post on social media. The caption reads:

> THEY LOVE US & HATE US. They love us when we are a caricature. An object for their entertainment. But when we are human beings, when we want to be treated as equals, that's when we have a problem. . . . On a similar note: We must address the issues of people putting their bodies on the front lines while "allies" take selfies, run from the police brutality, and take up much needed space, Allies. Take note. This is an indigenous lead struggle that needs bodies that help kill the black snake, not waste our time. #NoDAPL #standingrock #waterislife #MniWiconi #standwithstandingrock #nativeamerican #xicanx #genocide.[12]

Standing Rock refers to an Indigenous reservation located in North and South Dakota and home to the Lakota and Dakota nations who have been protecting tribal lands from an underground oil pipeline, which runs through four states: North and South Dakota, Iowa, and Illinois. The concerns of the Standing Rock Sioux Tribe address issues related to the environment, which includes "everything from farming and drinking water to entire ecosystems, wildlife and food sources."[13] Journalist Justin Worland's *Time Magazine* article "What to Know About the Dakota Access Pipeline Protest" offers important information regarding Standing Rock that will help to contextualize the post. Worland states, "The pipeline is to be built by Texas-based Energy Transfer Partners and is designed to transport as many as 570,000 barrels of crude oil daily from North Dakota to Illinois. The pipeline has united several different interest groups with a variety of objections, but Native Americans have been at the center of the opposition. The pipeline would travel underneath the Missouri River, the primary drinking water source for the Standing Rock Sioux, a tribe of around 10,000 with a reservation in the central part of North and South Dakota."[14] The impact of the DAPL became a national concern and led to protests, not just on the frontlines, but also within cities with strong ties to Native communities. Los Angeles was on the forefront of protests outside of the Dakotas.

FIGURE 34.2 Los Angeles to Standing Rock. Mujeres de Maiz Instagram.

Figure 34.2 shows three Mujeres de Maiz members, holding a sign that reads "NO DAPL WATER IS LIFE" hanging off the Los Angeles Main Street bridge over the 101 freeway. Behind the women is the Los Angeles courthouse and office of the National Relations Board. The location of the banner drop is an important aspect as the 101 freeway leads from Downtown Los Angeles to North Hollywood and has major access from the city to suburbs. The caption reads: "LOS ANGELES TO STANDING ROCK we say #NoDAPL #WaterIsLife #MniWiconi #losangelestostandingrock. Solidarity march in Los Angeles regarding the water pipeline that is being run through Standing Rock."[15] This image shows how communities in Los

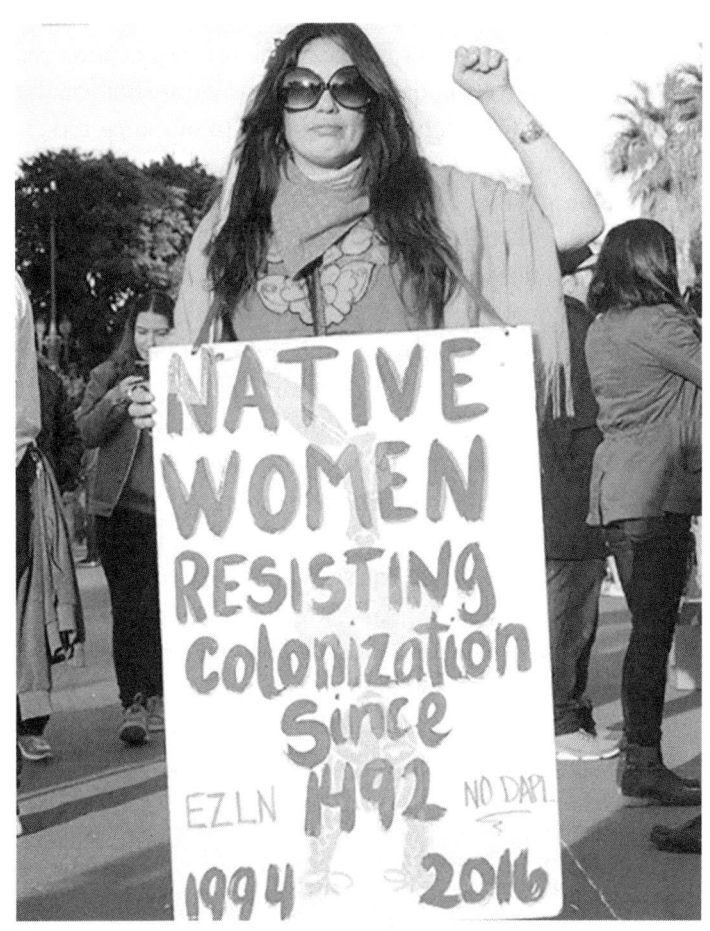

FIGURE 34.3 Native womxn resisting. Photo of Lilia 'Liliflor' Ramirez of MdM at NODAPL protest. Mujeres de Maiz Instagram.

Angeles stand in solidarity with the fight to stop the Dakota pipeline and how the impact of these fights goes beyond the frontlines of the pipeline to the streets of communities that fought similar social issues of displacement from land and access to water.

Figure 34.3 also addresses the protests on the Standing Rock reservation. This is a photograph of Lilia 'Lilifor' Ramirez, core member of MdM, painter, muralist, and papier-mâché sculptor. In this image, Lilifor is at the 2017 Los Angeles Women's March throwing a power fist with one hand, and in the other, she holds a sign that reads, "NATIVE WOMEN RESISTING Colonization Since 1492, EZLN 1994, NO DAPL 2016."[16] This image displays the message of resilience. The original caption reads: "I went to the WMLA as a reminder that #weexist. We are not your lackeys, we will wear a dress, we will pray, give thanks to our ancestors, I came to tell you 'welcome to our world,' and don't get comfortable because it's going to be a bit uncomfortable, my family will not be divided by a 'wall' we will build bridges with #loveandaction." The caption allows Liliflor to express her voice and the use of the words "we exist" show the resilience of the fight for not just women's rights, but rights of Native Americans and POC. Her caption and sign powerfully indicate that she will not back down, and she will fight just as her ancestors did.

Figure 34.4 is another image from the 2017 International Women's March that shows generations of Indigenous women and young girls protesting in the streets of Los Angeles and marching for women's rights, for equality, for acknowledgment of Indigenous women's rights—they stand side by side in a struggle for all. The signs they carry display Indigenous women activists with their years of birth and death, political prisoners' names, and other names of Indigenous women who have fought for the rights of their people. They hold a long white banner with the words "Indigenous Women Rise & Unite" displaying red, black, and yellow hummingbirds. The four colors (white, red, black, and yellow) represent

FIGURE 34.4 Indigenous womxn rise. Mujeres de Maiz Instagram.

the four directions of the medicine wheel. The word Indigenous is spaced so that the "o" is sideways with the word "US" below in red and bold. The caption on the Instagram post reads "INDIGENOUS WOMXN TAKING SPACE & HONORING ANCESTORS"; a powerful message that speaks to the context of the image. By marching, these women honor the women who fought before us, who fight with us, and who will continue to fight after us.[17]

Each of these images capture the essence of the time and struggle of marching and fighting for the equal rights of all women. The images are pieces of moments frozen in time where art becomes a political statement. The space that these images hold in a physical and digital format allows for the voices of women to circulate and live throughout the historical archive that is social media. Figures 34.1–34.4 visually allow followers to react and connect to the images; however, it is through each image's caption that followers are further educated via MdM's spiritual artivism. By using social media, MdM shares their holistic and transformative worldview through social justice education centered around Indigenous women's representation, allyship, sovereignty, land/water protection, and resisting settler colonialism. These images also allow MdM to further promote their teachings through a digital platform by providing insights and knowledge about the NoDAPL Movement, which allows a blending of artivist tools and community outreach by visually showing the impact around teaching and healing of the mind, body, and spirit through digital protest. These posts open up the conversation among MdM followers around the importance of community awareness and support for Indigenous feminist social and spiritual movements. The following section focuses on the ways MdM uses the reposting tool to open spaces for conversations around healing and reconnecting the mind, body, and spirit using an artivist framework.

REPOSTING TO RECONNECT THE MIND, BODY, SPIRIT

Reposting or sharing images allows users to reach a wider audience, and allows followers to connect with new accounts and broadens their followers. MdM has developed a strong social media following by reposting inspirational quotes and memes from other accounts that share a similar mission. Many reposts are about the long history of losing traditions within a settler society and reclaiming cultural knowledge, which allows a space for followers to connect to others who may be adjusting, healing, or transforming on a similar path. Reposting a meme, event information, or a call to action allows MdM to share content and inspire followers during their process to heal, transform, and reconnect.

On January 26, 2017, MdM reposted an image in bold black letters with flowers as the background that read "If It Doesn't Nourish Your Soul Get Rid of It," and the focal point being the word "Nourish."[18] This post encouraged followers to get rid of the negative energy that surrounds their soul or space. With 472 likes and a few followers tagging other accounts, this post is an example of how such statements have drawn interactions among followers, while the importance of tagging and sharing allows others to gain insight into a post. What I found important was one follower who commented "But that means I have to get rid of my internet"—a powerful comment that shows the effects of modern technology and connecting to a digital world. While this comment may seem like this follower is wanting to get rid of the digital piece that does not nourish their soul, it's the fact that they felt the power to make that comment that implies a negative impact of the internet and social media. However, the connection to technology is what allows them to see the post and understand that "something" needs to go in order to transform or "renourish" their spirit, whether it be their internet or something else in their life; the impact of this post is there within the follower's comment. MdM gave an opening to help this individual understand that their healing process must be transformed within some aspect of their life.

As I furthered my research, I came across what I felt was a powerful image reposted by the @womensmarch account by artist account @itmustbeeasign, which promoted the Women's March that was held on January 21, 2017.[19] The post states: "Somos Resisters! We Are Resisters" and features an image of various diverse women with black bold capital letters that read "RESISTERS" in the middle, a play on the words resist and sisters. The message is meant to embrace a racially and ethnically diverse sisterhood and promote the need to come together and bond to dismantle society's oppressions, an example of modern-day feminism within social media. The power of reposting allows for the statement, idea, or concept to travel through a wide range of social media accounts allowing for a faster form of action. In the article, "How Social Media Has Changed and Amplified the Modern Feminist Massage," author Katie McBeth states, "Modern day feminism combines issues of race, culture, social class, disability, sexual preference, and gender identity. This new feminism relies on the voices of women to share their frustrations, dreams, identity, and history." Social media accounts provide many modern feminist artivists an outlet for to express their voice. This is important, especially since many of these users would not have access to such a large public platform otherwise but are now given a digital space to voice and express issues among diverse groups of women and allow for ally support to stand in solidarity and to embrace the idea that "WE ARE RESISTERS."

Another example of digital spiritual artivism is the notion that "art is healing," a repost from punkinoo1.[20] The repost features bold black lettering that states: "Healing Is An Art, It Takes Time, It Takes Practice, It Takes Love." Stuckey and Nobel explain that art is healing because art allows individuals to bridge a connection between their mind, body, and spirit through the physical and emotional aspects to allow for healing.[21] What interested me about this repost were the comments from MdM followers who expressed their connection to the statement, quoting the words such as "It takes practice, it takes love," and "This is exactly what I need to hear today, thank you for sharing. Red heart emoji." The empowering message of post or repost can help change someone's mood, give them hope, and support them with their healing.[22] During my time assisting with reposting many followers would comment and send a DM (direct message) stating how empowering or useful a post was or how one post made their day seem so much brighter. Whether it be words or an emoji,[23] many comments have been made by followers to express how a post had impacted them, such as "Thank you," "Feel this," "That's the way it's got to be!!!!," and "OMG, I need to hear this."

For many diverse WOC and QWOC communities, the healing process takes years of struggle to unpack the long generational effects of trauma, as traditional healer/midwife and professor Patrisia Gonzales describes in her article "Trauma, Love, & History." She argues, "The impact of trauma is 'an impact that history has on our body, our families, our lands, our plants, and animals.'"[24] Intergenerational trauma is embedded within ourselves and our communities, however, art has been a venue for healing to help break from those traumas and this repost reminds followers that healing takes time, practice, and the love of ourselves and community. By promoting the concepts of soul nourishment, resistant sisterhood, and healing as an art, MdM's social media provides digital space to share medicinal art with other followers. These reposts allow for the process of healing through a digital platform, which adds to their tradition of programming and exhibition that celebrates and honors the intergenerational, intercultural work of holistic artivists, womxn, femme, and gender nonconforming artivists.

A NEW GENERATION OF SPIRITUAL ARTIVIST AND FEMINIST FOLLOWERS

Testimony by two MdM followers Betania Santos and Gaby Martinez allows us to further understand how MdM social media has impacted the community of WOC and QWOC. Betania, self-identified, Xicana says, "The community health advocacy posts have been important to myself and the community. MdM is not just about an art collective, but they are also about reaching communities . . . things that I learned about my healing process, I found through Mujeres de Maiz social media. . . . MdM posts give knowledge to others and still honors traditions, which helps to keep legacies and traditions alive."[25] This quote gives insight into the importance of MdM posts around community health and the impact of informational posts. Using social media to share health advocacy information such as Indigenous and feminist therapists and community healers, culturally relevant wellness tips, and inspirational quotes allows followers to gain knowledge of traditions, and for many individuals, this may be their only form of connection to ancestral teachings.

Gaby, a self-identified Disabled Xicana, adds, "[MdM's] social media platform has been used by all those communities and activism and education. . . . It's so impactful for communities, because they don't just post about women; they also post about other issues in the community. . . . MdM helps with that because they post about things that are going on and how you can get involved but they also remind you to take care of yourself and to put yourself first."[26] During our discussion, Gaby spoke on the significance of MdM social media platforms explaining how MdM works to bring awareness to issues that impact communities such as police brutality, violence in the community, and health care by reposting a meme or call to action with more information on how to get involved or help support in various forms. During the 2020 protests on police brutality involving the Black Lives Matter movement around the United States, MdM posts not only showed solidarity for the movement, but also how others can help/support by connecting their followers to other accounts and sharing information among their communities of followers. Gaby's comment about "taking care of yourself and to put yourself first" was an important message across MdM platforms. For example, 2020 showed that self-care and awareness are most important when educating yourself and others as protests emerged during a global pandemic. MdM shared information on how to get involved but also how to keep safe. Many would have liked to protest in the street, but the well-being of their

FIGURE 34.5 OG Medicina. Mujeres de Maiz Instagram. Artist Unknown.

health was a key factor, which led to educating followers on traditional medicines.

In addition to collecting the testimonies of two MdM social media followers, I was able to interview Felicia 'Fe' Montes, at the "Mujeres de Maiz: Twenty Years of Artivism and Herstory" exhibit located at the La Plaza de Cultura y Artes in Los Angeles, California, on May 29, 2017. Our discussion centered around how MdM social media accounts have formed into a platform for communication, artivism, and resistance, and Felicia's role as co-founder and social media account manager. During our dialogue, Felicia discussed the importance of having different social media accounts, and how each account reflects different aspects of MdM. For example, posting on Instagram is image-based, so a flyer with a meme would be the best format. Facebook has become more useful to promote and invite followers to MdM events and/or to other events that MdM supports. For example, Figure 34.5 is an old black-and-white photograph of two older Indigenous Mexican women, one is blowing smoke in the other's face while holding a bundle of plants (medicine). The captions reads, "OG Medicina . . . Medicina Comes in Different Forms: plants, pills, prayers. Whatever works for different folks. Platica about the Pirul tree."[27] This is an image from the MdM Instagram account that was posted to promote an event titled "Under the Pirul Platica with Bere of @Cantosdelatierra / @Hoodherbalism," on May 28, 2017, which Felicia talked about during our discussion. She starts to talk about the impact of posting an image on Instagram: "There was an image that showed an OG abuela photograph of an artist from 20–40 years ago taking a black and white picture, so we re-posted that image, which it's art but it's also art about wellness." She continues, "The image shares a story about a type of wellness people don't know or are not used to." By using this image, MdM introduces or reintroduces their followers to the knowledge of the ancestors, known as *abuela knowledge*," and allows for a dialog between followers. Felicia speaks on the impact and comments from followers, such as "'That's the only thing I trust' or 'That's mi abuela or curandera.' Things like that come out from that where people are kind of re-validating or validating their work or their families' connection or stuff like that." The context of this image speaks to the levels of how Instagram allows followers to interact with the image first before the textual context of that image.

Felicia speaks about how this is not just an image of a grandmother, but about the context of traditional healing and the idea of *"abuela knowledge,"* which is the passing down of generational knowledge from the grandmothers or elders within our families and communities such as herbal medicine, clean eating, and connecting the body to the elements of earth. It's through these practices and events that MdM has helped reclaim and share these traditions with communities who may have lost connections to these traditions or *"abuela knowledge."* Gaby illuminates this idea further when she shared, "I feel like Mujeres de Maiz is bringing mind, body and spirit into their posts by breaking down stigmas and stereotypes that are out there about *abuelita knowledge."* Allowing followers to connect to individuals that practice the traditions of the ancestors bridges the ideology of mind, body, and spiritual knowledge and social media is a tool to educate those who are looking to understand or reclaim the knowledge of their abuelitas. Felicia explained:

> We do our best to repost who we are to what we are about, which is being about those teaching or understanding of life or spirit. It might be about educational things or about taking care of the body, but just about options for people. For other accounts it is about spiritually, such as opening up our full moon circles to people and letting them know it's such a thing. If we repost an astronomer, or just say happy full moon, or come to our circle, it comes back to giving the knowledge and tools for individuals to choose and focus on what is important to them within their current path.

During our discussion of social media as an educational tool, Felicia explains how MdM has used their platforms: "We will post something to help educate, empower, and transform others. We always say, art educates, empowers, and transforms; well social media can educate, empower, and transform. In the comments, people will tell us: Thank you for posting that, I need this today. It's empowering, or motivating, or something that helps make people think about life or work; it's crucial, especially what's happening in this world."

The power of one post can impact and make a difference for someone within that moment. For example, one post can allow a reflection on an individual or impact the community. Felicia goes on to state:

On a political note, people would say, "Thank you for the information." "I wasn't aware this was happening" or "I signed a petition today." Even though people have stated that social media activism is more of armchair politics, we know that every little bit counts; if you're working, you're cooking for the community, taking pictures for the community, documentary for the community, or reposting for the community, everybody's role is essential. We don't try to judge those or rank them; it's what everybody does at their capacity, support, and ability. So, we try to remind ourselves about that so people can help to educate. So, in these terms, the art can be used as a social justice tool, empowerment for a generation.... We can repost that image and give the artist a shout-out.

As Felicia discussed, MdM's social media platforms allow followers to connect to content that MdM embraces as a collective as well as other like-minded collectives/individuals who promote spiritual activism within a digital environment.

CONCLUSION

"Social media, which is so easily accessible to us now, is something that we should all take advantage of, we can share the stories and thoughts or concerns that go around our community and make others aware of the issues we face, question, or simply want to inform others of or highlight around our community. We all end up reading someone else's side of the story, so why not share our own."

—AUTHOR UNKNOWN[28]

Since 2017, MdM's social media following has grown tremendously—their Instagram account has reached more than 109K followers alone and they began using their YouTube channel to promote current programming and past events including a Mujeres de Maiz docuwomxntary[29] from MdM's first year as a collective and an Oral Herstory Project from 2015 to 2016 that archived moments in MdM herstory.[30] Sharing these past projects allows many new and longtime followers to understand the importance of MdM's presence in Los Angeles. Over time, MdM has used various social media platforms to promote and share their programming, and with updates to Instagram and Facebook, MdM has been able to virtually broadcast their Live Art Show, exhibition, and workshops with the "Live" feature that can be shared throughout both platforms.

In a 2017 interview with Felicia, we imagined using social media platforms as a community-based educational tool to develop MdM's virtual offerings and expand their online programming. These ideas became a reality in March 2020 after MdM programming was cut short due to COVID-19, a worldwide pandemic that implemented stay-at-home orders that lasted nearly two years. Because of COVID-19, MdM had to shift their in-person spring programming to a fully virtual format, as did many other artists and community educators. Social media became a means to connect artists, educators, activists, and audiences worldwide. These virtual offerings provided healing for many who were isolated and heavily impacted daily with loss and grief. With the growth of a worldwide pandemic, MdM had to shift their weekly programming to be conducted using livestreams and various social media platforms including YouTube, Facebook, and Instagram, a reactivated Twitter (now X), and taking on a new platform called Twitch. These platforms allowed MdM to promote their workshops virtually to a wider audience and reintroduce weekly themes such as Mujeres Musica Mondays, Wise Words Wednesdays, Shopping Saturdays at the Mujer Mercado, and Self-Care Sunday—Art Sessions.

Beginning in April 2020, MdM created a fuller calendar for social media posting, such as Medicine Monday, where we talk about different Indigenous medicines; Monday Motivation, using a quote or a positive reflection to motivate followers; and Throwback Thursday, where we post a photo from a past event or never before seen images that highlight decades of MdM spiritual artivism, which is also a way to document and digitally archive MdM herstory, allowing generations to see the process of the collective. Felicia commented that "making things like that as a constant theme would be something we would like to incorporate." Although implementing these ideas will take time, it is important to document and archive twenty-five years of MdM spiritual artivism, allowing for a new generation to learn through the method of social media as a tool for education and healing. This highlights the importance of adapting curriculum for social media platforms geared toward women of color communities.

My experiences as an MdM intern, member, follower, and social media account assistant shape my perspective of how I have been personally impacted by images and informational posts and how others were able to connect and relate to similar posts. As a collaborator on the social media account, I was able to understand what ideas should be shared, such as memes on self-care, quotes on Chicana feminist theories, and event promotions. Not only was I learning the MdM ideology when assisting with posting, I was also impacted by those posts, by follower interactions, and by the positive feedback they would leave on a post. This was especially true of those that I had reposted, which reassured me that I was honoring MdM's ideology and allowing a space for others to gain the tools to educate, empower, and transform themselves on a path toward reconnection and healing.

Witnessing the rise of social media, I began to understand the importance and impact that MdM's platform will have moving forward. It has allowed for new ways to connect, for example going live, hosting weekly talks, and more expansive interactions through streaming from multiple platforms. Since 2012, MdM has created countless WOC and QWOC virtual spaces for followers to not just interact with comments and emojis, but to have full, live, accessible interactions within the form of digital activism through social media. The impact of a worldwide pandemic and mandatory physical social distancing created an opening for MdM to grow their digital presence allowing them to share their Indigenous Xicana feminist praxis and continue promoting spiritual activism and conversations on healing/restoring/reconnecting the mind, body, and spirit to a wider audience and a new generation of followers.

NOTES

1. My understanding of the interconnectedness between mind, body, spirit is informed by the following Chicana feminists texts: Dolores Delgado Bernal, "Using a Chicana Feminist Epistemology in Educational Research," *Harvard Educational Review* 68 (1998): 560; Elena Avila, *Woman Who Glows in the Dark: A Curandera Reveals Traditional Aztec Secrets of Physical and Spiritual Health* (New York: Penguin Putnam Inc., 1999); Patrisia Gonzales, *Red Medicine: Traditional Indigenous Rites of Birthing and Healing* (Tucson: University of Arizona

Press, 2012); Gloria Anzaldúa, *Borderlands: La Frontera the New Mestiza* (San Francisco: Aunt Lute Books, 1999); and Cherríe Moraga, *A Xicana Codex of Changing Consciousness: Writings, 2000–2010* (Durham, N.C.: Duke University Press, 2011).
2. Some of my Chicana feminist mentors include Dr. Dionne Espinoza, Dr. Ester E. Hernández, Dr. Alejandra Marchevsky, and Dr. Silvia Toscano.
3. Review chapter 32, "Conocimientos from the Mujeres de Maiz Oral Herstory Project."
4. Megan Pennings, "Restoring the Mind, Body, and Spirit: Mujeres de Maiz and Social Media as a Tool of Spiritual Activism and Education for Communities" (MA thesis, California State University, Los Angeles, 2017).
5. WOC is the acronym for womxn of color, and QWOC is the acronym for queer womxn of color.
6. Tags allow social media users to engage an individual, business, or any entity with a social profile when they mention them in a post or comment. In Facebook and Instagram, tagging notifies the recipient and hyperlinks to the tagged profile.
7. "Pride, Positivity & Power: 9 Instagram Accounts for Woke Latinxs," *Modern Tejana*, March 22, 2016, http://www.moderntejana.com/pride-positivity-power-9-instagram-accounts-woke-latinxs/.
8. Instafamous refers to Instagram users who have millions of social media followers.
9. Bart Cammaerts, "Social Media and Activism," htttp://eprints.lse.ac.uk, 2015.
10. https://www.mujeresdemaiz.com/.
11. AnaLouise Keating, "'I'm a Citizen of the Universe': Gloria Anzaldúa's Spiritual Activism as Catalyst for Social Change," *Feminist Studies* 34, no. 1–2 (2008): 53.
12. Mujeres de Maiz (@mujeresdemaiz), "They Love Us or Hate Us," Instagram, November 26, 2016, https://www.instagram.com/p/BNSHGdHh1nU/?utm_medium=copy_link. Illustration by Tyler Amato (@tyleramato).
13. Lauren Kimmel, "Does the Dakota Access Pipeline Violate Treaty Law?" *Michigan Journal of International Law* 38, Associate Editor, http://www.mjilonline.org/does-the-dakota-access-pipeline-violate-treaty-law/.
14. Justin Worland, "What to Know About the Dakota Access Pipeline Protest," *Time*, October 28, 2016, http://time.com/4548566/dakota-access-pipeline-standing-rock-sioux/.
15. Mujeres de Maiz (@mujeresdemaiz), "Los Angeles to Standing Rock," Instagram, November 4, 2016, https://www.instagram.com/p/BMZoibKhFT5/?utm_medium=copy_link.
16. Mujeres de Maiz (@mujeresdemaiz), "Native Womxn Resisting," Instagram, January 24, 2017, https://www.instagram.com/p/BPqy7Y2B0Aj/?hl=en&taken-by=mujeresdemaiz. Photograph of Lilia Ramirez by Kevin Tidmore.
17. Mujeres de Maiz (@mujeresdemaiz), "Indigenous Womxn Taking Space & Honoring Ancestors," Instagram, January 22, 2017, https://www.instagram.

com/p/BPlkZN7hVm_/. Photograph by Las Fotos Project Student Photographer Mary Reyes.

18. Mujeres de Maiz (@mujeresdemaiz), "If It Doesn't Nourish Your Soul Get Rid of It," Instagram repost @artevistafilms, January 26, 2017, https://www.instagram.com/p/BPvoX_uBZ8h/.
19. Mujeres de Maiz (@mujeresdemaiz), "Somos Resisters! We Are Resisters," Instagram repost @womensmarch, January 2017. Artwork by @itmustbeeasign.
20. Mujeres de Maiz, Instagram repost, @punkin0001, 2017.
21. Heather L. Stuckey and Jeremy Nobel, "The Connection between Art, Healing, and Public Health: A Review of Current Literature," *American Journal of Public Health* 100, no. 2 (2010): 254–63. https://doi.org/10.2105/AJPH.2008.156497.
22. Felicia 'Fe' Montes, Interview by Megan Pennings. Los Angeles. May 29, 2017.
23. An emoji is a small digital image or icon used to express an idea, emotion, and so forth.
24. Patrisia Gonzales, "Trauma, Love, & History," *Column of the Americas* (2006): 3–5.
25. Betania Santos, Interview by Megan Pennings, Los Angeles, June 6, 2017.
26. Gabriella Martinez, Interview by Megan Pennings, Video Recording Personal Interview, Los Angeles, June 10, 2017.
27. Repost image from Instagram account @cantosdelatierra. https://www.instagram.com/cantosdelatierra/ photographer unknown.
28. "Social Media: A New Perspective," CHST 404 Chicana Feminisms, http://citedatthecrossroads.net/chst404/2012/04/30/social-media-a-new-perspective/ (April 30, 2012).
29. Mujeres de Maiz Docuwomxntary, created by co-founders Claudia Mercado and Felicia 'Fe' Montes (1999), https://www.youtube.com/watch?v=uAutie1UMso.
30. Interviews conducted by students in Dr. Dionne Espionoza's WGSS 484 Chicana Narratives and Community History (Winter 2015) Cal State L.A. Review chapter 32 in this section.

35

The Bees. The Honey. The Humanity.

MARTHA GONZALEZ

THE WAREHOUSE on Ave 59 buzzed with energy. It was a beehive swarming with activity, and indeed we were building something equivalent to honey. Sweet. Nutritious. Necessary. The warehouse was the Popular Resource Center (PRC), and it was ready to explode into what would be the first of many Mujeres de Maiz events. The feeling and energy of the night were intoxicating, and I remember pushing through the crowd to see all of the work and art installations with excitement. I was also nervous as I anticipated my own performance piece.

My participation in the first MdM event consisted of being a part of "Las Eloteras." I also played with my band Quetzal. Las Eloteras was a dance mime group and I wrote and choreographed a myth creation piece around Coyolxauhqui the Aztec Moon goddess, titled "Coyolxauhqui y su Milpa." Honestly, I barely remember my participation, perhaps out of sheer nervousness. I mostly remember the feeling of excitement throughout the night. It felt like history was being made. We could not believe it was all coming together. So many people had shown up! The warehouse was packed with brown bodies dressed in their best Chicana shine. Bright red lips, intricate braided hairdos, denim jeans, piercings, Doc Martens, and style baby! There was lots of style.

Some of the most memorable pieces of the night were "La Tonantzina" by spoken word poet Marisol Lydia Torres, who stood on top of a clandestine radio station disguised as a shed. She was normally the quiet one of our bunch. But on this day, she was unleashed. We had never seen her like this before. On this powerful night, quiet Marisol with her high cheekbones, sad eyes, and long black hair demonstrated a side of herself none had ever seen. Shining in the spotlight we were all looking up as she took a Pachuca stance and recited her now classic poem for the first time. She had the entire audience cracking up! I thought, *Wow! Look at Mari go!* Then came Felicia 'Fe' Montes with her "Overcompensating Chicana Complex," and we all nodded our heads and recognized ourselves in her words. We were all starting out, but Felicia already knew where we were headed. She knew how to name our struggle. Felicia would later develop other personas like the "Ranchola," which is my personal favorite. But on that first night poetry group In Lak Ech was born, and I went on to produce their first poetry album.

Like Marisol and Felicia, plenty of artists, including myself, have come of age on the Mujeres de Maiz stage. My band Quetzal has played many times at MdM events over the course of the years. The MdM season gives us all a chance to create and reconnect to our creative selves year after year. Our human right to be creative beyond Western capitalist constructs was a means to challenge our understanding of art. In this way, MdM participation is a challenge to reflect on what it means to be an artist both in context and form. I believe that the subtraction of capital and centering art as a process was resonating in our minds as a group of us had just come from a life-altering trip to Chiapas, Mexico. In early August of 1997, we gathered with the Zapatista community of Oventic to hold *The Primer Encuentro Intercontinental por la Humanidad y Contra el Neoliberalismo*. In this way, Zapatista philosophy and particularly those five days of art-making in the mountains of Chiapas influenced MdM and the ways in which they think, pursue, and implement art-making. The philosophy that art and music are important community processes continues to be a central philosophy in our individual and collective efforts.

What is most gratifying to me is to have witnessed my son grow up around powerful women. For many years, he recited much of In Lak Ech's repertoire. While some sons wear capes and pretend to be superheroes, my son would wear pajama pants on his head in order to pretend he had long hair because he thought he was Cristina Gorocica! So much so that when I'd call him to the dinner table, I'd say, "Sandino ya es hora de comer!" He would very calmly walk up with pajamas on his head, look up at me, and say, "No mami yo no soy Sandino. Yo soy Cristina Gorocica." I would then reply, "Andale pues tu . . . Cristina Gorocica ya deja ese tambor y ven a comer!" Oftentimes he would wake my partner Quetzal and I in the mornings, singing In Lak Ech's "Woman Song." Beating the hand drum in perfect time he would sing, "Woman even though I cannot see you! I want to let you know I am with you heart and soul! Wei ya hei ya!" I think about these moments and it makes me laugh. I am grateful to have had my son be influenced by MdM and In Lak Ech's creative work and presence at such an early age.

The pollen and honey that has been shared for more than twenty years has been far-reaching and the subject of many dissertations and scholarly articles. I myself have taken the many lessons I learned in the MdM collective and applied it to my own doctoral studies. I received a PhD in Feminism from the University of Washington Seattle in 2013. I now teach at Scripps College and have recently published my first manuscript titled *Chican@ Artivistas: Music, Community, and Transborder Tactics in East Los Angeles* (2020). My work as an academic thus far has been about discussing the role of music in community, as opposed to music generated on the stage. My book is specifically about the contrast and tensions within these varying spaces along with the ethics, social, and economic parameters that delineate these spheres. *Chican@ Artivistas* quite simply narrates the change of music conception over time and it is collectives like MdM that have helped articulate an understanding from market-based art making to community-processed-based art.

Yes. MdM gathers us yearly and especially during the month of March and the East L.A. area buzzes with *energy y nosotras, pues nos transformamos como nahuales* into *abejas*. Like bees, we produce art, music, poetry, and dance—moving about collecting honey and pollen extracted from life experience. I suggest that our ART is "pollen" with all the social, historical, and political impetus that living beings shape to make their music and art. We are the bees and the pollen and honey extracted from life is our art. We live, we create, and we share for our own survival, but also for future generations. MdM is a revolutionary hive! It is an artist think tank challenging dominant ideas around race, class, gender, and sexuality. MdM participation is critical action, for they foster a space of collaboration for artists from different backgrounds. They summon us. They instigate. We are growing older as time relentlessly presses on. Our bodies are not so supple anymore. Our faces are beginning to wrinkle under the weight of lost loves, breakups, child bearing, and other life stresses. Nevertheless, we count on the yearly Mujeres de Maiz concert, art show, and various events that have been created over the years to bring us together. The yearly Mujeres de Maiz event reminds us that we have a space to run to, to express ourselves, our hearts, and our continued vision for hope and collective futures. I know that I will see my sisters on this day, some with their children in tow and others with their latest artistic creations. On these nights I am reminded that creative expression is more than a human right. It is a responsibility for my own health and the health of my community. Here is to many more years of making revolutionary honey with my MdM sisters today, tomorrow, and for generations to come!

36
Momma of the Soft Jersey T's

VICKIE VÉRTIZ

Momma of the soft jersey T's with tiny purple flowers sprinkling her breasts and pansíta
Dons a heroic pointy brassiere and a girdle you can see through
She birthed angels, cops, rebels, and poets
She birthed countless cocidos, caldos, camarones endiablados
She embroidered miles of bright-ass pink and orange flowers, green-stemmed, onto manteles, manta

Her manos are fuertes y calientitas and brown
Her hands smell like chile and ajo
Her strut: a sibilant soft waddle
A queen duck walking down La Loveland Street with a bag of grocerías for her ducklings, home asleep
from long nights of
Loving the wrong girl (again) and dancing to cumbias at the gay club
Her patitos absorbed her joie de vivre
developed sophistication for Corralejos and Cazadores
studied how to fine-tune love by watching mom dance norteñas

A wave of her magic manguera makes fuschia bougainvilleas and peach-colored
    nísperos explode in the
cement lawn
She's a té-de-manzanilla-heals-everything woman who's
healing herself
Who you can smell from the Bay
or a block away
Because she loves that Suavitel on soft jersey t's

Mujeres de Maiz, Flor y Canto: Cantando al Amanacer, no. 5 (2007): 7.

37
Revoloosonary Mama

PANQUETZANI

MY Revolution starts between
THESE legs
In THIS womb
with THESE: Brown Nipples
Loose-hanging breasts and potent
mind
with a Voice that Speaks Truth
SINGS of Liberation-Lullabies-oral tradition
All Our Relations

MY Revolution starts between moist
LIPS
I KISS to procreate—
Satiate sexual desire.
These SAME puckered lips
will kiss
my wet new baby—
Teaching gentle lessons daily.

THIS is a revolution of movement:
Swaying-rocking-bouncing—
ACTION.
Birthing, unconditional parenting
EATING delicious, nutritive foods,
Quenching the THIRST
of my microcosmic existence

This REVOLUTION
of a Woman—
a vessel, a MOTHER
is the
REVOLUTION
OF OUR PEOPLE

New LIFE
is NEW POTENTIAL for change
I bring with this open body
This vulva, these lips
This Revolution
in between THESE legs.

Compton, Calif.
Mujeres de Maiz, Flor y Canto: Soldadera de Amor, no. 9 (2011): 52.

38
I'm a Long Time Coming

PATRICIA PAZ MOYA AND PATRICIA ZAMORANO

I'm a long time coming
I am
The progression of my movements
I am steady and fluid
Like the winds
Of my past generations
India
Mestiza
Revuelta
Hembras machas
Are soaked through
My skin
Blood drenched
Saturated
By my mother's mother
And her mother's mother
I am the future
Strong
Bold
I walk with my ancestors

Not beside me
But alongside me
I adhere to the traditions
De la *fuerza*
Exercising customs
Traditions
Observing and acknowledging
Herstory's
Putting into practice
And opening
The next
Access

I'm a long time coming
I am
Brown skin
Burnt skin
Healing bones
Scars
Hard fingernails

Wrinkles
Sun kissed forehead
Wise eyes
Manos duras
Espalda fuerte
Moving swiftly
With strong steps
Cantando

Speaking words of wisdom
Telling tales
Weaving books
Into the minds
Of me
Of her
Dark wavy *pelo*
Bund
Trenzas
Teaching me
Teaching her
Learning
Discerning
Putting into practice
And opening
The next
Access

I'm a long time coming
I am
Mala hierba
Que nunca muere
Living off of

Frijoles de la olla
Nopales
Y arroz con pollo
Light brown eyes
Pelo andulado
Caderas de no acabar
Swishing back and forth
Eyes like an eagle
Making out the ways of the people
Preached long ago
I stride with vehemence
Educating
Schooling down
The next generation
Of fierce *Mujeres*
To breakdown
In laymen terms
The next portal
The next access
The next rite of passage.

Boyle Heights and Pasadena, Calif.
Mujeres de Maiz, Flor y Canto: Rites of Passage, no. 10 (2012): 50.

39

dreamseeds of the women of the corn

IRIS DE ANDA

IT WAS the summer of 1999, and I had decided to withdraw from UC Santa Cruz. I was nineteen and questioning everything. My last month in school, I decided to join a winter delegation heading to Chiapas, Mexico, to visit with the EZLN. The night I went to the meeting with those inviting us on this journey, I came back to my room in Kresge College and turned on my stereo. I had just acquired the new Manu Chao CD at Streetlight Records earlier in the week. As I listened to the songs and wrote in my journal, I was overtaken with emotion when one of the tracks featured the words of Subcomandante Marcos, saying, "Hermanos y Hermanas de otras razas y otras lenguas o aquél cuyas manos se acerque a este manifiesto que lo haga pasar a todos los hombres de esos pueblos." This was poetry. This was a truth that resounded inside every cell of my being. With only one year left until graduation, I packed my bass guitar and few belongings and returned to Los Angeles to tell my parents I would not be going back to college. There was no purpose in taking out loans for a creative writing degree. I thought, if you're a writer, then you write. No one can teach you that skill. Plus, there were more important things to do in life, I was a young punk who didn't want to be molded by the system. So, against the advice of my counselor, I left anyway. Also, my dreams had been telling me different things for awhile. There was something more out there that I needed to connect to. I wrote down one of the dreams in my journal. I remember being in a cornfield surrounded by a circle of women. We were all wearing rebozos and standing around a fire. We were singing songs and vibing with one another in the most profound way. I remember a name being given to me in the dream: the Women of the Corn. I wanted to find this feeling in my waking life, whatever it was, or wherever it was, and with whomever it was.

I returned to my hometown of El Sereno in Northeast Los Angeles to work at Warehouse Music and to save money for my trip down south. I picked up where I left off with my friends and soon enough one of them wanted to join me on the delegation. One day while walking down the street in our neighborhood, we encountered an older woman we used to work with at a restaurant in our teens and she asked how we were and what we were up to. We told her that we were planning to take a trip to Mexico. We would buy one-way tickets to Chiapas and work our way back up to DF. She looked at us and sighed, then stated, "Do it before you have a conscience." *What?* She said, "Do it before you have kids." With that being said, she gave us her blessing and we were on our way. Those words have stayed with me ever since. I continued to write daily and work all summer. My friend and I started collecting all the newspaper articles we could regarding the Zapatistas in *La Opinion* or the *LA Times*. We created a zine called *Revolucion* with clippings from these newspapers, the book *500 Years of Chicano History*, and our own photography and poetry. We cut out a full page from the *LA Weekly* that portrayed Zapata and Subcomandante Marcos and taped it to the wall behind the registers of the music store where we worked. We were consumed with reading and creating around this movement. One day, I arrived at work and my friend told me, "You just missed these two guerrilleros." I was confused. She told me they were musicians from Mexico City who recognized what our poster behind the counter represented. Some days later, I found the corazón card from La Loteria on the sidewalk as I was walking home from work. Some days after that I met Jovan, one of the musicians/guerrilleros and the rest, as they say, is herstory. This was love, intense and unapologetic, and we moved so fast. I never made it to Chiapas that winter. I moved in with Jovan and I was pregnant with my son, Xion, soon after that. I was ecstatic and scared all at once. Life took a different turn and a joyful routine set in. I had my daughters Isis and Ixchel in the years that followed and I continued to write in my journals for years. Then those words came flooding back, *"Do it before you have a conscience!"* because becoming a mother was one of the most powerful and humbling moments of my life. I remember thinking certain things would never be the same and that I would have to leave writing on the backburner, but the universe would connect me to a group of mujeres that held space in time for all of my words to flower.

Then in 2007, eight years after leaving Santa Cruz, I was browsing the internet at home and came across a call for submissions to a zine by a group called Mujeres de Maiz. I was immediately taken back to my dream of the Women of the Corn. I thought, *Is this a coincidence?* It couldn't be; it had to be synchronicity. So I submitted my poem *WE* for their 2008 zine, *Somos Medicina*. I was accepted into the publication and was so ecstatic to be in the company of so many powerful and talented wombyn. This was the first time I saw my words on paper outside of my journals at home on my bookshelf. I remember traveling to Mexico DF that year soon after receiving my contributor's copy and carrying it with me on the plane as one would a precious doll or keepsake. Feeling so proud to have contributed to this creation, it gave me a sense of empowerment to know my words fit somewhere. My words which come out split between Spanish and English tongue had found a home. I have been working with Mujeres de Maiz ever since. I continued to submit to their yearly zine and began attending their annual Live Art Show. I was published again and again in the zine over the coming years.

I started sharing my poetry once more at different community venues in 2010. It started in my neighborhood of El Sereno at Dose of Art Gallery for an event put together by Abel Salas, whom I later dubbed my poetry Padrino. He invited me to be part of a memorial reading for his mentor Raul Salinas, who founded Resistencia Books in Texas. Before this, my last reading had been at UC Santa Cruz over a decade before. So it's 2013 and I wanted to get involved on a deeper level, so I began to volunteer with the circle. It was then that I became involved with organizing the annual poetry night, which I've helped with to present day. Before my involvement, it had been organized for several years by Rebecca Gonzalez and Xitlalic Guijosa-Osuna. We celebrated the sixteenth anniversary of the event. I was so grateful to be part of the lineup that year. The poetry nights were a place of gathering voices of chingonas, sad girls, badass mothers, queers, and elders.

In 2013, I was also asked to help organize and lead the series of writing workshops for Mujeres de Maiz with Alejandra Sanchez and Olga Garcia. The "Weaving Words, Creating Words: Healing and Empowerment as Women Storytellers" writing workshops were held over a series of five Saturdays that spring at the Eastside Cafe. At the culmination, we had all the participants read at a Take Back the Night event with the Justice for My Sister organization at Mariachi Plaza. We had an amazing turnout for the entire session and I continue to be in touch with many of the mujeres that came through. The following year, I organized a series of five writing workshops once again, this time under my pen name IDEAlawriterunderground. Our guest writers Tara Evonne Trudell, Xanath Carranza, Ramona Pilar, Gloria Endiña Álvarez, and Sofia Rose Smith shared their craft with our circle, which took place at the Eastside Cafe once again. We continued the tradition of ending the series with a reading at Take Back the Night with Justice for My Sister. In 2015, we recreated the series with the help of Las Lunas Locas, an all-women writing circle at Here & Now Healing Arts Center in El Sereno which I co-founded with Cathy Uribe. Las Lunas Locas was envisioned by Karineh Mahdessian and Sophia Rivera after meeting at one of the Mujeres de Maiz writing workshops the year before. The corn seeds have spread in numerous ways.

I have been blessed to be part of various panels and presentations over the years with Mujeres de Maiz at different universities and community settings. I self-published my first poetry book *Codeswitch: Fires from Mi Corazón* in April 2014. I began hosting The Writers Underground Open Mic every third Thursday of the month at the Eastside Cafe in January 2014 until July 2017. I've been part of the Association of Writers & Writing Programs conference. I was a moderator for Poets Responding to SB1070: Poetry of Resistance. I've taken poetry road trip tours to the Bay Area, to the Southwest, to southern states, and to the East Coast. I've had the privilege of performing my poetry in Mexico and Cuba. In 2022, my second poetry collection *Roots of Redemption: You Have No Right to Remain Silent* was published with Flowersong Press. Following closely behind *Loose Poems*, a collection of B-side poems and songs was released in 2022 with Mutlimedia Militia. I continue to perform my poetry at universities and community venues. My cornstalk has come into full bloom, and I give thanks to Mujeres de Maiz for being some of that soil, some of my water, my air, and my fire. When I first attended one of the Coyolxauhqui full moon circles years ago, I remembered my dream and I thanked the Diosas for helping me find my SiStars in the flesh in my waking life.

women of the corn

came to me in dreamtime memory
many moons before the flesh
meeting around a sacred fire
in a cornfield we gathered
by circle and hands interlocked
under the light of coyolxauhqui
covered in rebozos of arcoiris
i remembered them from lives past
from the blue maiz
we learned of laughter
the things that matter
and tears for all the strife
sometimes mistaking one for the other
from the yellow maiz
we gained love of knowledge
and strength for the days ahead
to give thanks while breaking bread
from the red maiz
we carried the blood and the fire
and the roots to be grounded in
our cultura while the rose stood
as witness against the thorns before us
from the purple maiz
we sung the songs of the first
counting in languages of lost tongues
drums and rattles make for good medicine
so we continue the dance
soon the four directions

manifest in the womb of the wombyn warrior
seeds are planted and bloom
with time came the calling for the SiStars
to gather together across the nations
bring forth palabra y voz
cantos for the tierra
hope for those who are lost
now under the sixth sun
we rise in full form
remember to ancient wisdom reborn
in the raiz of all mujeres
our connections take hold
spiritual threads interwoven
in the art and the words that are spoken
by night and day
por noche y dia
we live with direct action por vida
to bring forth memory
in lak ech
you are my other me
whether with fists in the air
or fingers in the earth
chants at a rally
or planting herbs in our hearth
rising with el sol
or dreaming with la luna
we are true to our nature
fearless in freedom
standing in sisterhood
weaving waking stories
born of brujas
agua, tierra, aire, fuego
celestial beings incarnated
the council of our feminine
reaching out across the galaxies
into the mountains and deserts of
our grandmothers trenzas

we yearn for social justice
made manifest in the footsteps we conceive
and do believe in a new horizon
pachamama for the next seven generations
solar cycle of our world
where the word of the womyn
is the incantation of our elders
visions of the little ones
protecting each other
growing in the milpa of milagros
where the journey
extends into the future
of all life on this planet
as the medicine we carry
from our hearts to yours
transverses time and space
so it was we came again
to remember our place
all that we inspire in one another
gifts of grace under the altar of stars
with each kernel we exist and resist
reflections of us
ofrendas of ourselves
somos todas y nada
somos mujeres de maiz

40

Makeover Manifesto

IRIS DE ANDA

You & I are Boldly Beautiful
like turquoise beads
& feathers that fall
Seeking ways of self-expression
like braiding our hair
& punk mexica fashion

You & I are Shining Stars
like sterling earrings
& beauty scars
Adorning the spirit with light
like silver threads
& interior sight

You & I are Ultra Unique
like lines on our palms
& smokey eyes mystique
Connecting ourselves together
like stitched rebozos
& rustic leather

You & I are Womyn Warriors
like Itzpapalotl obsidian butterfly
& all the forebearers
Burning sage for clearing
like rearranging ideas
& soul dreaming

You & I are Mujeres of Maíz
like reflections of goddess
& rebellion reborn
Blessing curves with embroidery
like flowers on sweaters
& reclaiming our history

You & I are Lucid Lovers
like wear our hearts on our sleeves
& forgive others
Wearing rings of power
like rainbow moonstone
& being blessed empower

Los Angeles (El Sereno), Calif.
Mujeres de Maiz, Flor y Canto:
Identity Blinging, no. 11 (2013): 10.

CONTRIBUTORS

Margaret 'Quica' Alarcón, B.F.A, MEd.,M.F.A. is a professional Xicana artist and visual arts educator, born and raised in East Los Angeles. She is a formal artist with a comprehensive range of illustration and fine arts skills, including graphic design, mixed media, painting, drawing, printmaking, sculpture, and traditionally trained in papel picado. As an artist and educator, she brings decades of community activism through her art and work with Mujeres de Maiz. Her work has been included in many publications and exhibited in galleries and museums throughout the country including the Manetti Shrem Museum, Palos Verdes Art Center, Galeria Otra Vez in Self Help Graphics & Art, Avenue 50 Studio, the Láfia House Gallery Brewery Arts Complex in Los Angeles, the Snite Museum of Art in Indiana, the Fowler Museum at UCLA, and in the permanent collection of the Riverside Art Museum.

Angela Mictlanxochitl Anderson Guerrero, Ph.D., is the Executive Director of LIDERAMOS, a National Latino leadership development organization. She is a contemporary healer holding and guiding strategic change built in self-worth to regenerate radical compassion for a new world of equity, sustainability, and wonder. She completed her doctorate in transpersonal psychology and is an Abuela and Council Member of Danza de la Huitzilmeztli and Danza de Luna Xinachtli Meztli, transterritorial Mexica practices.

Skryb Anu was born in L.A. and is a multimedia artist who started off as an audio engineer/SFX editor. After a few years of industry work in the field, she began studying Cinema & Animation. Compelled by the desire to use these tools to express her POV in the world, she focuses on the things we often turn away from and suffer in silence.

Gina Aparicio was born and raised in the urban jungles of Los Angeles. Gina is a Xicana Indigena artist, teacher, and community organizer. She received her B.A. in Chicana and Chicano Studies from California State University, and her M.F.A. from Florida State University. She currently works as a professor of art at Sierra College in Rocklin, California. Her work has been exhibited in galleries and community spaces locally and nationally, including Manetti Shrem Museum, American Museum for Ceramic Art, Self Help Graphics & Art, Baltimore Clayworks, Yerba Buena Cultural Arts Center, Tropico de Nopal, Working Method Contemporary, Mission Cultural Center for Latino Arts and Women's Caucus for the Arts, and Indiana University. Her work has been published in *Queering Mesoamerican Diasporas* by Dr. Susy Zepeda, *Art Practical*, *Spectator*, and feminist studies journals, *Ceramics Monthly*, *Revista-Latinx Research Center* UC Berkeley, and Mujeres de Maiz *Flor y Canto* zines.

Povi-Tamu Bryant is a paranormal fiction connoisseur, a crafter, a parent, and Angeleno living on unceded Tongva land, where they were raised. As a Black queer and nonbinary person who has experienced housing insecurity and relied on public transportation, with limited income, they are dedicated to building and supporting communities who live at the intersections of multiple forms of oppression. Povi-Tamu is a migrant, with family roots from Chicago, and they have spent time in and around nonprofits in the Los Angeles area. Povi-Tamu is committed to building and strengthening the capacity of organizations to show up better for the people who work there. Their past work includes roles in Leadership Development in Intergroup Relations, a program of AJ SoCal, the LA Black Worker Center, and the board of Gender Justice LA. Povi-Tamu co-created Freedom Verses in the summer of 2018.

Maya Chinchilla is a Guatemalan, Bay Area-based writer, video artist, educator, and author of "The Cha Cha Files: A Chapina Poética." Maya received her MFA in English and Creative Writing from Mills College and she writes and performs poetry that explores themes of historical memory, heartbreak, tenderness, sexuality, and alternative futures. Her work, which draws on a tradition of truth-telling and poking fun at the wounds we carry, has been published in numerous anthologies and journals. Maya is a founding member of the performance group Las Manas, a former artist-in-residence at Galería de La Raza and La Peña Cultural Center, and is a VONA Voices, Dos Brujas, and Letras Latinas workshop alum. She is co-editor of "Desde El Epicentro: An Anthology of Central American Poetry and Art" and a lecturer at San Francisco State University, UC Davis, and other Bay Area universities. www.thechachafiles.com.

Marisol Crisostomo-Romo is an Indigenous woman of mixed heritage from northeast Los Angeles. Her family are fifth-generation Angelenos. She is a mama, wife, Nina, Tia, prima, hija, and registered nurse. She finds her joy through her children, her sweet old dog, her closest homegirls, and jingle dress dancing at powwows with her daughter. Her poetry has been published in various small publications and she is honored to have her poetry in the MdM anthology after first performing at an MdM event in 1998. She currently lives in the San Francisco Bay Area.

Liza Cohen Hita, Ph.D., is a mother, partner, writer, gardener, and clinical associate professor of psychology in the School of Social and Behavioral Sciences at Arizona State University. She engages in community-based participatory research focused on the dissemination and implementation of preventive interventions for families experiencing major life transitions, including high-conflict families, separating and divorced parents, bereaved caregivers, and families impacted by incarceration. She also studies decolonial methodologies, smart technologies, and counselor training, integrating them into her current research and practice on the online administration and cultural resonance of evidence-based parenting interventions and creating sustainable community-embedded supervision models. Her community work focuses on bridging health disparities through culturally restorative, holistic practices. She is a full spectrum doula sharing traditional prenatal, birthing, postpartum, and loss support and a student of Batok/Patik, which is the traditional art and healing practice of tattooing in the Philippines.

Iris De Anda, a Guanaca Tapatia poet, speaker, and musician who has been featured with KPFK and KPFA Pacifica Radio, organized with Academy of American Poets, performed at Los Angeles Latino Book Festival, CECUT in Tijuana, Casa de las Americas in Havana, Cuba, and is named one of Today's Revolutionary Women of Color. Author of *Codeswitch: Fires from Mi Corazon* (2014) from Los Writers Underground Press, *Roots of Redemption: You Have No Right to Remain Silent* (2022) from Flowersong Press, and *Loose Poems* a collection of B-side poems and songs (2022) from Multimedia Militia. http://www.lawriterunderground.com.

Mariela de la Paz originally took on oil painting as a form of therapy and self-healing, and her work is a dedication to her people––her native Chile of Mapuche ancestry. Primarily a self-taught artist, her painting career began in the mid-1980s. She has been mentored by accomplished Latin American contemporary painters, inspired in Buddhist Tanka style and her spiritual work with lama Pema tenzin and Tsewong Sitar Rinpoche of Bhutan, who have initiated her in the practices of the Dudjom Lingpa lineage, which involves high magic. This has been a continuation of her studies of Shamanism which began over thirty years ago and brought her to California to join the School of Contemporary Female Shamanism based out of Oakland in the early 1990s. Mariela has taught extensively, and her paintings are channeled pieces inspired by our cosmic union of our eternal soul and Mother Earth, concerned with spiritual transformation, and can be described as "inspired revelation."

Karen Mary Davalos, Professor of Chicano and Latino Studies at the University of Minnesota, Twin Cities, has published widely on Chicana/o/x art, spirituality, and museums. She has published four books: *Exhibiting Mestizaje: Mexican (American) Museums in the Diaspora* (2001); *The Mexican Museum of San Francisco Papers, 1971–2006* (2010), the Silver Medal winner of the International Latino Book Award for Best Reference Book in English; *Yolanda M. López* (University of Minnesota Press, 2008), the recipient of two awards; and *Chicana/o Remix: Art and Errata Since the Sixties* (NYU Press, 2017). With Tatiana Reinoza, she coedited *Self Help Graphics at Fifty* (UC Press 2023). With Constance Cortez (UTRGV), she launched a postcustodial, aggregating web portal, Mexican American Art since 1848, that compiles relevant collections from libraries, archives, and museum throughout the nation.

D'Lo is a queer/transgender Tamil-Sri Lankan-American actor/writer/comedian whose work ranges from stand-up comedy, solo theater, plays, films, and music production, to poetry and spoken word. He's been seen on HBO, Amazon, Netflix, and CW. His solo plays have toured nationally. His work has been awarded grants from Center Theater Group, City of Santa Monica, Durfee Foundation, National Performance Network, Ford Foundation, and the Foundation for Contemporary Arts. As a writer, he has been published in various anthologies and academic journals, and he is the creator of the "Coming Out, Coming Home" writing workshop series, which has taken place with South Asian and/or Immigrant LGBTQ Organizations nationally, which provide a transformative space for workshop participants to write through their personal narratives and share their truths through a public reading. He is also a Civic Media Senior Fellow through USC's Annenberg School of Innovation funded by the MacArthur Foundation.

Dionne Espinoza, Ph.D., is Professor in the Department of Women's, Gender, and Sexuality Studies at Cal State L.A. Her research centers the voices, archives, and critical theories of women of color writers and activists in social movements from the sixties to present with an emphasis on Chicana feminist thought and activism. She has coedited two books: *Enriqueta Vasquez and the Chicano Movement: Writings from* El Grito del Norte (with Lorena Oropeza) and *Chicana Movidas: New Narratives of Activism and Feminism in the Movement Era* (with Maylei Blackwell and María E. Cotera). A long-time oral herstorian, she developed, organized, and facilitated the Mujeres de Maiz Oral Herstory Project, a community partnership with MdM that involved Cal State L.A. students in conducting interviews with the artivists of Mujeres de Maiz for their twentieth anniversary.

Crystal Galindo is a California Xicana femme of Yaqui descent. With ties to the central valley, Arizona, Sonora, Texas, Tamaulipas, and Aguascalientes, her ideas and creativity mix a love of cosmic imagery and portraits intermingled with a longing for ancestral memories. Her artwork dates back to her days drawing on any blank surface as a toddler to her current practice as a full time mother and professional creator. Along with her large scale portraits, Crystal designs and makes jewelry, prints, and small works that provide accessibility to her community. She continues to create new and evolving works centering Black, Brown, Indigenous women/femmes/gnc people of all sizes and body types. Her social media presence has furthered her reach and raised awareness of inclusivity and representation among the fine arts community.

Amber Rose González is an Indigenous Xicana born and raised in the San Gabriel Valley, California, and ancestrally rooted in New Mexico. She is a transfer student who earned a B.A. in Gender, Ethnicity, and Multicultural Studies from California State Polytechnic University, Pomona, and a Ph.D. in Chicana and Chicano studies with an emphasis in Feminist Studies from the University of California, Santa Barbara. Amber is a wife, mami, and auntie, a Professor of Ethnic Studies at Fullerton College, a writer-researcher-organizer with Mujeres de Maiz, a certified yoga teacher, and co-author of *New Directions in Chicanx and Latinx Studies* (2023), published through the Open Educational Resources Initiative.

Martha Gonzalez is a Chicana artivista (artist/activist) musician, feminist music theorist, and Assistant Professor in the Intercollegiate Department of Chicana/o Latina/o Studies at Scripps/Claremont College. A Fulbright, Ford and Woodrow Wilson Fellow, her academic interest in music has been fueled by her own musicianship as a singer/songwriter and percussionist for Grammy Award–winning band Quetzal, who released "The Eternal Get Down" in 2017. Quetzal has made a considerable impact in the Los Angeles Chicano music scene and has been noted in a range of publications. In addition, Gonzalez, along with her partner Quetzal Flores, has been instrumental in catalyzing the transnational dialogue between Chican@s/Latin@ communities in the U.S. and Jarocho communities in Veracruz, Mexico. Notably, Gonzalez's tarima (stomp box) and zapateado shoes were acquired by the National Museum of American History.

Cristina Gorocica is the daughter of Luis and Teresa Gorocica. Her parents and most of her family are from Merida, Yucatan, Mexico. She is of Indigenous Mayan Yucatec descent. Gorocica is the youngest of four and she along with her brother Juan are the only ones born in the United States. She has two beautiful teenage daughters. She has been teaching for over fifteen years in inner-city schools throughout East Los Angeles. Gorocia started creative writing when she was in college and began writing songs after forming the women's poetry group of In Lak Ech and Mujeres de Maiz in 1998.

Virginia Grise is a recipient of the Alpert Award in the Arts, Yale Drama Award, Whiting Writers' Award, and the Princess Grace Award in Theatre Directing. Her published work includes *Your Healing Is Killing Me* (Plays Inverse Press), *blu* (Yale University Press), *The Panza Monologues* (co-written with Irma Mayorga; University of Texas Press), and *Conversations with Don Durito* (Autonomedia Press), an edited volume of Zapatista communiqués. Her interdisciplinary body of work includes plays, multimedia performance, dance theater, performance installations, guerilla theater, site-specific interventions, and community gatherings. She is a founding member of a todo dar productions, an alumnae of the Soho Rep Writer/Director Lab, the Women's Project Theatre Lab, and the NALAC Leadership Institute. Virginia has taught writing for performance at the university level, as a public school teacher, in community centers, women's prisons, and in the juvenile correction system. She holds an MFA in Writing for Performance from the California Institute of the Arts.

Xitlalic Guijosa-Osuna is a guayaba lover, swapmeetera, poet, hija de su madre, southeast-sider. She is inspired by her madre, padre, abuelas y bisabuelas, sobrinas, sobrinos, e historias del tianguis, tias, tios, and everyone that will meet her. Con la pluma en la mano she is ready to create a better world. Xitlalic has been writing since the age of seven and started sharing her poetry at the age of 20. She was part of the MdM poetry collective and committee and she has been published in the Mujeres de Maiz zine, Loud Mouth Magazine, Heart Break Anthology, UCLA Young Writers 98, and Voice of the Eagle 2000.

Lizette Hernandez is a mother, Salvadoreña born in the Bronx, New York and raised in South Central LA. She identifies as Indigenous (Maya/Xinca/Pipil) with African ancestry. She has over twenty-five years experience in community organizing, leadership development, and policy development and analysis. Quilombos Capacity Builders is her humble consulting practice where she works with community organizations and schools to foster transformative justice. Lizette mostly works in leadership development within Black/Indigenous/Latinx partnerships amongst immigrant workers throughout LA County. Lizette holds a Master's degree in City and Regional Planning from UC Berkeley and a Bachelor's in Civil and Environmental Engineering from UCLA. Lizette has been a dancer in Afro-Caribbean folkloric dance and she studies capoeira with her teen son. Lizette is a trained doula and a certified Reiki II Practitioner. Poetry has often been her lifeline when all else fails, and her way to stay connected to the Divine in times of utter chaos.

Celina Jacques is a Chicana artist and healer who specializes in using creativity and ritual for healing the heart, mind, and soul. Her offerings focus on decolonizing mental health through the intersection of creativity, psychology, and ancient wisdom. Her body of work ranges from sentimental portraits and visionary depictions of the Divine Feminine to bittersweet renditions of calaveras for Day of the Dead. Celina works, lives, and creates art in the greater Los Angeles. She holds an MA in Psychology, a BFA in Studio Art, and a BA in Psychology. Celina is a Board Certified Art Therapist, Licensed Marriage and Family Therapist, and Apprentice to a Curandera.

Luisa Leija is a poet, librarian, and cultural heritage worker. After over a decade working in the nonprofit youth development field, she became a librarian. Her work brings together her passions and expertise around community engagement, youth development, social justice, knowledge production, and cultural heritage, which enables her to provide a spectrum of services to historically marginalized groups. Luisa received her MSLIS degree from the University of Illinois at Urbana-Champaign in 2022. She also holds and MFA in writing from the California College of the Arts and a BA in Chicana/o studies from the University of California, Berkeley. Luisa resides in Southern California and is currently the Diversity, Equity, Inclusion and Multilingual Collections Senior Librarian at the Long Beach Public Library.

Michelle L. Lopez earned her MFA in Studio Art and MA in Art History from Cal State L.A. She is an educator, artist, curator, grant-writer, community organizer, and mom. Currently she teaches full-time in the Chicana/a and Latina/o Studies Department at Cal State L.A. She has worked with community organizations such as Mujeres de Maiz and Self Help Graphics & Art and co-curated *Mujeres de Maiz: 20 Years of ARTivism and Herstory en LA* and *Entre Tinta y Lucha: 45 Years of Self Help Graphics & Art* exhibitions. Michelle is a recipient of the CSU Chancellor's Doctoral Incentive Program fellowship and is working on her PhD in Leadership Studies at the University of San Diego.

Pola Lopez is a prominent painter and muralist whose acrylic paintings are driven by color and convey a multi-faceted array of symbolic, cultural and feminine imagery infused with spiritual vision and incendiary composition, establishing her as a key artist in the Latina/Hispana/Chicana/Mestiza genre. Born in Las Vegas, New Mexico, she identifies as an artist of mixed Jicarilla Apache and European heritage. An active and fulltime artist, she has operated studio galleries in Las Vegas, Taos, and in Santa Fe, exhibited in Contemporary Spanish Market and had the honor to represent New Mexico as the official portrait artist at the White House in Washington D. C. in 2006 when NM provided the People's Christmas Tree. Relocating in 2003 to California in search of the Chicano Art Movement, she maintained a public studio/exhibit space in Los Angeles for sixteen years. As a muralist, she produced individual, community, and student-assisted murals as a teaching artist. She returned home to Santa Fe, New Mexico in September 2020 due to the Covid-19 pandemic.

Roberto Q. Loza is a visual communication strategist and specializes in working with nonprofits, universities, small businesses, and artists. He has over a decade of experience in graphic design and website design. He has a passion for social justice and community empowerment and strives to use his skills to support businesses and organizations he believes in. He is always eager to learn new technologies and trends in the design industry and to share his knowledge and expertise with others. He is a Xicano raised in East Los Angeles and earned his B.S. in Business from Cal Poly Pomona and an M.A. in Communications from Cal State Los Angeles.

In his free time, he enjoys photography, art, and music. He enjoys the outdoors and traveling with his partner.

Gabriela Martinez, M.S.W., is a Disabled Xicana born and raised in Eastside, Los Angeles. At a young age, Gabriela developed a passion for helping her community. She is currently a bilingual macro social worker for a Peer Mentoring program at a national rehabilitation hospital. Gabriela is also a self-proclaimed advocate for self-care, and enjoys gardening and cooking decolonial plant-based meals during her spare time.

Maribel Martinez (all pronouns) is a Queer Chicanx P'urhépecha brainiac, storyteller, and dream warrior from East San José, CA. Maribel shapeshifts between public policy, higher education, and the arts. Maribel is a member of the Macondo writer's workshop, Califas en Comunidad writer's group, Primeras Paginas playwright's circle, The Multicultural Arts Leadership Institute (MALI) Silicon Valley, and was a founding member of La Peña's Hybrid Performance Experiment Ensemble and The Queerceañera Project SJ. Maribel is a recipient of the inaugural Movimiento de Arte Y Cultura Latino Americana (MACLA) Cultura Fellowship, the California Arts Council Emerging Artist award, and a Center for Cultural Innovation grant. Maribel's play for young audiences, *Becoming (MAR)*, premiered at Teatro Vision in 2023 and was broadcast on CreaTV San Jose. Its sequel, *Mar in the Middle*, had a staged reading at the School of Arts and Culture in 2023.

Norell Martínez is a Chicana fronteriza from the Tijuana/San Diego border region—the ancestral lands of the Kumeyaay people. She is Associate Professor in the Department of English and Chicana/o Studies at San Diego City College. She received a doctorate in Literature with an emphasis on Cultural Studies from UC San Diego. Norell is a community activist, an abolitionist, a Marxist, a scholar, and a mother. Her research is centered on Chicana/Latina, Indigenous, and Black feminism with an emphasis on so-called witches in the Americas, spiritual activism, and contemporary manifestations of bruja activism in the streets and in cultural production throughout the Americas. Her publications include "Brujas in the Time of Trump: Hexing the Ruling Class" in the anthology *Latinas and the Politics of Urban Space* (2021) and "A Pedagogy of Ofrendas" in *Voices from the Ancestors* (2019), among others.

Pedro Andres Martinez was born in Los Angeles and raised across the neighborhoods of Westlake, Koreatown, Northeast Los Angeles, and South Central. He received his B.A. from California State University, Los Angeles, in Chicana/o and Latina/o Studies as well as a minor in Women's, Gender, and Sexuality Studies. He is a nontraditional parenting student who is currently pursuing a master's degree in Chicana/o and Latina/o Studies with an interest in building an exploratory understanding of the precarities that racialized queer and transgender communities undergo, emote, express, situate, and process throughout their survival of geography, social life, gendered violence, sexual violence, kinship, and so forth, in South Central Los Angeles. Through Oral History, he ultimately hopes to build an expansive emotional register for witnessing this population's capacity to embody complex forms of survival, memory, and selfhood. Pedro spends his time trying to build joy alongside his daughter, his loved ones, and himself.

Lara Medina holds a doctorate in American History from the Claremont Graduate University and an M.A. in Theology from the Graduate Theological Union. She is a professor in Chicana/o Studies at California State University, Northridge where her teaching areas are Chicana/o religion, spirituality, and history. Her book *Las Hermanas: Chicana/Latina Religious-Political Activism in the U.S. Catholic Church* won a CHOICE Book Award in 2004. Other published works include "Communing with the Dead: Spiritual and Cultural Healing in Chicano/a Communities," "Chicanos and Religion: Traditions and Transformations," "Nepantla Spirituality: An Emancipative Vision for Inclusion," and "Nepantla Spirituality: My Path to the Source(s) of Healing." Lara is also a Reiki practitioner, temazcalli water pourer, and ritual facilitator.

Claudia A. Mercado is a multimedia documentary filmmaker, director, producer, writer, editor, and artivist born and raised in Highland Park, Los Angeles, California. She is a member of In Lak Ech and co-founder of Mujeres de Maiz. Claudia has exhibited her films in art houses, universities, museums, and film festivals; produced short documentaries for nonprofits and universities; and documented at the United Nations Permanent Forum on Indigenous Issues. Her short *Mujeres de Maiz/Women of the Corn—Chapter One: Regeneration, In Lak Ech and the Goddess of Corn in L.A.* was screened in 2019 at The Vincent Price Art Museum and her first documentary short on the South Central Farmers premiered at the Los Angeles International Latino Film Festival in 2006. Claudia earned a B.A. in Film Studies from UC Berkeley and an M.F.A. in Film, Television, and Theater from Cal State University Los Angeles.

Jo Anna Mixpe Ley is a Huichol Xicana from Boyle Heights Los Angeles, California, and she is currently raising her daughter in Boyle Heights too. Ley has been in education for nearly twenty years, and she is currently with Roosevelt MSTMA. She has taught sixth- to twelfth-grade English, the Arts, and a Chicana/o Studies course at UCLA. Ley graduated from UCLA with a B.A. in Chicana/o Studies and American Literature. She also received her M.F.A. from Cal Arts and her teaching credential in English from UCLA Extension. Additionally, she's a writer, founder, and actress in the theatrical group Las Ramonas. Ley is a community organizer, a published author, a marathoner and member of the Boyle Heights Bridge Runners, GirlLab of Run with the Lab, and a co-founder of Running Mamis.

Marilynn Montaño is a first-generation Chicana writer and artist from Santa Ana, CA. Montaño is a proud daughter of migrant parents from Puebla, Mexico. She is currently the event manager and an advisory board member for LibroMobile, a bookstore and literary arts co-op in Santa Ana, CA, and a Crear Studio fellow. In 2019, Montaño was named Poetic Influencer for OC Weekly's People's Issue. Her poetry was featured in *Mujeres de Maiz, Seeds of Resistance, Barrio Writers* anthology, *The Chachalaca Review*, and Sims Library of Poetry. Montaño has been featured at Beyond Baroque Literary Arts, The Ugly Mug, and Orange County Zine Fest.

Felicia 'Fe' Montes is a Xicana Indigenous artist, activist, community and event organizer, educator, FEmcee, designer, poet, performer, professor, and practitioner of the healing arts living and working in the Los Angeles area. Known throughout the southwest as an established Xicana cultural worker of a new generation, she creates with In Lak Ech, El Mercado y Mas, and La Botanica del Barrio, and is the founding director of Mujeres de Maiz. She has worked on various transnational art and organizing efforts, including work with the Zapatistas, Peace and Dignity Journeys, and La Red Xicana Indigena. Felicia graduated with a B.A. from UCLA in World Arts and Cultures with a minor in Chicanx Studies, an M.A. in Chicanx Studies from Cal State Northridge, and an M.F.A. from Otis College of Art and Design in Public Practice Art. In addition, she is an apprentice of Western Herbalism and Mexican Traditional Medicine. Check her out at http://feliciamontes.com.

mariana Aq'ab'al moscoso (elle/they/them) is a nonbinary detribalized and reconnecting Indigenous queer of Achi (Maya), Nicānāhuac, and Afro-Indigenous roots living on the occupied lands of the Nisenan, Maidu, and Miwok (colonially known as Sacramento, California). They are a cultural strategist, facilitator, liberation doula, storyteller, a budding cultural practitioner, digital artist, and community zine maker who centers Maya Cosmovision as a means to integrate balance and harmony into all they do. Mariana is a child of courageous parents who fled imperialist wars, a sibling, tia, and their most treasured role, solo parent, to a magically creative adult daughter. They are a co-visionary of Toj + Tijax: The Ritual of Myth Making an Indigenous queer healing space, while also working as the Associate Director of Artist Leadership at The Center for Cultural Power.

Patricia Paz Moya is an artist and a Marriage and Family therapist. Having moved from Chile to California as a young child, she became inspired by her surroundings and found an attraction to art and poetry. She takes from her life experiences to apply them to her artistic work, whether it be painting, or writing poetry that speaks to love, daily struggles, joy and pain.

Rachel Negrete Thorson is a multidisciplinary artist from the heart of the harbor of Los Angeles, California. She is a mother, wife, astrologer, bruja, and union longshore worker in the ILWU local 13.

Diana Pando is a poeta, writer, and storyteller from Chicagolandia with roots in Chihuahua, MX and Mexico City. Her poems have been featured in Cenzontle Literary Magazine, Pandora lobo estepario Press, Rebeldes: Proyecto Latina Anthology, and Mujeres de Maiz Flor y Canto. In the past, she has also been a featured poet at Guild Literary Complex, Logan's Run Reading Series and featured storyteller at 2nd Story. Her work has also been spotlighted on WBEZ's Afternoon Shift and her ten-minute play Thirst was presented at Teatro Luna's 10X10 play festival.

Panquetzani is a traditional herbalist, healer, and birthkeeper and the foundress of Indigemama: Ancestral Healing and her online school, Indigescuela. She breathes life into ancestral traditions, offering time-tested wellness practices, honoring the 4,500-year-old traditions of her foremothers, and integrating her lifetime of study into her private practice and daily life. Panquetzani comes from a matriarchal family of folk healers from the valley of Mexico (Tenochtitlan, Texcoco, y Tlaxcala), La Comarca Lagunera (Durango and Coahuila), and Zacatecas.

Megan Pennings is an Irish/Xicana artist who focuses on photography around storytelling within the areas of portrait, documentary, still life, and urban lifestyle. Megan received a dual B.A. in Sociology with an emphasis in inequalities and diversity and in Mexican-American Studies from California State Los Angeles. She received her M.A. in Mexican-American Studies and a graduate certificate in Women, Gender, and Sexuality Studies from California State Los Angeles. She is currently finishing her M.F.A. in Photography from the Academy of Art San Francisco. Megan's work is based on her interest in social media, culture, and community, and how identity and social expression are formed within photography.

Lilia Ramirez p.k.a Liliflor is an artist, muralist, cultural art educator using art as a tool for healing and transformation. Liliflor uses her own spiritual practice, indigenous knowledge passed on by elders to bridge engagement with the creative arts and well being outcomes. An "artivist hybrid visionary," she has been at the forefront serving the community since 1994. She was co-founder of the Peace and Justice Center (PJC) in 1995, an innovative youth run center in Los Angeles. In 1997 she co-founded Mujeres de Maiz, serving in various capacities in the organization such as curator, organizer, and director of annual exhibitions. A decade later she received her B.A. in World Arts and Cultural Studies from UCLA. Liliflor opened her first gallery First Street Studios in 2006. Currently she has her art studio housed at Kalli Luna Gallery in Boyle Heights.

Celia Herrera Rodríguez (Xicana/O'dami) is a painter and performance and installation artist whose work reflects a full generation of dialogue with Chicano, Native American, pre-Columbian, and Mexican thought. She is the co-founder and co-director of Las Maestras Center for Xicana[x] Indigenous Thought, Art and Social Practice at UC Santa Barbara, where she also teaches Chicana[x] art history and studio practice in the Department of Chicano and Chicana Studies. Originally from Sacramento, California, Herrera Rodríguez received her BA in art and ethnic studies from CSU Sacramento and an MFA in painting from the University of Illinois, Urbana-Champaign. In 1987, she went on to study art history, theory, and criticism at the Art Institute of Chicago. Her paintings, drawings, and installation work have been exhibited nationally and internationally, and her work is permanently housed in a number of private and public collections.

Natalina Ross is a native Xicana from San Antonio, Texas. She is honored to be the mama of a beautiful and talented Sun. She is candlemaker, tamalera, educator, and lover of all the flowers and seeds. With a tounge that stings like the píca of a chile pequín, she writes with the help of her ancestors and the gifts of their stories.

Faith Santilla is an award winning poet and has been a community and labor organizer for twenty-five years. She is the resident poet of the Beatrock music label, featured on songs with artists Bambu and Ruby Ibarra. Her work has been cited in numerous college courses and academic journals about Filipino American history and Hip-Hop. She was born and raised in the Boyle Heights area of Los Angeles, and lives in the San Gabriel Valley with her husband and two children.

Dr. Claudia Serrato, based in East Los Angeles, is a distinguished Indigenous culinary anthropologist and a professor of ethnic and food studies. With roots in P'urhépecha, Huasteca, and Zacateco heritage, she began her culinary journey in her youth, cooking alongside her elders. Dr. Serrato holds a Ph.D. in Sociocultural Anthropology from the University of Washington, Seattle, and has dedicated her life to preserving Indigenous culinary traditions and advocating for the decolonization of diets. Beyond her academic pursuits, she is a celebrated chef, recognized nationally for her contributions to the Native food sovereignty movement. In 2015, she received an honorary title from the Native American Culinary Association. Dr. Serrato co-founded "Across Our Kitchen Tables" and has been featured in prominent media outlets. Currently, she serves at California State University, conducts research on first foods, and offers specialized consulting. She remains a pivotal voice in food justice and sovereignty.

Marisol Lydia Torres (Xicana—Mexican/Nicaraguan) is a performer, visual artist, and writer. She began her career in theater and comedy in 1996 with nationally touring Chican@ theater company *ChUSMA* (1996–2007). Marisol is a co-founder of mujeres poetry and song group *In Lak Ech* (1997–present), as well as Xicana comedy theater troupe *Las Ramonas* (2007–present). As a visual artist, Marisol works as a painter, muralist, and paper mache sculptor. She received a B.A. in Latin American Studies; an M.F.A. in Television, Film, & Theatre; and works in Los Angeles as an educator.

Linda Vallejo creates work that visualizes what it means to be a person of color in the United States. Her works reflect her "brown intellectual property"—the experiences, knowledge, and feelings gathered over five decades of study in Latino-x, Chicano-x, and American indigenous culture and communities. Solo exhibitions include CSU San Bernardino, Fullerton Museum of Art, LA Plaza de Cultura y Artes, Texas A&M University Reynolds Gallery, UCLA Chicano Studies Research Center, Lancaster Museum of Art and History, Lancaster, Calif., and Soto Clemente Velez Cultural Center, NY. She was featured in ArtNews "Canon in Drag: Female Artists Reimagine Famous Works by Men," NY Times "Visualizing Latino Populations Through Art," and LA Times "Linda Vallejo and a decade of art that unapologetically embraces brownness." Selected permanent collections include the AltaMed Art Collection, Eileen Harris-Norton Collection, Museo del Barrio, New York, East LA College Vincent Price Museum, and the National Museum of Mexican Art, Chicago Ill.

Dra. Christine Vega is a first-generation Chicana from Pacoima, California. She earned her Ph.D. from the University of California, Los Angeles (UCLA) Graduate School of Education and Information Studies with a concentration on Race & Ethnicity. She is a #transferproud student from Los Angeles Mission College with B.A.s in Chicana/o and Central American and Women Gender Studies from UCLA and an M.Ed. from the University of Utah. She is the co-founder of Mothers of Color in Academia de UCLA and the Chicana M(other)work Collective. Dra. Vega is an Assistant Professor of Chicana/e/o Studies at San José State University. Her research and community work center Motherscholars, Parents, Activisms, Spirituality, and Transformational Counterspace(s).

Vickie Vértiz has been featured in the *New York Times* magazine, *Huizache*, the *Los Angeles Review of Books*, KCET Departures, and the San Francisco *Chronicle*, among many publications. Her second book *Auto/Body* won the 2023 Sandeen Poetry Prize from the University of Notre Dame. She is a recipient of fellowships from the Mellon Foundation, Bread Loaf Environmental Writers Conference, VONA, CantoMundo, and Macondo. Vértiz teaches writing at UC Santa Barbara. She lives in Los Angeles.

Patricia Zamorano (playwright and dramaturg) is a first-generation Mexican-American-Chicana, born and raised in Boyle Heights in the Aliso Village Housing Projects of Los Angeles, California. By day she is a Journeyman, heavy equipment operator and by night she is a story teller currently working on a full-length play. In 2019, she was invited by Abel Alvarado to be his dramaturg and producer for *ARENA A HOUSE MUSICAL*. She wrote two short films, *PUTA* (2021) and *MATRIARCHY* (2017) produced by Matriarchy Films. In 2007, she took Josefina Lopez's playwriting class where she wrote, co-directed, and produced two full-length plays, *YOU DON'T KNOW ME* (2008) and *LOCKED UP* (2014) at CASA 0101 Theatre. Since then she has written over a dozen short plays and monologues with Brown and Out LGBT short playwriting festival and Chicanas, Cholas y Chisme at Casa 0101. Patricia is honored to be included in the 50 Playwrights Project.

Susy Zepeda, Ph.D., is Associate Professor in the Chicana/o/x Studies department at the University of California, Davis (Patwin homeland). Her scholarly work is transdisciplinary, decolonial, feminist, community-centered, and grounded. Susy's research and teaching focus on Xicana Indígena spirit work, decolonization, critical feminist of color collaborative methodologies, oral and visual storytelling, and intergenerational healing. She established the courses Decolonizing Spirit and Food Justice at UCD. Dr. Zepeda's writing appears in the 2019 anthology *Voices from the Ancestors: Xicanx and Latinx Spiritual Expressions and Healing Practices* and the 2020 essay "Decolonizing Xicana/x Studies: Healing the Susto of De-indigenization," in *Aztlán: A Journal of Chicano Studies* as part of the *Dossier: Fifty Years of Chicana Feminist Praxis, Theory, and Resistance*. Susy's first book, *Queering Mesoamerican Diasporas: Remembering Xicana Indígena Ancestries*, was published by the University of Illinois Press in 2022, as part of the Transformations: Womanist, Feminist, and Indigenous Studies book series.

Nadia Zepeda is a queer Chicana interdisciplinary scholar-activist from Santa Ana, California. She's an Assistant Professor in the Department of Chicana/o Studies at California State University, Fullerton. Nadia received her B.A. in Chicano/Latino Studies and Spanish from California State University, Long Beach, and Ph.D. in Chicana/o and Central American Studies from University of California, Los Angeles. Through collaborative and community-based research, she traces the genealogy of healing justice in Chicana/x feminist organizing. Her teaching, research, and commitment to healing justice exemplify her investments in visions of transformative justice in the university and beyond.

INDEX

Note: **Bold** page numbers refer to figures

Abrego, Carmen, 339n3
abuela knowledge, 364–65
Abu-Jamal, Mumia, 155
Acjachemen-Juaneño people, 74
activism, 24n5, 67, 84, 86, 161–62, 165, 321; Black feminist, 192; Black Lives Matter, 281; and conocimiento, 308, 320, 337–43; cultural, 3, 47; Indigenous, 19, 53, 358; and In Lak Ech, 51, 57n17; in Los Angeles, 6, 35, 40; and Mujeres de Maiz, 31–33, 35–37, 43, 46, 54, 66, 80; relationship to artivism, 249; and social media, 349–70; spiritual, 19, 41–42, 178–200, 340, 343, 349–70; third-wave feminist, 268–89. *See also* artivism; *individual groups and projects*
activist research/activist-scholars, 20–23, 25n7, 308, 326–48
activists, 7, 11, 50, 140, 206, 317; and healing justice, 99, 113n14; in Los Angeles, 28–29, 205; and Mujeres de Maiz, 16, 71, 209; student, 206, 292, 311–13, 326, 333

aesthetics, 65, 182, 191, 249, 332; of altars, 12, 20, 268–89; decolonizing, 183, 253; participatory, 29; rasquache, 32, 34; and spirituality, 8, 14, 189–90, 275–76, 284
AF3IRM, 14
affirmative action, 46, 292–93. *See also* Proposition 209 (1996, CA)
Africa, 46, 48, 94, 127, 153, 191, 223
African Americans, 71, 154, 185, 192
African Arts Ensemble, 140
Afro-Brazilian dance, 344
Afro Innovator Exhibition, 156
Afro-Latinx people, 7, 25
Afro-Peruvians, 7
"Afterschool Freestyle Special," 295
Aguilar, Marlene, 98, 103–6, 109–10
Alaniz, Juanita Cynthia, 189
Alarcón, Margaret "Quica," 73–74, 180, 206, 209, 322n4; *Hermana de Maiz*, 247–48, **plate 3**; *Mujer de Maiz*, 248, **plate 2**; *Ojo de Maiz, Intaglio*, 248–49, **248**
Alcaraz Lopez, Lalo, 44

Alcatraz occupation (1969), 53
Alexander, M. Jacqui, 210, 219
alliances, 9, 11, 42, 74, 183, 185, 196n14, 250, 340
altarities, 270–71, 275–76, 287
altars, 5, 97–98, 108, 111n2, 112n5, 145, 188, 214, 258, 387; and artivism, 12, 20, 252–56, 268–89
alter-Native (term), 6, 24n1
Alurista, 43
Alvarado, Mary, 285–86
Alvarez, Adriana, 8
Álvarez, Gloria Endiña, 32, 384
Alvarez, Maritza, 74, 76, 78, 81n5, 222, 225
American Indian Movement, 53
American Indians, 120, 187, 242. *See also* Indigenous Peoples; Native Americans
Anderson Guerrero, Angela Mictlanxochitl, 17
Angelik Vagrants, 143
The Annals of San Francisco, 242
anthologies, 8, 15, 22, 117, 185, 191. *See also individual publications*
anticolonialism, 327, 344. *See also* decoloniality
anti-imperialism, 11, 17, 47, 176
anti-Semitism, 86
Anu, Skryb, 10, 18, 34, 43, 48, 72, 143
Anzaldúa, Gloria, 18, 55n1, 114n27, 117, 254, 272–73, 287, 288n3, 312; on conocimiento, 307–8, 317, 327, 337–40; on Coyolxauhqui, 100–101, 108, 238–39, 340; on inner work and public acts, 23, 193, 323; on nepantla, 44, 339; on new tribalism, 110, 114n36; on ritual, 9, 11, 250; on spiritual activism, 42, 180–83, 193, 353; *This Bridge Called My Back*, 185, 191; on virgen/puta dichotomy, 103
Apache People, 24n2, 211, 221, 246n7
Aparicio, Gina, 19, 72–77, **77**, 208, 216, 229n3; "Cihualmachiliztli, Woman of Wisdom," **plate 6**; "Cuica Maquixtia," 217–21; "In the Spirit of the Ancestors,"
212–17; *Ipan Nepantla Teotlaitlania Cachi Maztlcayotl*, 244, **245**
Aquí Estamos Y No Nos Vamos, 75, 81n8
Aquino, María Pilar, 182
Arizona, 81n7, 89, 216, 295; Tucson, 27n22
artisans, 10, 328, 329, 346n3
Artist Network of Refuse and Resist, 141
artivism, 11, 13, 16, 22, 25n7, 155, 164–65, 196n5, 205, 269, 330, 346n4, 373; of altars, 12, 20, 252–56, 268–89; Black queer, 151; digital, 196n14; and herstory, 28–57, 312–13, 322n3; and Mujeres de Maiz, 180, 193, 249–52, 306, 308, 312, 317–18, 321, 322n3, 328, 334; and social media, 21, 349–70
artSPEAK events, 141
ASCO, 32, 56n10
Association of Writers & Writing Programs, 384
Asturias, Miguel Angel, 289n5
Avenue 50 Studios, 39
Aztec codices, 52, 209
Aztec cosmology/deities, 48, 107, 112n7, 184, 243–44, 273, 279, 281–83, 371. *See also individual deities*
Aztec dance, 30, 44, 52, 97, 104, 111n3, 183, 188
AzTechas, 44
Aztec people, 113n19, 187, 220, 222, 228n1, 240, 256n1
Aztlán, 24n1, 24n2, 51, 173, 188, 212, 303; decolonization of, 215–17
Aztlán Cultural Arts Foundation, 10, 34, 161
Aztlan Underground, 11, 41, 155, 159

Baca, Judy, 32
Baca, Susana, 7, 78–79, **79**, 206; "Maria Lando," 206
Baca Zinn, Maxine, 337
Baker, Ella, 16
Balagtasan Collective, 14, 47
Baldwin Park, CA, 310
Barvosa, Edwina, 194

Basque People, 157
Beltran, Marlene, 10, 161, 164, 294
Benavidez, Max, 35
Ben Maltz Gallery, 199n48
Berkeley, CA, 140, 142, 143. *See also* University of California, Berkeley
Beverly Hills, CA, 138
Bikini Kill, 69
Blacc, Aloe, 78
Black Lives Matter, 250, 281, 363
Black people, 9, 31, 42, 138, 153, 288n1; Indigenous, 78; queer, 151. *See also* Afro-Latinx people
Blackwell, Maylei, 22, 27n25, 79, 217
black/white binary, 191
Blake, Debbie, 339n3
BlakHole, 155
Blossom, 234
Blues Experiment, 11
Boggs, Grace Lee, 16
Bolivia, 191
Bon, Lauren: *Another city is Possible*, **6**; *Not a Cornfield*, 5, 24n1, 76
Bonfil Batalla, Guillermo, 219, 229n10, 229n12
Boyle Heights (Los Angeles, CA), 81n9, 184, 250, 296, 312, 331; MdM shows in, 7, 12, 71, 152, 328
brown, adrienne maree, 16
Broyles-González, Yolanda, 56n5
Burning Spear, 155
Bush, George W., 155
butches, 147
Butchlalis de Panochtitlan, 72–73, **73**, 207
Byrd, Jodi, 122–23

Calderón, Dolores, 309
California, 27n22, 76, 81n7, 90, 108–9, 184, 187–88, 190, 216, 225, 271; racist propositions in, 9, 46, 158, 242; Southern, 39, 44, 49, 199n48, 330. *See also individual cities, neighborhoods, and universities*
California Community Colleges, 23
California State University, Long Beach, 27n22
California State University, Los Angeles, 306, 311–12, 321n1, 322n4, 349
California State University, Northridge, 179; Chicano House, 50
California State University system, 23
Calmécac, 187
Calvert, Kimberly, 143
Camacho Quintero, Maria, 80
Cambalache, 24n4
Cammaert, Bart, 352
Campbell, Nikki, 79
Campos, Emmet E., 309
Canada: Montreal, 112n8
@Cantosdelatierra, 364
capitalism, 176, 278, 372; critiques of, 19, 47, 90, 191, 274–75; gendered, 281–83; impact on Los Angeles, 9, 19, 271; and matrix of oppression, 182. *See also* neoliberalism
Carrillo, Graciela, 190
Casa de La Raza, 330
Casa del Mexicano, 207, 234
Castaneda, Cecilia, 181
Castañeda Quintero, Cecilia, 189
Castillo, Ana, 229n14, 272
Castillo, Celestina, 160
Catholicism, 55n4, 66, 86, 91, 99, 105, 137, 222, 229n6, 285; combined with Indigeneity, 102–3, 106, 186, 223, 243–44, 332, 346n7. *See also* Christianity
"Caught between a Whore and an Angel," 34
CAVA, 24n4
Cayleff, Susan, 323n8
Celebrating Words Festival, Written, Performed, Sung, 328–29
Central America, 158
Central Americans, 56n16, 67
Centro Regeneración/Popular Resource Center (PRC), 10–12, 17, 67, 69, 71–72, 80–81, 142, 158–62, 206, 301–3, 371

Centzon Huitznahua, 236
Cervantes, Lorna Dee, 27n22, 78
Cervantes, Susana, 190
Cervantes-Soon, Claudia G., 309
Cervántez, Yreina, 32, 38, 79, 189, 234, 243; *La Ofrenda*, 252–53; *Nepantla*, 241–42
Chao, Manu, 381
Charger, Harry, 122
Chavez, Rick, 49
Chávez-Arteaga, Alicia, 323n8
Chicana and Chicano studies, 332
Chicana feminism, 19, 180, 193, 309, 312, 323n8, 368. See also Xicana feminism
Chicana movement, 95
Chicana/o art movement, 28, 32
Chicana/o movement, 22, 25nn7–8, 30, 105, 180, 184, 186, 188–89, 194, 235, 292, 317
Chicana/o/x studies, 35, 55n1, 305, 310–11
Chicana por mi Raza, 313
Chicanidad, 35, 56n7. See also Xicanisma
Chicano nationalism, 19, 38, 105, 212, 215–17, 228
Chican/x (term), 25n7
Chicomecoatl, 79, 255
"Chihuahua in a Box," 295
China, 46, 136
Chinchilla, Maya, 274
Chomiha, 48
Christian, Barbara, 288
Christianity, 102–3, 168, 219, 229n11, 283. See also Catholicism
Chumacero, Olivia, 77, 163
Cihuateteo, 4
Cihuatl Tonali, 48
cisgender people, 114n28, 190
cissexism, 114n28
City Terrace, CA, 98, 107, 152–53, 184
Ciudad Júarez, Mexico, 47, 258, 282
civil rights movement, 31, 53, 68, 80, 140, 253
Clements, Marie, 179
Coatlicue, 37, 66, 332, 346n7; Coatlicue state, 240, 339n3, 340; and Coyolxauhqui, 107, 112n7, 236–37, 244, 343

Cohanim, 86
Cohen Hita, Liza, 10, 17, 33–34, 46–47, 68, 160, 302, 304
Cold War, 10
Collins, Patricia Hill, 339n3
Colombia, 30, 283
colonialism, 29, 78, 122, 212, 225–26, 229n6, 229n11, 235, 272, 275, 312; and Indigeneity, 94, 113n13, 119, 219–23, 229n10; and memory, 208–10; modern/colonial gender system, 230n22; neo-, 93–94, 165; and oral herstory, 316; and patriarchy, 80, 102, 108, 185, 218, 240, 320; settler, 181, 216, 227, 359. See also imperialism
Colorado, 216, 323n5
Comandanta Ramona, 12, 41, 47, 294, 314–15
Comisión Femenil Mexicana Nacional, 189
community-engaged research, 21, 326, 344
Community Service Organization (CSO), 12, 292
Concilio de Arte Popular: *Chisme Arte*, 27n22
conocimiento, 20, 306–25, 327, 337–40, 343–44, 353
Contreras, Sheila E., 113n19
Corazón del Pueblo, 186, 234, 331–32
Cormier, Chelsea, 323n8
corn/maiz, 21, 38, 69, 84, 118, 171, 187–88, 214, 239, 252, 254–55, 260, 282–85, 297; corn goddesses, 77, 79; and Mujeres de Maiz, 23, 37–38, 191, 248–49, 253, 396. See also Bon, Lauren, *Not a Cornfield*; Xilonen
Cotera, María, 100–101, 313, 324n13
COVID-19 pandemic, 14, 353, 363, 367–68
Coyolxauhqui, 33, 37, 48, 72, 235, 240–43, 245–48, 273, 304, 342, 371; and Coatlicue, 107, 112n7, 236–37, 244, 343; Gloria Anzaldúa on, 100–101, 108, 238–39, 340

Coyolxauhqui Full Moon Circle, 14, 17, 97–114, 184–85, 385
Coyolxauhqui imperative, 100–101
Coyolxauhqui mourning, 100–102
Coyolxauhqui Plaza, 184
Coyolxauhqui Remembered: A Journal of Latina Voices, 27n22
Crenshaw (South Los Angeles, CA), 153
Critical Latinx Indigeneities, 188
Cruz, Cindy, 113n16
Cuba, 158, 384
Cuica Maquixtia, 217–18, **218**, 220
cultural memory, 209, 212, 227, 286
Cuyuteca People, 157
cyber-toltecas, 44
Cypress Park (Los Angeles, CA), 66

Dakota Access Pipeline (DAPL), 354–57, **354, 356, 357,** 359
Dakota People, 277, 355
Danza Azteca, 30, 44, 52, 97, 104–10, 111n3, 183, 188
Danza Temachtia Quetzalcoatl, 329
Davalos, Karen Mary, 19, 56n5
De Anda, Iris, 21, 315–17, 322n4, 325n14, 384; *Codeswitch*, 325n14, 384; *Loose Poems*, 384; *Roots of Redemption*, 384
decoloniality, 8, 19, 27n22, 334; decolonial foodways, 180, 185, 187, 320; decolonial imaginary, 183; decolonial spirituality, 17, 107, 120–24. *See also* anticolonialism
decolonial methodology, 307, 309, 336, 390
decolonial motherhood, 189
decolonization, 25n7, 81, 95, 96, 118, 164, 174, 210, 215, 312, 314, 344; of art spaces, 20, 29, 234–57; of Aztlán, 215–17; of filmmaking, 224–27; of language, 221; and oral herstory, 307–20; and spirituality, 95
Deganawidah-Quetzalcoatl University (D-Q University), 198n32

deindianization, 99–101, 113n12, 209, 218–19, 221, 228. *See also* deindigenization
deindigenization, 118–19. *See also* deindianization
de la Paz, Mariela: "La Machi," **plate 10**
de la Riva, Osa, 189
de la Rocha, Zack, 81n2
Delgadillo, Victoria, 10, 34
Delgado, Manuel, 274
Delgado Benal, Dolores, 309
Del Pueblo Café, 330
Denim Day, 279
detribalization, 24n2, 99–102, 106, 218, 221, 228
Día de los Muertos/Day of the Dead, 12, 105, 254, 278–79, 285–86, 295
Diaz, Ella Maria, 198n32
Diaz Soto, Lourdes, 309
Diego, Juan, 244
differential consciousness, 181, 195
disability, 310, 362
disidentification, 192–93
Disturbing Silence, 143
D'Lo, 8, 152, 154, 156n1, 191, 207, 292
Doin' It in Public: Art and Feminism at the Woman's Building, 199n48
Dolan, Jill, 182
Dose of Art Gallery, 383
Duncombe, Stephen, 288

Eagle Rock (Los Angeles, CA), 66
East Los Angeles, CA, 8, 14, 17, 28–30, 71, 81n9, 84, 162, 186, 301; aesthetics of, 332; artivism in, 11, 26n9; Coyolxauhqui Full Moon Circle in, 17; Danza Azteca in, 104; Mujeres de Maiz in, 32–35, 38, 41, 44, 54, 71, 268, 271, 373; Womyn Image Makers in, 222
East Los Angeles College, 162
East Oakland, CA, 190
Eastside Cafe, 384
Eastside Los Angeles, CA, 14, 53, 234, 384. *See also* Boyle Heights (Los Angeles,

CA); East Los Angeles, CA; El Sereno (Los Angeles, CA); Lincoln Heights (Los Angeles, CA)
Eastside Luv, 7
El MERCADO y Mas (formerly Urban Xic), 29, 346n4
El Movimiento Estudiantil Chicano/a de Aztlán (MEChA), 140, 311
El Mundo Zurdo, 42
El Salvador, 10, 169–70, 191, 222, 230n18, 283
El Sereno (Los Angeles, CA), 71, 311, 315, 382, 383–84
El Teatro Campesino, 32, 37, 163
emergent strategy, 16
emplacement, 184, 197n27
Encuentro Cultural Intercontinental por la Humanidad y Contra el Neoliberalismo, 11–12, 40–41, 162, 314, 372
Encuentro Femenil, 27n22
Energy Transfer Partners, 355
Enomoto, Tylana, 24n4, 79
Entres Mujeres, 7, 24n4
EpiCentro, 222
epistemic violence, 19, 208
Espana, Frances Salome, 31
Esparza, Elena, 7
Esparza, Ofelia, 255
Espinoza, Analuisa, 181
Espinoza, Dionne, 20, 79, 309–10, 313, 317, 320, 322n4, 323n5, 323n8, 324n13, 349–50
Espinoza, Sara: *Warrior*, 244, **245**
Esplendor Azteca, 187
Estrada, Gloria, 24n4, 79
Estrada Courts, 196n14
ethnic studies, 23, 295, 312, 336
ethnography, 21, 326–27, 336, 346n1
Eurocentrism, 120–21, 193, 242, 246, 253, 255
"everything for everyone," 12

Facebook, 98, 111n4, 327–28, 330, 350, 353, 364, 367, 369n5

Facio, Elisa, 117
Farce of July, 40, 295
femicide, 282–83. *See also* gender violence; misogyny
feminism, 13, 27n25, 67–68, 88, 189–90, 199n48, 217, 263, 373; Black, 192; Chicana, 19, 22, 27n22, 51, 99, 107, 112n7, 118, 180, 193, 194, 215–16, 237, 268–89, 307, 309, 312–13, 323n8, 349–50, 368; Chicana lesbian, 194; Gloria Anzaldúa on, 18, 250; Indigenous, 50, 211, 308, 317–20, 327, 359; and International Women's Day, 71; Latina, 182, 216; and Mujeres de Maiz, 33, 55n1, 94, 150; queer, 99, 192, 194, 211; and social media, 349–70; and spiritual activism, 42; student activism, 341; and sustainability, 23; third-wave, 20, 268–89; Third World, 19, 195; and trans identity, 144–45; transnational, 17, 210, 249; women of color, 14, 19, 21–22, 24n5, 42, 47, 66, 80, 100, 186, 195, 230n22, 353; Xicana, 21, 56n7, 66, 107, 277, 326, 368; Xicanisma, 25n7, 35, 56n7, 272
feminist methods, 333–48
feminist of color praxis, 21–23
feminist studies, 330, 336
femmes, 18, 33, 56n6, 150n1, 362
femntors, 35, 56n6
Fernandez, Maria Elena, 48
Festival de Maíz, 187–88
Festivales de Flor y Canto, 25n7
Fiesta de Maíz, 187–88
Filipinxs, 25n7; Filipina-Jewish people, 17, 86; Filipinas, 46–47, 90–92. *See also* Pinay people
film studies, 66, 313
First Nations peoples, 179
Flores, Desire, 293
Flores, Quetzal, 373
Flores, Xochi, 24n4
Flor y Canto, 10, 95, 268–71 The Birth of la Diosa de Maiz, 10, 69, **70**, 94; Of

Mixed Waters, 12; *Seeds of Resistance*, 12; *Somos Medicina*, 383
Flowersong Press, 384
"for everyone everything," 41
Four Directions Wellness Clinic, 53
Fraser, Nancy, 27n25
"Freestyle Conspiracy," 295
Fregoso, Rosa Linda, 282–83
Frejo, Happy, 8
Frias, Isis, 383
Frias, Ixchel, 383
Frias, Xion, 382

Galindo, Crystal: "Coatlicue State," **plate 14**; *Coatlicue State: Josie Channels the Goddess*, 240; "29: Dolor," **plate 13**
Gallardo Josefina, 186, 189
Gallegos, Ixchel, 304
Gallegos, Tayecana Textli, 162, 304
Gallo, Juana, 74
García, Belinda, 323n5
Garcia, Joel, 56n17
Garcia, Olga, 384
Gaspar de Alba, Alicia, 24n2, 56n5
gender-expansive people, 107
gender violence, 20, 192, 210, 269–71, 276, 279, 281–83, 286. *See also* femicide; heteropatriarchy; patriarchy; sexual violence
Generation MEX, 44
Getty Foundation, 135; Pacific Standard Time: Art in L.A. 1945–1980, 199n48
Gilbert, Reid, 179
Global South, 18
Goeman, Mishuana, 121, 123
Golden State Freeway, 184
Goldman, Shifra M., 188
Goleta, CA, 330
Gómez-Barris, Macarena, 210
Gómez-Peña, Guillermo, 32
Gonzales, Patrisia, 212, 217, 361
González, Amber Rose, 196n4, 238, 249, 315–16, 320, 322n4

Gonzalez, Martha, 11, 21, 24n4, 33, 41, 51, 56n15, 74, 76, 79, 142, 160, 206, 292, 321n1, 328
Gonzalez, Rebecca, 383
Gonzalez, Rosalia, 74
González-Tenorio, Claudia, 24n4
"The Good Red Road: Cultural Conscious FEshion," 330
Gorocica, Christina, 10, 20, 33, 52, 68, 160, 373; "Sister in the Movement with an Attitude," 302
graffiti art, 6, 44, 253
Grand Park, 254
Gray, Jack, 119
Guatemala, 122, 191, 221–22, 283
Guerrero, Aurora, 17, 81n5, 154, 222–24, 226, 230n18
Guijosa Osuna, Xitlalic, 383
Gutierrez, Gustavo, 31

Habermas, Jürgen, 27n27
Hawai'i, 78
healing justice, 22, 99, 113n14
hemispheric solidarities, 25n7, 188, 191
Here & Now Healing Arts Center, 384
Hermanas Canto Cura, 8
Hernandez, Ester, 32, 190
Herrera Rodríguez, Celia, 31, 72, 211
Herron, Melissann, 323n8
herstory, 60–61, 67, 127, 144–45, 379, 382; of Mujeres de Maiz, 8, 14, 16, 21, 28–57, 69, 207, 277, 305–25, 366–67; oral herstory, 21, 306–25, 366. *See also* Women's Herstory Month
heteropatriarchy, 19, 99, 103, 108, 112n7, 123, 190, 192, 211, 215, 227. *See also* femicide; gender violence; patriarchy; sexism; sexual violence
Higgins, Elena, 8
Highland Park (Los Angeles, CA), 10, 66–67, 71, 84, 158, 301, 396
Hindus, 137
hip-hop, 7, 49, 51, 138–39, 143, 158

Hollenbeck Park, 184
Hollywood, 138, 167, 223
homophobia, 182, 185, 269–70, 288n1
Hood Herbalism, 14
@Hoodherbalism, 364
hooks, bell, 33
Huerta, Dolores, 49, 141, 252–53, 273, 293
Hugo, 143
Huitzilopochtli, 107, 112n7, 235–36, 238, 243, 244, 256n3

Illinois, 195n1, 355
imperialism, 80, 91, 221; critiques of, 19, 215, 224; US, 283. *See also* anti-imperialism; colonialism
Incan People, 228n1, 240
Indie Femme, 8
Indigeneity, 17, 99–100, 118–19, 187, 198n33, 312, 317; neo-, 188
Indigenismo, 74, 113n19, 224
Indigenous critical theory, 123
Indigenous epistemologies, 120, 123, 272
Indigenous pedagogies, 11
Indigenous Peoples, 9, 16, 24n2, 29, 47, 48, 55n4, 68, 78, 91, 191, 198n32, 289n5, 289n7, 303–4, 346n4, 362; and activist research, 21, 326–45; and artivism, 249–55; and Aztlán, 215–17; and Coyolxauhqui, 235, 238–48; and feminist art, 37–38, 50, 180, 211–28, 272–73; and feminist praxis, 317–20; and *Flor y Canto*, 269; and healing practices, 30, 183–90, 364, 367; and mestizaje, 100, 219; queer, 81n5; songs from, 51–53; and spiritual activism, 354–59, 368; and spirituality, 17, 19, 26n18, 30–31, 37, 41–42, 93–96, 99–114, 116–24, 183–86, 238–39, 275, 286–87, 346n7; Xicana, 10, 15, 17–19, 21, 25n7, 28, 32, 41, 50, 56n16, 74–76, 81n7, 174, 211, 308; and Zapatistas, 11, 17, 41, 205. *See also* American Indians; First Nations peoples; Native Americans; Pueblos Originarios; red road; United Nations, Declaration on the Rights of Indigenous Peoples; *individual nations and groups*
Indigenous rights, 158
Indigenous studies, 118, 336. *See also* Native studies
Indigenous Xicanas, 10, 14–21, 25n7, 28, 32, 41, 50, 56n16, 74–76, 81n7, 174, 211, 249, 308, 327–28, 344
In Lak Ech (collective), 17–18, 20, 40–41, 56n17, 66, 81n3, 84, 162, 206, 222, 292, 372, 386; "I Live," 52; *Mujeres Con Palabra*, 51–53; and Mujeres de Maiz, 10–11, 28, 33–35, 45–46, 48, 50–53, 68–69, **69**, 162–65, 303–5, 318; "Woman Song," 373; "Wombyn," 52
In Lak'ech (philosophical principle), 16, 26n18, 68, 94, 163, 180, 185, 192, 303
Inland Empire, CA, 98
Instagram, 369n5; MdM on, 21, 350–68
interdisciplinarity, 13, 38, 54, 55n1, 188, 191
intergenerationality, 10, 13, 38, 54, 77, 94, 180, 188, 191, 361–62
International Indigenous Grandmothers Gatherings, 74, 76, 78
International Monetary Fund (IMF), 91
International Women's Day, 12, 47, 48–49, 69, 71, 78, 160, 191, 293, 322n4
intersectionality, 11, 22, 27n22, 230n22, 312
Iowa, 355
Irwin, Katherine, 336
Italian Supreme Court, 279
@itmustbeeasign, 360

Jacques, Celina: "Labor of Love," **plate 15**
Jalisco, Mexico, 342
jarochas, 8
Jewish people, 17, 86, 139–40, 229n11
Jovan, 382
Juarez, Rufina, 76
Jupiter, Maya, 78–79
Justice for My Sister, 14, 384

Kahlo, Frida, 254, 302
Keating, AnaLouise, 182, 185, 308
K'iche' people, 122, 211, 221, 289n5
King, Rodney, 9, 154, 271
King, Susan E., 189
Korean Americans, 7
Kovach, Margaret, 336
Kukulkán, 186–87

La Colonia, 97
la cultura cura, 19
Lakota Nation, 104, 109, 117–18, 120, 122, 184, 223, 355
La Llorona, 103
La Malinche, 103
La Marisoul, 24n4, 79, 206
Lambert, Steve, 288n3
Lancaster, CA, 137–39
LA Plaza de Cultura y Artes, 14, 324n12, 364
Lara, Irene, 117, 119
Lara, Iuri, 97–98, 111n4
La Red Xicana Indigena, 74, 76, 81n7
La Santa Cecilia, 24n4, 206
Las Bomberas de la Bahia, 8
Las Eloteras, 371
Las Flores de Aztlan, 32, 181, 183, 186–89, 198n33
Las Hijas de Cuauhtémoc, 27n22
Las Lunas Locas, 384
Las Mujeres Muralistas, 33, 181, 190–91
Las Ramonas, 14, 18, 164, 294–95
Latin America, 158, 191, 211, 229n6, 251, 285
Latin American studies, 158
Latina/o/x studies, 45
Latinoamérica, 191
Latorre, Guisela, 190, 196n5, 196n14, 252
L.A. Womyn's Calendar, 186
Legacy L.A., 186
Legaspy, Karla, 225
Leimert Park (South Los Angeles, CA), 153
León-Portilla, Miguel, 42, 273

lesbians, 48, 151, 194
Licona, Adela C., 24n5
limpieza de sangre, 219, 229n9
Lincoln Heights (Los Angeles, CA), 10, 34, 66, 71, 161
Lippard, Lucy, 243
the Loft, 159
Lopez, Josefina, 8, 78
Lopez, Michelle L., 20, 322n4
Lopez, Pola: "Corn Mother," **plate 11**; "Queen Fly Stone," **plate 12**
Lopez, Yolanda, 32
Los Angeles, CA, 6, 17, 27n22, 47, 94, 105, 186–90, 205, 208, 211, 215, 221, 225, 333, 346n4, 352, 366, 381; activism in, 6, 9–10, 28–29, 35, 40, 205; artivism in, 25n7, 249–56; capitalism in, 9, 19, 271; community gardens in, 74–75; DAPL protests in, 355–59; Downtown, 14, 24n1, 47, 71, 76, 98, 155, 159, 253–54, 301, 353; feminist art in, 31–41, 143, 179; full moon circles in, 107, 110; Indigenous people in, 9; International Women's Day in, 69, 71; neoliberalism in, 226; queerness in, 81n5; social movements in, 317. See also *individual neighborhoods, organizations, and universities*
Los Angeles art world, 20, 52, 256
Los Angeles Contemporary Museum of Art, 56n10
Los Angeles Department of Cultural Affairs, 346n3
Los Angeles Indigenous Peoples' Alliance (LAIPA), 74
Los Angeles Mission College, 328–29
Los Angeles River, 24n1, 34
Los Angeles State Historic Park, 24n1, 76
Los Angeles Women's March, 357–59, **357**
Lugones, María, 230n22

Madre Tierra Press, 189
Mahdessian, Karineh, 384

Malagón, María C., 309
malintZINE, 27n22
Māori People, 8, 219
Maranon, Ymasumac, 47
Mariachi Plaza, 7, 331, 384
Martinez, Gabriela, 20, 309, 311–12, 315–19, 321–23, 325n14, 362, 365
Martínez, María Elena, 197n21, 219–20, 229n9, 229n11
Martínez, Norell, 12, 20
Martinez, Pedro, 20, 309, 311–17, 319–23
Matagalpa People, 157
matrix of oppression, 182
May, Diea, 279, 281, 286
Maya K'iche' People, 211, 221, 289n5
Maya Long Count Calendar, 24n3
Mayan codices, 209, 301
Mayan dance, 183, 188
Maya People, 11, 48, 183, 187, 188, 228n1, 255, 272, 304; and In Lak Ech name, 10, 26n18, 29, 34, 68, 122, 180–81, 183, 192, 303
Maya Quiché people, 122
May Day, 250
McBeth, Katie, 361
Medina, Lara, 17, 55n4, 79, 187
Mejia, Antonio, 49
Mendez, Consuelo, 190
Mendez, Dalila Paola, 81n5, 208, 222, 224–26
Mendoza, Sara, 74
Mercado, Claudia, 10, 12, 14–15, 17, 19, 94, 159–60, 162, 180, 206, 208, 302, 304; *Aquí Estamos Y No Nos Vamos!*, 75, 81n8; and In Lak Ech, 33; *Obsidian Mirror*, 81n1; in Womyn Image Makers, 81n5, 222; work on *Pura Lengua*, 229n17
Mesa-Bains, Amalia, 38, 255, 275
Mesa de las Madres, 253–54, **253**
Mesoamerica, 20, 25n8, 37, 93, 95, 124, 186, 209, 211, 289n5, 289n8; art/spirituality in, 93, 95, 269, 273; colonization in, 209, 229n10; cosmology/deities in, 37, 235, 270, 272, 286, 338; Indigenous people in, 217–18, 222; poetry in, 25n8
mestiza consciousness, 249, 323n5, 338
mestizaje, 100–101, 113n19
mestizo mourning, 100–101
mestizos, 113n19, 219, 221–22
Metabolic Studio, 5, 76; *Another city is Possible*, **6**
Mexican Americans, 25n7, 29, 97, 120–23, 222, 244
Mexican ancestry, 56n16, 66–67, 157, 184, 186, 191, 237, 254
Mexicana/os, 8, 46, 51, 60, 185, 222
Mexican Traditional Medicine, 30
Mexica people, 30, 108–9, 120–23, 184, 188, 191, 235–36, 243–44, 255, 256n3, 272, 289n8
Mexica Valley, 261
Mexicayotl tradition, 117–18
Mexico, 10, 24, 99, 111n1, 211–12, 223, 229n6, 240, 242, 251, 266, 273, 275, 384; Chiapas, 12, 30, 37, 41, 47, 84, 87, 105, 136, 155, 158, 161, 205, 271–72, 293, 294, 317, 372, 381–82; Chihuahua, 29, 295; colonization in, 78, 100–101, 216–17; femicides in, 283; full moon circles in, 107, 109; healing practices in, 117, 119; Indigeneity in, 220–22; Jalisco, 342; mestizaje in, 113n19; Mexico City (Mexico DF), 30, 98, 111n3, 229n12, 235, 282–83; Michoacán, 78, 104, 109; neoliberalism in, 10; Oaxaca, 30, 171; Tijuana, 155, 296; Veracruz, 8
Michán, Patricia, 236
Michigan Womyn's Music Festival (MichFest), 144
Middle East, 139, 191
mind-body-emotion matrix, 344, 346n1, 348n28
mind-body-spirit, 21
Miranda, Judy, 189

misogyny, 102, 106, 112n7, 270, 292. *See also* femicide; gender violence; sexual violence
Mixpe Ley, Jo Anna, 164
modern/colonial gender system, 230n22
Modern Tejana, 352–53
Montes, Carlos and Olivia, 30
Montes, Evelyn, 81n1
Montes, Felicia "Fe," 10, 68, 74, 76, 94, 117, 141, 161, 180, 206, 292, 294, 302, 306, 313, 317, 322n4, 326, 364; "America's Next Top Murder," 283–86; *Botanica del Barrio*, 251–52, **251**; on Coyolxauhqui, 238; on decolonization, 320; "Loteria Xicana," **plate 8**; on Mujeres de Maiz herstory, 16; at NACCS, 328; "Occupy LAcMAztlan performance art," **plate 17**; "Overcompensating Xicana Complex," 349–50, 372; *The Politricked Public Art Cart*, 250–52, **250**; "Who's That Grrrl?" flyer, **36**
Moraga, Cherríe, 31–32, 50–51, 55n1, 113n16, 114n27, 145–46, 209, 272, 293, 312; on Coyolxauhqui, 107; on In Lak Ech, 50–52; on theory in the flesh, 279; *This Bridge Called My Back*, 185, 191
Moreno, David, 184
Morgensen, Scott, 216
Morning Star Foundation, 74
movimiento, 194–95
Muchacha fanzine, 27n22
Mujeres Activas en Letras y Cambios Sociales (MALCS), 117, 179, 195n1, 229n3
Mujeres Contra La Rabia del Machismo (MCLRDM), 294–95
"Mujeres de Maiz: L.A. Artivism Live," 328
Mujeres de Maiz (MdM) Live Art Shows, 11, 13–18, 21, 34, 39, 70–71, 81n1, 81n3, 143, 150, 191, 206, 227, 234–35, 331, 346n6, 383; *Birth of La Diosa de Maiz*, 10, 69, 94; *Cihuatlatokan*, 74; *Danzando con el Fuego*, 72–74; *La Sagrada—She the Sacred*, 5, 75–78; *Mujeres de Maiz: The Roots of Herstory*, 12; *Of Mixed Waters*, 12; *Red*, 74; *Seeds of Resistance*, 12; and social media, 350–51, 353, 367; *Soldadera de Amor*, 328, 340–42; *Somos Medicina*, 75–76; *13-Baktun Return of the Wisdom of the Elders*, 7–8, 75, 78

"Mujeres de Maiz: Twenty Years of Artivism and Herstory," 364
Mujeres de Maiz: Twenty Years of ARTivism & Herstory en LA, 14
Mujeres de Maiz Oral Herstory Project, 21, 306–25, 366
Mujeres Unidas por Justicia, Educación y Revolución (MUJER), 341
Mujer Mercado, 7
Multimedia Militia, 384
Muñoz, José Esteban, 182, 192
Murphy, Jacqueline Shea, 119

Nahuatlaca People, 157
Nahuatlization, 220
Nahuatl language, 16, 48, 111n4, 124n2, 187, 217–21, 240, 272–73, 289n8
Nájera-Ramírez, Olga, 342
National Artist Network, 143
National Association of Chicana and Chicano Studies (NACCS), 195n1, 328–30
National Committee for Democracy in Mexico, 11
nationalism, 100, 227; Chicano, 19, 38, 105, 188, 212, 215–17, 228; cultural, 38, 105, 190, 212, 215–16; Mexican, 222; queering, 190–92
National Queer and trans Therapist Network, 113n14
Native Americans, 46, 48, 52–53, 56n16, 120, 186, 188, 198n32, 227–28, 229n6, 288n1, 355, 358; in La Colonia, 97; Two-Spirit people, 211; violence against, 216. *See also* American Indians; Indigenous Peoples

Native studies, 118. *See also* Indigenous studies
Navajo Nation, 8, 184
Negrete Thorson, Rachel, 10, 33, 68, 161, 234, 302; "Imix," **plate 4**
Nelly Vélez, Verónica, 309
neocolonialism, 93–94, 165
neo-indigeneity, 188
neoliberalism, 9–10, 12, 44, 118, 165, 225–26, 272. *See also* capitalism; Encuentro Cultural Intercontinental por la Humanidad y Contra el Neoliberalismo; North American Free Trade Agreement (NAFTA)
nepantla, 44, 241–42, 244, **245**, 338n1, 339n2, 342
nepantla spirituality, 55n4, 346n7
Nevada, 216
Nevel, Xochilt, 190
New Mexico, 81n7, 216
New Spain, 24n2, 219–20
new tribalism, 110, 114n36
New York City, 74, 143–44; Queens, 7–8
Nicaragua, 157
Nobel, Jeremy, 361
#NoDAPL, 355–57, **357**, 359
Nomadic Sound System, 56n17
NorCal (northern California), 139
North Africa, 191
North American Free Trade Agreement (NAFTA), 10, 205, 226, 267, 271
North Dakota, 355
Northeast Los Angeles, CA, 66, 301, 382
Northridge, CA, 195n1
Nuke, 11

OB, 143
Ochoa, María, 190
Olibis, Noni, 234
olin, 194–95
Olivo, Miriam, 190
Ollin, 11, 242
Omecihuatl, 97–98, 111n2, 111n4
Ometecuhtli, 111n4

Ometeotl, 111n4, 116, 119, 211
Opaskwayak Cree Nation, 334
Orange County, CA, 97–98
Oregon: Portland, 144
Otomí People, 249
Ovarian Psyco Bicycle Brigade, 186
Oventic, 11, 40, 87, 294, 372

Pachamama, 240–41, **241**, 387
Pando, Diana, 276; "Coyolxauhqui Rising," 273; "Mythology of Flesh and Turquoise Serpents," 258–59, 281–83
Panhe, 74
Paramount Ballroom (formerly Casa Grande Salon), 7
Parks, Rosa, 254
participatory aesthetics, 29
Pasadena, CA, 328
patriarchy, 20, 65, 107, 143, 184, 189, 226, 237, 243, 269–71, 273–75, 278, 282–83, 285; and colonialism, 80, 102, 108, 185, 218, 240, 320; hetero-, 19, 99, 103, 112n7, 123, 190, 192, 211, 215, 227
Pawnee people, 8
Peace and Dignity Journeys, 10, 30, 52, 105–6, 109
Peace and Justice Center, 37
Pedregon, Norma, 181
Pennings, Megan, 20–21, 309–10, 315–19, 324n11
Penny, 143
People's Yoga, 186
Perez, Irene, 190
Pérez, Laura, 241–42, 270, 274–78, 285
Pérez Huber, Lindsay, 309
Peru, 7, 78–79, 191
Petal, 234
Philippines, 47
Photoshop, 69
Piepmeier, Alison, 269, 285
Pilar, Ramona, 384
Pinay people, 14, 47, 91, 140. *See also* Filipinxs
platicar, 184

Poets Responding to SB1070: poetry of Resistance, 384
Ponce, Mary Helen, 189
Portillo, Antonio, 31
Portillo, Xochimilco, 31, 181
Posada, Gilda, 29
postmodernism, 44, 118
pre-colonial period, 29
pre-Columbian period, 51, 111n3, 272–73
Primera Taza Coffee House, 7, 332
Proposition 184 (1994, CA), 158
Proposition 187 (1994, CA), 9
Proposition 209 (1996, CA), 9, 46
Proyecto Jardin, 250
Pueblos Originarios, 120. *See also* Indigenous Peoples
Puerto Ricans, 8
@punkino01, 361

Quechua people, 47–48
The Queer Connection (TQC), 311
Quesada-Weiner, Rosemary, 189
Quetzal, 11, 24n4, 33, 41, 79, 160, 206, 328, 371–72
Quetzalcoatl, 242
Quiñonez, Juanita Naomi, 189
Quinto Sol, 11

racism, 41, 88, 158, 161, 182, 190, 215, 242, 252, 269, 272–75, 288n1; healing from, 100; internalized, 94; systemic, 185, 226. *See also* white supremacy
Radio Clandestina, 11, 17, 155; *Lucha Por Tu Voz*, 68
Rage Against the Machine, 81n2
Ramirez, Lilia "Liliflor," 10, 34, 37, 77, 81n1, 209, 322n4, 330, **357**; *Coyo Comes Alive*, 240, **plate 18**; *Mujer Bendita*, 243; *Mujer Maiz*, 255; *Xilonen: Angel of Los Angeles*, 255, **plate 9**
Ramírez, Omar, 11
Ramirez, Renya, 221–22
Ramirez, Rudy, 159
Rangel, Iram "Cui Cui," 8, 181

rasquache aesthetics, 32, 34
Raza Youth Conferences, 140
Reagon, Toshi, 144
red road, 3, 31, 50, 55n4
"The Red Road to the Xicana Kalli" 50
religious studies, 187
Research Cluster for the Study of Women of Color in Collaboration and Conflict, 229n3
Resistencia Books, 383
Revolucion, 382
Reynoso, Lilia: *Coyolxauhqui: Pachamama Lucharemos Contigo*, 240–41, **241**
Riot Grrrl, 271
Rivera, Sophia, 384
Rocha, Lisa, 10, 34, 330
Rodriguez, Anita, 189
Rodriguez, Melissa, 353. *See also* Modern Tejana
Rodriguez, Patricia, 190
Rodríguez, Roberto "Cintli," 118–19
Rodriguez, Rocky, 211
Rodriguez, Ruth, 190
Rodriguez, Sheila: *Madre de la Vida*, 246–47, **247**
Román-Odio, Clara, 183
Ronstadt, Marisa, 79
Rosales, Danny, 158
Rosencrantz, Sarah "Skinz," 46, 139, 292
Rovira, Guiomar, 37
Royal Chicano Air Force (RCAF), 187
Ruiz, Rosalinda: *Ascension*, 239–40, **239**

Sacramento, CA, 187
sacred transit, 120–23
Salas, Abel, 383
Salazar, Aida, 10
Salcedo, Bamby, 150, 207
Saldaña-Portillo, María Josefina, 100–101, 198n33
Salinas, Raquel, 32
Salinas, Raul, 383
Samoans, 8
Sanchez, Alejandra, 46, 143, 384

Sanchez-Arreola, Gloria, 330
Sanchez Brown, Olivia, 189
San Clemente, CA, 74
San Diego, CA, 187
Sandoval, Chela, 26n18, 42, 195, 196n5, 196n14, 344, 346n2, 348n28
San Fernando Valley, 157, 346n3
San Francisco, CA, 42, 187; Mission District, 181, 190–91
San Francisco Bay Area, CA, 8, 32, 187, 190–91, 222, 384; East Bay, 139
San Francisco State University, 27n22
San Gabriel Valley, 310
Santa Barbara, CA, 5, 328, 330–31, 333
Santilla, Faith, 47
Santos, Betania, 362
Santos, Lorena, 98, 103, 105–6, 110
Sarmiento, Carolina, 24n4
Scripps College, 373
Self Help Graphics & Art (SHG), 35, 39, 73, 76, 81n9, 105, 186–87, 234
self-love, 18, 127, 295
Seminole people, 8
Sendejo, Brenda, 183, 197n21
Seven Generations, 38, 277, 387
sexism, 41, 182, 183, 185, 242, 252, 269, 272, 275, 278, 288n1. *See also* femicide; gender violence; misogyny; sexual violence
sexual violence, 90, 126–27, 147, 179–80, 210, 219, 260–61, 266, 271, 279, 285–86
Silver Lake (Los Angeles, CA), 159
sisterhood, 32, 36, 39, 46, 68, 79, 87, 139, 150, 293, 349, 360, 362, 386
Sisters of Color United for Education, 323n5
Skim, 7, 72
Slate, Michael, 141
Smith, Andrea, 210, 216
Smith, Linda Tuhiwai, 113n16, 219
Smith, Sofia Rose, 384
socially engaged art, 193
social media, 12, 14, 20, 350–51; and artivism, 21, 349–70. *See also individual platforms*
social practice, 29, 193

Son del Centro, 24n4
South America, 67, 119, 236, 284
South Central Farm, 74–75, **75**, 81n8, 172, 205
South Central Los Angeles, CA, 71, 171, 271
South Dakota, 355
South Los Angeles, CA, 9
South Pacific, 90
sovereignty, 25n7, 85, 122, 359
Spanish Crown, 220
SPARC, 196n14
Sphear, 10, 34, 48, 143, 152, 154–55
spirit-darity, 31, 53
spiritual activism, 19, 41–42, 178–200, 340, 343, 349–70
spirit-work, 18
Spoken Wor(l)d Art Performance as Activism (SWAPA), 344, 348n28
Standing Rock Sioux, 355
Statewide Mass March Against Police Brutality, **280**
Stevenson, Jean, 112n8, 112n11
Stuckey, Heather L., 361
Sturken, Maria, 209
Subcomandante Marcos, 42, 381–82
Summer, 234
Sunrise Child, 48
survivance, 93
sustainability, 4, 23, 99, 179, 185, 353
Szymanek, Angelique, 193

Tagalog language, 16
Taíno people, 249
Take Back the Night, 295, 384
Tamil Sri Lankan Americans, 8, 18, 46, 48, 137–38, 140, 150, 152, 191
Tataviam people, 157
Taylor, Diana, 194, 209, 212, 228n1
Teatro ChUSMA, 41, 159, 164
Tejanas, 183–84, 190, 197n21. *See also* Modern Tejana
Templo Mayor, 98, 235
Tenochtitlan, 235, 256n3

Terry, Tash, 8
testimonios, 15, 17–19, 21, 120–21, 156n1, 307–13, 323n8
Texas, 129, 197n21, 216, 353, 355, 383; Austin, 118
Thahuicoatl Lara, Ana, 117
"That's What She Said," 295
theatre and performance studies, 179
Theatre of the Oppressed, 344
theory in the flesh, 279
third wave activism, 20, 268–89
Tía Chucha's Centro Cultural and Bookstore, 329, 346n3
TikTok, 52
Timoi, 234
"todos somos Marcos/Ramona," 12, 41, 305, 317–18
"todos somos Mujeres de Maiz," 12, 27n26, 305
Toltec people, 289n9
Tonalli Studio, 186
Tonantzin, 3, 37, 236
Tonawanda Seneca Nation, 121
Tongues (performance group), 72–73, 207
Tongues Magazine, 27n22, 81n5
Tongva-Gabrielino people, 23n1, 24n2, 76, 157
Torres, Marisol Lydia, 10, 13, 18, 33, 52, 68, 76, 234, 292, 294, 302, 314–18, 322n4; "In Lak Ech: Flor y Canto," **plate 5**; "La Tonantzina," 372
Traditional Chinese Medicine, 344
transgender people, 8, 18, 107, 113n14, 114n28, 142, 144–45, 149–50, 184–85, 191–92, 207, 322n3
transnationalism, 7, 17, 20, 22, 30, 191, 210, 223, 249
transphobia, 114n28, 144
transterritoriality, 17, 117–20
trauma, 107, 117, 160–61, 218, 228, 253, 269, 286, 302, 307, 339n3; healing from, 20, 99–100, 113n13, 205, 210, 214, 271; intergenerational, 361
Treaty of Guadalupe Hidalgo, 216

Tropico de Nopal, 39
Troy Café, 301
Trudell, Tara Evonne, 384
Trump, Donald, 242
Tubman, Harriet, 78
Tupina Yaotonalcuauhtli, Rosa, 118
Twitch, 353, 367
Twitter, 353, 367
Two-Spirit people, 211
Tzitzimime, 4
Tzul, Gladys, 122

United Farm Workers (UFW), 49, 252, 253
United Nations (UN), 76; Declaration on the Rights of Indigenous Peoples, 41; Permanent Forum on Indigenous Issues, 74
University of California, Berkeley, 66, 104; Mujeres en Marcha, 68
University of California, Los Angeles (UCLA), 10, 35, 45–46, 84, 98, 139–40, 141, 154, 161, 293
University of California, Santa Barbara (UCSB), 330, 332, 341
University of California, Santa Cruz, 211, 381
University of California system, 23
University of Southern California (USC), 161
University of Washington Seattle, 373
Untitled, 154–55
urban Indians, 9, 24n2
Uribe, Cathy, 384
US Bureau of Indian Affairs, 56n16
US Religious Freedom Restoration Act, 121

Valdez, Luis: "Pensamiento Serpentino," 26n18
Vallejo, Linda, 31, 180–81, 183, 186, 189–90, 199n48; *Flores de Aztlan Danza Cosmica*, **plate 1**; *Madre Celestial*, 246, **plate 7**
Vega, Christine: *Walking the Red Road: Sisterhood Transformation*, **plate 16**

veganism, 185
Venegas, Sybil, 94
Venezuela: Caracas, 190
Vietnam, 136
Villareal, Elizabeth, 309
Virgen de Guadalupe, 37, 44, 103, 128, 244, 332
virgen/puta dichotomy, 103
Vizenor, Gerald, 93

Wadda G (Women Aware, Deep, Dark & Gay), 48, 143, 152–55
Washington: Seattle, 144, 328
Water, Renee Link, 113n13
Waziyatawin (Angela Wilson), 319
We Are the Land, 254–55
Weaving Words, Creating Words workshops, 384
WE RISE LA, 14
Wheeler, Sarah, 323n8
White Memorial Hospital, 250
white supremacy, 9, 19, 216
Wildcat, Daniel R., 277
Wilson, Pete, 242
Wilson, Shawn, 334
Women of Color Film and Video Festival: Regenerations, 211, 214, 217
women's, gender, and sexuality studies, 310, 311, 312
Women's Graphic Center, 189
Women's Herstory Month, 12, 191
Women's History Month, 49
@womensmarch, 360
Women's March (Los Angeles), 250, 357–58
women's studies, 55, 55n1, 142
Womyn Image Makers (WIM), 48, 72–73, 81n5, 176, 186, 222–24; *Pura Lengua*, 225–27; *Viernes Girl*, 81n5, 230n18
Wood, W. Warner, 193
Worland, Justin, 355
"a world where many worlds fit," 18, 42, 165, 317–18
Wounded Knee occupation (1973), 53

xenophobia, 9, 29, 158, 271
Xicana feminism, 21, 56n7, 66, 107, 277, 326, 368. *See also* Chicana feminism; Xicanisma
Xican@ Records and Film, 40
Xicanisma, 35, 56n7, 272. *See also* Chicanidad; Xicana feminism
Xilonen, 77, 255, **plate 9**
Xion, 382
Xiuhtecuhtli, 282

Yaanga, 5, 23
Yellow Bird, Michael, 319
Yescas, Florencio, 187
YouTube, 353, 366–67

Zapata, Gabriela: *Malinalxochitl, Mi Primera Luna*, 244
Zapatista Army of National Liberation (Ejército Zapatista de Liberación Nacional, EZLN), 10–11, 17, 19, 37, 40, 87, 105, 141, 161, 180, 205, 271–72, 294–95, 314, 357, 372, 381, 382; "todos somos Marcos/Ramona," 12, 41, 305, 317–18; "a world where many worlds fit," 18, 42, 165, 317–18. *See also* Comandanta Ramona; Encuentro Cultural Intercontinental por la Humanidad y Contra el Neoliberalismo; Subcomandante Marcos
Zapotec people, 193
Zaragoza-Wong, Sylvia, 189
Zavella, Patricia, 337
Zepeda, Nadia, 17
Zepeda, Susy, 19
Zepeda, Zuleica: "Justice for My Daddy," 280–81, **280**
Zibechi, Raul, 119
zines, 8, 15, 19, 21, 25n8, 26n15, 34, 45, 57n19, 84, 162, 165, 179, 206, 211, 212, 293, 318, 382–83; and artivism, 12, 20, 268–89; and counterpublics, 22; definition, 24n5. *See also Flor y Canto*; *individual zines*